International Competitiveness and Technological Change

International Competitiveness and Technological Change

Marcela Miozzo
Professor in Economics and Management of Innovation, Manchester Business School, University of Manchester, UK

Vivien Walsh
Professor in Innovation Management, Manchester Business School, University of Manchester, UK

OXFORD
UNIVERSITY PRESS

Library
University of Texas
at San Antonio

OXFORD

UNIVERSITY PRESS

Great Clarendon Street, Oxford OX2 6DP

Oxford University Press is a department of the University of Oxford.
It furthers the University's objective of excellence in research, scholarship,
and education by publishing worldwide in

Oxford New York

Auckland Cape Town Dar es Salaam Hong Kong Karachi
Kuala Lumpur Madrid Melbourne Mexico City Nairobi
New Delhi Shanghai Taipei Toronto

With offices in

Argentina Austria Brazil Chile Czech Republic France Greece
Guatemala Hungary Italy Japan Poland Portugal Singapore
South Korea Switzerland Thailand Turkey Ukraine Vietnam

Oxford is a registerd trade mark of Oxford University Press
in the UK and in certain other countries

Published in the United States
by Oxford University Press Inc., New York

British Library Cataloguing in Publication Data

Data available

Library of Congress Cataloging-in-Publication Data

Miozzo, Marcela, 1963-
    International competitiveness and technological change/Marcela
Miozzo, Vivien Walsh.
        p. cm.
    Includes bibliographical references (p.) and index.
1. Technological innovations–Economic aspects. 2. Competition.
3. International economic relations. 4. Industrial organization.
I. Walsh, Vivien. II. Title.
HC79.T4M56 2006
338'.064–dc22   2006006152

Typeset by SPI Publisher Services, Pondicherry, India
Printed in Great Britain on acid-free paper by

ISBN 0–19–925923–2   978–0–19–925923–6
ISBN 0–19–925924–0 (Pbk.)   978–0–19–925924–3 (Pbk.)

1 3 5 7 9 10 8 6 4 2

⬚ CONTENTS

CONTENTS

☐ LIST OF FIGURES

☐ LIST OF TABLES

☐ LIST OF BOXES

LIST OF ABBREVIATIONS

AFME	l'Agence Française du Management de l'Energie
CAD	computer-aided design
CAM	computer-aided manufacturing
CNA	Confederazione Nazionale dell' Artigianato
CNRS	National Centre for Scientific Research
FDI	foreign direct investment
FTC	Fair Trade Commission
GATS	General Agreement on Trade in Services
GATT	General Agreement on Tariffs and Trade
GMOs	genetically modified organisms
GPNs	global production networks
GVC	global value chain
ICT	information and communication technology
IPR	Intellectual Property Rights
KIBS	knowledge-intensive business services
MIT	Massachusetts Institute of Technology
MCI	Ministry of Commerce and Industry
MITI	Ministry of International Trade and Industry
MM	Ministry of Munitions
NCI	National Cancer Institute
NIH	National Institutes of Health
NSF	National Science Foundation
OECD	Organization for Economic Co-operation and Development
TRIPS	Trade-Related Aspects of Intellectual Property Rights
USPTO	United States Patent and Trademark Office
WIPO	World Intellectual Property Organization
WTO	World Trade Organization

☐ ACKNOWLEDGEMENTS

Many colleagues have contributed to the book by stimulating us to examine particular issues, by criticising our ideas, by providing us with pre-publication copies of their work, and by writing some of the important contributions on which we attempt to build. Of course, any errors remain our own responsibility. In particular we would like to thank: Jonathan Aylen, Michael Best, Michel Callon, Maurice Cassier, François Chesnais, Michel Delapierre, Paul Dewick, Chris Freeman, Jean-Paul Gaudillière, Andrew Glyn, Jordan Goodman, Ken Green, Damian Grimshaw, Thomas Hatzichronoglou, Cori Hayden, Jeremy Howells, Philippe Larédo, Bill Lazonick, Andres Lopez, Jill Lovecy, Ilana Löwy, Bengt-Åke Lundvall, Silvia Massini, Andy McMeekin, Stan Metcalfe, Philippe Mustar, Richard Nelson, Mary O'Sullivan, Keith Pavitt (†), Woody Powell, Ruth Rama, Paulina Ramirez, Judith Reppy, Luc Soete, Marilyn Strathern, Gindo Tampubolon and Andrew Tylecote. Several generations of students who have attended our courses provided us with important feedback. We acknowledge permission to reproduce data, tables and figures from OECD, Francois Chesnais and Andrew Glyn. Particular thanks are due to Chris Freeman, Bruce Tether, Jonathan Aylen and Matias Ramirez who read the manuscript in whole or in parts and gave us very valuable comments. We would like to acknowledge the contributions from the Anglo-German Foundation, British Academy, the ESRC, the EPSRC, Nuffield Foundation, Scottish Homes, and the Wellcome Trust who supported some of the research that this book reports. Many thanks to the Centre de Recherche Medecine, Sciences, Santé et Société in France for providing Vivien Walsh with an intellectually stimulating environment while some of the chapters were being prepared, and the CNRS for making her stay there possible. Also, many thanks to the Buenos Aires office of the United Nations Economic Commission for Latin America for hosting Marcela Miozzo while this book was being prepared. Finally, we are especially grateful to Alison Smith for preparing the manuscript for publication with speed, efficiency and a considerable amount of management skill.

Part I
Introduction

In recent years there has been a revival of interest in the issue of international competitiveness and a renewed concern with the sources of the wealth of nations, a concern raised 250 years ago by the economist Adam Smith. Today, however, this interest in international competitiveness is accompanied by at least a suspicion that innovation (new technologies and new forms of organization) must play a central role in competitiveness and long-run economic change. Indeed, technological competition is the main form of competition under capitalism (and firms not responding to this demand tend to fail). Innovation opens up new business opportunities and sets the stage for economic transformation. Innovation is important to the survival and growth of firms and national economies and ensures a continuing rise in the living standards of the citizens of the region or country whose firms are competitive in world markets.

This book synthesizes the rapidly growing body of research into industrial innovation and its effect on economic change and growth by scholars from a number of disciplines. This body of literature has made an effort to conceptualize industrial innovation, to outline its key features and its outcomes for economic growth. Similarly, there is an understanding that innovation tends to cluster in some industries. Moreover, firms do not innovate in isolation, but depend on extensive interaction with networks of institutions in the regional and national economy. There is also evidence that the character of the institutional structure for the effective development and exploitation of innovation depends on the underlying technologies, the nature of demand, and the characteristics of the organizations that supply them. These factors, moreover, differ from sector to sector. In addition, research shows that globalization, which brings increasing interdependence of economic organizations across countries and regions, affects the development and diffusion of innovation across national borders.

Chapter 1 sets the context for the book by developing a perspective on the relation between innovation and economic development, drawing on the work of Schumpeter and Marx. From this perspective, capitalism is seen as a dynamic system, with innovation as its main engine of change. Innovation tends to cluster in certain sectors which grow more rapidly, implying structural changes in production and demand, and, eventually, organizational and industrial change. As such, the basis of competitiveness and shifts in industrial leadership are questions of structural change, and, rather than rely on aggregate comparisons between countries, is better explored by examining the efforts to develop technological and organizational changes at the level of firms and industrial sectors. Competitiveness depends on the ability of firms to develop and use new technologies and organization and also on the institutional environment in which firms operate.

Chapter 2 considers the main source of innovation: research and development (R&D) activity. It considers where the inventions and innovations come from in terms of the countries that specialize in their production, the institutions carrying out R&D and the institutions which provide the sources of the relevant research and development funding. We examine the evolution of science and technology from being an activity carried out by very few people with a private income or an activity sponsored by patrons, to the professionalization of science and technology and the evolution of the in-house corporate R&D laboratory. The chapter examines the amount and nature of government-funded R&D, defense-related R&D, and industrial R&D in different countries.

1 Technology and Competitiveness

Introduction

'Technology' and 'competitiveness' are two of the most popular buzzwords of our time. Technology is high up the agenda in both policy and academic debates. The capacity of firms to use new technologies and improved organizational methods is central in explaining industrial leadership and the competitiveness of regions and countries. Nevertheless, the relation between industrial innovation, scientific research, organizational change, and competitiveness is not clear. The extent and manner in which innovation occurs in an economy depends on the development of new production and business capabilities, institutions, and infrastructure—factors which are, in turn, contingent (among other things) on business strategy and government decisions on public research funding.

Governments are increasingly concerned with national competitiveness. Rapid liberalization and deregulation of trade and investment flows, falling transportation and communication costs, and increasing rates of technological change are exposing all countries to an unprecedented level of international competition. The increasing concentration of production in the worldwide intracorporate networks of multinationals, and changes in the location and sourcing of scientific and technological activities of multinationals, present new demands on countries and regions. The preoccupation of governments with competitiveness is further reinforced by country league tables, such as that of gross domestic product (GDP) per capita, and a perception that some countries (notably Japan) may have climbed up such tables during the 1970s and 1980s by the systematic use of competitiveness policies (Krugman 1994a; Greenaway 1997).

The study of competitiveness is now a flourishing industry producing a variety of outputs: from serious academic analyses to management consultancy reports, ideological tracts, and impressive but (in the words of Lall [2001]) 'futile' economic models. Among the indicators produced are those using as measures of changes in countries' competitiveness the relative price or cost indices regularly published by the International Monetary Fund (IMF) and the Organization for Economic Co-operation and Development (OECD), or the absolute measures produced by the World Economic Forum (WEF) and the Institute for Management Development (IMD) (Boltho 1996; Krugman 1996). These are discussed later in the chapter.

In this book, we approach the study of technology and competitiveness by focusing on the capacity of firms to develop better technological and organizational capabilities. We also examine the support that firms receive from the wider network of institutions in the private and public sectors, the activities and interaction of which initiate, import, modify, and diffuse new technologies and organizational capabilities in regions and countries. We place our focus on the firm because the development of economies depends on the development of firms. Firms are unique in the role they play in articulating technologies to productive effect. They are also unique in having to combine knowledge of technology with organizational capabilities and knowledge of the market. Moreover, they are unique as problem generators and locations for technological, organizational, and economic learning.

Mainstream economics (also known as neoclassical economics) offers little help in understanding the connection between the development of the firm as a productive unit (and, in particular, its ability to develop and exploit innovation effectively) and the development of the wider economy. The main problem is that mainstream economics lacks a theory of innovation and competitiveness. In economic growth theory, technological change is traditionally treated as a residual factor, or the contribution to growth that is left over when the effects of variables such as inputs of labour and capital, which economists understand and can measure, have been taken into account. Our book, however, following a growing body of literature critical of mainstream economic theory (sometimes called evolutionary or neo-Schumpeterian economics, see Nelson and Winter 1982; Dosi et al. 1988; Freeman and Soete 1997) is based on the view that innovation is an important economic phenomenon. Furthermore, a fundamental point of departure is that innovation is very far from being the outcome of a linear process which begins with investment in basic research and leads through applied research, development, pilot plant construction, and market launch to an economic effect (of success and profit, or failure to make a return). Technology and innovation need to be considered as the outcome of the complex relation between scientific and technological research, development of production capabilities and business and industrial organization. Furthermore, the development of the firm and its technological and organizational capabilities depend on the support of the wider institutional context that makes it possible for firms to access knowledge to develop and exploit those capabilities. There is, therefore, an important role for public policy to create the framework and opportunities that influence the behaviour of firms and drive innovation and competitiveness.

This chapter is organized as follows. The first section discusses the limitations of mainstream economics in dealing with innovation. The second section presents an alternative view of the relation between innovation and economic development. The third section discusses long-term fluctuations in economic development. The fourth section examines the limitations of the most popular indices of competitiveness. The final section explores the concept of competitiveness.

Innovation: why mainstream economics cannot help

One of our main arguments is that mainstream economics has little to offer in clarifying the extent and manner in which innovation occurs in an economy and its impact on economic development and the competitiveness of regions and countries. This is caused, in part, by the neglect by mainstream economics of the competitive strategies and attributes of firms. Drawing on the contribution of a number of non-mainstream economists, we summarize here the main problems of mainstream economics to deal with innovation:

- **Methodological obsession with equilibrium.** Mainstream economics relies on a static comparative methodology. Capitalism is seen as a system that reverts to equilibrium after small departures from it (Rosenberg 1986). The method and conceptual framework of mainstream economics cannot explain the widespread economic effects and irreversibilities in the economy (David 1985; Arthur 1989) caused by the commercialization of radical new products and processes such as the introduction of nylon by DuPont or mainframe computers by IBM. Technology operates over the long run and changes things forever. Firms with better technologies challenge their rivals and this generates winners and losers, the exit of less efficient firms and entry of new firms.

- **Ideological obsession with markets.** Mainstream economists argue that in a well-functioning capitalist economy, it is market coordination that determines the allocation of productive resources (in response to scarcity), with business enterprises adapting to changes in market prices, subject to given technological constraints. The so-called 'Harvard tradition' in industrial organization in the 1960s and 1970s stressed the importance of relatively invariant features of production technologies (e.g. economies of scale) as determinants of observed structures and performance, with market structure determining conduct and performance (Bain 1956; Mason 1957).[1] In line with mainstream economic theory, markets are typically emphasized as the best, or even the only efficient way of organizing and governing an economic system. The market is not seen as one among many social organizational forms found in the economy but the 'protean manifestation of social order itself' (Mirowski 1981: 606). However, as Nelson

(2003) argues, market organization may be far more complex, and with more varied forms, than is suggested by mainstream economics. At the same time, an increasing number of situations exist in which the market is not a very satisfactory way of governing and coordinating behaviour or allocating resources. Regulations and other non-market elements may be necessary to make market governance work, while for many activities it is, or would be, socially more desirable or economically more efficient to use other modes of organization and governance. This obsession with markets obscures important issues associated with the dynamics of capitalism. In particular, firms do not always simply adapt to a given economic environment. For example, firms, such as Ford in the early twentieth century and Intel in the 1990s, adopted organizational and technological innovations that enabled them to change their economic environments and *create* markets by producing completely new products, processes, or services that enabled people to do things that had never before been possible, or which changed the methods of production of a very large number of firms and industries in most national economies. The market is an important institution in capitalism, but it is the interplay between market processes and innovating firms which characterizes capitalism.

- **Technology is given.** Mainstream economics regards technology and science as exogenous, that is, a phenomenon coming from *outside* the economic system, possibly with an impact on the economic system, but essentially a matter for scientists and engineers rather than a business problem or something generated by or influenced by social and economic forces. In practice, however, as this book will go on to elaborate, firms' and countries' competitiveness relies on their ability to access and use new technologies, new rules and modes of doing business, and new abilities to cooperate with other economic actors, innovators, and knowledge institutions (Freeman and Perez 1988). Technology is thus at the heart of economic development and competitiveness of firms and countries, while mainstream economic analysis places it on the periphery (important in its impact, certainly, but not the subject of economic understanding and analysis).

For many decades, thinking about science and technology was dominated by a linear research-to-marketing (or discovery-push) model. In this model, the development, production, and marketing of new technologies followed a well-defined and causal time sequence that originated in research activities, involved a product development phase, then led to production and eventual commercialization. Following this model, federal spending on research and development (R&D) and increases in the education of scientists and engineers became the USA's de facto industrial policy before the Second World War (Best 2001). In the USA, France, and the UK, relatively large expenditures on R&D[2] were justified in the 1940s and 1950s with the expectation that these would benefit the national economy (Freeman 1987). The focus in these three countries was very much on building up a strong research capability in nuclear technology and weapons systems, corresponding to the demands of the Cold War, and support for fundamental research. British policy particularly emphasized government support for basic research rather than civil industrial technology. It soon became clear to policymakers that the model was inadequate, however, when the performance of Britain was compared with that of Japan for example (with a smaller share of world R&D, a concentration on civil and not defence technology, and a much more rapid rate of economic growth in the 1960s). The British economy was clearly not benefiting from the relatively high level (and high-growth rate) of R&D.

Another linear model, known as a 'demand-pull' model, in which innovations were stimulated by market signals, was also proposed, but found to be equally one-sided. Parallel to this change in hypotheses about the determinants of innovation, the emphasis of science policy in the late 1960s and 1970s became increasingly based on a focus on the general economic environment rather than expanding the research and development system (Freeman 1987: 119). This, too, corresponded to the changing needs of OECD countries: increasingly a buyers' market represented pressures for increased efficiency and better competitive performance in international markets, while policymakers were aware that the growth of R&D spending could not be sustained indefinitely.

Debate in the innovation literature about the relative importance of demand-pull and discovery-push forces in stimulating innovation resolved itself around a consensus that innovation is in fact a coupling process between technical possibilities and market demands or opportunities, though at different times in the life cycle of a technology or industry one or other might be the prime mover (Walsh 1984). Today, the innovation process has finally come to be recognized as characterized by continuing interaction and feedback—emphasizing the role of design—the feedback between upstream and downstream phases and between firms and the wider science and technology systems (e.g. Kline and Rosenberg [1986] and Rothwell's 'fifth generation' innovation model [1992]; see Faulkner and Senker [1995] for a review of such models). These models mean that innovation requires attention to be paid to linkages, especially relations between firms and their suppliers and users of their products and services (Lundvall 1985, 1988; von Hippel 1988) and collaborative research relations between firms and universities (Nelson 1998).

- **Ignores the organization of production.** In mainstream economics, the firm is regarded as a 'black box' that will mysteriously but effectively produce output of a given quantity and quality once sufficient material inputs are provided (Rosenberg 1982). Mainstream economics fails to analyse the way in which new knowledge is produced and its interaction with the strategy and behaviour of the firm, or, more generally, fails to recognize the connection between the development of the firm as a productive unit and the development of the wider economy. In Rosenberg's words:

Economists have long treated technological phenomena as events transpiring inside a black box. They have of course recognized that these events have significant economic consequences. ... Nevertheless the economics profession has adhered rather strictly to a self-imposed ordinance not to inquire too closely into what transpires inside that box. (Rosenberg 1982: vii).

Our purpose, instead, and that of the evolutionary or neo-Schumpeterian tradition in which we write, is to break open the black box and examine the processes by which technological change is generated and study the business, organizational, and technological capabilities of the firm, the processes that cause differential growth between firms and the interactions with sectoral and national institutions that support the development of these capabilities in the firm.

- **Focus on price competition.** Conventional economic theory of trade is based on the idea that countries have comparative advantages in certain resources or factor endowments, such as cheap sources of energy, cheap or abundant labour and skills, cheap or abundant raw materials, or readily available capital, and therefore a comparative advantage in the production of certain goods. Countries might thus be expected to specialize in the production and export of these goods, and import those they have less of an advantage in producing.

  This is based in turn on the idea that competition is essentially about the *price* of goods. Since the Second World War, however, an accumulation of evidence about patterns of trade does not fit the comparative advantage theory. For example, the USA (with the most expensive labour and the most capital-intensive economy) was expected to export capital-intensive goods and import labour-intensive goods. The Leontieff paradox (Leontieff 1953) was the observation that, in fact, the USA was exporting goods that were more labour intensive than its imports. Furthermore, the work of various authors collected by Pavitt (1980) suggests that the UK often imported goods that were more expensive than home-produced ones because they were better in some other way (e.g. they were more reliable, performed more functions, or were more innovative).

An alternative approach to innovation

To explain the manner in which innovation occurs and its relation with economic development and competitiveness, this book draws on the contributions of two economists from very different persuasions but whose views on capitalism, innovation, and economic development had much in common: Joseph Schumpeter and Karl Marx. The idea that it is technological change rather than price competition that matters most in the success and growth of firms and economies in capitalist economies was argued by Schumpeter (1942) (see Box 1.1) and Marx (1887) (see Box 1.2) before him. We need not accept all the conclusions reached by Marx or Schumpeter to recognize the importance of their major insights into the process of capitalist development. An alternative to that presented in mainstream economics, on the relation between innovation and economic development, and which draws on the legacy of Schumpeter and Marx has the following characteristics:

- **Capitalism as an evolutionary process.** Capitalism can never be stationary, but is constantly undergoing a process of change and its dynamics are rooted within the system. Capitalism has its own logic and is self-transforming (Rosenberg 1986). If we are willing to take historical analysis seriously, it makes no sense to see economic development simply in terms of firms adapting in response to market forces. Instead they both evolve and change in interaction with each other, and shaping each other. The analysis needs to focus on capitalism as an evolutionary process—the variations in performance of firms in relation to their international competitors, the selection processes that transform firm diversity into structural changes in domestic and international economies and the processes that generate variation in behaviour and performance among firms.

- **Innovation as central to economic change and development.** Introduction of new or cheaper ways of making things or the introduction of wholly new things is central to economic development. In Britain, for example, by the 1960s, a great variety of reasons were being advanced (in sources from the mass media to serious academic analysis) for the relative decline in the country's economic health, including the high prices of British goods compared to competing products, the exchange rate, the number of strikes, the lack of commitment by the workforce, absenteeism, aggressive trade unions, bad management, and long holidays. Essentially these were all variants on *price* factors and the argument that UK goods *cost more* than competing products due to inefficient production, low productivity, and high manufacturing costs. This argument, in turn, is related to mainstream trade theory's concept of 'comparative advantage', discussed earlier. International trade theory underwent a profound change in the 1960s (Freeman 1979). It was perhaps Posner (1961) who first spoke explicitly of 'non price factors', including innovation, in contrast to price and cost factors which had previously dominated trade theory, but Schumpeter (1942: 84) made the same point earlier when he said: '[t]he problem that is usually being visualized is how capitalism administers existing structures, whereas the relevant problem is

Box 1.1 Joseph Alois Schumpeter

Schumpeter (1883–1950, born in Austria) was a conservative scholar who wrote *The Theory of Economic Development*. This book launched him on an academic career (including teaching at Harvard) interrupted by a brief foray into government and business. In this book he argues that the introduction of technological and organizational innovations—new or cheaper ways of making things, or ways of making wholly new things—generates a flow of income that cannot be traced either to the contribution of labour or to the resource owners. The innovating capitalist receives a 'rent' from the differential in his cost. This rent derives from the innovating activity of the entrepreneur and disappears as soon as other capitalists learn the trick of the pioneer. On the heels of the innovators comes a swarm of imitators. The innovation is generalized through the industry, and a rash of bank borrowing and investment gives rise to a boom. But the very generalization of the innovation removes its differential advantage. Competition forces prices down to the new cost of production; profits disappear as routine takes over. As profits decline, so does investment, leading to busts, until the next wave of innovations appears and the whole process starts again.

However, the depression of the 1930s cried out for reasons why new innovations were failing to arrive on time. In his *Business Cycles* he argues that there are three kinds of business cycles—one of quite short duration, a second with a rhythm of seven to eleven years, and a third with a fifty-year duration with epoch-making innovations like the steam locomotive and automobile (and he argued that all three cycles were touching their respective low-points at the same time during the depression of the 1930s). Schumpeter argued that the expectation of profits played an important role in motivating the entrepreneur to innovate (this is sometimes called 'Mark I' model of innovation, associated with Schumpeter (1934), originally published in 1912), but in a later version of his theory gave an important role to corporate R&D and the institutionalization of the capacity for innovation (known as 'Mark II' model with Schumpeter (1942), as he moved from the world of owner-managed firms in turn-of-the century Vienna to the world of large US corporations in the 1930s and 1940s).

In *Capitalism, Socialism and Democracy*, Schumpeter turns his pen towards the only opponent he sees as truly worthy—Marx (notice that Schumpeter is a contemporary of Keynes but he hardly addresses Keynes's arguments). Contrary to Marx, Schumpeter sees capitalism as an economic success, describing capitalist innovation as a 'perennial gale of creative destruction' (Schumpeter 1942: 84) in which the agents of innovation are monopolies (in contrast to other analyses that regard monopolies as sclerotic, or rigid and not readily adaptable, organizations). Capitalism is seen as an economic system caught up in a process of continuous self-renewal and growth. However, when forced to answer whether capitalism would survive, Schumpeter conceded that Marx was right in saying that it would not. Capitalism might be an economic success, Schumpeter argued, but it is not a sociological success:

'Capitalism creates a critical frame of mind which, after having destroyed the moral authority of so many other institutions, in the end turns against its own; the bourgeois finds to his amazement that the rationalist attitude does not stop at the credential of kings and popes but goes on to attack private property and the whole scheme of bourgeois values' (Schumpeter 1942: 143).

He thus argued that the capitalist 'mentality' (rather than its economic logic) brings down the system (what Schumpeter called 'crumbling walls'). For Schumpeter, the main fact about the modern corporation is that managers cannot fill the strong role played by the entrepreneurs. Socialism will succeed, because without the entrepreneurs to guard capitalism, a new class of socialist intellectuals and government officials eventually take over.

Source: Heilbroner (1953), Schumpeter (1934, originally published in 1912), Schumpeter (1942), Philips (1971).

Box 1.2 Karl Marx

Marx (1818–83, born in Germany, and from 1849 resided in London) was a radical scholar and journalist who founded an international working class movement with Friedrich Engels, and paved the way for Lenin, the architect of socialism. His aim was to understand the logic of capitalist development, including the role of scientific knowledge and new machinery, but from the point of view not of the manufacturers but of the workers. He developed a critique of the economic theories of classical economists such as Adam Smith. His book *Capital* examined the intrinsic tendencies of capitalism and concluded with a pessimistic outlook for the survival of the capitalist economy (pessimistic, that is, from the point of view of the manufactures and owners of capital). His dialectical materialist theory of history incorporates Hegel's idea of inherent change, but, unlike Hegel, his theory is not grounded in the world of ideas but in changes in economics (specifically, in the mode of production and exchange). He argued as follows:

'Economic categories are only the theoretical expressions, the abstractions of the social relations of production .... Social relations are closely bound up with productive forces. In acquiring new productive forces men change their mode of production; and in changing their mode of production, in changing the way of earning their living, they change all their social relations. The hand-mill gives you society with the feudal lord; the steam mill, society with the industrial capitalist' (Marx [1867] 1956: 122).

He argued that as organizational and technological forces of production change (as factories destroy handicraft industries, for example) the social relations of production (and social classes) change too, and conflict develops (e.g. the feudal lord fights the rising merchant and the guild master opposes the young capitalist). Gradually, however, the classes in society (and wealth distribution) are rearranged.

In *Capital* he erects a model of pure and abstract capitalism (a capitalism with no monopolies or unions) which he uses to argue that even the best of all possible capitalisms is heading for disaster. This is because one particular commodity, labour power, is different from all others. Workers sell their labour power for its 'value', or wage, that will cover their subsistence but make available to the capitalist the value it produces in a full working way, which is longer than the hours for which he paid, resulting in 'surplus value', the source of profits. While all capitalists have profits, they are also all in competition and as they try to expand their scale of production, wages tend to rise and surplus value tends to fall. Capitalists meet the threat of rising wages by introducing labour-saving machinery, throwing workers into the street. This industrial reserve army of the unemployed competes wages down to their former 'value'. As profits shrink, more labour-saving devices are introduced, reducing profits and leading to bankruptcies and crisis. When capitalists reduce the proportion of workers; however, they are reducing their source of profits and 'killing the goose that lays the golden eggs'. After a crisis, there is a renewal but each renewal leads to the same ending, with more labour-saving technology and large firms absorbing the smaller ones.

Source: Heilbroner (1953), Marx ([1867] 1956).

how it creates and destroys them'. He argued that to define capitalism simply as an economy with private property, market exchange, and competition did not capture its essential ingredients. It was not price competition but innovation that mattered in capitalism, as follows:

Economists are at long last emerging from the state in which price competition was all they saw.... But in capitalist reality as distinguished from its textbook picture, it is not that kind of competition which counts but the competition from the new commodity, the new technology, the new source of supply, the new type of organization (the largest-scale unit of control for instance)—competition which commands a decisive cost or quality advantage and which strikes not at the margins of profits and the outputs of existing firms but at their foundations and their very lives (Schumpeter 1942: 84).

- **Inevitability of crises in capitalism.** Capitalist accumulation is irregular and cyclical, with big structural transformations that tend to lead to crises. Marx regarded crises as a necessary expression of the main contradictions of the capitalist mode of production: the contradiction between the social character of production (factory production and so on) and the capitalist form of appropriation (the owner of the means of production appropriates products which have been exclusively made with the labour of others). Marx argued that, in the search for profits, capitalists reduce the applied volume of live labour (by replacing it with labour-saving innovations) and reduce wages to a minimum (facilitated by the pressure of the industrial reserve army on the labour market leading to cycles of phases-crisis, depression, trade revival, boom, and so on).

Schumpeter also developed a theory to explain booms and bust in terms of innovation in what is called 'long waves'. We will develop this theory in the next section, but before we turn to that it may be worth mentioning that it is Keynes who is best known for addressing the problem of business cycles. While Schumpeter started out as a neoclassical economist who broke with the tradition in two important ways—in developing a theory of economic development and in giving a key role to technological change in his theory—Keynes (see Box 1.3) criticized neoclassical theory but from within. He attacked in particular the view of mainstream economics that the proper role of state intervention is laissez-faire, arguing that state intervention could be used to ensure the full utilization of productive resources so that capitalism could work. Based on the work of Keynes, there is a consensus among economists that one of the main sources of cyclical fluctuations in the economy is the instability of investment. Nevertheless, Keynes did not recognize fully the dominant influence of technological change on investment. As argued by Freeman and Perez:

... in the early stages of radical technical innovation uncertainty prevails, so that Schumpeterian entrepreneurship and Keynesian animal spirits[3] are necessary for the first steps. Once diffusion is under way, even though diffusion itself involves further innovation, the excitement generated by rapid growth of markets and/or exceptional profits of innovations may generate rising confidence and waves of imitation, provided the social and institutional framework and the infrastructure favour these developments (Freeman and Perez 1988: 43).

Box 1.3 John Maynard Keynes

Keynes (1883–1946, born in Britain) was a civil servant and a liberal Cambridge scholar. He accumulated his private wealth effortlessly by dealing in international currencies and commodities, and also generated money as a Bursar of King College. He was gifted in many ways and had varied interests: he was a member of the Bloomsbury group (of avant-garde intellectuals including Lytton Strachey and Virginia Woolf), chairman of a life insurance firm, a collector of modern art, and a writer for the *Guardian*; he ran a theatre; and he was a director of the Bank of England. He wrote a number of influential books but *The General Theory of Employment, Interest and Money* was perhaps his more revolutionary contribution. He set out to explain the Great Depression of the 1930s by arguing that there are no safety mechanisms in the economy. While neoclassical theory tells us that when savings are abundant, interest rates fall and investment increases, this failed to happen in depressions. He argued that savings and investment are undertaken by different groups (on the one hand, savings depend on income and, on the other, investment on confidence, expectations, and 'animal spirits' of businessmen). Uncertainty prevents investment from being a dependable engine for the economy. When the business outlook is poor, businessmen will not invest— paving the way for a possible depression. If savings are not invested by expanding business firms, incomes decline. Capitalism is thus uniquely 'vulnerable' in comparison to other modes of production where there was control of economic life from above:

'Ancient Egypt was doubly fortunate and doubtless owed to this its fabled wealth, in that it possessed two activities, namely pyramid-building and the search for precious metals, the fruits of which, since they could not serve the needs of many by being consumed, did not stale with abundance. The Middle Age built cathedrals . . . . Two pyramids, two masses for the dead are twice as good as one; but not so two railways from London to York. Thus we are so sensible, have schooled ourselves to so close a semblance of prudent financiers, taking careful thought before we add to the "financial" burdens of posterity by building them houses to live in, that we have no such easy escape from the sufferings of unemployment' (Keynes [1935] 1964).

The dismaying conclusion of his work was that there was no automatic safety mechanism in capitalism to solve the problem of unemployment. He proved wrong the assumption that when savings became abundant, they would be cheaper to borrow, and that businessmen would be encouraged to invest. The economy could remain in 'equilibrium' despite the presence of unemployed people and underutilized plant. This is because the economy operates not to satisfy 'wants' but 'demands'. He thus advocated an active role for government policy and public responsibility for the overall level of investment and employment to maintain overall prosperity.

Source: Heilbroner (1953), Keynes ([1935] 1964).

Rooted in the contributions of Schumpeter and Marx, the study of innovation has advanced our understanding of the major trends and patterns of technological change and their links to economic change and development. An important advance is the understanding of the nature of major long-term fluctuations in economic development (these long-term fluctuations were previously identified by the Russian economist Kondratieff ([1925] 1935), and are often known as Kondratieff 'long waves',[4] to which we turn later.

Techno-economic paradigms

Scholars engaged in innovation studies have identified long-term fluctuations that cannot be explained simply in terms of conventional short- and medium-term business cycles. While Keynes, the main contributor to the literature on business cycles, said that depressions reflected the state of expectations of businessmen, his theory did not require him to account for the reason why their 'animal spirits' (confidence to invest) were low. Schumpeter dealt with this problem, and explained booms and busts by the bunching of innovations and the swarming of secondary innovators and businessmen seeking to bring to the market improved versions or new methods of producing the initial, radical innovation. He became famous for explaining long-term development in terms of waves of technological innovation. These waves were fifty years in duration (longer than Keynes' business cycles).

Freeman and Perez (1988) draw on Schumpeter's work and call these long waves 'techno-economic paradigms' ('technological revolutions'), which have such far-reaching effects that they can have pervasive effects throughout the economy, leading not only to the emergence of new products, services, systems, and industries but also affecting almost every other branch of the economy.[5] They affect the input cost structure and conditions of production and distribution, and the general 'technological trajectories' (Dosi 1982; Nelson and Winter 1982), which exert a dominant influence on the outlook of engineers, designers, and managers by defining the path of development within a technological field, the definition of the relevant problems to be tackled, and the specific knowledge related to their solution. Schumpeter's long waves or cycles ('gales of creative destruction') can be seen as a succession of 'techno-economic paradigms' whose diffusion is accompanied by structural crises, in which social and institutional changes are required to bring about a better 'match' between the new technology and the institutions in the economy.

In each techno-economic paradigm, a particular input, which can be described as a key factor, fulfils the following conditions: low and rapidly falling relative cost; unlimited availability of supply over long periods; and pervasive application in many products and processes throughout the economy. This combination of characteristics holds today for microelectronics. It held until recently for oil, which together with synthetic materials, underpinned the post-war boom (the fourth Kondratieff upswing). Before that, the role of key factor was played by low-cost steel and electricity in the third Kondratieff wave, by coal and steam-powered transport in the Victorian boom of the nineteenth century (the second Kontratieff wave) and by cotton and pig iron in the industrial revolution (the first Kondratieff wave) (see Figure 1.1 and Table 1.1).

The new techno-economic paradigm is characterized by a number of features. While mainstream theory puts emphasis on various combinations of labour and

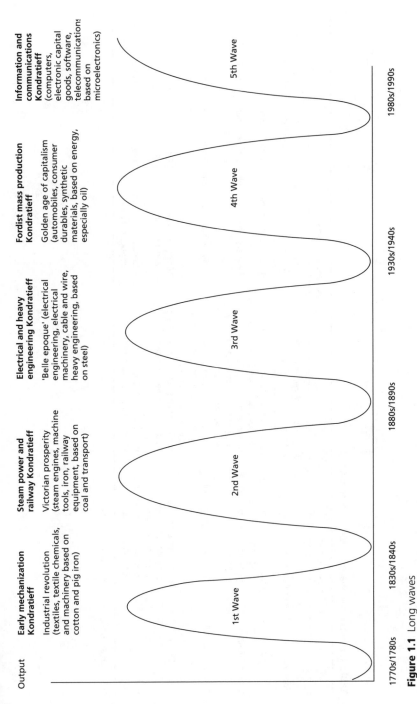

Figure 1.1 Long waves

(*source*: adapted from Freeman and Perez 1988)

Table 1.1 Successive waves of technical change

Long waves or cycles		Key features of dominant infrastructure			
Approx timing	Kondratieff waves	Science, technology, education, and training	Transport, communication	Energy systems	Universal and cheap key factors
First, 1780s–1840s	Industrial revolution: factory production for textiles	Apprenticeship, learning-by-doing, dissenting academies, scientific societies	Canals, carriage roads	Water power	Cotton
Second, 1840s–1890s	Age of steam power and railways	Professional mechanical and civil engineers, institutes of technology, mass primary education	Railways (iron), telegraph	Steam power	Coal, iron
Third, 1890s–1940s	Age of electricity and steel	Industrial R&D labs, chemicals and electrical, national laboratories, standards laboratories	Railways (steel), telephone	Electricity	Steel
Fourth, 1940s–1990s	Age of mass production ('Fordism') of automobiles and synthetic materials	Large-scale industrial and government R&D, mass higher education	Motor highways, radio and TV, airlines	Oil	Oil, plastics
Fifth, 1990s–?	Age of microelectronics and computer networks	Data networks, R&D global networks, lifetime education, and training	Information highways, digital networks	Gas/oil	Microelectronics

Source: Freeman and Soete (1997, Table 1.3, p. 19).

capital and on substitution between them, the approach from Schumpeter (and neo-Schumpeterians) stresses major changes in the price of new inputs and new technologies. Once a new technology is widely adopted the change is generally irreversible (the principal actors become 'locked in' by the pervasive economic and technical advantages and complementarities) (David 1985; Arthur 1989).[6] A new techno-economic paradigm emerges only gradually as a new 'ideal type' of productive organization, to take full advantage of the key factor that is becoming more and more visible in the relative cost structure. The new paradigm has the potential to generate a productivity jump and opens up a range of new investment opportunities (Freeman and Perez 1988).

Techno-economic paradigms are a useful tool to explain shifts in technological leadership or longer-term competitiveness. The emphasis on the role of structural change in economic development, and especially during periods of paradigm change, when the characteristics of innovation undergo transformation, may be especially relevant in explaining the existence of windows of opportunity for some countries when catching up. During those periods, firms in leading countries may experience difficulties to adjust to the new conditions, and the firms in countries that lie behind may find their institutions and organizations more conducive to grasping the opportunities opened by the new paradigm.

This book combines the insights from scholars working on innovation studies (e.g. Nelson and Winter 1982; Dosi et al. 1988; Freeman and Soete 1997) with the insights of economists who specialize in the study of industrial development and international competition (e.g. Best 1990; Lazonick 1991). While the strength of the contributions from scholars working on innovation from an evolutionary and neo-Schumpeterian perspective is their focus on the role of technology in industrial development and change (as we can see, for example, with the contribution on long waves), their weakness is how business capabilities and organization fits into the story. For that reason, we complement the insights of innovation scholars working from a neo-Schumpeterian perspective with the insights from business history, sociology, and economics on the relation between organizational structure and context in the process of innovation. Economic development is regarded here as a structural process that combines business innovation strategy with organizational capabilities to create new economic possibilities.

Competitiveness indices

The concern with competitiveness has spawned a large industry aimed at policymakers, analysts, and firms. The best known product is the competitiveness indices presented in *The Global Competitiveness Report* of the WEF elaborated by Michael Porter and the *World Competitiveness Report* of the International Institute for Management Development (see Table 1.2).

The Geneva WEF has been producing the *Global Competitiveness Report* since 1980 (World Economic Forum 2003). It combines quantitative data (indicators of countries' economic performance, technological capacity, and infrastructure from published data) and an executive opinion survey conducted each year by the WEF from around 4,800 businessmen in 59 countries. The index reflects eight main factors: openness to foreign trade and investment; government expenditure and competence; finance; infrastructure; usage and spread of technology; management quality; costs and efficiency of labour; and quality of institutions. Lall (2001) has commended its emphasis on the

Table 1.2 Top thirty competitiveness rankings by the Institute for Management Development and the World Economic Forum for 2002

Country	IMD competitiveness index	WEF growth competitiveness index	WEF microeconomic competitiveness index
USA	1	1	1
Finland	2	2	2
Luxembourg	3		
Netherlands	4	15	7
Singapore	5	4	9
Denmark	6	10	8
Switzerland	7	6	5
Canada	8	8	10
Hong Kong	9	17	19
Ireland	10	24	20
Sweden	11	5	6
Iceland	12	12	17
Austria	13	18	12
Australia	14	7	14
Germany	15	14	4
UK	16	11	3
Norway	17	9	21
Belgium	18	25	13
New Zealand	19	16	22
Chile	20	20	—
Estonia	21	26	30
France	22	30	15
Spain	23	22	25
Taiwan	24	3	16
Israel	25	19	18
Malaysia	26	27	26
Korea	27	21	23
Hungary	28	29	28
Czech Republic	29	—	—
Japan	30	13	11
Portugal	—	23	—
Slovenia	—	28	27
Italy	—	—	24
South Africa	—	—	29

Source: World Economic Forum (2003) and Institute for Management Development (2002).

microeconomy as the vital determinant of competitive performance, while pointing out some analytical, methodological, and quantitative weaknesses. One of the most important of these is that there is an underlying assumption that markets are efficient and policy intervention, where necessary, must be 'market friendly'. Government measures to strengthen capabilities and promote the exploitation of externalities[7] or overcome the costs and coordination problems of learning are not considered, and relations between free markets and technological development are not seen to vary according to the level of development. As a result, the indices assign uniformly higher values to freer trade, stronger intellectual property protection, and more liberal capital accounts across countries. The conclusion is that the complete solution lies in faster integration with global markets and greater deregulation. In particular, there is no indication as to how to overcome the enormous problem of structural transformation in less-developed countries (Lall 2001).

The Lausanne Institute for Management Development (IMD) produces the *World Competitiveness Yearbook* annual report on the competitiveness of nations based on statistics and executive opinion survey data (of local and foreign enterprises operating in a given country, and local executives as well as expatriates) published since 1989, covering 49 countries and 314 criteria (Institute for Management Development 2002). The IMD places emphasis on survey questions (80 per cent of 174 criteria in 2001 and 40 per cent of 314 criteria in 2002). The *World Competitiveness Yearbook* uses the following factors to rank economies in terms of competitiveness:

• Economic performance: macroeconomic evaluation of the domestic economy (including size and growth of domestic economy, international trade, international investment, employment, and prices).

• Government efficiency: extent to which government policies are conducive to competitiveness (including public finance, fiscal policy, institutional framework, business legislation, and education).

• Business efficiency: extent to which firms operate in an innovative, profitable, and responsible manner (including productivity, labour market costs, and availability of skills, bank and stock market efficiency, management practices, and impact of globalization).

• Infrastructure: extent to which basic, technological, scientific, and human resources meet the needs of business (basic infrastructure, technological infrastructure, scientific infrastructure, health and environment, and value system).

While it is a welcome attempt to include issues of competitiveness and innovation, technological development is considered a question of 'infrastructure' rather than the result of the development of firm capabilities and business strategy and the support from broader institutions in the innovation systems. In the infrastructure criteria, there are some questions on funding and application for technological development and technological cooperation (although perhaps the most concrete question on technology policy is the enforcement of patent and copyright protection).

As in the *Global Competitiveness Report*, the factors related to government efficiency assume that state intervention in business activity should be minimized, with the government role being the creation of adequate macroeconomic conditions and educational resources (see Box 1.4). Government efficiency is measured by openness of public sector contracts to foreign bidders, access to local capital markets to foreign firms, non-discrimination of foreign companies by domestic legislation and flexibility of labour regulations (hiring or firing practices, minimum wage). Business efficiency is mostly about finance and productivity. There is a neglect of the internal production organization of the firm and the combination of this with business capabilities. There is little concern about the strength of firms' technological, organizational, and business capabilities, or how these may differ at different stages of development in different countries. There is also little concern with the links between firms and the wider science and technology infrastructure. There is one question on how relocation of R&D facilities affect the future of the economy but most questions refer to the ease of credit flows to business, development of banking services, and the definition of rights and responsibilities of shareholders. A more general critique of the approaches discussed in this section concerns the emphasis in mainstream economics on numbers as indicators of performance, at the expense of considerations of well-being, quality of life, and the way in which the benefits measured might be distributed throughout the population.

For our purpose of understanding the relation between innovation and competitiveness, these reports offer little help. The reason for the weakness in the most popular competitiveness indices relates to the difficulty of economics in dealing with the concept of competitiveness, a problem to which we now turn.

Economics and the relation between innovation and competitiveness

At the level of the firm, competitiveness refers to the ability of a firm to increase in size, market share, or profitability relative to other firms offering similar products and services (OECD 1992). In mainstream economic theory, comparative costs of production determine relative competitiveness; that is, competitiveness can be increased by reducing the prices of goods and services, which in turn can be done by reducing production costs, for example, by cutting labour costs. Table 1.3 indicates a range of price and non-price factors which can affect the competitiveness of firms. Since the late 1970s, a series of

Box 1.4 Principles of world competitiveness

I Economic Performance

1. [The] prosperity of a country reflects its past economic performance.
2. Competition governed by market forces improves the economic performance of a country.
3. The more competition there is in the domestic economy, the more competitive the domestic firms are likely to be abroad.
4. A country's success in international trade reflects [the] competitiveness of its domestic companies (provided there are no trade barriers).
5. Openness for international economic activities increases a country's economic performance.
6. International investment allocates economic resources more efficiently worldwide.
7. Export-led competitiveness often is associated with growth-orientation in the domestic economy.

II Government Efficiency

1. State intervention in business activities should be minimized, apart from creating competitive conditions for enterprises.
2. Government should, however, provide macroeconomic and social conditions that are predictable and thus minimize the external risks for economic enterprise.
3. Government should be flexible in adapting its economic policies to a changing international environment.
4. Government should provide adequate and accessible resources of quality and develop a knowledge-driven economy.

III Business Efficiency

1. Efficiency together with ability to adapt to changes in the competitive environment are managerial attributes crucial for enterprise competitiveness.
2. Finance facilitates value-adding activity.
3. A well-developed, internationally integrated financial sector in a country supports its international competitiveness.
4. Maintaining a high standard of living requires integration with the international economy.
5. Entrepreneurship is crucial for economic activity in its start-up phase.
6. A skilled labour force increases a country's competitiveness.
7. Productivity reflects value-added.
8. The attitude of the workforce affects the competitiveness of a country.

IV Infrastructure

1. A well-developed infrastructure including efficient business systems supports economic activity.
2. A well-developed infrastructure also includes information technology and efficient protection of the environment.
3. Competitive advantage can be built on efficient and innovative application of existing technologies.
4. Investment in basic research and innovative activity creating new knowledge is crucial for a country in a more mature stage of economic development.
5. Long-term investment in R&D is likely to increase the competitiveness of enterprises.
6. The quality of life is part of the attractiveness of a country.

Source: Excerpt from Institute for Management Development (2002: 665).

Table 1.3 Price and non-price factors

Price factors	Price of goods and services, labour costs, raw material and energy costs, costs of production, marketing and consultancy, exchange rates, costs of operating product, cost of repair and maintenance of product, availability and cost of credit for purchase, cost of customer help lines
Intrinsic or product-related non-price factors	Innovativeness, technological sophistication, performance, good design, aesthetic quality, reliability, durability, safety, ease of maintenance, user-friendliness and ease of use, number of functions, ergonomic quality, environmental friendliness
Associative or firm-related non-price factors—related to organization and production of the goods	Delivery time, after sales service, company reputation, distribution network, ease of obtaining spare parts, bundling with other products, ease of access to retailer, customer services, technical services, advertising and packaging, ethical behaviour (e.g. not made where human rights abuses take place, products not tested on animals)

Source: Walsh et al. (1992).

studies have pointed to the importance of these non-price factors in competitiveness. Non-price factors include: human resource endowments (skills and worker motivation), technical factors (R&D capabilities, ability to adapt, and use technologies), and managerial and organizational factors (not only within the firm but also regarding relations to other firms, customers, suppliers, and public and private research institutes) (Clark and Guy 1998). These non-price factors can either increase the efficiency of production or enable a firm to produce a product or service that did not exist before, thereby not simply increasing market share, but creating a whole new market.

The first difficulty in dealing with the concept of competitiveness is it originated in microeconomics and was later transferred, with some awkwardness, to the level of national economies. The second difficulty is that macroeconomic competitiveness has traditionally been viewed as being principally a question of prices, costs, and exchange rates and therefore simply a matter of conventional macroeconomic policy (OECD 1992). Here, however, the emphasis is on the institutional and structural dimensions of competitiveness, to which we turn later.

First, however, we will consider the difficulty mentioned earlier, the problem of transferring of the notion of competitiveness from the firm to the level of countries. Professional economists argue that competitiveness is a meaningless word when applied to national economies. And in the view of Krugman (1994*b*: 4) 'the obsession with competitiveness is both wrong and dangerous'.[8] Krugman argues that the pattern of international trade and specialization largely reflects historical circumstance rather than underlying national strength, and that the prospects for successful 'strategic' industrial and trade policy to enhance competitiveness (e.g. picking winners, nurturing selected industrial sectors and firms) are not very good (see Chapter 8). This, he argues, is because there is no evidence that it can produce large gains, that reaching a practical consensus on which sectors are really strategic is very difficult and that attempts at introducing strategic trade policy turn into thinly disguised interest-group politics (Krugman 1994b, 1996). However, others have argued that this scepticism is misplaced and that there is a legitimate role for analysis and policy to enhance competitiveness (Lall 2001). Indeed, Lall argues that economics has always been concerned with most issues related to competitiveness—investment, skills, clusters, information, competition policy—even though they have not been integrated under the generic label of 'competitiveness' (Lall 2001).

The second difficulty with the concept of competitiveness, which we mentioned earlier, is that, from a macroeconomic perspective, competitiveness has traditionally been seen as a question of prices, costs, and exchange rates. Its measurement is most often based on changes in market share. There is, however, a problem in equating international competitiveness solely with indicators of relative unit costs or prices. This practice has been sometimes justified by the absence of data on so-called 'non price' factors, although case study data on the importance of non-price factors began to appear in the late 1970s (Blackaby 1979; Pavitt 1980). Kaldor (1978, 1981) pointed to a number of paradoxes arising from this price-dominated approach. Contrary to received theory, a fall in relative unit wage costs and export prices was correlated with loss of export market shares in manufacturing in the USA and UK, and, conversely, a rise in relative unit wage costs and export prices took place alongside an increase in export shares for Germany and Japan. There were other factors that these analyses did not capture (such as the role of skills, production and technological capabilities, and quality of the products).

Similar paradoxes emerged with regard to the direct link assumed between productivity growth and competitiveness. During the 1980s, it was shown that non-material investment (such as improved organization of work and production practices and improved skill of the workforce) contributed significantly to productivity gains (see the example of the Japanese automobile industry in Womack et al. 1990). Nevertheless, the new growth models continued to resort to traditional calculations of productivity growth to explore the relation between productivity and growth (Mytelka 1999). New paradoxes appeared such as rising productivity levels going hand-in-hand with declining sectoral competitiveness, or dramatic export growth in countries like China and Korea without dramatic productivity growth.

In the neo-Schumpeterian or evolutionary tradition, a number of 'new technology trade theories' began to appear following empirical studies that showed more expensive products can outsell cheaper ones (e.g. sector studies including agricultural equipment and textile machinery, see Pavitt [1980]). The factors besides price (non-price factors) that influence purchasers are related to quality. Dosi and Soete (1988) argue that some countries have what appears to be a competitive advantage that allows them to produce goods that are *qualitatively* different. However, they argue, these advantages are not the result of any 'endowment' (such as raw materials or readily available capital) but the outcome of what is essentially *a learning process*: innovative advantages established by gradual accumulation of capital and technology. Furthermore, these are not freely available, but firm specific, and both the result and cause of technological specialization in certain areas.

As argued earlier, with the notable exception of Schumpeter, most economic thinking on technical change has treated it as an exogenous variable. The early work of Solow (1957) found that an exogenous 'residual' associated with technical change accounted for up to one-half of the US economy, according to calculations that related national output to capital and labour inputs only. Since then, econometric models analysing the link between R&D expenditure and productivity growth, or between patents and world trade flows, were developed. Griliches (1995) included a weighted sum of past R&D expenditures, where the weights reflect both delays in the effects of recent R&D and declining returns from earlier expenditures. The results show consistent high rates of return to R&D. Soete (1981) considered the relationship between numbers of patents issued in the USA by various foreign countries and their shares of world exports. Fagerberg (1987) looked at the effect of R&D and world patenting on productivity, using cross-sectional data (yearly averages) for a number of countries for the 1973–83 period. Both authors found an important role for innovation in export performance. Fagerberg found that both R&D and patenting yielded very significant results statistically, with the correlation between productivity and patenting being closer than that between productivity and R&D.

An attempt to represent technical change as an integral part of the development process, through the notion that improvements in technology are frequently incorporated or 'embodied' in new plants and machinery, was included in the so-called 'vintage' class of growth models (beginning with Salter 1962; see Silverberg et al. 1988). The development of evolutionary or neo-Schumpeterian economics brought to the fore the relation between technical change and economic progress. Nelson and Winter (1977) regard innovation as purposive but inherently stochastic (or something that can be analysed rather than precisely predicted), with R&D strategies of firms not following profit-maximizing criteria (one of the central assumptions of neoclassical theory of the firm) but rules of thumb. They also argue that there are powerful intraproject heuristics or problem-solving strategies when technology is advanced in certain directions, with payoffs from advancing in that same direction (or technological trajectory). They also developed the concept of the 'selection environment' to explore the institutional complexity and variety surrounding innovation, including the motivation of firms in the sector in which they operate and the kinds of innovation a firm will find profitable to undertake, the way in which consumers (or other parties) constrain firm behaviour and the mechanisms for information sharing and imitation among firms (Nelson and Winter 1977). The selection environment is the environment into which an innovation is launched. It is a wider concept than that of the market, which includes the market but also other institutions and individuals which determine whether or not a market can exist, such as government regulations, industry standards, and intermediates who test and recommend innovative products (as doctors do in the case of drugs) (Nelson and Winter 1977).

These contributions have made scholars aware of the need to look into the effects of the development of technological and organizational changes at the level of firms and industrial sectors to understand the source and nature of competitiveness. A good example of this is the collection of essays in Mowery and Nelson (1999) that show detailed historical case studies of the evolution of national industries and investigate the factors that have allowed industries at the national level to gain leadership. The evidence points to the importance of the nature of the domestic markets in determining the course of industry development (but, rather than focus on the local availability of natural resources, as the theory of comparative advantage would suggest (see Chapter 8), they focus on the advantages created by firms and policy such as access to high-skilled labour, general infrastructure expenditure, as in university funding and the development of venture capital).

Debates as to whether the organization of national industry matters for competitiveness have pitted Reich (1991) against Porter (1990a, 1990b) (see Lazonick 1993). Reich stresses the importance for countries to invest in the education of its population in order to find employment in world oligopolies (Reich 1991). He argues against the proposition that organization of national industries and national economies matter in global competition in the shift from a high volume to a high-value economy (based on flexible production and demand). He then argues that the government needs to increase education spending to induce entrepreneurs to bring capital to the country and hire 'symbolic analysts'—employees who make contributions derived from education, experience, and expertise and who command high levels of remuneration. These contributions include problem solving (research, product design, and fabrication), problem identifying (marketing, advertising, and customer consulting), and brokerage services (financing, searching, and contracting). However, Lazonick (1993) argues that since the 1970s there has been an increase in education in the USA but decreasing living standards, and it may be wrong to say that the fate of national enterprises does not matter; Reich therefore avoids asking why national competitiveness might have decreased.

In contrast to Reich, Porter (1990a, 1990b) argues that because of intensified global competition, nations have become more rather than less important. He focuses on the importance of industry clusters or cohesive

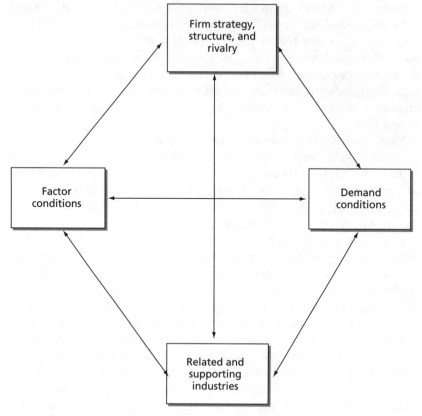

Figure 1.2 Determinants of national advantage
(*source*: Porter 1990a: 77)

industrial and technological communities in national economies. He argues for the need to build specific industries and industrial segments (more technology and skill intensive than the national average) within regions and countries. There are four attributes of a nation that create an environment which promotes clusters (connected by vertical and horizontal relations) of competitive firms (see Figure 1.2):

- factor conditions (skilled labour, infrastructure, specialized scientific institutes, and venture capital), the stock of which is less important than the rate and efficiency of their creation;
- demand conditions, or the nature of the home market demand for the industry's products (the need for sophisticated buyers);

- related and supporting industries such as suppliers which are not 'captive' and are internationally competitive; and

- firm structure, strategy, and rivalry or how firms are created and managed and domestic rivalry among them.

Geographic concentration magnifies cooperation and domestic rivalry. As nations pass through different stages of economic development, government roles shift (encouraging change, promoting domestic rivalry and cooperation, and focusing on specific factor creation).

The studies mentioned previously, which (together with a myriad of case studies) explore the relation between innovation and economic performance, suggest the need for countries to deepen industrialization and widen their linkages to the science and technology infrastructure (see Chapter 2), a point captured in the literature on 'national systems of innovation' (see Chapter 6). 'Structural' competitiveness refers to the fact that 'while the competitiveness of firms will obviously reflect successful management practice by entrepreneurs or corporate executives, their competitiveness will also stem from country-specific long-term trends in the strength and efficiency of a national economy's productive structure, its technical infrastructure and other externalities on which firms build' (OECD 1992: 243). Underlying the national systems of innovation literature is a resurgence of interest in innovation and a reconceptualization of the firm as a learning organization embedded within a broader institutional context (Freeman 1987, 1995; Lundvall 1992; Nelson 1993; Edquist 1997; Laredo and Mustar 2001). From this perspective, competitiveness can be seen as the outcome of a continuous process of innovation that enables firms to stay ahead or keep up as technology and the mode of competition change (Mytelka 1999). Thus, national competitiveness is not just the sum of the efficiency of firms in a country, but also the synergy and externalities generated by collective learning processes. As we will see later, the concept of national systems of innovation point to the systemic elements that influence the effectiveness with which its firms master and operate technology.

Conclusion

Competitiveness of firms is based on factors other than cost of labour, with 'non-price' factors playing an important role. Sound macroeconomic policies remain a factor in competitiveness, but a country's relative unit labour costs do not reflect national competitiveness. Also, while competitiveness is situated at the micro-level, at the level of the firm, in its ability to use better technology and organization, it also depends on the institutional environment in which firms operate. Government policy can affect national competitiveness, in particular though supporting the infrastructure and collective governance outside the scope of individual firms and facilitating the formation of linkages, networks, and interactive connections (OECD 1992).

The rest of the book develops the ideas discussed in this chapter. Part II examines historically the shifts in international leadership as a result of new technology and organization since the late-nineteenth century to the present. Part III examines the strong sectoral specificity and specialization of innovation institutions and the influence of national systems, including national organizations and institutional frameworks and policies, which support the development of firm production and innovation capabilities. Part IV explores the process of globalization, which has obviously a number of implications for innovation and the competitiveness of domestic economies.

Notes

1 The dominant paradigm in industrial economics (e.g. Scherer 1980) is that the structure of an industry (number and size of the producers in it) is on a spectrum from perfect competition at one extreme to monopoly at the other. These structural characteristics are then seen as the principal influence on the behaviour or strategy of firms in terms of pricing, product differentiation, allocation of resources, and collusion (and by implication R&D strategy). In turn, the conduct of the firm determines the profits (or performance) of firms. Although there are many refinements of this model which allow for reciprocal relationships between structure, conduct, and performance, essentially the direction of causality is *from* external factors *to* the behaviour of the individual firm.

2 Figure 2.1 shows that the level of R&D spending in the UK in 1966 was 7 per cent of the world total, which (together with France, also 7 per cent) was the largest after the USA, and higher than that of Germany (6 per cent) and Japan (5 per cent). This share had declined by 1989, while those of Germany and Japan had considerably increased, as shown in Figure 2.2.

3 'Animal spirits' is a term used by Keynes to capture the idea that entrepreneurs or firms take decisions, especially about investment in risky ventures, not only based on careful calculations of likely costs and expected profits but also something less tangible which may be related to the history and philosophy of the firm or the confidence of the entrepreneur in the future. As argued by Keynes (1936: 161–2): 'Animal spirits ... a spontaneous urge to action rather than inaction ... not as the weighted average of quantitative benefits multiplied by quantitative probabilities ... so that the thought of ultimate loss which often overtakes pioneers ... is put aside as a healthy man puts aside the expectation of death.' This is one of the reasons why mainstream economics, which assumes an objectively rational decision-maker who calculates the optimal course of action based on accurate knowledge of costs and benefits, is inadequate in providing a theory of firm behaviour, and for accounting for the wide variety of firm strategies, even within the same industry in a similar economic environment. Other reasons relate to the impossibility of knowing in advance what costs and benefits will turn out to be, which depend in turn on the behaviour of other actors, including competitors, the buoyancy of the economy, and the uncertainty of the outcome of research and development activities.

4 Freeman (1996) surveys the controversies surrounding Schumpeterian theories of long waves.

5 Freeman and Perez (1988) classify innovations into incremental innovations (which occur more or less continuously and generally pass unnoticed, and do not result from deliberate R&D but from improvements suggested by engineers and others engaged in production), radical (discontinuous events, the result of deliberate R&D activity, e.g. nylon and nuclear power), changes in 'technology systems' (combinations of incremental, radical, organizational, and managerial innovations affecting several branches of the economy, for example, the group of synthetic material innovations, petrochemicals innovation, machinery innovations in injection moulding and extrusion) and the most dramatic, the changes in 'techno-economic paradigms' described in this section.

6 David (1985) explains why particular technologies can dominate or become 'locked in' despite not being 'optimal'. He illustrates his argument through the example of the QWER-TYUIOP keyboard arrangement, which has prevailed since its development despite generations of criticisms based on ergonomics. This particular technological arrangement came into being because of chance solution to a design problem (it was designed in the 1860s to slow the typing as there was a tendency of the typebars to clash and jam in typewriters if struck in rapid succession) but then became an element of a 'of a larger, rather complex system of production that was technically interrelated' (manufacturers and buyers of typewriting machines, the advent of 'touch' typing, and the development of a variety of both private and public organizations which trained people in this skill), leading to scale economies (as more users were using this dominant technology) and making the choice of this particular technological arrangement irreversible.

7 An externality occurs when a decision causes costs (e.g. pollution) or benefits (what economists call 'free lunches', for example infrastructure, free education) to stakeholders other than the person making the decision. In general, welfare economists are concerned with negative externalities as these may lead to market inefficiency.

8 This is because in mainstream economics, greater success in some industries will, through the operation of dynamic comparative advantage, involve less market success in other industries, as, for example, exchange rates adjust to reflect the balance of payments consequences of the competitive process.

2 The Science and Technology System

We have argued in Chapter 1 that innovation is of fundamental importance to the survival and growth both of firms and of national economies. A large part of the business activity of firms is based on the introduction and sale of products that did not exist before, of improved products, of new ways of making products, and of new and improved services. We discuss this more fully in Chapter 7. This chapter considers where the inventions and innovations come from in terms of the institutions and parts of the world which specialize in their production, and which provide the sources of the relevant R&D funding.

Essentially innovations come from R&D activity. But the relationship between R&D and innovation is not necessarily a straightforward one. It may be either a long time—or quite a short time—after the necessary R&D activity generates new knowledge or inventions, before any of this becomes part of an innovation. Taxol, for example, the world's best selling anti-cancer drug ever made, until competition from generic products started in 2000, took thirty years from its discovery in the bark of the Pacific yew tree to its approval by the US Food and Drug Administration (Goodman and Walsh 2001). That is a long time for the commercialization of an innovation by any standards.

Furthermore, the R&D may not necessarily have been done, or not all done, by the innovating firm. In fact the firm introducing the new product or service may have done nothing but coordinate all the activities necessary to get something new on to the market—they may have bought in all the expertise necessary and subcontracted production, marketing, and distribution. Chapter 9, on networks of collaboration in the innovation process, discusses further the way innovation can take place as a very widely distributed activity. To continue with the example of Taxol, inventive and innovative work was conducted across a huge network of public and private sector actors. It was first a product of public sector research, carried out by chemists, botanists, cell biologists, and clinical practitioners, in a number of universities and hospital research centres, coordinated and largely funded by the US National Cancer Institute (NCI). Also part of the network were the US Department of Agriculture, logging firms, bulk chemical suppliers, and other subcontractors. Finally, it was commercialized by an industrial firm, Bristol

Myers Squibb, under a series of Cooperative Research and Development Agreements with the National Cancer Institute, US Department of Agriculture and US Department of the Interior, signed after the clinical trials had demonstrated significant positive results against ovarian cancer.

Finally, it is important to take into account the many other extremely important inputs to the innovation process in addition to R&D, including marketing, promotion, packaging, and advertising; production efficiency; finance; the management of the whole process; the efficiency of the organization; and the skills of the staff. All these affect the efficiency with which the scientific and technical knowledge and skills may be developed and turned into new products, processes, and services. We will discuss these issues further in Chapters 6 and 7.

But, with those qualifications, innovation does depend in the final analysis on R&D. And the reason for doing R&D, or at least for paying for it to be done, is the expectation that sooner or later it will lead to the creation of wealth and the improvement of competitiveness. Industrial firms pay for R&D in the belief that wealth will be created for the firm, in the form of profits on investment, and/or that their market share will increase. Governments pay for R&D in the belief that the balance of trade will improve and that wealth will be created for the nation, and sometimes also to contribute to national prestige and security. Improved wealth not only creates a feeling of well-being in a large enough proportion of electors to keep governments in office, but provides the means with which those governments can pay for health care, education, welfare services, and all the other aspects of national infrastructure.

An idea of the potential, at least, for innovation and the creation of wealth may be obtained by looking at where R&D is done: in which countries, by which industries, and by which organizations (e.g. industry, university, public R&D labs, or private non-profit research institutes); and who pays for it, with what sort of goals. This chapter illustrates general trends and how countries/ industries differ. During the life of the book the exact figures will, of course change, but the relative picture will change more slowly: for example those countries where government pays for a lot of R&D and those where industry pays for a much higher proportion; or the industries that are very R&D intensive. These data can be updated by referring to the latest editions of the OECD's *Main Science and Technology Indicators* which comes out every year,[1] and for a larger number of countries, UNESCO's *The State of Science and Technology in the World* which appears much more irregularly.[2]

The OECD was an organization originally formed in 1960 by the USA, Canada and most of the West European countries, with the view of promoting economic growth and employment, and therefore increased standards of living, in its member countries, while maintaining financial stability (OECD 2003a). It also had the goals of contributing to economic growth in the rest of the world and the expansion of world trade, 'on a multilateral, non-discriminatory basis in accordance with international obligations' (OECD 2003a: 2). Thus it was a kind of club for the economically advanced capitalist countries. The less developed, newly industrializing, and centrally planned (also known as communist) economies were not members. Japan joined the OECD in 1964, Finland in 1969, and Australia and New Zealand in 1971 and 1973. Then, after a gap of more than twenty years, a group of the more economically advanced of the less developed and formerly centrally planned (now market) economies joined: Mexico in 1994, the Czech Republic in 1995, Hungary, Poland, and Korea in 1996, and the Slovak Republic in 2000.

The reason for using the statistics published by the OECD is that, for the countries covered, the figures are reasonably comparable. The OECD publishes a range of statistical publications, not only those containing science and technology data. For the latter, *The Frascati Manual* details exactly what the member governments should include or exclude in each category (OECD 2002). Full details of the data and the methodology used for compiling the tables are given in each of the statistical publications. The OECD also started collecting some R&D data from a few non-member countries in the 1990s (Argentina, Israel, China, the Russian Federation, Romania, Singapore, Slovenia, and Chinese Taipei[3]).

Where in the world is most R&D done?

Figure 2.1 is based on figures published by UNESCO, and includes less developed and newly industrializing countries (NICs), but not the centrally planned economies. At the time these countries either did not produce comparable statistics, or they were not considered to be reliable, so the figure represents not the whole world, but just the market economies or capitalist world. The figures are for 1966, at the height of the post-Second World War economic boom and the take-off of the fourth Kondratiev (see Chapter 1). At the time, 98 per cent of all R&D done in the capitalist world was done in the economically advanced countries and only 2 per cent in developing countries. By 1989 (see Figure 2.2, based on figures from a similar group of countries) that had gone up to 4 per cent.

It is reasonable to assume that most of the R&D done in the advanced countries is directed towards the demands or anticipated demands of people in those countries—making goods and providing services that people will pay for—rather than the perhaps more elementary needs of the majority of the world's inhabitants. Of course, there are institutions that carry out research in the richer countries which is designed to benefit the poorer ones: for

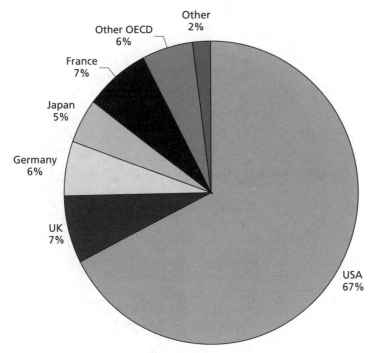

Figure 2.1 Worldwide distribution of R&D by country of performance, 1966 (market economies only)
(*source*: Green and Morphet 1977).

example on tropical medicine or breeding drought resistant crops. Many goods and services produced by business firms are traded on a worldwide basis, though not necessarily designed with the world's poor in mind, and often more readily available to the better off in the poorer countries. The implication for developing countries is that they have to find some mechanism for getting R&D done, aimed at their own problems and needs, and/or transferring some of the results of work done elsewhere to themselves. According to the Declaration on Science and the Use of Scientific Knowledge (quoted by UNESCO 2001: 6):

Most of the benefits of science are unevenly distributed, as a result of structural asymmetries among countries, regions and social groups, and between the sexes. As scientific knowledge has become a crucial factor in the production of wealth, so its distribution has become more inequitable. What distinguishes the poor (be it people or countries) from the rich is not only that they have fewer assets, but also that they are largely excluded from the creation and the benefits of scientific knowledge.

Figure 2.3 (for 1996–7) is based on a different set of figures, this time including a much larger proportion of the world. In particular, China, the

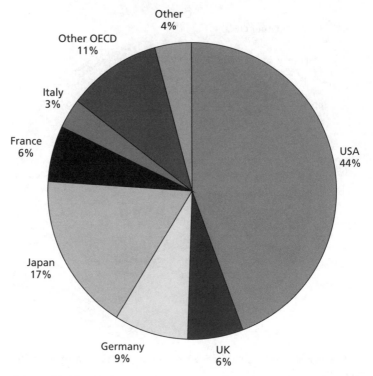

Figure 2.2 Worldwide distribution of R&D by country of performance, 1989 (market economies only)

Note: Freeman's source is the National Science Foundation whose sources in turn include UNESCO and OECD.

(*source*: Freeman 1992)

former Soviet Union, and the formerly centrally planned economies of eastern Europe are all included. According to the authors of the UNESCO report on which it was based, they have used statistics from 83 countries, representing 82 per cent of the world's population and 92 per cent of global GDP (UNESCO 2001: 45). However, due to the grouping of countries in the UNESCO tables on which Figure 2.3 is based, we cannot accurately compare categories such as 'rest of the world' with the earlier figures. Figure 2.4 (based on data in OECD 2003a) gives data for a more recent period, although fewer of the world's economies are included. However, since the OECD's membership expanded in the 1990s (as detailed earlier) and since the OECD has begun publishing statistics for a number of non-member countries, Figure 2.4 gives a reasonable coverage of the world for most purposes. Using both the UNESCO and OECD reports, we have calculated that the share of R&D carried out by the same groups of countries as in the category

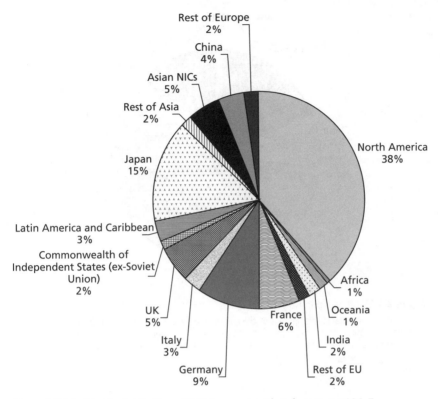

Figure 2.3 Worldwide distribution of R&D by country of performance 1996–7

Note: The world total for this figure comes from all the countries for which UNESCO collects data.

(*source*: calculated by authors using data from UNESCO [2001] and OECD [2003a]).

labelled 'rest of the world' in Figures 2.1 and 2.2[4] had reached about 13 per cent by 1996–7. This is still a very small proportion, bearing in mind the fact that the whole 'pie' now includes the former centrally planned economies[5] (not included in Figures 2.1 and 2.2), and especially if we take into account the populations represented in these countries. But it is nevertheless a huge growth in relative terms. According to UNESCO (2001: 6–7), less developed countries had 77.7 per cent of the world's population, 38.9 per cent of its GDP and 15.6 per cent of its gross expenditure on R&D. Chapter 5 discusses these issues further, and considers the question of latecomer industrialization and 'catching up'.

At the height of the post-war economic boom (Figure 2.1), two-thirds of the R&D done in the capitalist world was carried out in the USA. The reason why such a large share took place in the USA is, of course, partly because it is a large country (though less than 5 per cent of the world's population)[6] with more resources than any other (GDP was 21.8 per cent of the world total in 1996–7). Among the economically advanced countries Japan had the next

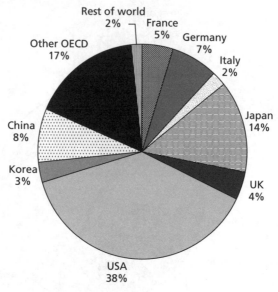

Figure 2.4 Share of world R&D, 2001

Note: The 'world' total in this figure is all the countries for which the OECD collects data, i.e. member countries plus China, Argentina, Israel, Romania, Russian Federation, Singapore, Slovenia, and Chinese Taipei. Excluded are thus India, Africa, the rest of Latin America, and the rest of Asia.

(*source:* OECD 2003a)

largest population but in the 1960s it did a much smaller proportion of the world's R&D. By 1989, the shares had changed quite considerably (Figure 2.2). The USA was doing only 44 per cent of the total R&D though still by far the largest share of any one country. Japan's share by then was approaching around half that of the USA, with around half the GDP as well. This is a very big growth in the resources devoted to R&D in Japan, and a major decline in that done the USA in relative, though not necessarily in absolute, terms. The UK also had a decline in its share of total R&D, and France had a small decline. There was a substantial growth in Germany's share (the effects of reunification were not reflected in OECD statistics until 1991) and that of 'other OECD' (especially the share of the smaller advanced countries such as the Netherlands and the Nordic countries).

The most notable addition in the data for the 1996–7 (Figure 2.3) are the contributions from the Asian NICs (in which Korea's share was particularly important) and China. Figure 2.4 shows that China's level of R&D spending had reached the third highest place in the world by 2001, at nearly US$60 billion or 8 per cent of all the countries for which statistics are collected (see also OECD 2003a: 14 and Appendix Table 1), after the USA (US$282 billion and

38 per cent of those in Appendix Table 1) and Japan (nearly US$104 billion or 14 per cent of those in Appendix Table 1) and above Germany (nearly US$54 billion or 7.3 per cent of Appendix Table 1). R&D spending in China has grown rapidly since 1996–7 when it was US$21 billion (4 per cent of the world total) compared to the USA's US$199 billion (36 per cent of the world total), and Japan's US$83 billion (15 per cent of the world total) (UNESCO 2001: 7). In the same period China's R&D spending has grown from 0.6 per cent of GDP in 1996 to 1.1 per cent in 2001 (with 60 per cent coming from companies, both domestic and foreign (Marsh 2003).

Table 2.1 shows that as a percentage of GDP (representing national income) the USA still spends a lot, but not as much as Sweden, Finland, Japan, Iceland, and Korea. Some small countries are proportionately large spenders when their R&D expenditure is considered as a percentage of GDP—Sweden, Finland, Iceland, Switzerland, and Denmark are all in the top 10, indicating the relative importance given to R&D even if the country has limited resources. Among NICs, Korea has increased its R&D spending massively as part of a deliberate strategy. Figure 2.4 shows that Korea now spends 3 per cent of the world's total R&D funds. (Recall that all the 'rest of the world' combined accounted for only 2 per cent of the world's total R&D spending in 1966.) In absolute terms, Korea had by 2001 a higher proportion of the world's R&D expenditure than all the other OECD countries except the USA, Japan, Germany, France, and the UK, although its GDP was only in 10th place.

Table 2.1 Gross domestic expenditure on R&D as percentage of GDP, 2001 or latest year

OECD country	%	OECD country	%
Sweden	4.27	Canada	1.85
Finland	3.40	Norway	1.62
Japan	3.09	Australia	1.53
Iceland	3.04	Czech Republic	1.30
Korea	2.96	Ireland	1.17
USA	2.82	Italy	1.07
Switzerland	2.63	New Zealand	1.03
Germany	2.50	Spain	0.96
France	2.20	Hungary	0.95
Denmark	2.19	Portugal	0.78
Belgium	1.96	Greece	0.67
Austria	1.94	Poland	0.67
Netherlands	1.94	Slovak Republic	0.65
EU	1.93	Turkey	0.64
UK	1.90	Mexico	0.43
	OECD Total 2.33		

Source: OECD (2003a).

The institutions carrying out the R&D

In a book first written in the 1960s, de Solla Price (1986) estimated that about 80–90 per cent of the scientists who had ever lived were still alive then, compared to about 95 per cent of the people in the world who had ever lived, who were dead by that time. Thus at a conference of physicists attended by a great many of those who had made epoch-making discoveries, one of the speakers was able to say: 'Today we are privileged to sit side-by-side with the giants on whose shoulders we stand' (Price 1986: 1).

Although there are now some billion or so more people in the world than there were in the 1960s, and the percentage of people alive today, out of those who have ever lived, is slightly higher, the general argument that the growth of science is a very recent phenomenon has not changed.

The stereotype of a scientist was once an eccentric professor or at least some kind of academic, or perhaps a lone inventor. Today we can see from Table 2.2 that academic scientists represent a minority of those responsible for R&D, and of invention and innovation. In the case of the lone inventor, as we shall see later, they represent a tiny minority of those responsible for invention (never mind innovation) today. Table 2.2 shows that most R&D is done by business enterprises: over half in all the countries in the table, though with national variations (see Chapter 6 on national innovation systems for more discussion on these variations): it is nearer three quarters in the USA and Japan, about two-thirds in the UK, a bit less in France, a bit more in Germany and only just over half in Italy. In all the countries for which the OECD provides statistics (see Appendix Table 1) only the following have under half of their R&D done by firms: Australia, Greece, Hungary, Mexico, New Zealand, Poland, Portugal, Turkey, and Argentina. Over 70 per cent is done

Table 2.2 R&D resources by sector of performance, 1985 and 2001

Country	Year	Industry	Government	Other including higher education	Total (%)
USA	1985	72.6	11.7	15.7	100
	2001	74.4	7.0	18.6	100
UK	1985	62.5	19.9	17.6	100
	2001	67.4	9.7	22.9	100
Japan	1985	71.8	9.8	18.4	100
	2001	73.7	9.5	16.8	100
France	1985	58.7	25.3	16.0	100
	2001	62.4	13.4	19.9	100
Germany	1985	73.1	12.9	13.9	100
	2001	70.5	13.4	16.1	100
Italy	1985	56.9	23.9	19.2	100
	2001	50.1	18.9	31.0	100

Source: OECD (2003a).

by firms in Belgium, Finland, Germany, Iceland, Japan, Korea, Sweden, Switzerland, the USA, Israel, and the Russian Federation.

In the UK, France, the USA, and Italy, the share done by government has gone down since the mid-1980s, while in Germany and Japan it has remained about the same. In the UK and some other countries this partly reflects the privatization of certain government laboratories as well as reduced government budgets overall. France and Italy have a particularly high share of R&D carried out by government organizations. Although in these countries government research laboratories, such as CNRS, INRA, and INSERM in France and CNR in Italy, employ people who would be classified as part of the university sector in the Anglo-Saxon countries, in fact this is not a complete explanation of the high level of government R&D, since in practice the OECD includes CNRS (France) in its classification of the higher education sector, although CNR (Italy) is included in the government sector (OECD 2003a: 75).

The professionalization of science and technology

In this section we shall briefly examine the evolution of science and technology from being an activity carried out by very few people, either with private incomes for whom science was a hobby (though often a very serious undertaking) or an activity sponsored by patrons in much the same way as art and music.

In the Renaissance, the political and religious cultural environment encouraged alchemists and other experimentalists to keep secret the knowledge they generated, in case it put power over material things into the 'wrong' hands—and especially into those of the 'vulgar multitude' (David 2001). At the same time, knowledge which was obviously potentially profitable, like geographical knowledge relevant for trade routes, or technological 'recipes', was also kept from the public domain, for example as the craft and guild 'mysteries' of the industrial arts. Meanwhile, priests or aristocrats who practiced science were seen as having no 'sordid' material motives, because they did not need external sources of money (Shapin 1999; Calvert 2002).

David's paper mentions this environment for discovery at the time of the Renaissance, as a starting point for analyzing the transition to a period in which the institutionalization of 'open science' took place. By 'open science' he meant the open pursuit of knowledge by members of state-sponsored academies, such as the Royal Society and the Academie Royale des Sciences—which emerged in the seventeenth and eighteenth centuries—together with the associated norms of disclosure and demonstration, and the formation of active networks of correspondence which gave way to the publication of learned journals. The appearance of 'co-operative rivalries' in the revelation of new knowledge was also a feature of this development.

Court and ecclesiastical patronage of the arts and sciences had two motives: the generation of useful, practical knowledge to solve problems such as those associated with warfare, food production, or transport; and the gaining of prestige as a result of science's claims to reveal the secrets of nature. This in turn promoted reputation-building by scientists in various ways—though the term 'scientist' had not yet been adopted and they were known as natural philosophers—and this stimulated the growth of peer appraisal and collective evaluation.

In addition to the identification of a recognizable body of practitioners with agreed forms of recognition and evaluation, the professionalization of science meant securing adequate funding for those who practiced it. Table 2.3 contains a selection of scientists listed in Gascoigne's book (1987), who were born during the fifteenth to nineteenth centuries, indicating their source of funding and how this evolved. The table is intended to be illustrative, rather than a representative sample, and the scientists listed were selected to include well-known scientists from a variety of disciplines and countries. It can be seen that the earlier names in the table are frequently those of scientists (or natural philosophers) who relied on royal, aristocratic or church patronage or who had independent incomes themselves. An example is Robert Boyle in the seventeenth century, who was an Anglo-Irish aristocrat and landowner, though Isaac Newton, born only fifteen years later, was an early example of a natural philosopher with an academic job. Patronage began to give way to private scientific societies and later state-sponsored academies as supporters of science. France began the process of transforming science from a hobby to a profession: when the Ecole Polytechnique was founded, students were taught science by people who were active in research. Increasingly over time, we can see that those listed in Table 2.3 were reliant on other sources of income, though not very often to begin with on science itself as gainful employment. Several were doctors, Scheele was an apothecary, and Priestley was a nonconformist minister of religion. During the nineteenth century it became more common for natural philosophers to be employed in positions related to the practice of scientific research, for example giving public lectures, and increasingly in university teaching jobs, although Charles Darwin, in the middle of the nineteenth century, was a late example of a scientist who lived the life of a country gentleman, and as a young man worked unpaid as a naturalist on *The Beagle*.

Only a small proportion of scientists are employed, even today, as full time academic researchers. The majority are employed in industry. Among scientists employed in non-industrial laboratories, a minority are employed full-time on research in some countries. For example, in the USA and UK academic scientists are normally either university teachers who may have permanent contracts but do research part-time, or full-time researchers

Table 2.3 Selection of scientists and their employment (in chronological order by date of birth)

Name	Dates	Important discovery	Main job
Nicholas Copernicus	1473–1543	The 'Copernican revolution' in astronomy—sun-centred universe.	Canon of Frauenburg cathedral (Poland).
Tycho Brahe	1546–1601	Astronomical observations which supported theory of sun-centred universe.	Supported by patrons: the King of Denmark, then the Holy Roman Emporer in Prague. Made astronomical instruments.
Galileo Galilei	1564–1642	Properties of a pendulum; Independence of weight and rate of fall; astronomical observations which gave support to Copernican theory.	Made telescopes for the Grand Duke of Tuscany.
Robert Boyle	1627–91	Relationship between pressure and volume of gases.	Anglo-Irish Landowner.
Isaac Newton	1642–1727	Gravity, paths of moving bodies, movement of planets, trajectories.	Professor of mathematics at Cambridge University.
Carl von Linné (Carolus Linneus)	1707–1859	Classification of plants and animals.	Doctor who went into botany via medicinal plants.
Joseph Black	1728–99	Latent and specific heat.	Doctor; professor of medicine at Glasgow University.
Joseph Priestley	1733–1804	Discovery of dephlogisticated air (oxygen).	Non-conformist minister.
James Watt	1736–1819	Major improvement to steam engine	Shipbuilder, instrument maker.
William Herschel	1738–1822	Discovery of Uranus.	Professional musician, then astronomer to the British King. Made telescopes for sale.
Carl Scheele	1742–1786	Discovery of fire air (oxygen).	Apothecary.
Claude Berthollet	1748–1822	Reversibility of reactions.	Physician to Duc d'Orléans; then inspector of dyeworks at Les Gobelins tapestry factory; later senator.
Antoine Fourcroy	1755–1809	Chemistry of plant alkaloids.	Director general of public instruction (reformed French higher education) and professor of chemistry.
Alexander von Humboldt	1769–1859	Scientific voyages, plant collections, work in earth sciences.	Independent income; mining inspector for Prussian government; later lord-in-waiting to the Prussian King.

(*Continued*)

Table 2.3 (*Continued*)

Name	Dates	Important discovery	Main job
Han-Christian Oersted	1777–1851	Relationship between electricity and magnetism.	Gave public lectures, then professor at University of Copenhagen.
Humphry Davy	1778–1829	Work on electricity, heat and light.	Gave public lectures at the Royal Institution.
Louis-Joseph Gay Lussac	1778–1850	Combination of gas in simple proportions by volume eg showed that water was made from two parts hydrogen and one part water.	Taught at Ecole Polytechnique; worked for Napoleon's government—director of national gunpowder factory, chief assayer at the Mint, discovery of lead chamber process for sulphuric acid.
Michael Faraday	1791–1867	Electricity.	Assistant to Humphry Davy (i.e. washed up, copied out lecture notes, more like a servant); later director of research at Royal Institution.
Justus von Liebig	1803–73	Application of chemistry to agriculture.	Professor of Chemistry.
Charles Darwin	1809–82	Scientific voyages, theory of evolution.	Country gentleman—not expected to work for a living.
Louis Pasteur	1822–95	Molecular asymmetry, fermentation, vaccine for rabies	Schoolteacher, then university administrator.
Gregor Mendel	1822–84	Foundation of genetics.	Monk.
Lord Kelvin (William Thomson)	1824–1907	Theories of heat, work on electricity and magnetism.	Professor of Natural Philosophy, Glasgow University.
James Clerk Maxwell	1831–79	Electromagnetism; differential equations.	Professor of National Philosophy at Aberdeen, then London; lived for a while as landed gentleman in Scotland, then established Cavendish Laboratories at Cambridge (experimental physics).
Dmitry Ivanovitch Mendeleev	1834–1907	Periodic table of the elements.	Professor of chemistry St Petersburg.
William Henry Perkin	1838–1907	Discovery of aniline purple (mauve), 1st synthetic coal-tar dye. Founder of synthetic dye industry.	Assistant to Hofmann at Royal College of Chemistry; owner-entrepreneur of dye firm from age 18; retired at age 36 and continued in full-time research, funded by the profits of his firm.
Marie Curie	1867–1934	Radium, polonium, radioactivity.	Professor of Chemistry at the Sorbonne, Paris.

Source: Selected and assembled by the authors from Gascoigne (1987).

employed only on fixed term contracts. In other countries, such as France and Italy, it is more normal for researchers to be permanent, full-time civil servants[7] employed by organizations such as the Centre National de la Recherche Scientifique[8] or the Consiglio Nazionale delle Ricerche. This is discussed further in Chapter 6.

In addition to funding, the professionalization of science also involved promoting it as an activity 'in its own right', formalizing a definition of what it was, and what it was not, generating a sense of self-awareness or specialness (like a 'corporate identity') among practitioners, and promoting loyalty and accountability to the discipline and other members of the group. The name 'science' was chosen, as in the British Association for the Advancement of Science established in 1831 (which was presented as quite distinct, too, from the 'aristocratic' Royal Society).

According to Francis Bacon, the natural philosophers' success at exercising power and dominion over nature attracted the attention of entrepreneurs, who adapted the methods of natural philosophy to gain power and dominion over human productivity in the context of various industries emerging during the eighteenth century. This, in turn, stimulated the industrial revolution (Aikenhead 2003). During the nineteenth century, according to Aikenhead (2003), natural philosophers made efforts to distance themselves from technologists, portraying them as merely those who applied the abstract knowledge of natural philosophy, and thus representing 'pure science' as superior to practice, and the pursuit of knowledge as a vocation rather than simply a job.[9] Furthermore, scientists had to find sources of finance, while technology led to economic returns. However, in our view, this separation was more of an Anglo-Saxon trend: engineers had higher status elsewhere.

To turn now from professionalization of pure science to that of technology, we focus on the evolution of the in-house corporate R&D laboratory. Freeman and Soete (1997) have argued that this was one of the most important organizational innovations to be introduced over the century that began in the 1870s. At the time of the industrial revolution, when industry was dominated by cotton, iron and coal, railways and heavy engineering, and Manchester and Birmingham were among the high-tech centres of the world, new machines—innovations—were often produced by the people who worked with the machinery, based on observation, imagination, trial and error (Freeman and Soete 1997: 9). See also the discussion on this in Chapter 3.

Skilled craftsmen with experience of adjusting their machines could often imagine new ways in which the machine might be made to work more efficiently. New arrangements of levers, pulleys, cogs, and wheels are not difficult to imagine if you are used to working with them. Some people are good at fixing and improving equipment, machinery, and mechanical things without necessarily having any theoretical knowledge of the principles on which those things work, rather as those who are said to have 'green fingers' are good at making plants grow. Alternatively, new machinery was sometimes made by engineers who specialized in design but were still essentially crafts-men. Very occasionally, insights that contributed to new machinery would come from outside: from science or natural philosophy.

The steam engine, by posing the question of power as the most important technical issue of the nineteenth century, stimulated the search for under-standing the principles that related work, power, and energy in the laws of thermodynamics. It was not the other way around: steam engines were not designed because someone had come up with the laws of thermodynamics in the abstract (Lilley 1949). Although, of course, there was an interaction between the new understanding and new knowledge on the one hand, and the innovation process on the other, and new designs were subsequently made to take advantage of the theoretical understanding of mechanical efficiency and other contributions of the laws of thermodynamics.

The institutional innovation of the in-house R&D laboratory was intro-duced by the chemical industry, and quickly taken up by the electrical industry. This was not an accident. Imagining new machinery was one thing. Imagining new chemicals, and later electrical innovations, was an entirely different matter. Some abstract conception from quite fundamental science, of atoms, molecules and bonds and their arrangement in space, or of the movement of electrons through matter, was necessary to chemical and electrical innovation. For a production worker, it was not possible to imaginatively 'design' a new arrangement of atoms or way of moving elec-trons around, as a result of ingenuity and day-to-day experience (Walsh et al. 1992: 120). Accidental discoveries that led to chemical and electrical innov-ations could still happen: for example Perkin's discovery of aniline purple, the basis of the take-off of the synthetic dye industry, happened when he was trying to make quinine from coal tar. But the rate of dye innovations began to decline again until a new development in academic chemistry, in the form of Kekulé's proposal for the structure of benzene, opened up a new range of opportunities (Walsh et al. 1992: 120). While innovation in engineering stimulated the development of a new branch of science, innovation in chem-istry was itself stimulated by advances in the science of organic chemistry.

Developments such as these encouraged a period of close collaboration between academic research chemists and inventor/entrepreneurs and then that in its turn promoted the desire for more direct control over the science that was being carried out. German chemical firms established their own R&D labora-tories from the 1870s, quickly followed by American electrical firms, but long before the same kind of pressure was felt by engineering firms. That these developments took place in Germany and the USA rather than elsewhere was the result of the particular combination of institutional arrangements in those countries, as discussed in Chapters 3 and 6.

By internalizing R&D, the firm was able to increase its control over the rate and direction of technological change, reduce some of the risks and uncertainties involved in it, and appropriate new areas of knowledge. The firm was therefore able to negotiate and control some aspects of its environment, rather than simply respond to it. The in-house R&D laboratory revolutionized the way firms compete and change their technological bases, and it increased the firm-specific and cumulative nature of technology (Coombs et al. 1987; Freeman and Soete 1997). Thus firms were more easily able to build up competencies based on previous successes, experiences, learning-by-doing, and probably some failures, which were particular to any given firm because no other firm would have the same set of people, talents and skills, knowledge, experiences, or personalities.

In most industries and countries in-house R&D was quite limited before the First World War. Mowery (1983) has analyzed the important role of independent research organizations in the USA in the early years of the twentieth century, showing that they employed more than 15 per cent of private sector professional scientists in 1921 and still nearly 7 per cent in 1945, (see Table 2.4). Over the century, the in-house laboratory became the main form of private sector organization for R&D. While R&D was overwhelmingly the work of independent individuals in 1900, it had become dominated by business enterprise by 1950. In the field of plastics, Table 2.5 shows the decline in number of patents taken out by individuals in comparison with corporate patents, from 43 per cent of the total before 1930 to 8 per cent in the period

Table 2.4 Employment of scientific professionals in independent research organizations as a percentage of the employment of scientific professionals in all in-house and independent research laboratories in USA, 1921–46

Year	Scientific professionals in independent research organizations
1921	15.2
1927	12.9
1933	10.9
1940	8.7
1946	6.9

Source: Mowery (1983).

Table 2.5 Patents on plastics: Percentage taken out by individuals and organizations, 1791–1955

Date	Individuals (%)	Organizations (%)	Total (%)
1791–1930	43	57	100
1931–45	15	85	100
1946–55	8	92	100

Source: Delorme (1962) cited by Freeman and Soete (1997: 117).

1946–55. The real take-off of organized industrial R&D was after the Second World War, after which time the statistical data available show the concentration of R&D in industry. These issues are discussed further in Chapter 3.

Organizations which fund R&D

Perhaps more significant in terms of the goals of the research and the influence over the rate and direction of technological change, is who pays for it, rather than who does it, see Table 2.6. In the USA, France, and the UK, the percentage of funds coming from government sources has gone down sharply since 1985. At the same time, the share of funds from industry has gone up from 50 to 68.3 per cent in the USA and from 41.4 to 52.5 per cent in France, but has not changed significantly in the UK. Instead, in the UK, the share from the category 'other' has significantly increased from 10.5 to 23.6 per cent of R&D funds. This category includes charitable trusts, foundations, and other non-profit making organizations such as the Wellcome Foundation and Cancer Research UK, which pay for a lot of medical research in Britain, as do a large number of smaller charities associated with particular illnesses, such as the Muscular Dystrophy Society and DebRA (the national charity working on behalf of people with the genetic skin condition Epidermolysis Bullosa). Indeed the reduction in share of funding from Government appears to have been replaced by funds from such sources, and industry's share of R&D funding in Britain is still under half, while in other countries, most notably the USA, Government's share has been replaced by industrial funding. In France, Callon and Rabeharisoa (2003) have studied the role of organizations of patients and their families in shaping research in the illnesses which concern

Table 2.6 R&D resources by source of funds 1985 and 2001

Country	Year	Government	Industry	Other	Total (%)
USA	1985	48.3	50.0	1.7	100
	2001	26.9	68.3	4.8	100
UK	1985	43.4	46.0	10.5	100
	2001	30.2	46.2	23.6	100
Japan	1985	19.1	74.0	6.9	100
	2001	18.5	73.0	8.5	100
France	1985	52.9	41.4	5.6	100
	2001	38.7	52.5	8.8	100
Germany	1985	36.7	61.8	1.5	100
	2001	31.5	66.0	2.5	100
Italy	1985	44.7	51.7	3.6	100
	2001	51.1	43.9	5.0	100

Source: OECD (2003a).

them, and the share of R&D funds from these sources is also significant in that country, as it is in Japan, though much smaller than in the UK. The increase in industry funding has been more important than 'other' sources in making up for the reduction in share of government funding in France. Indeed, although the share of R&D paid for by industry is only just over half in France, the growth in that share has been quite remarkable over the past 20–30 years: earlier OECD statistics indicate that industry paid for only 38 per cent of French R&D in 1975. This is discussed further in Chapter 6.

In Germany and Japan government funding was lower to start with (especially in Japan) and has not gone down very much, while industry pays for two-thirds and nearly three-quarters of R&D, respectively. In Italy the share from government has gone up, and the share from industry has gone down. Appendix Table 2, which gives figures for all the countries for which the OECD provides statistics, shows that in the following countries, industry pays for less than 50 per cent of R&D: Australia, Austria, Canada, Greece, Hungary, Iceland, Italy, Mexico, New Zealand, Poland, Portugal, Spain, Turkey, the UK, Argentina, Romania, and the Russian Federation. Of these, it is less than one-third of the total in Greece, Mexico, Poland, Portugal, and Argentina. Industry pays a high proportion, over 70 per cent of the total, in Belgium, Finland, Japan, Korea, and Sweden, and over 60 per cent in Germany, Iceland, Switzerland, the USA, Israel, and Chinese Taipei, the OECD mean being 63.6 per cent.

The era of cutting back on public spending, and of public policy oriented towards encouraging market forces, began seriously in the 1980s under many national governments, most notably those of Ronald Reagan in the USA and Margaret Thatcher in the UK. This trend started later in France—in fact in the early 1980s France was embarking on a new phase of nationalization during François Mitterrand's first term of office, just at the time when the trend elsewhere was to cut back on public spending and in some cases to privatize sectors which had previously (or in the case of some sectors, always) been in public ownership. Privatization in France began in 1986 under the first 'cohabitation' (of a socialist president [Mitterrand] and a conservative government), but the major wave was in the 1990s, following the Law of 19 July 1993 and the privatization of twenty-one major enterprises such as the chemical and related products firm Rhône Poulenc.

The relative shares of R&D paid for by government and by industry can be very significant as a reflection of any country's public policy towards industry, towards promotion of innovation, and concerning the role of government. These shares are also reflected in the success or failure of such policies. These issues are discussed in more detail in Chapter 6. A longer term indication of the changes in industry-funded R&D is given for the USA, Japan, the EU, and the OECD as a whole in Figure 2.5. As a percentage of GDP, industry-funded R&D in Japan has been higher than in other countries, and has continued to grow overall, though there was a short period of decline in the early 1990s.

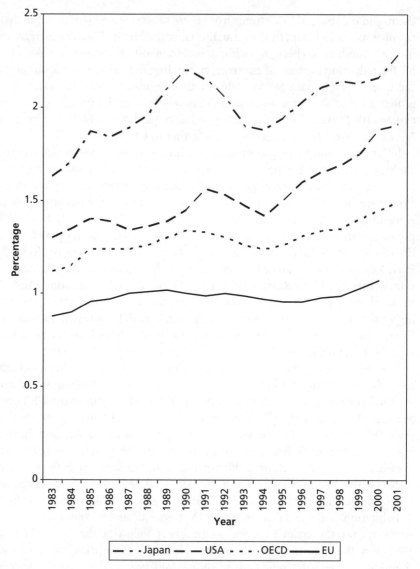

Figure 2.5 Industry-financed GERD as percentage of GDP, 1983–2001

(*source*: OECD *Main Science and Technology Indicators,* various years)

The greatest rate of growth has been that of the USA. Industry-funded R&D has grown as a percentage of GDP in the EU, though very little during the 1990s, despite the rather more rapid rate of decline of government-funded R&D as a percentage of GDP shown in Figure 2.6.

The OECD (2003a: 16) shows that the gross domestic expenditure on R&D (GERD) has grown in the OECD area 1983–2001 as a percentage of GDP,

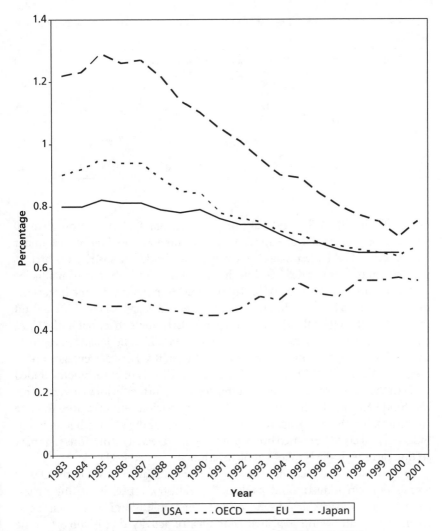

Figure 2.6 Government financed GERD as percentage of GDP, 1983–2001
(*source*: OECD *Main Science and Technology Indicators,* various years)

though it was not significantly greater in 2001 than it was in 1990 for the OECD as a whole, for the EU and especially for the USA,[10] due to the decline in these areas in the early 1990s. Japan was an exception, with a growth over the whole period (despite fluctuations) to approximately 3 per cent of GDP in 2001.

Table 2.7 indicates the sources of funds for research carried out by industry, from which it is clear that business firms also do quite a lot of R&D paid for by governments, as well as from their own investments, Japan being an exception with less than 1 per cent in this category. Japan, Germany, and Korea are all countries in which industry funds more than 90 per cent of the R&D it carries

Table 2.7 Sources of funds for research carried out by industry (%), 2001 or nearest year available

OECD country	Industry	Government	Other national sources	Abroad	Total
France	81	9.9	0.1	9	100
Germany	90.6	7.1	0.2	2.1	100
Italy	80.7	12.2	0.2	6.9	100
Japan	97.9	0.8	0.8	0.5	100
Korea	91.2	8.1	0.2	0.6	100
UK	64.4	11.9	0	23.7	100
USA	89.1	10.9	0	n/a	100
EU	83.7	7.8	0.1	8.4	100

Source: OECD (2003a).

out itself. The UK, USA, and Italy, on the other hand, all have more than 10 per cent of industrial R&D funded by government, and France just under 10 per cent. The largest share of government-funded industrial research is generally in the area of defence, but the end of the Cold War has seen a major decline in this area (OECD 2003a: 16). Figure 2.6 shows the decline in government-funded R&D from the mid-1980s, except in Japan where it started off much lower than the OECD mean and particularly lower than that in the USA, and has risen slightly, so that the figures for the USA, EU, and Japan appear to be converging (though Japan's government funding of R&D as a percentage of GDP is still less than the OECD mean). The major decline is in government-funded R&D in the USA. We discuss defence-related R&D further below. Governments also fund R&D in infrastructural industries (e.g. in telecommunications in some countries), health and agriculture, although much of the latter, while useful to industry, is likely to be carried out in public sector research institutions. The next section deals with the breakdown of government-funded R&D.

To summarize this section, in general the largest share of R&D in the OECD area is done in industry and paid for by industry, especially in the richest countries and those which do most R&D. The implication is that science and technology in the world is primarily an area of activity that is subject to the pressures, demands, and stimuli of a market economy and the corporate strategies of firms. Firms' decision processes in planning and organizing R&D are thus not only of vital importance for the success of the firms themselves, but for the success of the scientific and technological effort in the country as a whole. They have the major impact on the rate and direction of technological change.

GOVERNMENT-FUNDED RESEARCH AND DEVELOPMENT

Governments also still play a very important role in determining the rate and direction of technological change, not simply as a result of policies which influence firm behaviour, or demand for products and services, or the supply and training of scientists and engineers, but also as a result of the direct funding of R&D. This is so despite the relative decline in government funding since the mid-1980s, although it is especially true in countries where the proportion of R&D funded by government is still high, either relative to GDP, or compared to the proportion funded by other sources. Some of the newly industrializing and poorer European countries and former centrally planned economies are in this category, as mentioned in the last section.

Governments attempt to use their influence to direct technological change both via spending and by less direct methods, which are part of the political process. Different countries, at different times and with different parties of government, of course, vary in the methods used, from encouraging market forces to direct intervention. We return to some of these questions in Chapter 6, although a fuller treatment is outside the scope of this book and rather to be found in a discussion of science and technology policy. This chapter will just briefly examine the ways in which the R&D funds from governments are divided up according to different goals (see Table 2.8).

First, Table 2.8 (based on OECD data) divides government-funded R&D into that with Defence and Civil objectives, discussed further in the next section. The OECD then divides civil R&D funds into various objectives: economic development, health and environment, space programmes, non-oriented research and general university funds. In the USA, health and environment accounts for a huge 55.2 per cent of civilian R&D funded by government. The majority of these funds are channelled via the various national institutes of health (NIH), of which the first and possibly best known is the National Cancer Institute (NCI),[11] established in 1937 with a scale of funding that changed dramatically after the Second World War in response to public concern about the growing death toll from cancer, and once again in 1971 when President Nixon famously declared 'war against

Table 2.8 Government funding of R&D: Defence vs. civil objectives, 2002 or latest year

OECD country	% Civil	% Defence	As % of civil R&D				
			Economic development	Health and environment	Space programmes	Non-orientated	General university funds
France	76.8	23.2	16.9	13.4	12.8	25.8	28.1
Germany	94.7	5.3	20.9	14.5	5.1	17.4	42.1
Italy	96	4	16.8	16.2	7.6	13.9	45.5
Japan	95.9	4.1	33.8	7.7	6.3	16.0	36.3
Korea	84.7	15.3	53.3	17.3	3.8	25.6	n/a
UK	69.7	30.3	14.1	32.1	2.9	19.3	31.1
USA	45.6	54.4	12.1	55.2	13.4	11.7	n/a
EU	84.9	15.1	20.6	16.2	6.2	17.4	38.3
OECD total	70.2	29.8	22.3	27.1	8.5	15.8	24.5

Source: OECD (2003a).

cancer'. Analogies were made with the Manhattan Project (for the atomic bomb), and cancer was seen as something that had to be tackled by a major effort on a national scale to be managed by the state. Economists justify this kind of intervention in terms of market failure: the failure of normal operations of market forces, operating efficiently, to generate the necessary resources.

The US state has since the mid-1950s funded and also managed, not just the relevant basic research but also applied research, development, formulation, toxicity testing, and clinical trials of many new drugs in the anticancer field—that is, all the R&D necessary to take a potential drug almost to the point of full scale production and market launch. A great deal of the public research on molecular biology, for example, was justified by the possibility of its generating fundamental knowledge which might contribute to the development of cures or treatments for cancer. The research on molecular biology, in turn, provided the most important part of the foundation from which biotechnology start-up firms were launched in the early 1980s, and an extremely important body of knowledge on which the pharmaceutical and other industries depended.

The USA has had the largest amount spent on health-related research by any country in the world in both absolute and relative terms (as a percentage of the population or GDP), and in the USA it is second only to the defence R&D budget (Walsh et al. 1995). When the sums spent by the OECD countries are compared using purchasing power parities, the USA spends on health and the environment more than twice that spent in these areas by all the EU governments and the Japanese government put together (OECD 2003a: 49). In comparison, the USA's GDP is only approximately three quarters of the combined total of the GDPs of those countries. Furthermore, the sum spent by the USA on health and the environment is over 70 per cent of the total spent in the whole of the OECD in this category, although the USA's GDP is only 36 per cent of the combined GDPs of the OECD countries (OECD 2003a).

Despite the high levels of spending on health and environment R&D, however, most other indicators of health show the USA lagging behind many other countries which spend less, either on R&D or on provision of health care in general. For example, the USA has a relatively high infant mortality rate, exceeded in the OECD only by Hungary, Korea, Mexico, Poland, the Slovak Republic, and Turkey (OECD 2002: 10–11). The USA has a more unequal distribution of health care than most advanced countries: for example a high proportion are not covered by health insurance.

In the area of economic development, however, the countries which have high levels of government spending on relevant R&D are Japan, Germany, and Korea, which are also the countries in which the share of total R&D funds from government is particularly low, and from industry high. The USA spends very little under the heading of economic development (under 12.1

per cent compared to 33.8 per cent in Japan, 20.9 per cent in Germany, and 53.3 per cent in Korea), and less than two-thirds the OECD average.

American culture and public opinion is strongly associated with individualism, entrepreneurship, and opposition to government intervention (or 'interference') in the affairs of industry.[12] Arnold and Guy (1986) pointed out in 1986 that the USA had no explicit industrial policy, or ministry or department of industry, as most other countries did. This is still the case today, and the USA is, if anything, even more strongly committed to non-intervention by government. In the 1980s, when the OECD statistics for government R&D spending were classified into categories that included 'industry oriented' research as a separate category from 'infrastructure' (such as energy and telecoms), the percentage shown for the USA in this category was zero, by definition. Now infrastructure and industry-oriented categories are combined under the heading of 'economic development', but the US share of federal government spending in this category is still a small share of total government funding of R&D.

In fact, a substantial amount of industrially related R&D comes from Department of Defense spending under the heading of 'national security', as that is more likely to be supported in Congress. And 10 per cent of all federal support for basic research comes from the Department of Defence (30 per cent in computer science and engineering). Arnold and Guy (1986) concluded, from an examination of defence projects, that many of them would be called industrial projects in any other country (where government support of industry was more acceptable): they could only be called strictly 'defence-related' by the greatest stretch of the imagination. That is, a significant amount of defence R&D could be considered to be disguised industry-related R&D. This is discussed further in the next section. Pavitt used to say that US government policy was influenced by two major fears: Fear of Communism, and Fear of Cancer.[13] The first generated the defence procurement and spending on defence-related R&D, see next section (which underwrote the microelectronics and computer industries); the second gave rise to the high levels of expenditure on the life sciences that gave an impetus to the biotechnology industry. Both were examples of exceptions to the general US opposition to government intervention, and would often be justified in terms of market failure.

On the other hand, Japan spends more on space and defence-related projects than appears in the statistics, as military procurement contracts are excluded from the data for defence R&D spending in Japan (OECD 2003a: 78). According to the terms of the post-Second World War peace treaty, Japan no longer had a defence industry of any significance, and for many years OECD statistics showed government allocations for defence-related R&D as zero or close to zero, although in the footnotes estimates would be given for some degree of spending in this area. It became established culture that Japan did not officially spend on defence as USA did not officially spend on support for industry.

DEFENCE-RELATED R&D

Table 2.8 shows that the USA is by far the largest funder of defence R&D among the countries for which the OECD provides statistics, with over 50 per cent of government R&D funds in this category in 2002. The next highest shares come from the UK and France, which allocate 30.3 and 23.2 per cent of government-funded R&D to defence-related objectives. Figures for Italy, Germany, and Japan are almost an order of magnitude smaller, at 4.0, 5.3, and 4.1 per cent respectively. The former Soviet Union, USA, France, and Britain all pursued national policies based on investment in military-related technologies, while Japan encouraged a strong civilian technology base. In the former, military R&D dominated government spending for R&D for most of the post-Second World War period, and indeed in many developing countries defence has also been given a major role in technology development (Reppy 2000).

During the 1980s there was a great deal of debate about the impact of the R&D effort for military technology on the economy more generally, some of which is reported by the OECD (1992: 246–8). Pianta (1988), for example, refers to the contradictory effect on economic and technological development of large expenditures on military R&D:

The 'positive' effects of military research have been described as civilian 'spin-offs', while the 'negative' effects can be summarized as a distortion of the research priorities, the pattern of innovation and the orientation of technological change.

The US Defence Department's R&D and procurement programmes created a major stimulus to the development of new technologies financed by the public, from both the supply and the demand sides. Reppy (2000) observes that, to many commentators, the obvious explanation of US dominance of high-technology markets after the Second World War was the 'cross subsidization of its civilian technology by investments in military R&D. Aircraft design, space technology, nuclear power, and solid-state electronics are examples of areas that benefited from large-scale military spending, either for R&D or for procurement, or both' (p. 9). She gives the further example of management and accounting innovations that originated in the US defence sector, especially the techniques for managing large scale, complex programmes. Langlois (2002) and Mowery and Langlois (1996) have examined in particular the role of US defence procurement in stimulating the early microelectronics, computer, and software industries.

On the other hand, as several authors have pointed out, the concentration of innovative activity in the area of defence meant the diversion of resources and skills away from commercial technologies, and an increase in competition for limited R&D resources. Reppy goes on to say:

Whether we regard the outcomes as a by-product of security policies that emphasized technological supremacy or as the result of a conscious policy to base industrial policy on investments in military technology, the privileging of the defence sector produced innovation systems that were simultaneously enlarged by high levels of government spending and distorted by the demands of military procurement. (Reppy 2000: 15)

Pianta (1988) has also noted that funding for basic research and procurement contracts played an important role in the development of some new technologies, giving the example of half the total US sales of semiconductors in the early 1960s as being due to military procurement. But he then goes on to observe that this share had fallen dramatically by the 1980s and that there were also many examples of commercially *unsuccessful* spin-offs from military technologies (e.g. in supersonic aircraft) (Pianta 1988; see also Rosenberg 1986: 18). Rosenberg (1986: 29) suggested that distortions created by the US level of defence R&D had contributed to a declining international level of competitiveness, while Kaldor (1982: 1) has argued that defence R&D has 'successively eroded the economy of the USA and the economies of those countries that have followed in her wake', the defence innovation systems of the USA and Britain being biased towards trends in innovation which are ever more baroque or embellished, and ever more isolated from civilian needs and markets. Defence markets, she says, can be more secure outlets for production of uncompetitive firms, with resources, energy, and the development of skills concentrated on unnecessary technological embellishments, while neglect of user needs and market constraints is allowed to persist (Kaldor 1980).

Reppy (2000) has analyzed the 'Military Industrial Complex' in the USA, which includes the interlocking and self-reinforcing interests of the armed forces, defence contractors and subcontractors, government laboratories, and members of Congress, together with academic researchers, federally funded R&D centres and consultants in technology assessment and programme analysis. This network is protected by its role in national security, and supports high levels of government spending. A similar situation also exists, on a smaller scale, in other countries with large military R&D budgets. In France, the Ecole Polytechnique generates close linkages among students who go on to become the civil servants responsible for military procurement and the engineers who work on the defence contacts in industry, as well as the officers in the armed forces (Chesnais and Serfati 1992: 69).

The end of the Cold War removed the justification for high levels of defence spending: a powerful enemy with technologically advanced weapons. But new dangers come from what Kaldor (2001) describes as a new type of warfare waged by armed networks of non-state as well as state actors, including paramilitary groups, terrorists cells, fanatical volunteers, organized criminal groups, mercenaries and private military companies as well as units of regular forces and other security services. New technology is still important in 'new warfare', and modern communications technologies have become of central significance not only in organizing the networks but also in mobilizing support via propaganda.

In the ten years after the fall of the Berlin Wall, world military spending fell by one-third. Military budgets were cut, new weapons programmes were deferred or cancelled and, in the USA in particular, the industry underwent a massive restructuring, with the major contractors reduced to only four companies (Reppy 2000).[14] Kaldor (2001) argues that American military spending then began to rise again after 1998. From 2000, she says, it was as high again in real terms as in 1980. Meanwhile, spending on military R&D declined less than military spending overall, and has gone up more rapidly since 1998. US military R&D spending is 47 per cent higher in real terms than in 1980 (SIPRI 2001). Instead of disarmament, downsizing, and conversion, says Kaldor, the end of the Cold War led to a 'feverish technological effort to apply information technology to military purposes', generating an interaction between systems for information collection, analysis, and transmission with weapons systems, known as the 'Revolution in Military Affairs' (Kaldor 2001: 5). She further suggests that during downturns in the US military procurement cycle, military R&D is always sustained, designing and developing the systems to be procured in the next upturn. The expensive development and procurement phases have always coincided with renewed preoccupation with various threats. In the area of biological weapons, National Institute for Allergy and Infectious Diseases (NIAID) funding increased 403 per cent from the period 1996–2000 to the single year 2005 (Sunshine Project 2006).

As we have noted in the previous section, countries with heavy investment in defence are able to provide an alternative form of resource for their governments when the political environment is hostile to government intervention. Thus, during the Thatcher government in Britain and the Reagan-Bush years in the USA, as Reppy (2000: 15) points out, 'industrial policy initiatives for the civilian sector were routinely disparaged as doomed to failure and ideologically incorrect'. But government spending for innovation within the framework of national security could not be criticized in the same way, and

government programs such as Sematech and the Very High Speed Integrated Circuits (VHSIC) program in the United States—programs clearly intended to bolster the civilian micro-electronics industry in its competition with Japanese firms—were funded from the DOD budget. Even under the Clinton administration, which came into office with a declared intention of revitalizing the U.S. industrial base, the practice of linking technology programs to the DOD budget continued, and dual-use programs have emphasized military applications of civilian technologies rather than the reverse. Technology transfer programs designed to transfer defence technologies into the civilian economy have had only limited success. (Reppy 2000: 15)

Defence R&D has not only had an impact on innovative activity but also on the structural and rhetorical aspects of government policy.

INDUSTRIAL R&D

Expenditure on R&D differs greatly between industrial sectors. Table 2.9 shows that the vast proportion of R&D is done in just a few high technology or research intensive sectors: electronics, drugs, computers, scientific instruments, certain services and aerospace, compared with all the other manufacturing industries such as pottery and ceramics, textiles, cutlery, food processing, printing, furniture, heavy engineering, automotive, shipbuilding, glass, chemicals and many others, and primary sectors such as agriculture and mining. The high-technology sectors tend to be the fastest growing, and those with the most potential contribution to make to economic growth at the national level.

The pattern of sectors which spend the most on R&D also varies between countries. Countries where a high proportion of R&D is carried out by the electronics, office machinery, and computer industries include Japan, Korea, and Italy, with the USA and France in the medium range. The UK has a particularly low proportion of its industrial R&D in this area, but a higher proportion than other countries in pharmaceuticals (higher even than the 'other' category which includes all sectors not specifically mentioned), the next highest being France (whose drug industry accounts for half this level, relative to the national level of R&D spending). A great many non-British-based pharmaceutical firms have important R&D activities in Britain, owing to its highly qualified but relatively low paid (compared, e.g., to the USA) scientific staff.

US industry spends the largest share on scientific instruments, while Italy, the UK, and France have the most industrial R&D in the area of civil aerospace, Japan having a particularly low level of spending in this sector. Over half the industrial R&D in Germany and Japan, and over 40 per cent in France, is in the 'other' category, which includes medium-technology sectors,

Table 2.9 Business enterprise research by sector of performance (%), 2001 or most recent year

OECD country	Aerospace	Electronics	Office machinery and computers	Pharmaceuticals	Scientific instruments	Services	Other	Total (%)
France	10.9	14.7	1.6	13.3	7.3	11.4	40.8	100
Germany	7.3	12.0	2.1	6.8	5.5	8.7	57.7	100
Italy	11.9	21.5	1.3	9.5	4.7	23.4	27.7	100
Japan	0.8	18.4	10.6	6.7	4.4	2.1	56.9	100
Korea	4.3	40.4	8.7	2.5	1.6	14.1	28.6	100
UK	11.9	9.8	1.0	28.7	4.6	22.4	21.6	100
USA	5.5	13.7	5.5	6.9	10.2	36.3	22.1	100
EU	7.3	13.1	1.7	0.0	4.5	12.5	60.9	100

Source: OECD (2003a).

such as cars, railway engineering and other engineering-based industries, and the chemical industry, which are innovative and competitive in those countries. A variety of high-, medium-, and low-technology activities, from hairdressing, child minding, and retailing to banking, finance, and the writing of software, are traditionally included together in the 'service' sector. Some of these sectors are traditional activities with little scope for technological innovation, while others are high tech, innovative, and research intensive, with a great deal of scope for innovation in information and communication technologies in particular (see Chapter 7 for further discussion). The USA, UK, and Italy have the highest proportions of industrial R&D in services, US industry in particular having more than one-third of all R&D in this category (compared, e.g., to only 22.1 per cent in 'other' sectors).

Conclusion

In this chapter, we have analyzed the professionalization of science and technology, and the emergence and growth of the industrial R&D lab as an organizational innovation. We have examined the relationship between R&D and innovation, using statistics from the OECD and UNESCO. As a result we have concluded that most of the world's science and technology is produced by just a few countries, which has implications for the countries that produce far less. Some of the small industrialized countries (e.g. Switzerland, the Netherlands, and the Nordic countries) are proportionately large spenders on R&D proportionate to their GDPs, while some of the NICs, Korea in particular, have increased their spending massively as a result of deliberate strategy. As a result of a very rapid growth since 1996–7, China now has the third highest level of R&D spending in the world, after the USA and Japan and greater than that of Germany. Most of the world's R&D is orientated towards certain goals, which we have analyzed. Most of the world's R&D, too, is done in industry with over 70 per cent of R&D done by industry in the USA, Germany, Japan, and Korea. The UK relies more than other countries on charitable trusts, foundations, and other non-profit making institutions, with nearly a quarter of its R&D funding coming from these sources. R&D is concentrated in just a few industrial sectors known as the 'R&D intensive' or 'high tech' sectors. These vary from country to country with Japan and Korea focusing on IT-related sectors, the UK and France specializing in pharmaceuticals and Germany and Japan performing over half their industrial R&D in engineering-based sectors. Finally, we have considered the way in which defence spending has an impact in stimulating or distorting other areas of R&D.

Notes

1 In writing this book we have used the 2003 edition.
2 The most recent version of this publication was produced in 2001, with statistics for the year 1996–7. The previous version was called *World Science Report* and was published in 1998, with figures for 1994 (http://www/uis.unesco.org/en/pub/doc/WS_report_2001.pdf)
3 This is the name which was given by the People's Republic of China to the country also known as Taiwan. It is now also the name used by the OECD and UNESCO. Taiwan or Chinese Taipei calls itself the Republic of China.
4 For example those excluding the former centrally planned economies: Asian NICs, rest of Asia, Latin America and the Caribbean, India, and Africa.
5 If we exclude the centrally planned economies from the 'pie' in Figure 2.3 for comparison with Figures 2.1 and 2.2, the 'rest of the world' accounts for 15 per cent of total R&D.
6 Asia has 60.8 per cent of the world's population (38.6 per cent without China).
7 Researchers in France officially became designated as civil servants in 1984, although CNRS and the other state research bodies existed well before then. Teaching is, however, often carried out by researchers. It is not an obligation, it is normally paid in addition to the researcher's salary, but at the same time it is usually expected that the researcher will teach, rather as university teachers in the UK are expected to do research, and, in a similar way, it is one of the factors taken into account in evaluation exercises.
8 Recent changes have taken place in France in the employment of non-industrial research scientists and in a move towards the separation of funding and performance of research. For example, the Agence Nationale de la Recherche (National Research Agency, ANR) was established in February 2005 to distribute funding to projects chosen by peer review on the basis of scientific excellence, a new departure in how research is funded in France. See http://www.gip-anr.fr
9 A view which continues to be expressed, e.g., *Nature* (1996) cited by Calvert (2002: 1).
10 Though some individual countries have a high level of GERD as a percentage of GDP, see Table 2.1, these are not given in the OECD figures quoted here.
11 A complete list of the National Institutes of Health may be obtained from www.nih.gov
12 Whether there is a contradiction between entrepreneurship and the freedom of industry to 'make a buck' without government interference, on the one hand, and American goals of individual liberty, on the other, is a matter for debate even before US foreign policy is taken into account.
13 One occasion was in the course of his presentation at the conference Technologie et la Connaissance dans la Mondialisation, 10–11 September 1998, Université de Poitiers.
14 Lockheed-Martin, Raytheon-Hughes, Boeing-MacDonald, and—a distant fourth—Northrop-Grumman (Reppy 2000). Apart from Boeing, with its large commercial aircraft business, these companies now concentrate almost entirely on the defence market, having sold or spun off many of their civilian subsidiaries. They are thus now considerably *more* dependent on defence business than before (Reppy 2000).

Part II
Organizational and Technological Capabilities and Growth

Part II describes the way in which organizational and technological capabilities have changed over the past century and how these changes explain the shifts in international industrial leadership. We examine how industrial dominance shifted from Britain in the late nineteenth century, to the USA in the early twentieth century, to Japan after the Second World War and to the USA again more recently. We also examine the organizational and technological capabilities behind the rise of the successful East Asian newly industrializing countries.

Evidence of the shifting dominance of industrial economies shows two important features of innovation and economic growth. First, institutions that favour growth and take-off of new technology systems in one period may hold it back in another. Indeed, countries that have risen to positions of international industrial dominance on the basis of earlier forms of business and production organization may not be able to make the transition to more powerful forms of business and production organization when new technologies open up new opportunities. The very institutions that formed the foundations of industrial dominance in one period may become barriers to industrial change in the previously dominant economies because of vested interests and the lack of ability to compete by making adaptive responses to old technologies and forms of organization. Second, the evidence confirms the view of capitalism as a system where change is uneven and discontinuous (see Chapter 1), and in which there are no steady linear steps to success.

Table II.1 Forms of business and production organization in leading economies

Business and production organization	Representative economy	Period of growth
Proprietary/ competitive capitalism	UK	Late nineteenth century
Managerial/ corporate capitalism	USA	1920s–70s
New competition/ collective capitalism/ flexible specialization	Japan and European industrial districts (Third Italy)	1950s–80s
Systems integration	US high-tech regions (Silicon Valley)	1980s–

Table II.1 presents the shifts in industrial dominance as characterised by changes in the forms of business and production organization in the leading industrial economies. In Chapter 3 we focus on the institutions of the nineteenth century that enabled Britain to become a leading industrial economy (proprietary capitalism) but impeded in the twentieth century the adoption of technological and organizational innovations. We also describe the consolidation of new sets of institutions in the early twentieth century in the USA and Germany (managerial capitalism) which led to important leaps in productivity and competitiveness. These institutions comprise the rise of the modern corporation and managerial coordination of mass distribution and production.

Chapter 4 describes the new forms of business and production organization in Japan and the Third Italy (new competition) which exposed the limitations in production organization of managerial capitalism. These include 'networks' of firms (large corporations in Japan and small firm industrial districts in Italy), interfirm relations, new production concepts such as just-in-time and the role of industrial policy. The problems of this form of business and production organization are also described. We also examine the business and production organization forms responsible for the resurgence of US high-tech industry (network-based systems integration).

Chapter 5 explores the institutions of late industrialization. It discusses the different nature and role played by technological knowledge in industrialization in the nineteenth and the twentieth century. Using South Korea and Taiwan as the main examples, we describe industrialization in the twentieth century as 'industrialization by learning', involving well coordinated government intervention, a particular strategy, structure and operation of leading firms and a competitive focus of enterprises.

3 Organizations and Technology in Proprietary and Managerial Capitalism

Introduction

One of the fundamental arguments on which this book is based is that changes in organizational and technological capabilities are responsible for shifts in industrial leadership. Here we illustrate the way in which changes in organizations and technology account for the changes in industrial dominance from Britain in the late-nineteenth century to the USA and Germany in the early twentieth century. Already by the early twentieth century, Britain was lagging behind other countries in manufacturing productivity growth and exports. Between 1870 and 1913, Britain's share of world trade fell from over 40 to 30 per cent and the growth of industrial output and productivity failed to match that of her major competitors (Walker 1980). Indeed it has been argued that:

... by 1870 the 'workshop of the world' possessed only between one quarter and one fifth of the world's steam power, and produced much less than half its steel. By the end of the 1880s the relative decline was visible even in the formerly dominant branches of production. By the early 1890s the USA and Germany both passed Britain in the production of the crucial commodity of industrialization, steel .... Indeed among the industrial powers it was the most sluggish and the one which showed most obvious signs of relative decline. (Hobsbawm 1968)

While some authors have argued that this lag was due to cultural conservatism and entrepreneurial failure (Landes 1969; Weiner 1981), others argue that this lag is not just a problem of entrepreneurial failure, but that, instead, for an understanding of what went wrong in Britain, we must first look at the reasons for its success during the nineteenth century, a period in which Britain was the world's leading economic power. This is because the decline in Britain can be attributed to the failure of the economic and social institutions of the nineteenth century (that were very successful in producing the First Industrial Revolution, see Chapter 6) to adapt to changed conditions at the end of the nineteenth century and beginning of the twentieth century (Walker 1980; Elbaum and Lazonick 1986).

Institutions connected to firm and market organization, industrial relations, education, and finance provided an optimal environment for the take-off and diffusion of a wave if innovations and, in turn, the boom in the production of textiles, iron, coal mining, shipbuilding, and engineering during the nineteenth century (during the first and second Kondratieff long waves described in Chapter 1). However, the entrenchment of these institutional structures in the early twentieth century impeded Britain from adopting further technological and organizational innovations (in the third and fourth Kondratieff long waves). This has been called the 'British disease' (Elbaum and Lazonick 1986).

In the early twentieth century, we see the consolidation in the USA and in some parts of Europe, notably Germany, of a new form of business and production organization. This was the large enterprise, coordinated by managers, and capable of high-speed throughput and reduced units costs, with divisions and functional specialization, including the R&D laboratory. This organizational form dominated the industrial landscape during the third and fourth Kondratieff waves.

This chapter is organized as follows. The first section describes the main features of organizations and technology of proprietary capitalism. The second section examines organizations and technology in managerial capitalism. The conclusion summarizes the main challenges facing the US production system.

Organizations and technology in proprietary capitalism

The main institutions of 'proprietary' or 'personal' capitalism—the terms that characterize the economic and social institutions prevailing in Britain in the nineteenth century—are described by Elbaum and Lazonick (1986). Box 3.1 summarizes the main features of the organizations and technology of proprietary capitalism. British industry was very atomistic, with numerous firms with small market shares. Firms had a high degree of vertical specialization. Distribution of intermediate and final products relied on well-developed market mechanisms, often involving specialized merchant firms. Most enterprises were single-plant firms that specialized in particular lines of manufacture of intermediate or final products. Industries exhibited a high degree of regional concentration based on geographical advantages as well as external economies provided by local access to skilled labour, transport

---

Box 3.1 Organizations and technology in proprietary capitalism

Proprietary capitalism in Britain in the nineteenth century was characterized by the following features:

- Small firms
- Owner-proprietors, small managerial staff, crude methods of cost accounting, and production control
- Market coordination
- Regional concentration
- Vertical specialization
- Finance from personal family fortunes, retained earnings, some local banks
- Strong links between scientists and entrepreneurs
- Strong local investment by landlords in transport infrastructure (canals and roads, later railways)
- Reduction or elimination of internal and external barriers to trade
- Dissenters' academies and some universities provide science education. Mechanics trained in new industrial towns on a part-time basis.
- Industrial techniques based on trial and error
- Organization of work by skilled labour

Sources: Elbaum and Lazonick (1986); Freeman and Soete (1997).

---

facilities and distribution networks, capital and product markets. Relying on the market to coordinate economic activity (the 'invisible hand' described by the Scottish economist Adam Smith), nineteenth century British firms were relatively simple in their internal organization. Firms were run by owner-proprietors or close family associates. Managerial staff were relatively few, and methods of cost accounting and production control were crude or non-existent. Mechanical ingenuity and experience enabled engineers and craftsmen to make improvements as a result of observation, imagination, trial and error, and small-scale experiment. Development of industrial techniques did not rely on systematic in-house research, but on the more patchy and random contributions of production engineers, private inventors (who sometimes established the firms to commercialize their inventions), or the workmen who actually operated the machinery.

Until the 1870s the long-term finance for these firms came mainly from family wealth and retained earnings and, to a more limited extent, local banks (Best and Humphries 1986). The economic crisis of the late 1870s saw the collapse of many local banks that were over-committed to regionally specialized industries. Subsequently, there arose a national branch banking system that had little explicit involvement in the long-term finance of British industry.

Firms relied on skilled labour to organize work. After periods of bitter dispute over the right to form trade unions, the British workforce won a certain amount of protection by union agreements and training was generally carried out 'on the job' by more experienced members of the workforce. Responsibility was delegated to foremen or overseers (generally promoted from the shop floor) for day-to-day production management, quality control, cost accounting, hiring, training, and disciplining the workers (during the second Kondratieff this was widespread throughout USA and Europe too, see Nelson 1980). Because of their intimate practical knowledge of production methods, workers were able to keep imperfect machinery running steadily and to contribute to minor technological improvements. This had the advantage of low-fixed costs not only for individual firms but also for the British economy as a whole (Lazonick 1991).

The evolution of industry structures characterized by small, atomistic firms, regional concentration, and high vertical specialization, together with employers' reliance on skilled labour to organize work on the shop floor, did not provide a stimulus for firms to invest in the development of managerial structures and organizational capabilities. Meanwhile, an alternative form of organizing business—managerial capitalism—was emerging in the USA and Germany in response to the growth of firms beyond a size that could be managed by a single owner-entrepreneur. New management structures developed differently in the USA and Germany, but became the dominant modes of business and production organization in each country, allowing them to respond more effectively to new economic conditions. In both countries, as we will see, these new forms of business organization were based on large firms administered by professional managers, and especially involving specialist managers such as cost accountants and professional engineers. The new structures were stimulated by innovations in production techniques and by the integration of industrial and finance capital since they involved expensive equipment which required complex maintenance and repair, new forms of coordination, and sophisticated accounting (Schumpeter 1939; Chandler 1977)[1]. The dominant electrical firms, AEG and Siemens (Germany) and General Electric and Westinghouse (USA), among the world's largest firms in any industry, particularly needed the participation of strong financial interests to assist in the development of network systems (like the railways before them). The new 'professionalization' of management characteristic of both Germany and the USA, although in very different forms, hardly touched the higher levels of British firms until much later (Freeman 1989). While in the decade before the First World War, the large electrical firms in the USA and Germany employed up to 80,000 staff,[2] no British firm employed more than 10,000 (and even then the largest UK firms were subsidiaries of Westinghouse, General Electric, and Siemens) (Hannah 1983 cited by Freeman 1989).

Vested interests in the old forms of business and production organization proved to be important obstacles to the transition from proprietary to managerial capitalism in Britain. In effect, as argued by Elbaum and Lazonick (1986), British industrialists clung to family control of their firms. British bankers lacked direct involvement in industry and had little ability or incentive to use financial leverage to reorganize business or production organization.

The concentration of banking in the City of London also gave rise to a relatively cohesive class of finance capitalists with much more coherent influence over national policy than industrial capitalists who were divided along enterprise, industry, and regional lines. Problems of industrial competitiveness were aggravated by the policy favoured by bankers of maintaining the value of the pound sterling and protecting the position of the City as the financial centre of the world (Elbaum and Lazonick 1986).

Furthermore, as Tables 3.1 and 3.2 show, a much higher proportion of the national product was invested in domestic industry in the USA and Germany (and some of the then 'newly industrializing countries' such as Italy and Sweden) than was the case in Britain, for which foreign investment was more than 50 per cent of net capital formation (Freeman 1989). Landes (1969: 349) said: 'The British had capital. But those who channelled and dispersed it were not alert to the opportunities offered by modern technology; and those who might have used it did not want or know enough to seek it out.' Freeman (1989) points out that the British Empire and British 'spheres of influence' overseas offered opportunities for more profitable investment, for example in plantations, mining, or railways, and 'well-established and relatively secure channels of shipment, distribution, finance and communications'. The strength of the City of London in financial services meant that finance capital and overseas portfolio investment, rather than manufacturing, increasingly dominated in economic policymaking as well. The impetus to bring about a different kind of institutional change, that would provide

Table 3.1 Gross-fixed investment as a percentage of GNP

Country	1889/90	1899/1900	1906/7	1912/13
UK	11.9	11.5	13.4	13.9
Germany	18.3	19.5	19.6	18.3
USA	20.0	19.8	20.5	18.3
Total	17.3	17.4	18.8	17.4

Source: Freeman (1989).

Table 3.2 Foreign investment as percentage of total net capital formation, current prices

Germany		UK	
1851/5–1861/5	2.2	1855–64	29.1
1861/5–1871/5	12.9	1865–74	40.1
1871/5–1881/5	14.1	1875–84	28.9
1881/5–1891/5	19.9	1885–94	51.2
1891/5–1901/5	9.7	1895–1904	20.7
1901/5–1911/5	5.7	1905–14	52.9

Source: Freeman (1989).

more of a stimulus to the renovation of British industry and technology, was greatly weakened, while financial services in the USA and Germany were oriented predominantly to the rapidly growing needs of their domestic industries (Hobsbawm 1968).

The British educational system in turn hampered industry by failing to provide appropriately trained managerial and technical personnel. The small size of the higher education sector in Britain reflected the modest level of state support: between 1880 and 1900 the German educational subsidy was ten times that of Britain (Rose and Rose 1970: 29). In any case the British higher education system was not oriented towards the pursuit of business and applied science (Wrigley 1986) but on educating the gentry in areas such as classics, and preparing them for the church, the armed forces, or colonial administration. The British system did not supply enough people with the necessary skills for entrepreneurship, management, and technological development in the new industries. By 1913 Britain had only 9,000 univeristy students compared to 60,000 in Germany; Germany produced 3,000 graduate engineers per year while in England and Wales only 350 graduated in all branches of science, technology, and mathematics with first and second class honours (Hobsbawm 1968: 152–3). Very few institutions equivalent to the series of great new Technische Hochschulen in Germany and Institutes of Technology in the USA were established in Britain until much later (Cardwell 1957).[3]

Even more seriously, Britain had not developed systematic education and training in middle and basic craft skills. The tradition of training on-the-job (above) may have been adequate for developing techniques based on mechanical ingenuity, observation, experience with machinery and learning-by-doing during the Industrial Revolution, when innovation was very much a matter of imaginative redesign of the arrangements of levers, pulleys, cogs, and pistons, which can be visualized relatively easily (see Chapter 2).[4] This approach was increasingly inappropriate for the skills associated with the new technologies, especially electrical and chemical engineering, which required a certain level of theoretical and methodological understanding of physics and chemistry, and hence the movement of electrons and atoms, which cannot be visualized in the same way, as well as practical experience with machinery and equipment.

In addition, the informal linkages between higher and technical education and industry, which proved to be very important in the industrial research systems in the USA and Germany, failed to develop in Britain. Therefore, British firms were run with little understanding of production technology or management techniques. Indeed, Albu (1980) pointed out the historical lack of demand by the engineering industry, causing low levels of status, pay, and education of British engineers. Furthermore, there has been a separation of engineering education and training in Britain, with university education much more of an academic than a vocational subject, and the vocational side of training a matter of short courses and the completion of professional training left to industrial employers. Even in the post-Second World War period the average British manager still had inferior educational and technical competence compared with his or her equivalent in other industrialized countries (Swords-Isherwood 1980). A British government report as late as 1980 (Committee of Inquiry into the Engineering Profession 1980) underlined the need for more and better professionally and technologically competent managers and engineers in manufacturing industry, a deficiency that it dated back to well before the First World War.

While in Britain the existence of unions prior to big business provided some limitation to the powers of management to reorganize work according to mass production (Best 1990; Lazonick 1991), in the USA and Germany efforts to increase work intensity and repressive policies towards trade unions are evident in various laws (Germany) and management strategies used against unions (USA) (Freeman 1989).

A crucial factor in the economic decline of Britain was the poor innovation record of British industry—in particular, low levels of R&D during 1900–50 (see Box 3.2). The level of research intensity in British firms was on average about one-third of its level in US manufacturing during that period (Mowery 1986). Managerial capitalism included the absorption into the firm of industrial research, one of its most important organizational innovations, which was introduced in Germany in chemicals and high-voltage electricity and adopted by the US electrical industry. This innovation allowed for a more effective exploitation of the complementarities between research and production activity. It was particularly the organic chemicals industry that relied on long-term relations between firms and university professors and the in-house laboratory (Lehrer 2005). In Britain, the reorganization of major firms occurred later than in the USA or Germany, and was less complete; for example, ICI was formed in 1926 from the merger of various firms in the UK chemical industry including British Dyestuffs (mentioned later), as a deliberate strategy of emulating IG Farben in Germany and DuPont in the USA.

There was little pressure to transform the UK system as highly atomistic firms could not afford to hire specialized technical personnel and were further reluctant to support industry-wide research institutions that would benefit competitors as well. Elbaum and Lazonick (1986) point out that at the onset of the First World War, concern over the inability of British industry to supply technologically sophisticated materials of strategic military importance (such as optical range finders for guns, various items of precision engineering equipment and synthetic dyes for uniforms) led to policy initiatives in areas of R&D. For example, the Department of Scientific and Industrial Research (DSIR) was established, and the British Dyestuffs Corporation was formed with capital of £3 million, part of which came from Treasury funds, and £100,000 of which was allocated to scientific research (Rose and Rose 1970).

Box 3.2 Technology and the decline in British international competitiveness

---

The collection of chapters in Pavitt (1980) stresses how British innovative activities declined notably in the twentieth century, and fell behind competing countries. During 1886–90, the ratio of UK to German patenting was 1.6. By 1901–5, it had been reduced roughly to 1.0, and by 1910–15 reached 0.8. After the First World War it fell to 0.6 in 1936–40. By the 1970s this ratio was just above 0.5 (Pavitt and Soete 1980: 43). This pattern of decline is mirrored in R&D expenditure statistics. In 1967, industrial R&D in the UK was roughly the same as in Germany, and well above France and Japan. By 1975–6, it was not much more that half of the German and Japanese levels and only about 20 per cent above the French level (Pavitt and Soete 1980: 43–4).

Sectoral studies confirm these general trends. Rothwell (1980) shows the decline in Britain from its previous prime position in textile machinery production. He points out that while technical innovation is an important determinant in the export competitiveness of textile machinery, the UK textile machinery has been less innovative than its main European rivals (except for the 'new' machinery areas of texturizing, carpet tufting and computerized control knitting machines). Indeed, the total number of scientists and technologists employed in the UK textile machinery industry fell by nearly 14 per cent between 1968 and 1973, and R&D expenditure fell by 30 per cent during the same period (Rothwell 1980: 140). Also, lack of market intelligence in many world markets and the poor links between product design and production engineering exacerbate the problems.

Similarly, while until the 1880s Britain was the world's foremost producer of steel and leading innovator (with developments such as Bessemer steel-making), by 1890 it was surpassed by the USA and by 1900 by Germany. By 1980, Britain ranked in eighth place (its productivity ranking below European competitors, half that of the USA and a third that of Japan) (Aylen 1980: 200). Aylen (1980) suggests the British steel industry adopted process innovations more slowly than its Western competitors. Britain took the wrong route in oxygen steel-making in the 1960s, in part because it was unwilling to step outside established practices to the same degree as steel industries in other countries.

A number of other deficiencies have been pointed out as responsible for loss of competitiveness for Britain in other sectors, such as heavy electrical equipment and nuclear energy (Buckley and Day 1980; Surrey et al. 1980). In particular, the dependence of industrial firms for development and design capabilities on government agencies has been seen as explaining the reduction in the capacity to compete successfully internationally.

Twenty-four industrial research associations were set up for the promotion of cooperative R&D by firms in the private sector, with 50 per cent of funds coming from industry and 50 per cent from government. However, British Dyestuffs was handicapped by the lack of trained chemists in top management positions and a reliance on chairs in universities for research efforts. Government-sponsored cooperative research proved an inadequate replacement for in-house R&D of modern corporations, in particular, because firms lacked in-house technical expertise to evaluate and employ the results of extramural research (Elbaum and Lazonick 1986).

As a result, because of the legacy from nineteenth century institutions, Britain did not make the transition to mass production and managerial capitalism along with the USA. Britain continued instead to manufacture traditional products using traditional technologies, and producing to order.

British competitiveness was long based on price competition in traditional industries, originating in the advantages of the Empire (cheap raw materials, domination of trade routes, and secure markets). There was a lack of incentive to compete or innovate in newer markets (such as steel, electrical equipment, and chemicals) that the USA and Germany dominated in world markets (Walker 1980).

Organizations and technology in managerial capitalism

By the end of the nineteenth century, US industry assumed an important role in the world. The USA became an important producer of consumer products, mass-produced light machinery, electrical equipment, and standardized industrial machinery mostly for the domestic market, but also for export. But while the USA led the world in the establishment of new management practices, it remained behind Germany in scientific and technological achievements until after the First World War. And in some of the new, 'high tech' sectors of the time (e.g. new materials) US production did not overtake that of Germany until the eve of Second World War (Walsh 1984). It was after the Second World War and until the beginning of the 1970s that the USA consolidated its position of world leadership in advanced technologies. During that period, output per worker was higher than any other advanced nations (by 30–50 per cent), total factor productivity (in aggregate and in almost all industries) was nearly as large, and it had the largest share of world trade in its products (Nelson and Wright 1992). These achievements can be attributed to the effect of the consolidation in the early twentieth century in the USA of a new form of business and production organization—'managerial' or 'corporate' capitalism. Small, traditional family firms were replaced by large firms administered by salaried managers. This was the main instrument for managing mass production and distribution. What Chandler (1977) calls the 'visible hand' of managerial coordination, enabled leaps in speed and volume throughput by mass-production technologies. These relied on the new, cheap, and flexible energy (electricity generated initially from coal and soon [in the USA at least] from oil) and infrastructural development in transport (railroads) and communication (telephone and telegraph), and were derived from particularly favourable access to natural resources and the world's largest domestic market.

Chandler (1977) provides an account of the range of institutions associated with managerial capitalism. As we argued in the previous section, in the nineteenth century, the traditional business firm under proprietary capitalism had a single unit, single function, and single product line and was located in one geographic area and coordinated by prices. Nineteenth century owners of plantations, mills, shops, mines, and factories hired salaried employees to administer these simple organizations. By the 1840s there were still no middle managers (managers that supervized the work of other managers and in turn reported to senior executives). However, by the early twentieth century we see the development of a new type of business institution in the USA, the so-called 'big business' (see Box 3.3). Similarly, in Germany, firms such as Krupps had become the largest private industrial undertaking on the European continent (in coal, iron, steel, armaments, ship and submarine building) while chemical firms BASF, Bayer, and Hoechst (merged together as IG Farben 1926–45) dominated the world market for chemicals, and AEG came to a cartel agreement with General Electric in which they divided the world between themselves in the electrical equipment markets (Freeman 1989; Lehrer 2005).

General Motors and DuPont in the USA created what has come to be known as the multidivisional (M-form) structure.[5] In this type of structure, autonomous divisions integrated production and distribution by coordinating flows from suppliers to customers in different, clearly defined markets. Figure 3.1 shows the multidivisional structure of a manufacturing firm (DuPont), in which each divisional office had its own accounting, purchasing, production, sales, R&D, and traffic offices. Each division had its own administrative office (with middle management) and books and accounts that

---

Box 3.3 Organizations and technology in managerial capitalism

Managerial capitalism in the USA and Germany during the 1920s–1970s was characterized by the following features:

- New business institution: big business (multidivisional firm).
- New type of 'economic man': the manager (hierarchical managerial bureaucracy).
- New economic function: visible hand (administrative coordination of mass distribution and mass production).
- Increases in throughput and productivity by mass production (involving the principles of interchangeability and flow), cheap and flexible energy, and market expanding infrastructural developments in transportation and communication.
- Vertical integration of production and distribution.
- Integration of industrial and financial capital.
- Abundant natural resources in USA exploited with heavy investment and economies of scale, e.g., in steel and oil.
- Import of science and technology from Europe to USA via immigration.
- Systematic research and development within the firm and in specialist research organizations.
- Increased output of trained managers and engineers from new educational institutions.
- New specialist management functions, including cost accounting, sales and marketing, production management.

Source: Chandler (1977), Best (1990), Lazonick (1991); Freeman and Soete (1997).

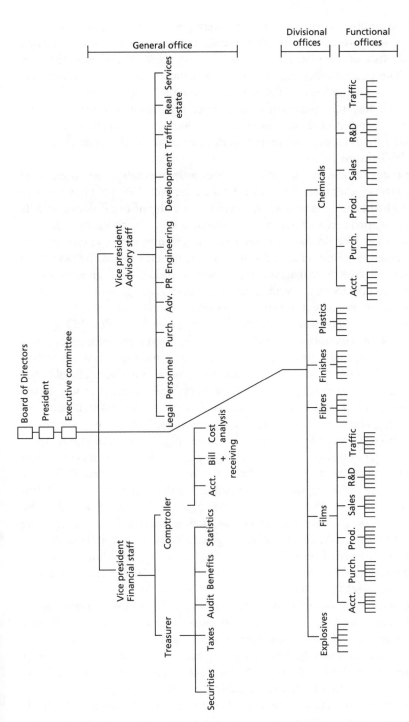

Figure 3.1 Multidivisional structure of a manufacturing firm

(*source*: Chandler 1977: 458)

could be audited separately. Divisions were given decentralized responsibilities for their own operations, while overall strategic decisions were made by a general office of top managers, assisted by large financial and administrative staffs. The general office monitored the divisions to ensure that flows were attuned to fluctuations in demand and that they had similar policies in personnel, research, purchasing, and other functional activities. The top managers concentrated on planning and allocation of resources and also evaluated the financial and market performance of the divisions (Chandler 1977; Williamson 1985).

For the first time, coordination activities were internalized and monitored by managers rather than the market. By the First World War, big business was the dominant business unit administered by a cadre of professional, middle and top salaried career managers, who attended special schools, and had their own journals like doctors and lawyers. Importantly for economic theory, management became separated from ownership. This raised the possibility that the objectives of management and owners could differ. Career managers may prefer policies that favour long-term stability and growth of the enterprise rather than current profits (dividends).

Noble (1977) shows that as 'scientific management' (see Box 3.5) split up production into its component procedures, reducing the worker to an appendage of the machine, a great expansion of technical and supervisory personnel took place in order to oversee the productive process as a whole. The old-style entrepreneur, who managed most of the firm's operations, gave way to the university-trained manager, often an engineer. The professionalization of engineering and the establishment of engineering education as a recognized branch of higher learning forged a link between big business and university.

The modern business enterprise took the place of the market mechanism in coordinating the flow of goods. The visible hand of management (Chandler 1977) progressively replaced the invisible hand of market forces (Adam Smith). During the 1870s and 1880s, this coordination was achieved in the USA first in the marketing of farm crops, such as grain and cotton, requiring fewer capital goods than manufacturing firms used. The capital goods were mainly in the form of grain elevators, cotton presses, and warehouses. This led to increases in profits through increases in stock turn (rather than because of increases in size) (Chandler 1977).

The first revolution in business organization in the USA was in mass distribution (Chandler 1977). The mass marketeers (such as the department story Macy's and the mail order house Sears, Roebuck and Co.) coordinated the flow of goods administratively. Changes in organization reduced the number of transactions involved in the flow of goods, increased the speed and especially the regularity of that flow, reducing costs, and increasing productivity. The revolution in production came more slowly than did the revolution in distribution, for it required further technological as well as organizational innovation.

Mass production required the invention of new machinery and processes. The first 'big businesses' in American industry were those that united the types of distributing organization created by the mass marketeers with the types of factory organization developed to manage the new processes of mass production.[6] One of the important features of German success was the enormous sales effort made by manufacturing firms, and the large variety of innovations in sales methods. Another was the role played by standards institutions, especially in precision, optical, and electrical engineering. The National Standards Institute founded in Berlin in 1886 became an important national research laboratory, and gave rise to a series of national laboratories, the Kaiser Wilhelm Institutes, which played an important role for the vast majority of firms which did not yet have their own in-house R&D as the large chemical and electrical firms did.

Critical for opening up new opportunities for innovative firms in the USA was the development in the middle of the century of a national communications network based on fast all-weather transport (the railroad) and improved postal services and telegraph. In addition to providing manufacturing firms with better access to raw materials and product markets, improved communications facilitated the rapid population of the USA's vast spaces, increasing the supply of labour with various skills available to firms while fostering the rapid growth of aggregate demand (Chandler 1977). In principle, infrastructural developments could have generated external economies that could have encouraged the growth of fragmented industrial structures as in Britain. In contrast, however, some US manufacturing firms seized the opportunity to transform business organization and production giving way to managerial capitalism.

The communications infrastructure enabled a large and steady flow of raw materials into, and finished products out of, a factory, making possible unprecedented levels of production. The realization of this potential required, however, the introduction of new machinery and processes. Once these were developed, manufacturers were able to place within a single establishment (internalize) several processes of production. Mass-production technologies enabled leaps in speed and volume of throughput. Mass production allowed firms to carry out several processes in one factory (first in processing liquids and semi-liquids, such as crude oil, later in a number of mechanical industries, including those processing tobacco and grain and more slowly in the metal-making and metal-working industries). This began in the USA with Rockefeller in petroleum, Carnegie in steel, and various textiles firms in Massachusetts (Chandler 1977).

The early advancement of the US machine tool industry, which emerged from machine shops linked to New England textile mills in the 1820s and 1830s, was very important for mass production. In the machine tool industry, new skills and techniques were sequentially developed or perfected in response to the demands of specific customers and once they were acquired, the machine tool industry became the main transmission centre for the transfer of the new skills and techniques to the entire machine-using sector (Rosenberg 1976).[7]

Mass production was underpinned by two principles: interchangeability of parts and flow. Interchangeability of parts was developed nearly a century before mass production at the Springfield Armory, Massachusetts, in the early 1800s (see Box 3.4). In the words of Max Wollering, whom Ford hired from the machine tool industry, 'There is nothing new (about interchangeability) to me, but it might have been new to the Ford Motor Company because they didn't have much experience along that line' (Hounshell 1984: 221). The production of standardized parts brought with it the production of specialist machines, product, and process engineering (see Box 3.4).

The second principle behind mass production is flow. Henry Ford's plants were organized according to the principle of flow, with plant layout designed to maximize throughput efficiency (Best 1990). The production-organizing concept for Ford and his engineers was timing. The challenge was to regulate material flow so that just the right amount of each part would arrive at just the right time. Best (2001) argues that in Ford's plant, making few parts would slow the flow, while making too many would produce waste in the

---

Box 3.4 Interchangeability and the 'American system of manufactures'

Manufacturing in the USA developed in the first half of the nineteenth century along distinct lines that English observers in the 1850s referred to as the 'American system of manufacture'. This American system grew and developed into 'mass production' by the 1920s, the most prolific production system ever known.

Developed at the Springfield Armory in Springfield, MA, by Eli Whitney (and to a lesser extent by Samuel Colt in the Colt armory at Hartford, CT), the American system of manufacture involved the use of standardized, interchangeable parts (Hounshell 1984). Interchangeability was achieved through careful adherence to a rational jig and fixture system and a refined model-based system of gauging. Without interchangeability, each firing pin on a rifle was hand-filed and armories would still need to employ a regiment of hand-fitters to repair arms (Best 2001).

The American system of manufacture also involved mechanization through the sequential operation of special-purpose machines. Mechanization provided a means for quantity production rather than interchangeability (Hounshell 1984). Interchangeability of parts, combined with machine production was called the 'armory system' or 'armory practice'. These principles were later applied to the production of Singer sewing machines, woodworking, Mc Cormick agricultural reapers, bicycles and later perfected for the production of automobiles by Ford (see Hounshell 1984).

Best (2001) points out that during this period, product and process engineering emerged as a range of specialist machines had to be designed and built to convert the principle of interchangeability into practice. Product engineering emerged as a set of standard procedures, an organizational capability, and an occupational category to specify, identify, design, and operate efficiently the machines required. The rudiments of process engineering also appeared as methods were established to lay out, interface, standardize, measure, operate, and trouble-shoot machining activities along a production line (Best 2001).

form of inventory. The vision of a flow line concentrated the attention of engineers on barriers to throughput. A bottleneck would occur wherever a machining operation could not process material at the same pace as the previous operation. The machine responsible for the bottleneck constrained not only the throughput at that particular machine but the production system as a whole. Increasing the pace of work on any other machining activity could not increase output, only inventory. William Klann, the head of Ford's engine department, described the origins of flow: 'We combined our ideas on the Huetteman and Cramer grain [conveying] machine experience, and the brewing experience and the Chicago stockyard. They all gave us ideas for our own conveyors' (Hounshell 1984: 241). Mass production was a revolutionary concept, but it was built from inventions and machinery working in other industries. Indeed Hounshell (1984) describes how Ford brought together existing technologies from granaries, breweries, foundries, bicycles, canning, and meat packing to create mass production.

In mass production, as in mass distribution, economies resulted more from speed than from size. It was not the size of a manufacturing plant in terms of number of workers or the amount and value of productive equipment that enabled economies, but the synchronization of production that drove the rate of throughput up and the per-unit costs down, and linking up an assembly line was a final step. Before this, there was a need to equalize the cycle time for each operation (a cycle time is the time it takes to complete a single operation, usually on a single piece-part). Failure to synchronize operations appears as inventory build-up in front of the slower operation. As argued above, the way to increase the flow of material is not to speed the pace of the conveyor belt but to identify the slowest cycle time (bottleneck) and improve this. When bottlenecks were reduced, productivity and throughput increased. This meant that Ford had to develop two things. First, he could not simply purchase machines in the market. His machines needed re-gearing, re-tooling, and re-designing and his engineers had to develop a plant layout to achieve the narrow timing specifications required by the principle of flow. Second, he developed innovation in electric power generation so that power could be distributed to individual machines and machines could be arranged on the factory floor according to the logic of product engineering and the material conversion process (Best 2001) (this shows how important was the development of electricity as such a flexible source of power compared to steam). Indeed, Ford increased the rate of production by technology management rather than by 'scientific management':

The Ford approach was to eliminate labour by machinery, not as the Taylorites customarily do, to take a given production process and improve the efficiency of the workers through time and motion study and a differential piece-rate system of payment (or some such work incentive). Taylor took production hardware as given and sought revisions in the labour process and the organization of work; Ford engineers mechanized work processes and found workers to feed and tend their machines. Though time and motion studies may have been employed in the setup of the machine or machine process, the machine ultimately set the pace of work at Ford, not a piece-rate or an established standard for a 'fair day's work'. This was the essence of the assembly line and all the machinery that fed it. While depending upon certain elements of Taylorism in its fundamentals, the Ford assembly line departed radically from the ideas of Taylor and his followers (Hounshell 1984: 254–5).

Best (2001) agrees with Hounshell (1984) and is critical of the oversight in much of the literature of Ford's main contribution, the 'principle of flow', and the lack of attention to the link between Ford's contribution and the later development of 'lean production' at Toyota in Japan:

Ford, unlike American industrial followers, had no interest in labour productivity, conducting time and motion studies, or devising piece-rate systems .... Ford increased the rate of production by technology management: bottlenecks were eliminated and standardized cycle times were driven down. Unfortunately, the principle of flow was not written into industrial engineering manuals which, instead, adopted the 'scientific management' paradigm .... The concept of flow penetrated into management thought, and, less often, practices, in the early 1990s masquerading as 're-engineering' and 'lean production'. (Best 2001: 35)

Henry Ford was open about the organizational structure, sales and production methods of the Ford Motor Company and invited technical journalists to his factory. As a consequence of this openness, Ford production technology diffused rapidly through US manufacturing. Within a decade, many household appliances such as vacuum cleaners and radios were assembled following his principles. Ford thus contributed to educating the technical community on the principles of mass production (Hounshell 1984).

Big businesses also engaged in forward and backward integration, especially with raw materials or components production and with the distribution of financial goods to make the best use of mass distribution and production if their suppliers or distributors had not developed these methods. Ford pursued vertical integration because he developed mass production earlier than his suppliers. Indeed, he owned a rubber plant in Brazil, did not trust banks, owned iron mines in Minessota, owned ships to carry iron ore and coal through the Great Lakes to Rouge and a railroad to connect production facilities in the Detroit region (Best 1990). However, this degree of vertical integration was only necessary because his suppliers had not mastered mass production yet.

Also, managerial capitalism was based on the integration of financial and industrial capital. The early twentieth century saw the limitations of family capital. Ownership became scattered—managers did not own the firms and stockholders had no knowledge of management. Increasingly fragmented individual share ownership resulted in substantial delegation of corporate

---

Box 3.5 Mass production and consumption and its contributors

Mass production can be defined as the manufacturing of standardized products in high volumes using special-purpose (dedicated) machinery and predominately unskilled labour (Hirst and Zeitlin 1991). The following names have contributed to the development of mass production and consumption:

- **Henry Ford**: Ford argued that the key to mass production in the factory of the Ford Motor Company was not so much the assembly line (an idea he borrowed from the meat cold storage plant), which help to bring regularity to the Ford factory, but complete interchangeability of parts and the principle of flow. Ford and his engineers experimented continuously, patiently rearranging and redesigning machines until the flow of parts and the speed and the intervals along the assembly lines meshed into a perfectly synchronized operation (Hounshell 1984; Best 1990).

- **Alfred P. Sloan Jr.**: Sloan introduced the organization of firms into decentralized divisions serving clearly defined markets/products. At the head of General Motors, he developed close links to banks (such as Morgan). He also developed early marketing and advertising techniques (especially through the annual model change) (Womack et al. 1990). In terms of throughput efficiency, however, General Motors was a step backwards from Ford, since it produced multiple products without multiple-product flow (see Best 1990: 151).

- **Frederick W. Taylor**: Taylor developed the system of scientific management—segmenting work processes and routinizing work tasks by breaking them down into 'foolproof' steps to be performed over and over again by dedicated machinery eliminating the responsible involvement of the workforce. The main significance of Taylorism was the development of a new management style based on professionalization and specialization of the functions of management (cost accounting, production engineering, sales management, public relations, market research, etc.).

- **John Maynard Keynes** (see Box 1.3): Keynes was important for managerial capitalism because he emphasized the need to support aggregate demand. By supporting the balance of consumption and production, the costs of investment in production through special-purpose equipment could be amortized.

---

control to professional managers. This delegation enabled many large firms in the USA to develop long-term innovative capabilities that built on the organizational and technological capabilities that firms already possessed (Lazonick and O'Sullivan 1996).

A number of industries took advantage of the opportunities for mass production and mass marketing offered by national rail and telegraph in the early twentieth century. These included new branded and packaged consumer products (cigarettes, canned goods, flour and grain products, beer, dairy products, soap, and drugs), mass-produced light machinery (sewing machines, typewriters, and cameras), electrical equipment, standardized industrial machinery (boilers, pumps, and printing presses) and obviously the automobile industry, the most spectacular US success story (Nelson and Wright 1992).

Corporate capitalism involved the transition from an age of innovation led by independent inventors to the age of corporate laboratories (see Box 3.6) in

---

Box 3.6 Science for industry

The electrical and chemical industries were the first to establish research as a systematic part of the business. The primary purpose of these early laboratories and those which later sprang up in the nascent rubber, petroleum, automotive, and pharmaceutical industries, were applied research and development (process-testing, routine chemical analysis, cost-cutting, and quality control). In time, however, some of the giant companies which dominated these industries extended their activities into the area of fundamental scientific research. Nearly all of the basic research done by industry, as well as the bulk of applied research, was restricted to large firms with ample financial resources, since they alone were able to provide researchers with a relatively stable working situation and adequate facilities . . .

Before 1900 there was very little organized research in American industry, but by 1930 industrial research had become a major economic activity. In a 1928 survey of nearly six hundred manufacturing companies, 52 per cent of the firms reported that research was a company activity, 7 per cent stated that they had established testing laboratories, 29 per cent were supporting cooperative research activities of trade associations, engineering societies, universities, or endowed fellowships, and 11 per cent of those doing little or no research indicated that they intended to introduce research work. In less than three decades American industry had clearly become infatuated with scientific research. The major reason for this rush to science is not hard to fathom: there was money in it.

Source: Excerpt from Noble (1977: 111).

---

which the education of engineers and scientists was a critical component. Federal government support for university programs in agriculture and the practical arts, starting with the Morrill Land Grant College Act of 1862, provided stimulus to countrywide engineering education. The number of graduates from engineering colleges grew from 100 in 1870 to 4,300 in the First World War (Nelson and Wright: 1942). The wave of mergers of 1897–1902 that established the large businesses that are still known today, saw also the expansion of the private research laboratories. General Electric, DuPont, American Telephone and Telegraph (AT&T), and Kodak all set up R&D labs before the First World War, developing by the 1910s the chemicals and electrical engineering industries, despite the fact that USA had no advantage in fundamental science, and lagged behind Europe in patents and knowledge in these areas. Indeed, many of the early innovations, as well as inventions and discoveries in fundamental science, which were important in fuelling the third Kondratieff upswing had been made in Britain (Hobsbawm 1968: 152); it was the institutional, organizational, and managerial innovations which promoted the rapid take-off and diffusion of these innovations that were adopted more readily in Germany and the USA than in Britain. The development of the industrial laboratories depended on and fostered a huge expansion in engineering and science education (Mowery and Rosenberg 1989). The employment of scientists and engineers in industrial research laboratories in US manufacturing firms expanded by ten times between 1921 and 1940 (from 2,775 to 27,777) (Mowery and Nelson 1996: 196). As such, industrial research was not only an effect, but also a cause of the development of the modern corporation. The logic at the time was that funding science would generate technological breakthroughs that would usher in new products and new industries that, in turn, would drive growth. As argued in Chapter 1, federal spending on the education of scientists and engineers became America's de facto industrial policy (Best 2001). However, it is to be noted that many of the industries in which the USA had leadership, including non-electrical machinery, steel, and vehicles, were not science-based (and the USA did not surpass Germany, Britain, or France in scientific Nobel prizes until after the Second World War) (Nelson and Wright 1992). Lead in high-technology industries (such as electronics) was new, and as the result of massive private and public investments in R&D and scientific and technical education after the Second World War. The USA did not begin to undertake R&D in pharmaceuticals in a serious or systematic manner until the Second World War when the needs of the wounded provided a demand stimulus to a large scale cooperative research project coordinated by the government and aimed at finding a commercial process for production of penicillin. Indeed, pharmaceuticals is still a sector where as many European as US firms are in the top ten (see Chapter 7). Germany, on the other hand, had been a leading pharmaceutical innovator since the turn of the twentieth century (and an important player since the turn of the nineteenth century).

To conclude, these institutions led to the evolution of a few vertically integrated firms that quickly dominated the US economy. They exploited increases in output per unit of labour, capital, and materials through speed and throughput but also economies of scale (decrease in fixed costs per unit of labour and capital by spreading these over high volumes) and economies of scope (decrease in fixed costs by spreading these over a number of related product lines). These relied on US advantages of natural resources and the largest domestic markets. The growth of these big businesses, however, rested on the coordination of production and distribution rather than on their size and on mastering interchangeability and flow of production on the shop floor. As we have argued, Germany developed along different lines from the USA. State bureaucracies in Prussia and other German states were well developed in comparison to the USA and Britain (Weber [1922] 1978) and imparted a particular character to German industrialization (Kocka 1994; Freeman and Louçã 2001). Not only did the state play a more important role in the industrialization of Germany than in USA or Britain, but the management bureaucracies that developed in the large firms such as Siemens were influenced by procedures in the state bureaucracy regarding salary scales, recruitment, administrative procedures, and qualifications. A high proportion of employees in the beginning of the twentieth century were 'Angestellte'–salaried employees who expected a career in the firm, and many of these were professional engineers (Kocka 1994; Freeman and Louçã 2001). Highly qualified professional engineers in the electrical industries and chemists in the chemical industry dominated management culture and influenced long-term product development and investment (Freeman and Louçã 2001). The development of professional associations and higher education institutions contributed to the formation of engineers. For example, in 1856, the association of German Engineers (the Verein Deutscher Ingenieure (VDI)), was established, as the leading institution for training and technology transfer among experts, which stressed theoretical background as well as practical knowledge. Also, new institutions of higher education (the Technische Hochschulen) were responsible for the high number and good quality of engineers, which played an important role in German industrialization (see Chapter 6).

Conclusion

This chapter gives an account of how changes in organizational and technological capabilities over the past century are responsible for shifts in industrial leadership. The British enterprise, atomistic and coordinated by prices in the market, was ill-equipped to compete with the US or German enterprise coordinated administratively by management. British firms could not drive down costs and improve throughput and productivity as could management teams with organizational and technological innovation. The US and German large oligopolies facilitated long-run planning, particularly where large-scale capital investments were involved. Managerial coordination of product flows within the vertically integrated enterprise permitted the achievement of high-speed throughput that in turn reduced unit costs. Vertical integration of production and distribution provided the direct access to market outlets that was a condition for the effective utilization of mass-production methods. Managerial control over job content and production standards in turn facilitated the introduction of new high-throughput technologies. Integration of financial and industrial capital (through the start of bank lending to industry, as best represented by the relation of General Motors and Morgan, see Box 3.5), along with managerial bureaucracy, made possible the geographical mobility of capital and the rapid expansion of capacity to produce for new or growing markets. Systematic R&D provided the main source of technological innovation, particularly in such science-based sectors as the electrical and chemical industries. The production side of the managerial enterprise was the diffusion of the principle of flow from cars to supplier industries, including petrochemicals and steel, and a range of consumer durables. The vertically integrated, managerial enterprise became the new business model. The new business model integrated the economies of mass production with those of mass distribution and brought in the age of mass consumption.

However, as we will see in the next chapter, the principles of production and organization which underpinned the growth of US industry eventually became obsolete (Piore and Sabel 1984; Freeman 1987; Lazonick 1991). The USA also failed to transform its business and production organization in the 1980s and in many industries lost dominance in favour of the Japanese business and production organization. The loss of US market share in the traditional mass-production labour-intensive industries to lower wage regions was a consequence of advances in production capabilities elsewhere. Japan's success in high-volume manufacturing industries such as cars and electric appliances was consistent with the spread of mass-production technologies. But it became a shock when US enterprises began losing market share in high-tech industries such as semiconductors. The publication of the Massachusetts Institute of Technology (MIT) book *Made in America* in 1989 (Dertouzos et al. 1989) signalled the growing concern that US industrial leadership was under severe attack and US industry was threatened with a hollowing out process (the shift from producing in the USA to just assembling in the USA components produced abroad) (see also Nelson 1990). The book analyses US competitiveness in a number of sectors: America's falling share of microelectronics market such as in semiconductors (except for computer software and large well-financed firms in the computer industry such as IBM, Digital Equipment, and Hewlett-Packard); problems of sales despite technological leadership in commercial aircraft; retreat in consumer electronics; erosion of competitiveness in steel production; increased foreign ownership of a large part of the successful chemical industry; problems in the mass markets of US textile manufacturers; the challenge of flexible manufacturing by Japan in the automobile industry; and the failure of the machine tool industry which lacks support from sophisticated users or government.

Chapter 4 examines the challenge to the US organizations and technology. The US business model designed around a particular logic of specialization, limited management efforts to develop and commercialize technological breakthroughs originated in the laboratories. This business model came under increasing competition from a new model (the 'new competition') capable of assimilating new technologies into the production system.

Notes

1 Chandler writes about the USA and Schumpeter about Germany.
2 In the case of Siemens.
3 Rose and Rose (1970) report that one MP demanded the establishment of thirty state science colleges, of which only three were eventually founded in London: the Royal School of Science, the City and Guilds Technical College, and the School of Mines (descended from the Royal College of Chemistry). They were intended to produce the scientists, engineers,

and technically minded industrialists that the country needed, together with Owens College in Manchester and University College, London. Even then some intervention by Prince Albert (who was, of course, German) was necessary—and at one stage a Principal had to be recruited from Germany (see also Beer 1959).

4 As we pointed out in Chapter 2, the development of machinery based on steam technology, which raised questions of power, energy, and efficiency, gave rise to a new branch of science: thermodynamics (rather than the other way around) (Lilley 1949). Which is not to say, of course, that a great many improvements were not made possible, at a later stage, as a result of the increase understanding provided by a knowledge of thermodynamics.

5 The multidivisional form evolved after vertical integration, professional managers, and expanded product lines. In large firms, the M-form replaced the unitary organizational form (U-form)—in which corporate functions were centralized—gaining administrate efficiency, as the general office was responsible for strategic decisions and the divisions for operations decisions. This was an advantage when firms started developing and acquiring different products and services.

6 Franklin Delano Roosevelt was aware of the way in which a new prolific system of production was developing in USA. The following quote attributed to him illustrates this: 'If I could give every Russian just one American book, I would choose the Sears, Roebuck catalogue' (Noble 1977).

7 Rosenberg (1976) shows that the firearms industry in the USA in the first half of the nineteenth century was decisive in the development of specialized, precision machinery jigs, fixtures, taps and gauges, and the systematic development of die-forging techniques. The sewing machine industry during 1950–70 adopted many of the processes of firearms production and also contributed with additions to machine-cutting (notably the universal milling machine), which in turn were applied in the production of other metal-using products, especially the bicycles and automotive sectors. The production of bicycles used these techniques and developed further techniques, such as for making ball bearings, which had an important effect in reducing wear and friction on all machine processes. Automotive production in its early stages depended on machine tools development and induced innovations across the whole spectrum of machine tools: drilling and tapping, milling and lathe work.

4 Organizations and Technology during the Periods of 'New Competition' and 'Systems Integration'

Introduction

In Chapter 3 we described the way in which changes in organizational and technological capabilities accounted for shifts in industrial dominance from Britain to the USA in the early twentieth century. This chapter examines the challenges to US firms' organizational and technological capabilities from the large Japanese firms and the small-firm industrial districts of the 'third Italy'.

While economies all over the world went into recession in the late 1970s and 1980s, frequently accompanied by a deterioration in labour and social conditions and rising unemployment, a few regions stood out as showing remarkable resilience and even growth. In Japan, large firms, supported by a central government pursuing an active industrial policy, achieved a dominant domestic market share and international competitiveness. Their success was supported by strong networks of manufacturing, trading and supplier firms, and banks with cross-ownership links which developed production capabilities in high-volume manufacturing industries such as cars and semiconductors. Networks were also central to the success of industrial districts in Italy (and also Germany), where technologically sophisticated, highly flexible small- and medium-sized manufacturing firms are engaged in a variety of industries, including traditional labour-intensive ones, in a context of strong unions and left political parties (we return to a discussion of networks in more detail in Chapter 9). These networks of small- and medium-sized firms operate in a range of traditional but design-led industries such as clothing, shoes, and furniture in North-central and North-eastern Italy (Tuscany, Veneto, and Emilia-Romagna, sometimes called the 'Third Italy') (Brusco 1982; Piore and Sabel 1984; Pyke et al. 1990) (and in machine tools and metalworking regions in Baden-Wurttemberg in Germany, see Sabel et al. (1989)). In all cases, they receive financial and commercial support from quasi-government regional institutions.

During this period, the US economy suffered a paradox—its technological progress was combined with a productivity slowdown. This can be explained by the deterioration of US production capabilities and a failure to convert its technological advances into high-quality low-cost products. Japan and the 'third Italy', in contrast, derived a manufacturing competitive advantage from the upgrading of production capabilities through strong networks. Both Japanese firms and the industrial districts in Italy were able to achieve good performance standards in cost, quality, flexibility, and/or design that could not be matched by US managerial capitalism. The tables turned again in the 1990s, with a new rise in productivity in high-tech regions of the USA (Best 2001). Firms like Intel reinvented production around a new 'open systems' business model, which has given rise to a new regional model of innovation based on the decentralization and diffusion of research and design. This regional innovation model has also developed in other high-tech sectors such as software and biotechnology. What these examples demonstrate is that the large, multidivisional firm with centralized, large in-house R&D labs may no longer be the only key driver of regional growth dynamics. Instead, entrepreneurial firms and their networks of research across firms and universities, together with the development of market opportunities may also play a central role in shaping economic prospects for regions and countries.

This chapter is organized as follows. The first section describes the main features of organizations and technology prevailing in Japan and the 'Third Italy'. The second section examines organizations and technology in what has been termed 'systems integration'. A conclusion identifies the policy challenges of the developments described in the chapter.

Organizations and technology in the period of the new competition

Much of the decline in US competitiveness is explained by the emergence in Japan and the 'Third Italy' of a new model of organizational and technological capabilities, which has been called the 'new competition' (Best 1990), collective capitalism (Lazonick 1991), and the 'second industrial divide' (Piore and Sabel 1984). These terms are used to embrace interfirm complexes which range from groups of small Italian firms linked by cooperative associations for joint marketing, technological advance, and financial underwriting to giant Japanese organizational structures coordinating trading companies, banks, and manufacturing firms. Box 4.1 summarizes the main features of organizations and technology associated with the 'new competition'. It represents a contrast to managerial capitalism, in which innovation strategy was pursued within a separate, and in some cases large, R&D department with its own budget and staff of product and process engineers that specialized in the design of new products and processes. Firms in the new competition promote a strategy of continuous improvement and integrate thinking and doing within production (with the work of the R&D department being closely related to the work of production engineers and process control, and almost indistinguishable from one another). Rather than exploit economies of time in throughput as in managerial capitalism, firms in the new competition exploit economies of time in process and product design. They also forge long-term consultative relations with a few suppliers. Moreover, they have received support from national or local government committed to high growth and are involved in sector cooperation and competition (see Box 4.2).

Box 4.1 Organizations and technology in the 'new competition'

The 'new competition' in Japan and the 'Third Italy' which prospered in the 1950s to 1980s is characterized by the following features:

- Entrepreneurial firm (networks with the flexibility of small firms and the capacity to invest productively of large firms)
- Flexible specialization (economies of time in process and product design) (see Box 4.6)
- Consultative relation with suppliers
- Strategic industrial policy (target strategic sectors, sector cooperation, and competition)

Source: Best (1990).

Box 4.2 Four dimensions of the 'new competition'

The new competition can be distinguished from the old in four dimensions:

- **The firm: the collective entrepreneur**. The entrepreneurial firm ... builds on the idea of Schumpeterian competition. The first feature of the entrepreneurial firm is a strategic orientation: a strategically oriented firm chooses the terrain on which to compete; a hierarchical firm takes the terrain as given. The second ... is that the goal of the entrepreneurial firm is to gain strategic advantage by continuous improvement in process and product; the goal of the hierarchical firm is to gain minimum production costs by continuity in production operations, product runs, and product design .... Mass production is about one form of time competition: economies of time in throughput. Time competition has entered into two dimensions beyond the reach of the hierarchical firm. The first is about process time, or the time that materials take to be processed within a plant .... The second is an extension of Schumpeterian competition: economies of time in the implementation of new product designs ...

- **The production chain: consultative coordination**. Ford's external supplier relations were market driven. Nissan's external supplier relations are design driven .... At full capacity a

---

Box 4.2 (*Continued*)

Nissan assembly plant will work with only 120 suppliers . . . . The difference is that the struggle over prices goes on within the context of a long-term relationship based upon established norms of mutual responsibility.

- **The sector: competition and cooperation.** Intense local price competition can reduce global competitiveness, particularly in high fixed cost industries, by limiting the capacity of the sector to invest in its future . . . . Strategically managed inter-firm associations can promote the long-term development and competitiveness of a sector . . . . If, for example, members of different firms cooperate in labour training, export marketing, or financing research, they may also develop the capacity to adjust mutually to new challenges and respond collectively to new opportunities.

- **The government: strategic industrial policy** [T]he task of industrial (including antitrust) policy is not to establish an ideal as defined by the neoclassical theory of perfect competition but to administer a paradox: cooperation alone can ensure that commitments are made to the long-term infrastructural development of a sector; competition alone can ensure that business enterprises remain innovative . . . . Three elements of successful industrial policy activities in Japan and the Third Italy stand out. The first element . . . is a creative use and shaping of the market . . . . The market, it has been said, is a good servant, but a bad master. Second, successful industrial policy has a production as opposed to a distributional focus . . . . Third, Japanese industrial policy has been strategically focused. It is about the targeting of industrial sectors to maximize industrial growth . . .

Source: Excerpt from Best (1990: 11–20).

THE THIRD ITALY

One of the cases that best represents the 'new competition' is the network of small independent producers in north-central part of Italy, which is sometimes called the 'Third Italy' because it is neither the northern industrial heartland triangle of Milan-Turin-Genoa, home of the car and chemical industries, and large multinational firms, nor the agricultural south. In this area, small firms in industrial districts are involved in continuous innovation, use flexible production methods, have complementary production activities, and share common services. Best (1990) describes the industrial district as acting as a 'collective entrepreneur'.

While industrial districts have been identified in many parts of Italy and in the Baden-Wurttemberg region of Germany (and in such varied locations as Denmark, Sweden, Spain, and Los Angeles in the USA) (Sabel et al. 1989; Herrigel 1993; Malecki 1997), the Emilia-Romagna region is the one that has received greatest attention. Brusco (1982) lists examples of industrial districts in the region of Emilia-Romagna which include knitwear in Modena; clothes and ceramic tiles in Modena and Reggio; shoes in Bologna; buttons in Piacenza; tomato canning and ham in Parma, and pig breeding in Reggio Emilia. However, he argues it would be a mistake to think that this phenomenon is confined to consumer goods. Industrial districts are also common in engineering: the production of cycles, motorcycles, and packaging machinery in Bologna; agricultural machinery and special oleodynamic engineering apparatus in Modena and Reggio; woodworking machine tools in Capri; and food processing machinery in Parma.

The 'Third Italy' is often quoted as a small firm economy success story where success has taken place without the industrial giants. In the early 1970s to the mid-1980s, Italy had the fastest rate of growth of the four big European economies, and overtook France and Britain in size of national output to be the fourth largest in the world after USA, Japan, and Germany. The fastest growing region was Emilia-Romagna, the area around the city of Modena, where 90 per cent of firms had fewer than 99 employees, small firms accounted for 58 per cent of employed workforce, and more than a third of the workforce were self-employed. Emilia-Romagna had the most industrial exports in vehicle, ceramics, clothing, machinery, and metalworking products. The economic performance of Emilia-Romagna has been distinctly superior to that of other regions in Italy: from 1970 to 1979, money income per head in Emilia-Romagna grew at an annual rate of 18.5 per cent (compared to an average rate for Italy of 17.5 per cent per year); and Emilian income rose to 5.6 million lire per head in 1979 (compared with the average Italian income of 4.4 million per head). Also, exports rose from 5 per cent of total Italian exports in 1963 to 9.4 per cent in 1971. Moreover, the region showed a large participation of the labour force. This was 46 per cent in 1980, 6 per cent higher than the national average (Brusco 1982: 167–8).

The Emilian model has been presented by Piore and Sabel (1984) as a paradigmatic example of flexible production, based on small craft shops using highly versatile machinery operated by polyvalent operatives (see Box 4.3). Two factors have accounted for the decentralization of production. First, the rise of trade union power forced large firms to disintegrate production vertically to smaller, less unionized firms. Second, since the mid-1960s there was the emergence of demand for more varied and customized goods which could not be met by mass production (Brusco 1982).

These networks of small firms have been capable of resisting foreign competition, especially from cheaper Third World producers. There are three main reasons for this. One is that the flexibility of labour and the regulatory environment favours family over hired help; it integrates home and workshop; and it established the artisan as a hybrid figure placed between capital and labour (Lazerson 1990). A second reason is the higher technical level of the machinery employed. The flexible use of labour facilitates the introduction of innovation, even when they are labour-saving. A third reason is that these networks enhance the capacity to develop new products and machinery by the proximity of entrepreneurs and extensive collaboration between skilled workers and technicians within each firm. However, while some regard the network of independent producers as a positive alternative to

---

Box 4.3 The 'second industrial divide'

The brief moments when the path of technological development itself is at issue we call industrial divides. At such moments, social conflicts of the most apparently unrelated kinds determine the direction of technological development for the following decades . . . . Industrial divides are therefore the backdrop or frame for subsequent regulation crises.

In our view, the first industrial divide came in the nineteenth century. At that time, the emergence of mass-production technologies—initially in Great Britain and then in the United States—limited the growth of less rigid manufacturing technologies, which existed primarily in various regions of Western Europe. These less rigid manufacturing technologies were craft systems: in the most advanced ones, skilled workers used sophisticated general-purpose machinery to turn out a wide and constantly changing assortment of goods for constantly shifting markets . . . .

[W]e are living through the second industrial divide. Extrapolating from current developments, we see two potentially contradictory strategies for relaunching growth in the advanced countries. The first strategy builds on the dominant principles of mass-production technology; but it requires a dramatic extension of existing regulatory institutions, including a redefinition of economic relations between the developed and the developing worlds. The second strategy veers sharply from established technological principles and leads back to those craft methods of production that lost out at the first industrial divide. This second strategy requires the creation of regulatory mechanisms whose association with bygone forms of economic organization apparently discredits them as instruments of modern industry.

Source: Excerpt from Piore and Sabel (1984: 5–6).

---

large bureaucratic organizations (Lazerson 1990), others argue that it perpetuates racial, gender, and skill divisions (with the 'quality craft work' reserved for middle-class Emilian men) (Murray 1987).

Best (1990) discusses three main types of small firm. The first are the traditional firms producing for the local market, such as butchers and bakers, pasta-makers, cheese and ham producers whose competitive edge is based on quality—for example they do not use preservatives or freezing (and do not need to for a local market). In Italy, as in France, the quality of food is very important relative to the price, and there is still a strong tradition of buying from specialist firms and market stalls, such as bakers, butchers, pasta shops, cheese shops, fishmongers, and greengrocers, rather than at the supermarket. The second type are design-dependent firms which subcontract to lead firms, the latter shaping the product design and controlling an important phase in the production chain such as assembly or retailing. An example of a lead firm might be the manufacturer of clothing Benetton (Belussi 1989; Belussi and Arcangeli 1998) (see Chapter 9). The lead firm interacts with regional, national, or international markets (or all three) and the subcontractor competes with other subcontractors on the basis of price. The subcontractor does not normally have independent design or marketing capacity though it is the design that is often the key to international competitiveness (as in clothing and furniture). The lead firm competes on quality and design and its ability to respond to changes in fashion. The third type are design-independent suppliers, firms which design themselves or at least modify designs and therefore shape products and markets. They may not produce their own brands (which may be the retailer's brand) but they are not tied to the designs of assembly or retailing firms.

A critical feature of the industrial district in Italy is its capacity to promote specialization as new technologies develop, and to keep on doing it. The health of an industrial district can be measured by the rate of creation of new firms as spin-offs. One of the key characteristics of the industrial district is its ability to restructure in order to seize new opportunities, without the creation of a managerial hierarchy. A new firm may be set up as a spin-off from the old firm, by someone leaving to start their own business. The two firms may remain closely linked as customer and supplier and with personal contact. This contrasts the US experience at the turn of the century in which small family firms were unable to hold their own in competition with the emerging U-form firm (see Chapter 3), with its central office, functional departments, and managerial hierarchies. Instead, production was rationalized into the large M-form business firms engaged in mass production in managerial capitalism.

The Third Italy, in contrast, is very strongly based on both productive decentralization and social integration. Networking allows for economies of scale or scope, and a changing balance between activities which take place within the firm and those which are done externally. The network allows for economies of scale from joint solutions to the development and diffusion of technology, for example, in the development and use of new process equipment and new materials or dyes; and marketing via trade fairs and export arrangements. It also allows for economies of scope, in which small firms band together to purchase integrated manufacturing systems such as assembly, handling and control equipment which would be beyond the means of individual small firms. At the same time the small firms also compete strongly with each other.

While Italian industrial districts are strongly characterized by networks of small firms, Italian multinationals are also often involved in network structures in which a few large and modern firms with a strong regional base are linked to a very large number of small traditional firms. The network structure avoids the organizational and financial burden of a fully integrated structure. In the case of these networks, in contrast to the large company groups to be found in the USA, functional specialization exists between the core and the periphery, rather than between the departments of the one enterprise. The core firms are usually specialized in overall planning, strategic management, monitoring of manufacturing and commercial units, the electronic network, R&D, design, and advertising. The periphery is likely to specialize in manufacture of precisely specialized components or products, and sales (see the case of Benetton in Chapter 9).

It is worth noting that industrial districts are often located in regions where one political party—either the Communists or the Christian Democrats—dominates. The local authorities in the industrial districts of Emilia-Romagna, Tuscany, and Umbria are dominated by the Communist party, while those in Veneto, Friuli, and the Marches are controlled by the Christian Democrats. These political forces have provided firm support for small business both by legitimizing them and by introducing specific policies (Brusco and Pezzini 1990).

In the Third Italy, it has been the influence of quasi-public institutions at the regional level which has supported the industrial districts. The Confederazione Nazionale dell' Artigianato (CNA) is a confederation of trade associations that does more than lobby the government. It provides business services for which there are substantial economies of scale. Membership of the CNA allows member firms to cooperate in the provision of collective services while remaining autonomous in decision-making and finance. CNA supplies administrative services to artisan firms, including accounting services; financial services; and assistance in the development of property facilities, in the creation of business service centres in industrial districts, and in establishing cooperatives to solve general problems for a group of firms, such as quality control or bulk purchasing of raw materials or export marketing (Best 1990).

JAPAN

We now turn to the most impressive example of 'new competition'—the case of Japan. From 1946 to 1976, Japanese manufacturing production increased 55-fold (see Johnson 1982, Table 1, pp. 4–5). Several explanations have been offered for the economic growth experienced by Japan. These include: the 'national character' explanation (which argues that the Japanese have a unique, culturally derived capacity to cooperate with each other), the 'miracle' explanation (which argues that Japan has three key institutions explaining the unique growth record: lifetime employment, a seniority wage system, and enterprise unionism), the market forces explanation (which argues that Japan benefited from the availability of capital, labour, and markets with government providing nothing more than an environment for economic growth), and the 'free ride' explanation (which agues that Japan was the beneficiary of its post-war alliance with the USA through lack of defence expenditures, access to major export markets, and relatively cheap transfer of technology).

However, this chapter argues that it is the particular organization of firms and types of industrial policy that enabled the adoption of organizational and technological innovation which have been responsible for Japan's high growth (Johnson 1982; Freeman 1987, 1988; Best 1990) (Box 4.4). It is also important

---

Box 4.4 Institutions of high growth in Japan

During the period 1949 to 1954 the Japanese forged the institutions of the high-growth system. In 1954 ... MITI (Ministry of International Trade and Industry) put the system into effect .... Some of the elements of what became MITI's high-growth system derived from the government's selection of industries for 'nurturing', perfection of measures to commercialise the products of these chosen industries, and development of means for regulating the cut-throat competition that the first two sets of policies generated. The tools in the hands of economic bureaucrats included control over all foreign exchange and imports of technology, which gave them the power to choose industries for development; the ability to dispense preferential financing, tax breaks, and protection from foreign competition, which gave them the power to lower the costs of the chosen industries; and the authority to order the creation of cartels and bank-based industrial conglomerates ... which gave them the power to supervise competition. This high-growth system was one of the most rational and productive industrial policies ever devised by any government, but its essential rationality was not perceived until after it had already started producing results unprecedented for Japan or any other industrialized economy.

Source: Excerpt from Johnson (1982: 198–9).

---

to stress that virtually all of these institutions date from the twentieth century (and usually no earlier than the First World War) and do not just spring from Japanese 'culture' and 'national character' (Johnson 1982). The organizational and technological changes crucial to Japanese growth, were not a 'free ride' but the result of the deliberate development of this particular set of institutions (Johnson 1982; Best 1990).[1]

For more than seventy years the Japanese state gave first priority continuously and consistently to economic development. Johnson (1982) explains how the Japanese state acted as a true 'development' state as the Ministry of Commerce and Industry (MCI), Ministry of Munitions (MM), and Ministry of International Trade and Industry (MITI) mobilized the nation for economic development. Japan's achievement started with the financial crisis of 1927 and ended with the oil shock of 1973. However, state influence is still felt in attempts beyond the 1970s to change industrial structure to post-industrial 'knowledge intensive' industries. According to Johnson (1982) the main elements of the success were a small, inexpensive but elite bureaucracy staffed by the best managerial talent (not in terms of salaries but academic competence), a political system in which the bureaucracy was given sufficient scope to take initiatives and operate effectively (and fend off the numerous interest groups which would distort the priorities of the developmental state), the development of an industrial policy that preserved competition to avoid the inefficient loss of incentives, corruption, and bureaucratism of state control, and a unique pilot organization—MITI.

MITI originated from the MCI from the separation of agriculture and commercial administration. It developed by adding industrial functions while shedding commercial ones, obtaining planning capability, and gaining control over energy. It also obtained micro-level intervention powers (through its Enterprises Bureau) and control of international trade. MITI has had influence over key industries—steel, electric power, and chemicals in the 1950s, automobile and appliances in the 1960s, advanced electronics in the 1970s, computers, robots, and new sources of energy in the 1980s. It has had no jurisdiction over transportation, agriculture, construction, labour, or finance, although it has had a strong influence over them, particularly over finance, through such institutions as the Japanese Development Bank. The features and functions of MITI set it apart from other organizations in any other developed or less developed country. These features include: small size, indirect control of government functions, 'think-tank' functions, 'vertical bureaus' or sector planning agencies for carrying out sector-specific rationalization plans, and internal democracy (Johnson 1982). MITI continued with sector-specific deliberation councils composed of private and public officials who met on a permanent basis. The success of these vertical bureaux depended on orchestrating a private–public consensus around a sector development plan. Since the passing of the Foreign Capital Law in 1950, the government was in charge of technology transfer. This was a complex process of public–private interaction that has come to be known as 'industrial policy' (Johnson 1982). MITI was the main Japanese government agency charged with the implementation of industrial policy. As argued by Johnson:

The importation of technology was one of the central components of post-war Japanese industrial policy, and to raise the subject is to turn the discussion to MITI and the Japanese government's role. Before the capital liberalization of the late 1960s and 1970s, no technology entered the country without MITI's approval; no joint venture was ever agreed to without MITI's scrutiny and frequent alteration of the terms; no patent rights were ever bought without MITI's pressuring the seller to lower the royalties or to make other changes advantageous to Japanese industry as a whole; and no program for the importation of foreign technology was ever approved until MITI and its various advisory committee had agreed that the time was right and the industry involved was scheduled for 'nurturing' (Johnson 1982: 17).

Best (1990) lists a number of instruments used by MITI to set the path for industrial change: tariffs and quotas; control of foreign exchange; influence over credit allocation in public and private banks; technology import licences; accelerated depreciation allowances; land subsidization; influence over cartel legalization with the Fair Trade Commission (FTC); and the creation of joint private–public companies. The effectiveness of MITI was improved by the loss of its absolute powers of state control following the expiration in 1952 of the Temporary Materials Supply and Demand Control Law. MITI did not lose all controls—it still exercised complete control over foreign trade and the introduction of foreign technology—but after 1952 it had to learn to employ indirect methods of intervention in the economy. This differentiated it from both the Ministry of Finance and the Ministry of Agriculture and Forestry, and promoted a true public–private cooperation in the industrial sector. The period 1952–61 was the ministry's golden age (Johnson 1982). Using the Fiscal Investment Loan Plan, the Development Bank, the Industrial Rationalization Council, and several other powerful institutions, the Enterprises Bureau single-mindedly turned the Japanese industrial structure from light, labour-intensive industries (textiles, toys, footwear) to steel, ships, and automobiles, of which Japan is today the world's leading producer.

The guidance of MITI shaped the long-term pattern of structural change in the Japanese economy and this influence was made on the basis of judgements about the future direction of technological change. It is interesting to note that in the immediate post-war Japan specifically rejected long-term development based on traditional theory of comparative advantage (see Chapter 8), which was advocated at that time on several fronts and especially by the Bank of Japan (which argued for a specialization in areas of 'natural' comparative advantage, such as low labour cost labour-intensive industries such as textiles). The discussion mainly concerned whether Japan could have a role in the automobile industry, but eventually extended to all industrial and trade policies (Freeman 1988). MITI established a mode of working that relied on continuing dialogue on technological developments, with industrial R&D personnel and with university scientists (Freeman 1987). The Japanese system included informal and formal forecasting that allowed the formulation of technology and industrial policies not so much on the basis of particular products or existing statistics or weight of established firms and industries, but on those new technologies which are likely to transform the established pattern. As pointed out by Freeman:

In this context the organizing and energizing role of the Japanese forecasting system is important. The 'visions' of the future produced by STA, MITI, NIRA, and other government and private sources do not pretend to be accurate predictions, nor do they commit companies to inflexible plans. They chart the broad direction of advance for the economy and for technology and give companies sufficient confidence in this vision to make the long-term investments in research, development, software, equipment and training (Freeman 1988: 344).

Once these 'visions' were in place, the policies of MITI enabled sequential targeting of sectors to maintain industrial competitiveness. Resources have shifted from unskilled-labour-intensive sectors through raw-material-intensive and skilled-labour-intensive sectors and eventually to knowledge-intensive sectors. Japanese industrial policy has been successful at integrating these shifting sectoral patterns with the competitive strategies and organizational capabilities of individual firms. MITI makes informed investment decisions, anticipating relative rates of growth of sectors and negotiating sectoral investment guidelines (see Figure 4.1).

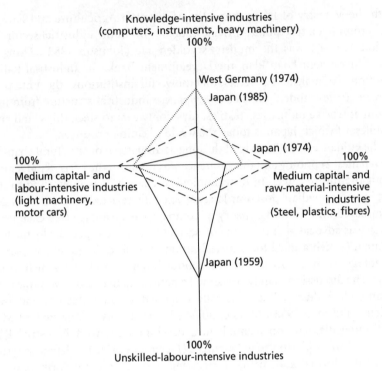

Figure 4.1 Evolution of Japanese industrial structure
(*source*: Best 1990: 190)

Best (1990) and Freeman (1987) describe the evolution of production strategies in Japan. The Japanese policy of forbidding foreign direct investment (FDI) and putting responsibility in the local firms for technology acquisition contrasts with the policies in many less developed countries of obtaining technology transfer through the entry of subsidiaries of multinationals (see Chapter 5). First, given the lack of resources in the immediate post-war, and the need to generate the foreign exchange needed for food and raw material imports, planners channelled resources into exports of labour intensive low-priced goods, made by low-wages workers (such as textiles, toys, and footwear). Soon, however, policymakers became aware that labour-intensive industries were not the basis for a high growth economy. During this period, MITI's influence was through direct physical controls and allocations, giving priority to key industries, such as energy, steel, and chemicals, and to the development of mass and flow production technologies (Freeman 1987). While in the 1950s USA produced 70 per cent of the world steel and Japan none, by the 1980s Japan had eight of the world's ten deep water steel plants of capacity over 10 million tons and the USA had none (Best 1990: 141). By 1976, Japan had a large share of OECD exports: 90 per cent of motorcycles,

70 per cent of televisions and radios, 43 per cent of ships, 23 per cent of watches, and 20 per cent of cars were exported (Best 1990: 141).

After this period, however, MITI shifted to indirect policies, such as fiscal and financial incentives. MITI recognized that the 1960s path of energy and materials-intensive growth was facing limitations and placed instead emphasis on information technology. In the 1970s, MITI promoted the development of the computer industry, the telecommunications industry, and the semiconductor industry (such as large-scale integration and very large scale integration) (Fransman 1990). Japanese producers focused on high volume segment and established production facilities that reduced overhead costs (costs of material handling, inventory, quality control, inspection, warehousing, and resource planning). As a response, Western competitors retreated to high value segments. Japanese producers realized high profits based on lower overheads and eventually followed into the lower volume market as well. Finally, in the 1970s, Japanese producers developed flexible production (see Box 4.5) which involves the production of a range of products on the same production line without increasing indirect labour costs. These involved new production concepts including 'just in time', decrease in inventory, reduction in change-over times, lead times, source inspection, self-stoppage machines, integration of planning and doing, and consultative supplier relationship (Best 1990) (see Box 4.6). Competitiveness was thus sought by upgrading product, process, and organization continuously dealing a blow to US and European higher value goods production.

These transformations relied on important changes in production organization and strategy. The shift from low wages to scale economies focused on reducing indirect labour (while direct labour is the work involved in the alteration of the physical characteristics of the material as it is transformed into a product, indirect labour, on the other hand, is the work involved in performing support functions to direct labour activity such as maintenance, scheduling, inspection, and supervision).[2] The shift from the focus on overhead economies to flexible production involved the absorption of foreign technology and the development of an endogenous capacity of Japanese firms to improve continuously (Best 1990). Although the Japanese firms were not the major contributors to the original radical innovations in computers and telecommunications, the Japanese technological forecasting system did identify the main elements of the emerging microelectronics paradigm at the beginning of the 1970s and, earlier than elsewhere, enabled Japanese firms to exploit robotics, computer numerically controlled machine tools, flexible manufacturing systems, construction and financial services (Freeman 1987).

To understand those broad changes, we must look to the way in which large firms were ready to make long-term investments in new technology organization. The typical business groups in Japan include a big bank, several industrial firms, and a trading company. The bank plays an important role

---

Box 4.5 Flexible specialization/Toyotism and its creators

The new production system known variously as 'flexible specialization', 'JIT', the 'Toyota Production System', and 'lean production' can be defined as the manufacture of a wide and changing array of customized products using flexible, general-purpose machinery and skilled, adaptable workers (Hirst and Zeitlin 2002). This production system is based on the principle of multi-product flow. Three names can be associated with this new production system:

- **Taiichi Ohno**: Ohno was the assembly manager and eventually executive vice president for Toyota. In the 1940s and 1950s he introduced many improvements that eventually became the Toyota Production System. He applied the principle of flow of Ford to a range of products. He equalized cycle times for every part. Flexibility (variation of the product mix in response to demand shifts) comes from three sources: first, adjusting the number of workers in cells; second, quick set-up and changeover in machines and, third, the employment of multi-skilled workers. Each worker must operate not one machine, but three to four machines, and also do set-ups (and maintenance activities) on the machines. What was revolutionary about the way of producing in Toyota was not 'just-in-time' production but the idea of single-minute exchange of dies. To produce multiple products on the same line, is necessary to make the machines capable of being programmable (mechanically or electronically) for different products. The challenge of Toyota was to go beyond multiple products on the same line to multiple products on the same line in batch sizes of one. This required cellular manufacturing—with machines laid out and reconfigured according to the routing sheets or flow charts but in U-cells and without a conveyor line.

- **Sakichi Toyoda**: Toyoda was a weaver who, in 1924, invented a loom that would detect any error and automatically stop production, preventing the creation of defective goods. He later sold the patent on his machine to a British firm for about $150, 000. That money was used to help his son found a start-up, Toyota, which would become the world's second-biggest auto producer. Toyoda's innovation of instilling human judgement on machines (also known as 'automation' or 'Jidoka') would be adopted in Toyota and then in almost every industrial enterprise, cutting down on waste, improving customer relations, revealing problems and conserving resources.

- **W. Edwards Deming**: Japanese system forsook Taylorist information for another type, that of statistical quality control championed by W. Edwards Deming. While the purpose of Taylorist information is to minimize direct labour costs in the production of a standardized product, the purpose of Deming's information is to provide a basis for continuous upgrading of production methods and product quality. Deming's message was that quality and productivity are positively related, contrary to the trade-off presumed in mass production. Statistical quality control is based on the premise that defective products are usually caused by poor systems rather than by bad workers. He argued that the concentration of US firms on measurable aggregates introduces a powerful bias towards output quotas and against product quality. Deming stressed purpose and worker self-respect as a source of motivation for the worker and competitiveness for the firm.

Source: Womack et al. (1990), Best (2001).

---

during upswings in economic activity by supplying capital to the members, and the trading company plays a key role during downswings in economic activity by importing raw materials on credit and promoting fiercely the export of products that cannot be sold domestically. The American occupation at the end of the Second World War broke up the old zaibatsu trading

Box 4.6 New production concepts

The new production concepts of Japanese producers include the following:

- **Process over operational efficiency**: Operational efficiency is about concentrating efforts on productive time—the time during which material is transformed by machining operations. Process efficiency includes both productive and unproductive time. Unproductive time is the time materials spend in inventory or other non-operational activity such as handling, moving, inspecting, reworking, counting and repacking. Operational throughput efficiency, the indicator of success in mass production is measured in terms of productivity per labour or machine input hour. In contrast, process throughput efficiency is the ratio of time a product is being transformed to the time it is in the production system. Process efficiency has led to the creation of a new set of performance indicators. One indicator is the work-in-process (WIP) turn: the ratio of WIP to annual sales (WIP is the value of inventories that a plant requires to maintain production; it does not include inventories of produced goods waiting to be shipped, it is a subcategory of inventory readily ascertained from a firm's balance sheet). Toyota was at the forefront in driving up WIP turns—in the late 1970s when Western automobile firms had WIP turns of around 10, Toyota's WIP turn was greater than 300 per year (and it is estimated that every doubling of the WIP turn increases labour productivity by 38 per cent).

- **Just-in-time (JIT) for material resource planning**: The idea of Toyoda (founder of Toyota Motor Works, formerly a textile firm) is that inventories can be virtually eliminated in the production process. His idea was to model the assembly line after the US supermarket. Instead of producing to pre-planned orders, suppliers would produce to sales figures. Rather than 'pushing' products through the production system, JIT 'pulls' them through. The JIT communication system is in the form of actual consumption figures of the following stage, not of orders from a planning staff anticipating future demands.

- **Fast changeover**: Japanese producers can produce a range of products economically with short changeover times. In contrast, the longest changeover time is the nine months it took to convert from Ford's Model T (at Highland Park) to Model A (at River Rouge). Long runs are operationally efficient but process inefficient—while one product is assembled, materials for others are produced for inventory. However, the barrier to short runs is the time required to change over the configuration and settings of machines from product to product. Long runs minimize changeover, during which production is stopped, but generate rising non-production costs. In mass production, changeover times were treated as fixed constraints and batch sizes were determined by economic order quantities or by the quantity of output at which the rising cost of inventories were equated to the unit decreasing changeover costs. The Japanese engineers managed to drive changeover times so that small batches could be run with minimal interference to the principle of flow.

- **Self-stopping machines**: In Toyota, machines were designed to detect abnormalities and stop automatically before any defective products were produced (see Toyoda's design of self-stopping looms in Box 4.5). A single worker could now oversee several machines without fear that defective products would go undetected or that an expensive machine might be damaged because a part entered at a wrong angle. Multi-machining based upon machines laid out in U-shapes with a single worker overseeing a group of machines around him/her. Increase in labour productivity is not based on worker speed up. Also, to avoid that machines would shut down, workers became 'problem solvers' rather than 'machine minders'. To facilitate this, the internal mechanisms of machines were exposed so that workers could improve them.

- **Quality control**: Deming inspired managers to focus on the management of interrelationships as well as the plan-do-check-act management of Total Quality Management. Continuous

---

Box 4.6 (*Continued*)

---

improvementof product and process (Total Quality Management, kaizen, small group activity, self-directed work teams) sought to integrate thinking and doing on the shop floor. The purpose of statistical process control was not only to distinguish systemic from special causes of defects but also to focus attention on improvement of the organization a way to advance quality and productivity.

Source: Best (1990).

---

companies, which were big, diversified, family-owned businesses (such as Mitsui, Mitsubishi, or Sumitomo) and which often had government or military links. The Americans were motivated by their strong opposition to trust-like structures. But as soon as the occupation was over, MITI busily rebuilt the zaibatsu into the modern-day keiretsu through its licensing powers and ability to supply preferential financing. MITI cut down about 2,800 trading companies to 20 big ones (Johnson 1982: 206). As with the zaibatsu, the function of the new groups was to concentrate capital on key developmental projects, pioneer the commercialization of modern technologies in Japan, and obtain economies of scale in manufacturing and banking. However, in contrast to the zaibatsu, the internal organization of the keiretsu was more businesslike, they were freed from family domination and they competed fiercely with each other. The keiretsu today are groups of enterprises linked together through reciprocal shareholdings, credit relations, trading relations, and interlocking directorships. Where the zaibatsu were linked by holding companies which were the groups' headquarters, the keiretsu are loose federations of independent companies. Members of the keiretsu groups are not normally subsidiaries or minority-controlled associates of particular parents. Many have no dominant shareholder, but other members of the keiretsu will be among their largest shareholders and collectively hold substantial blocks of shares. The controlling participants form stable and long term relationships with other members of the keiretsu. Loan capital is provided by the group bank (see the finance section in Chapter 6 for more details) and sales are handled by the group trading company. The members of the keiretsu are therefore united by economic bonds and by their common orientation to the idea of the group. This group orientation is expressed through the power of the presidents' club—a committee made up of the presidents of the member firms. It meets regularly, say once a month, and develops the policy for the group as a whole.

In addition to the set of network relationships within the group, there are interfirm relationships with component suppliers and industrial subcontractors.[3] This is the basis of the new production concepts (see Box 4.6) and especially JIT supply—the suppliers of components and subassemblies have ICT links to the hub firm so can have components and subassemblies delivered as they are required, eliminating the need for extensive storage. There is also widespread interfirm cooperation in R&D and technology within the keiretsu, between keiretsu and involving non-industrial organizations, such as universities and public laboratories. Members of a group are coordinated through their relationships with the same major bank and major trading company, and through equity links and management working groups, and are able to share research facilities, accountants, marketing staff, and production capacity, of some of these, if it is appropriate. The keiretsu are, therefore, involved in three kinds of networks: the keiretsu itself, the hub firms' supplier networks, and R&D networks. The keiretsu has both the advantages of scale and coordination of the large vertically integrated firm of managerial capitalism and the flexibility of decentralization. Its aim is cooperation and mutual flow of information between the parts, rather than rigid top-down hierarchy.

Japanese firms obtained and improved upon imported technology mainly through 'reverse engineering'. Japanese education and training systems were key enablers in the process. This was a result of the large absolute numbers of young people acquiring secondary and higher levels of education, especially in science and engineering; and, second, the scale and quality of industrial training carried out at enterprise level. Because of 'reverse engineering', managers, engineers, and workers grew accustomed to thinking of the entire production process as a system and to collaborating closely with suppliers to understand and improve on imported technology. Japanese engineers used 'the factory as a laboratory' (Freeman 1987). Many ideas for improvement came from the shop floor and the work of the R&D department was very close to the work of production engineers and process control. Indeed, careful training and rotation of jobs are also important features of these firms.[4] In particular, rotation of workers from R&D to production in the case of engineers, or from one shop to another in the case of production workers, is more common than in other countries. It is also not uncommon for engineers in the development team to transfer to the production department to work on integrating new products and processes into production after mid-career (Aoki 1990). Therefore, R&D staff tend to be more familiar with the technological needs of production and marketing and their innovations tend to be easier to manufacture and more commercially relevant (Odagiri and Goto 1993).

While Japanese firms tended to introduce few product innovations, their organization was advantageous to the introduction of many incremental innovations which raised productivity and quality especially in shipbuilding, motor vehicles, and colour televisions. The emphasis on high quality of products owes much to 'reverse engineering'. In the 1950s the first automobiles, television sets, or machine tools were often of very poor quality. A determined effort to overcome these defects led to the social acceptance of 'quality circles' (originally an American innovation) and to the development of greatly improved techniques of quality control not simply at the end of the production run but at every stage, including the testing of all components from subcontractors. Some of the most important Japanese innovations have been on-line inspection, test and quality control equipment, and instrumentation arising in this process (Freeman 1987).

It has been argued that the new Japanese production model extends the principle of flow to multiple products on the same production line and new product development (Best 1990; Womack et al. 1990). The challenge to management, engineers, and workers is to drive down cycle times for multiproduct production and new product development. The development of flexible production methods enables firms to achieve higher product quality, lower costs, and faster delivery times. Technology management is integrated into shop-floor work practices in the form of incremental and continuous improvement of the process of production; this involves the development of new manufacturing methods, self-directed work teams, and continuous improvement work practices. This organizational capability enabled Japanese manufacturing enterprises to gain market share rapidly in many industries in the 1970s and 1980s.

Japan's looser capital market constraints than in the USA or UK, with reciprocal shareholdings between banks and firms, make it more unlikely for shareholders to interfere in the running of a firm unless the firm is in trouble. Managers normally have discretionary power, are typically promoted from within the firm, and tend to represent the employees rather than the shareholders. The material rewards between managers and permanent workers are much lower than in the USA or Europe, which also strengthen the identification of managers with the interests of employees. As argued by Johnson:

Morita Akio, chairman of Sony Corporation, believes that the emphasis on profitability has been a major cause of American industrial decline, 'The annual bonus some American executives receive depends on annual profit, and the executive who knows his firm's production facilities should be modernized is not likely to make a decision to invest in new equipment if his own income and managerial ability are judged based on annual profit.' Morita believes that the incentive structure of post-war Japanese business has been geared to development goals, whereas the incentive of American business is geared to individual performance as revealed by quick profits ... In post-war Japan the living standards of top executives and ordinary factory workers have differed only slightly (Morita observes that the American president of Sony's US subsidiary makes more corporate salary than Morita himself received from Sony). (Johnson 1982: 313–14)

This, together with the system of annual bonus related to company performance and long-term employment, means that Japanese managers have a strong motivation towards firm growth, for the employees are most concerned with the long-term survival and performance of the firm and prospects for promotion. Also, a large proportion of directors, in contrast to those in the UK and the USA, are full time insiders who come from production and technology departments, followed by marketing ad export (rather than from finance and accounting), generating a more favourable understanding and attitude towards R&D and commercial relevance (Odagiri and Goto 1993). Box 4.7 and Table 4.1 show the different operational and incentive schemes

---

Box 4.7 The M-form and the J-form structures

Aoki (1990) developed a model to explain the logical connection between the Japanese mode of internal operation and coordination, on the one hand, and the employment system, on the other. Also he argues that bank-oriented business finance is related to the internal structure of the Japanese firm. He contrasts the American multidivisional (M) form and the Japanese (J) form in three areas, as follows:

- **Operational practices**: In the J-form, horizontal coordination among operating units based on knowledge sharing rather than skill specialization is an important characteristic whereas in the M-form an office at the top makes production plan based on management's prior knowledge of market demand. The production process in the M-form is divided into a series of specialized standardized functions. This is followed by an ex-post adaptation to actual market conditions accompanied by adjustment of product and in-process inventories. In contrast, in the case of Japanese auto producers, for example, the central production planning office drafts the quarterly and monthly production plans based on market demand forecast and presents procurement plans to outside suppliers. This is only a general guide, however. An integrated production/delivery plan for ten days is prepared on the basis of orders from regional and overseas dealers. In response to the plan, the engineering office prepares a sequence of daily production schedules. The daily schedule is adjusted two days prior to actual production in response to actual customers' orders transmitted from dealers to factory by an online network system. On the final assembly line, the sequence of production of varieties of cars is scheduled to minimize inventory. Cars are delivered to customers in 8–12 days after customers order them. Also, in the J-form there is more interaction in product development between design engineers and plant engineers at the early phase of design and it is difficult to say where the phase of prototype fabrication and testing actually starts. Rotation of engineers between design and plant facilitate 'informal' information sharing. Design engineers are transferred to plant as line managers to avoid engineering problems at the manufacturing phase. Aoki (1996) argues that there are advantages to the M-form when the environment is extremely uncertain, involving new concepts and highly specialized scientific approaches, or when it is stable and facilitates the large-scale production of standardized commodities, but not in the intermediate situation, where small, batch production of products in a high volume assembly process is required and thousand of steps have to be coordinated.

- **Incentive scheme**: In the M-form, operating tasks are separated from coordinating tasks and divided into specific functions. The valued operational skills in the M-form are specialized skills. The J-form depends on employee competition to achieve higher status within hierarchies of rank as a primary incentive device. Each rank carries certain level of pay, but not a specific job. Criteria for promotion include years of service and merit, which are not related to specific job but broadly defined problem-solving abilities. The personnel department controls promotion and rotation (the personnel department is itself subject to

Box 4.7 (*Continued*)

rotation). Protest by 'exit' (Hirschman 1970) is very costly, hence the enterprise union 'voices' grievances. Aoki (1990) argues that the hierarchical nature of incentives complements the non-hierarchical tendency in daily operations.

- **Financial control**: In contrast to the M-form controlled by the market for securities, the J-form has a bank-oriented financial system. Banks are allowed to hold a maximum of 5 per cent of stock of non-financial firms. Because equities held by banks tend to be stable, the management of the J-form is insured from take-over raids by the open market. The bank is the major stockholder and lender but does not exercise vertical control over management. If the firm faces a business crisis, the main bank assumes the responsibility of rescue operations, including rescheduling of loan payments and emergency loans.

Table 4.1 M-form and J-form compared

Models	M-form	J-form
Operational practices	• Hierarchical separation between planning (coordination) and implementation (operation) • Economies of specialization	• Horizontal coordination among operating units • Knowledge sharing
Incentive scheme	• Decentralized market approach (clear employment contract relating specific jobs to competitive wages)	• Rank hierarchy (long-term employment and seniority promotion not automatic) • Personnel department and union
Financial control	• Securities markets	• Autonomy from external financial interests if firm is profitable

Source: Aoki (1990).

between the Japanese firm and the multidivisional form structure in managerial capitalism.

Doubts have been raised about the viability of the Japanese model as a result of the Asian crisis. As argued by Lazonick (1999), Japan's successful emphasis on 'retain and invest', where Japanese firms continuously reinvest in plant, equipment, and employees, to generate innovative processes and products, and then share gains with employees, distributors, suppliers, and communities, is being called into question, with voices calling for a 'corporate restructuring' towards the 'downsize and distribute' Anglo-Saxon model, shedding labour and distributing corporate revenues in the form of dividends and stock repurchase to shareholders. Lazonick (1999) suggests that Japan's economic problems of the 1990s—unemployment, unstable banks, underconsumption and underfunded pensions—are in fact the result of the country's successful economic development. The problem was due to the changed relation of the banking sector to the industrial sector in the 1980s. As the wealth of the Japanese economy grew, the banks were flooded with corporate and household deposits. At the same time, the successful industrial firms were able to reduce bank debt, diminishing the need for the banks to play their traditional intermediary role. Banks became sources of easy money, accepting the market value of borrowers' stocks and land as collateral, permitting the land and stock speculations of the late 1980s bubble. The recession of the 1990s meant that existing problem loans became more problematic and many new prudent loans turned bad (Lazonick 1999). He argues against the calls for Anglo-Saxon-style 'corporate restructuring' and for an attempt at corporate reform in keeping with the Japanese model (Zysman 1983; Coates 2000).

An additional challenge to the 'new competition' in Japan is the relative neglect of those industries associated with basic research.[5] The next section describes the recent resurgence of these industries in the USA, and the main features of organizations and technology explaining their development.

Organizations and technology in the period of systems integration

The 1990s saw the resurgence of US industrial leadership across a range of high-tech industries. In particular, the case of Silicon Valley in North California has received particular attention as a site for high-tech industries. This region generated 150,000 new technology-related jobs between 1975 and 1990. In 1990 the region exported electronics products for $11 billion (almost a third of the country's total) and was the home of 39 of the nation's 100 fastest-growing firms (Saxenian 1994: 2).

This model, that enables the development of superior regional innovation capabilities, has been called 'system integration' (Best 2001) (see Box 4.8). In

---

Box 4.8 Organizations and technology in network-based systems integration

High-tech industries in the USA based on systems integration since the 1980s are characterized by the following features:

- Entrepreneurial firm
- Importance of personal networks
- Start-ups pioneered by venture capital with technological knowledge and involvement in new firms
- Industry/university partnering models (Stanford University and colleges) for integrating product development and R&D
- Development of related and supporting sectors
- Teamwork
- Decentralization and diffusion of research and design capabilities (multidisciplinary teams in experimentation plants)

Source: Saxenian (1994), Best (2001).

Chapter 3 we argued that innovation in managerial capitalism was carried out through research in stand-alone labs. In the 'new competition', instead, innovation was extended to incremental changes in production processes and product design. More recently, high-tech regions in the USA have developed capabilities for rapid design changes and industrial innovation that integrate basic research into production. Regions such as Silicon Valley have developed regional innovation capabilities embedded in virtual laboratories in the form of broad and deep networks of operational, technological, and scientific researchers which cut across firms and universities (Best 2001).

Saxenian (1994) describes the unique features explaining the development of a vibrant semiconductor electronics industry in Northern California's Silicon Valley (and contrasts it with developments in Boston's Route 128) (see Box 4.9). First, personal networks were crucial to regional innovation in Silicon Valley. In the 1960s, many engineers in Silicon Valley had worked in Fairchild Semiconductor Corporation. This shared professional experience served as a powerful bond. Silicon Valley was distinguished by unusually high levels of job hopping (during the 1970s, average annual employee turnover exceeded 35 per cent in local electronics firms and was as high as 59 per cent in small firms) (Saxenian 1994: 34). Individuals moved both within and between industry sectors: from semiconductors to personal computers or from semiconductor equipment to software and from established firms to start-ups and vice versa. This continual reshuffling tended to reinforce the value of personal relationships and networks.

Box 4.9 Silicon Valley (North California) versus Route 128 (Boston, MA)

Silicon Valley has a regional network-based industrial system that promotes collective learning and flexible adjustment among specialist producers of a complex of related technologies. The region's social networks and open labour markets encourage experimentation and entrepreneurship. Companies compete intensely while at the same time learning from one another about changing markets and technologies through informal communication and collaborative practices; and loosely linked team structures encourage horizontal communication among firm divisions and with outside suppliers and customers. The functional boundaries within firms are porous in a network system, as are the boundaries between firms themselves and between firms and local institutions such as trade associations and universities.

The Route 128 region, in contrast, is dominated by a small number of relatively integrated corporations. Its industrial system is based on independent firms that internalize a wide range of productive activities. Practices of secrecy and corporate loyalty govern relations between firms and their customers, suppliers, and competitors, reinforcing a regional culture that encourages stability and self-reliance. Corporate hierarchies ensure that authority remains centralized and information tends to flow vertically. The boundaries between and within firms and between firms and local institutions thus remain far more distinct in this independent firm-based system.

Source: Excerpt from Saxenian (1994: 2–4).

Silicon Valley's venture capital industry emerged out of the region's base of technology enterprises. As successful entrepreneurs such as Fairchild's Eugene Kleiner and Don Valentine reinvested their capital in local start-ups, they created a new type of financial institution. Silicon Valley's venture capitalists became unusually involved with their new ventures, giving advice on business plans, finding co-investors, recruiting managers, and serving on boards of directors. The start-ups pioneered by venture capital were more successful in Silicon Valley than in Route 128 despite the fact that more money was invested in the Route 128 venture capital sector. The reason for this was that, in contrast to venture capital in California, the Route 128 venture capital sector was established by old-line East Coat financiers and managed by professional bankers rather than entrepreneurs, who would not have the same knowledge and involvement in the technologies and organization of the new ventures.

A second key feature of regional innovation in Silicon Valley is the relationship with the university. Saxenian (1994) argues that Stanford University, which actively promoted local technology start-ups during the years following the Second World War, is far more deeply integrated into its regional surroundings than MIT. Other research and training institutions, such as the California State University and the community college systems were also integrated into the regional production system. While Stanford established a licensing office in 1969 to encourage the commercialization of technology developed at the university, MIT did not set up such an office until the late 1980s. This neglect of the region's emerging technology enterprises was partly the legacy of MIT's relations with established corporations such as DuPont, Eastman Kodak, and Standard Oil. Saxenian (1994) notes that while the MIT Industrial Liaison Programme charged firms a US$50,000 annual fee for access to university research findings, the Stanford Industrial Affiliates programme charged five times less, which allowed relatively smaller firms to participate in the research network.

A third feature of regional innovation in Silicon Valley is the development of related and supporting sectors. As the disk drive industry flourished in Silicon Valley, so have independent suppliers of disk equipment and materials and small design firms, contract manufacturers, metalworking shops, and software developers. Semiconductor firms cross-licensed their patents liberally to competitors during the industry's first three decades. This ensured that technical advances diffused quickly and that the industry as a whole progressed. Also, second-sourcing arrangements, in which producers ensured the development of alternative suppliers of their products, similarly contributed to spread technological capabilities within the region's industrial community. Technology exchange agreements and joint ventures were also common in Silicon Valley before they became staples of US industry.

A fourth feature is that Silicon Valley's entrepreneurs sought to avoid hierarchical structures. William Hewlett and David Packard, and later Intel's

Robert Noyce, pioneered management styles based on teamwork, openness, and participation. This may explain the absence of labour unions in Silicon Valley's technology firms. In contrast, most executives in Route 128, such as DEC's Ken Olsen, An Wang and Data General's Edson DeCastro, remained in charge of the firms they started for several decades. Start-ups in Route 128 hired managers from the established corporations who were typically in their fifties and sixties and well equipped to implement the organizational structures and operating procedures of managerial capitalism. This is in contrast to the start-ups in Silicon Valley, the managers of which were in their twenties and thirties and experimented openly with organizational alternatives.

Nevertheless, if the boundaries between firms and between firms and local institutions were blurring in Silicon Valley, the boundaries of firms in Route 128 such as DEC and Data General were strictly defined, remaining secretive and self-contained. It is true, however, that the leading Silicon Valley firms also sacrificed organizational flexibility as they grew. In their efforts to become the 'big three' of the semiconductor industry, National, Intel, and AMD also tended to build bureaucratic organizations that undermined the autonomy of the independent business units (Saxenian 1994).

The differences between the regions became obvious in the 1990s. The Massachusetts area was revitalized in 1980 when large minicomputers manufacturers—DEC, Data General, Wang, Honeywell, and Prime—controlled two-thirds of the minicomputer markets. Their growth led to the creation of 100,000 net new jobs between 1970 and 1985. However, the crisis of the minicomputer industry in the 1970s and 1980s led to decline in Route 128 (and that of commodity semiconductors producers in Silicon Valley). This reveals the danger of betting on one single product in a time of rapid technological change. While Route 128 had little prospects for recovery, in Silicon Valley, start-ups and a restructuring stream of high value-added semiconductors, computers, components, and software-related products led to Silicon Valley surpassing Route 128 as the national centre of computer systems innovation. The ease of new firm formation meant that more technical paths were pursued in Silicon Valley than would have normally been possible in a single firm or region (Saxenian 1994).

By 1990, the semiconductor industry consisted of two sectors: the production of memory and other commodity devices (produced by a small number of very large Japanese firms making long-term investments and continuous improvements in quality and yield in high-volume manufacturing) and the production of high performance, high value-added and customized semiconductors (produced by flexible firms in Silicon Valley where access to leading edge customers, design, and specialized suppliers is important). The balance of these segments reversed in the 1980s. Commodity chips generated 80 per cent of the worldwide semiconductor industry revenues in 1983, but by 1990 this share had fallen to 33 per cent (Saxenian 1994). Silicon Valley had to respond by increasing its flexibility through relying more on partnerships with suppliers (not only to deliver reliable products but to continue designing and producing high quality up-to-date components and software).

The new principle characterizing Silicon Valley and the revitalization of the US high-tech industries has been called 'systems integration' by Best (2001). Systems integration involves open systems networking, industry/university partnering models for integrating product development and R&D, decentralization and diffusion of design, technological diversity, and new firm creation. Systems integration is both a driver of new product development and a characteristic of production activities. It is facilitated by multidisciplinary teams. While for Ford and Toyota the challenge was to synchronize production by equalizing cycle times, for Intel, the challenge was to integrate all of the technologies required to make a chip along an emergent technology trajectory in which productivity is advancing 50 per cent every eighteen months. This is not simple, as many of the activities are rooted in different science and technology domains. Indeed, Best (2001) argues that this decentralization of design and production affords a competitive advantage to US over Japanese firms, since the latter are highly concentrated (with twelve companies accounting for 75 per cent of sales), and have built-up customers in the form of consumer electronics, computer, and communication divisions, designed for 'lean production' but not for the development of diffused design capabilities.

Intel is symbolic of America's manufacturing recovery, as Ford was for the introduction of mass production. The following quote by Best illustrates the key drivers of production in Intel:

Whereas Ford pursued process integration and synchronized a range of machines, Intel pursues systems integration and integrates over 600 activities embodying an array of technologies with deep roots in various technology and science research programmes being conducted outside the firm. The production challenge addressed by Intel is not to achieve economies of scale for a given technology but to achieve higher productivity and lower costs by sustained technological change .... Systems integration is about building the organizational capability to incorporate rapid technological change in components into complex products. This involves simultaneous advances in integrated circuit design tools, production technologies, and miniaturization capabilities (Best 2001: 49).

An interesting point is that Intel has never owned a stand-alone R&D lab (Best 2001). However, Intel's R&D budget exceeds US$1 billion annually. Instead of stand-alone laboratories, Intel opted for development research to be conducted in the manufacturing facility through the construction of full-scale experimentation plants. Technology integration teams (educated in a range of engineering and science disciplines) operate the experimentation plans.

Best (2001) also points out that instead of designing its own equipment or complementary components for the various uses of microprocessors, Intel establishes and publicly discloses parameters for producers of chip-making equipment and for users of Intel chips for the next generation of micropro-cessors. Following design modularization, equipment manufacturers build to published interface design rules and performance requirements established by Intel. Suppliers and equipment manufacturers invest heavily in design because Intel is the standardsetter. Intel, along with Microsoft, establishes the technol-ogy platform for the PC. The computer makers, Microsoft, and applications software producers must design next year's products according to the perform-ance parameters of the central processing unit. The risk to component sup-pliers of not participating overwhelms the risk of loss of intellectual property.

As argued by Best (2001), Intel depends upon, and reinforces, an industrial district constituted by multiple nodes responsible for the design of new products. Intel not only partners with a vast array of specialist producers and research institutions but also draws upon an extended industrial high-tech district with an extraordinary capacity to conduct experiments, carry out innovations, and conduct research. Intel divides research into two types: research that requires integrated manufacturing capability and research that does not require state-of-the-art semiconductor technology. Intel focuses on the former and networks with universities to get the latter. Silicon Valley project teams are continuously combining and recombining across a population of 6,000 high-tech firms, making it an unparalleled ICT industrial district.

As a model of industrial organization, Silicon Valley breaks with the tendency of ever increasing concentration of technological research within a few big labs during the heyday of managerial capitalism. What Best (2001) calls 'open system networks' mean that research is not limited to laboratories but becomes a regional capability embedded in a complex of regional institutions.

Conclusion

This chapter gives an account of how changes in organizational and techno-logical capabilities in the last decades are responsible for shifts in industrial leadership. The firms in the traditional sectors in the 'Third Italy' are collect-ively entrepreneurial, with decentralized production and diffusion of design capability. The development of industrial districts suggests two important lessons. First, it has shown that technological innovation is just as possible within 'mature' sectors as within high-tech sectors as electronics. Second, it is not necessarily true that traditional sectors will become the exclusive preserve of low-wage less-developed countries. However, the production practices of the 'Third Italy' industrial districts and Japan are not enough to force the pace of technological change in industries associated with basic research. This requires the development of new 'systems integration' capabilities. While Japanese firms extended technology management capabilities to incremental changes in the production process, 'systems integration' as developed in Silicon Valley enables rapid product development. 'Systems integration' drives new product development and production through multidisciplinary teams, linking networked groups of firms by 'open systems' product architecture. Also, basic research has been integrated into new product development in the form of a regional model of innovation and technical skill formation through adequate supply of engineering graduates to technology-driven firms in the region (Best 2001).

Notes

1 This is not to say that there are no features of the Japanese system of innovation (see Chapter 5) that pre-dated the First World War. For example, during the Tokugawa era (1603–1868) there were already high levels of technological development (machine engineering) and elementary education and in the Meiji era (1868–1911), emphasis was placed on engineering education. Also, the 'network' firm in Japan dates back to pre-Meiji restoration merchant houses (the Meiji restoration of 1868 was the occasion when Japan opened up to foreign trade after more than 200 years of seclusionism and a non-feudal government was inaugurated to modernize the country) (Odagiri and Goto 1993).

2 The Japanese system of production distinguishes between productive and unproductive time. Engineers are concerned with the amount of time that workers are transforming material as a percentage of the total production time. Whereas mass production emphasizes operations engineering—the reduction of time required per machine or labour hour—new competition emphasizes process engineering—the reduction of time required to move materials from entry point to plant exit point, and to transform new product ideas into products. Mass production cost accounting systems measure operations time but ignore processing time, thus obscuring inefficiencies in the production process (Best 1990).

3 Suppliers in the Japanese production system have independent design and problem-solving capabilities. Japanese automakers, for example, deal directly with far fewer parts makers: whereas General Motors deals with 3,500 suppliers, not including materials suppliers, Toyota deals directly with 300 components suppliers, which, in turn, deal with 5,000 second-tier suppliers, that, in turn, coordinate 20,000 third- and fourth-tier suppliers (Best 1990). Moreover, these suppliers are not captive suppliers. In the USA, automakers provide blueprint specifications to a range of potential parts makers, who bid on the basis of price. A contract enforceable by court is the instrument to ensure that suppliers meet the specifications in the blueprints. In contrast, Japanese automakers tend to provide components performance requirements. Part makers have design capabilities to solve problems jointly with the automaker. Instead of writing a price and quality standard into a contract in advance of the development, the automaker and parts maker agree a 'target cost performance' and a 'target quality performance'.

4 It has been argued that the lack of adoption of the multidivisional form in Japan has facilitated rotation among divisions (Odagiri and Goto 1993).

5 This concern has triggered changes in research and innovation policies since the 1990s, expanding government R&D (doubling the public budget by US$130 billion over 1995–2000) with restructuring of ministerial and advisory bodies and a reorganization of the public research system by making them more autonomous and exposing the universities to external evaluation (Sato 2001).

5 Organizations, Technology, and Less Developed Countries: East Asia and Latin America

Introduction

Industrial development requires a broad range of technological and organizational capabilities, which can only be acquired through a long process of deliberate accumulation of resources, including skills, knowledge, and production-enhancing institutional structures. Investments in human and physical capital are not the only factors driving industrial transformation. An emphasis solely on investment assumes that technological knowledge is fully embodied in machinery and codified in blueprints, and that all less developed countries need to do is to access these and adopt them at relatively low cost. Instead, only part of the technology required by less developed countries is codified in blueprints and machine manuals. Much of it is tacit and requires a painstaking and difficult process of learning by doing and using.

Scholars in the field of innovation studies stress the partly tacit, cumulative, and path-dependent nature of the learning processes of firms (Nelson and Winter 1982; Rosenberg 1982; Cohen and Levinthal 1989). The very nature of technological and organizational knowledge precludes perfect transfer from developed countries. Katz (1984) has warned us of the way in which a number of social, organizational and economic characteristics make replicating 'off-the-shelf' technology from developed countries uneconomic. For example, smaller market size may force firms in less developed countries to adopt a lower degree of automation. In scale-intensive industries with continuous flow, many less developed countries produce a highly diversified output mix, with higher down times and idle capacity then developed countries' firms. Moreover, imperfect subcontracting markets induce a higher degree of vertical integration at the individual firm level with negative consequences for product and plant design and the type of equipment selected (Katz 1984). The learning process is highly technology specific and capabilities built up in one activity are not easily transferable to another (Lall 2001). The costs of technological exploration, the importance of basic technology and science, and the institutions supporting knowledge accumulation are different in each case. Different technologies have different potential for further technological advance, including knowledge leakages for other sector or technologies. The building of firm capabilities occurs at all levels—the shop floor, process or product engineering, maintenance, inventory control, logistics, and R&D. R&D is at one end of the range of technological activities and it becomes more important as more complex technologies are used (Lall 2001).

Industrial latecomers cannot tap global markets and technology simply by opening up to foreign investments and markets. Technology imports are not a substitute for the development of domestic capability. Both the absorption of imported technology and the success of local technological efforts depend on the nature of the supporting national innovation infrastructure as much as they do on the capabilities of individual firms. There is also a wide diversity of development experience and potential. The technological capabilities achieved by firms and the technology policies adopted in Taiwan and South Korea are very different from those in Brazil, Argentina, or Mexico, for example. Although there are no simple rules for innovation and industrial policy in less developed countries, research shows that there is a role for public policy in less developed countries in supporting dynamic technological capability formation in local firms (Teubal 1996; Lall and Teubal 1998).

In this chapter we examine how East Asian countries became industrialized, and we explore the contrast between industrialization in East Asia and Latin America since the 1970s. While it is instructive to draw lessons for competitiveness from East Asian newly industrializing countries (Lall 2001), it is important to remember also that the context for policy making has changed significantly over the past decade or so. The international rules of the game are very different, and exercise much greater influence on what governments can and cannot do. In the 1960s and 1970s, when the East Asian newly industrializing countries built up their industrial bases, pervasive government intervention was the accepted norm and there were few external pressures against selective policies. Today, many such policies are ruled out: selective import protection, local content requirements, export subsidies, direct credit and differential interest rates, performance and entry rules for foreign investors, and the copying of foreign products are unacceptable to the World Trade Organization (WTO) and major trading partners. Although there may be some benefits from WTO measures (including the prevention of inefficient interventions, allowing greater access to OECD markets and international capital and technology flows, and providing stable rules and uniform governance standards), at the same time, however, these policies constrain governments from several interventions that are in their legitimate economic interest—and that most presently developed nations used freely during a similar stage of their own development. Manufacturers in the industrially developed countries were also able to benefit from weak or non-existent environmental and occupational health and safety standards during their own development. All governments have to take the new rules as the parameters within which they design their competitive strategies. This is not the only change. Latecomer countries are also under pressure to encourage technology inflows embodied in FDI and traded products to a much greater extent. Participation in production systems dominated by multinationals is more important than it was in the post-war period as a way to boost competitiveness and keep up with fast-moving technology. All these changes present new challenges to less developed countries.

This chapter is organized as follows. The first section examines the debates on industrialization in the nineteenth century and draws lessons for industrialization in the twentieth century. The second section addresses how East Asian countries caught up with the more advanced countries. The third section compares the differences in organizations and technology in Latin America and East Asia that are responsible for Latin American countries falling behind. A conclusion draws lessons for the understanding of the relation between organizations, technology, and less developed countries.

Debates on industrialization in the nineteenth century: does British history trace the development path for Germany and Russia?

Economic historians' ideas about industrialization are dominated by Karl Marx's thesis that it is the history of advanced industrial countries (at the time he wrote this he referred to Britain) which traces out the road of development for the 'backward' countries (these referred in particular to Germany and Russia). Two contributions that have challenged the Marxist thesis have been very influential in economic development studies. The first contribution was that by Rostow (1960), who proposed that economic development is a linear (rather than dialectical) historical process, consisting of five consecutive stages. He argued against Marx's idea that changes in methods of production generated revolutionary class conflict and that within each stage a new stage emerged with its own technologies, property relations, and antagonistic classes, which would lead to its destruction. In Rostow's argument, instead, there was no conflict and the stages (traditional society, the transitional stage or precondition for take-off, the take-off stage, the drive to maturity, and the stage of high mass consumption) were the same for all countries, no matter where they started off on the road to development. This theory influenced development strategies and US and international aid policies in the 1960s, with international agencies searching for the right time in the development of certain sectors to inject foreign aid to 'backward' countries.

The second contribution was that of Gershenkron's (1952), which challenged the Marxist thesis in a different way from Rostow's, and also challenged Rostov's idea that all countries had to go through the same stages in the process of development. He argued that different degrees of backwardness (as represented by different levels of output, technological progress, skills of the population, degree of literacy, corruption in business, and investment 'horizons' of entrepreneurs) resulted in considerable differences not only regarding the speed of development (the rate of industrial growth) but also to the productive and organizational structures which emerged from those processes. These differences were the result of the development of institutions for which there was little need or counterpart in established industrial countries. In addition, the ideology or intellectual climate accompanying industrialization differed. He shows how the industrialization of European latecomers in the nineteenth century such as Germany and Russia differed in fundamental respects from the British industrial revolution, largely because of the magnitude of the challenge in the 'catching-up' effort of latecomers. As we see later, these countries developed new institutions—in particular banks and an active state—for which there had been no need in Britain.

First, Gershenkron (1952) argues that industrialization in Britain proceeded without any substantial use of banking for long-term investment. In Britain, the more gradual nature of industrialization and the accumulation of capital from colonial trade, from modernized agriculture and later from industrialization itself, obviated the pressure of developing any special institution for the supply of long-term capital to industry. In contrast, latecomers applying the most efficient techniques and larger average size plants in sectors with relatively high ratios of capital to output and with scarcer entrepreneurial talent, required the development of banking for the supply of capital. Indeed, the development of industrial banking (the Credit Mobilier) in France under Napoleon III and the cartelization of German banks and industry are examples of this process.

Second, Gershenkron (1952) illustrates the development of the state as the primary agent supporting economic progress by referring to Russia. In the 1890s, the magnitude of the challenge for Russia—the scarcity of capital, the corruption in business, and the need to finance large-scale heavy industry— was so great that no banking system could succeed in attracting capital to finance industrialization. The state, moved by military interest, assumed the role of sponsoring industrialization through taxation, directing income from consumption to investment.

Box 5.1 Lessons for twentieth century industrialization from European industrialization in the nineteenth century

The story of European industrialization in the nineteenth century would seem to yield a few points of view which may be helpful for appreciation of present day problems . . . .

[T]he tendencies in backward countries to concentrate much of their efforts on introduction of the most modern and expensive technology, their stress on large-scale plant, and their interest in developing investment-goods industries need not necessarily be regarded as flowing mainly from a quest for prestige and from economic megalomania.

What makes it so difficult for an advanced country to appraise properly the industrialization policies of its less fortunate brethren is in fact that, in every instance of industrialization, imitation of the evolution in advanced countries appears in combination with different, indigenously determined elements. If it is not always easy for advanced countries to accept the former, it is even more difficult for them to acquiesce in the latter. This is particularly true of the institutional instruments used in carrying out industrial developments and even more so of ideologies which accompany it. What can be derived from a historical review is a strong sense for the significance of the native elements in the industrialization of backward countries.

Source: Excerpt from Gerschenkron ([1951] 1966: 26).

Thus, because of the specific methods of catching-up, Germany, Russia, and France developed along very different lines from Britain. In addition, the ideology required to spur industrialization was different (in France the socialism of Saint Simon and the philosophy of Rousseau, in Germany the nationalism of List, and in Russia orthodox Marxism). These ideologies were not required to spur Britain's industrial revolution.[1] Gershenkron's work reinforces the idea that there may be more than one path to industrialization and provides lessons to understand industrialization in the twentieth century (see Box 5.1). One of the most important lessons is that different countries at different stage of development may need to develop different institutions and instruments to cope with their particular challenges.[2]

Debates on industrialization in the twentieth century: how Korea and Taiwan caught up

A small number of late industrializing countries have experienced dramatic economic growth since the Second World War (especially South Korea and Taiwan). These countries succeeded despite having no competitive asset of pioneering technology. The nature of technology differentiates industrialization in the UK, Germany, and the USA on the one hand, from industrialization in the twentieth century on the other hand (Amsden 1989). While industrialization in Britain, Germany, and the USA proceeded through innovation (with Britain introducing the main inventions, including the mule, the steam engine, the spinning jenny, and the USA and Germany developing specific institutions to commercialize innovations, see Chapter 3), late industrializers after the Second World War industrialized through 'learning'. These latecomers (the more successful countries like Korea and Taiwan but also the less successful ones like Argentina, Brazil, and Mexico) industrialized by borrowing and improving technology that had already been developed by experienced firms from more advanced economies, realizing lower costs, higher productivity, better quality in what she calls 'mid-technology' industries by incremental product and process improvements. Amsden (1989) argues that the imperative to industrialize exclusively on the basis of learning is responsible for general properties in common in a subset of less developed countries, otherwise very different in resource endowment, history, and culture.

While the conventional explanation for the outstanding economic growth of Korea and Taiwan is that they have conformed to free market principles, and that these economies have liberalized and opened up to international trade and investment, industrialization in East Asia has been the result of three particular set of institutions (Amsden 1989). The first involves the developmental role of the government, which intervened to get relative prices 'wrong' to stimulate economic activity (e.g. through subsidies and strict monitorable performance standards). This is contrary to mainstream economics suggestions that countries should get their 'prices right', that is, the prices (e.g. interest rates or exchange rates) should reflect true scarcities, for example, that money should be expensive in labour-rich and capital-poor countries. The second is the competitive focus on enterprises, which concentrated on shop floor incremental product and process improvements in mid-technology industries. The third is the strategy, structure, and operation of leading firms, with diversified business groups operating in technologically unrelated areas (see Box 5.2).

The case of successful late industrializers in East Asia shows that considerable technological effort is involved in industrial development. As argued earlier, technology does not flow freely, is not fully codifiable in blueprints or manuals, is costly to absorb, and depends on prior investments in knowledge. Building technological capabilities is a long, costly, and risky process and technological knowledge has to be combined with the accumulation of complementary organizational and business capabilities. The acquisition of technological capabilities depends on the nature of the supporting national innovation infrastructure as much as it does on the capabilities of individual firms.

Another lesson from industrialization in East Asia is that despite the rising share of services in income, the main challenge for less developed countries is to build an internationally competitive manufacturing sector. Manufacturing has traditionally been the engine of growth and for transforming the economic structure of less developed countries (UNIDO 2002). This is because

---

Box 5.2 Institutions of late industrialization in East Asia

Amsden (1989) argues that the institutions of large industrialization that underscore the success and the absence of which are responsible for delay in the industrialization of late-comers are as follows:

- **Developmental role of the state**. In successful late industrializers, there has been a high degree of well-coordinated government invention to get the relative prices 'wrong' and interfere with market forces to create profitable investment opportunities. The state has intervened with subsidies to stimulate economic activity but exercised discipline over subsidy recipients (i.e. they were not 'giveaways'). In exchange for subsidies, the state imposed monitorable performance standards on private firms. In Taiwan, the subsidies to export were tied to targets such as R&D spending and personnel training. In South Korea, licences to expand or enlarge the scale of operations were contingent on performance in exports, R&D or the introduction of new products. Poor performers were penalized (e.g. in Korea in the construction, the shipbuilding, and the auto industry) and good performers were rewarded. There has been a refusal to bail out poorly managed firms. This poor performance was not assessed in financial but in production and organization of management terms. This process may have been highly politicized, with government 'friends' taking over troubled enterprises but heavy investment in the education of civil servants meant that performance standards were applied rigorously.

- **Competitive focus of enterprises**. The agent of expansion in late industralization is the modern industrial enterprise. With the non-dynamic bottom end of the market vulnerable to lower wage countries and the top end impenetrable due to technology entry barriers, successful late-industrializing countries have deliberately targeted scale-intensive 'mid-technology' industries where technology, although expensive, is available from international suppliers (historically, electrical machinery, basic chemicals, automobiles, consumer electronics, and commodity semiconductors more recently). The shop floor has been their strategic battleground, where they must make the technology work through continuous improvement. The role of engineers has been very important in late industrializers (as important as managers had been for managerial capitalism).

- **Strategy, structure, and operation of leading firms**. The late-industrializing firm is unable to protect itself by diversifying around a core technology family. It grows by diversifying into many technologically unrelated sectors. In contrast to the multidivisional firm of managerial capitalism which is large in scale, administered by a hierarchy of salaried managers and the basis of diversification of which is its core technology that it exploits in related industries, firms in late-industrializing countries do not have a core technology but develop diversified technological and organizational capabilities exploiting them in technologically unrelated areas. This applies to the large firms in less developed countries, including the Korean 'chaebol' and Latin American 'grupos'. The case of Samsung illustrates this unrelated diversification. Samsung invested first in sugar manufacturing, woollen textiles, life insurance, and then in the 1970s in shipbuilding, electrical manufacturing, and petrochemicals. The trend of diversification is intensified by the bandwagon effects of oligopolistic behaviour (if one business group sees a business opportunity in one sector, the other groups follow).

---

manufacturing is the main vehicle for applying technological progress to production, it is the main source of R&D, it is a vital source of new skills and entrepreneurial capabilities, and it is the main source of direct demand that stimulates the growth of many modern services (UNIDO 2002). In particular, it is machinery production that seems to be one of the bases of industrialization.

The importance of machinery sectors for economic development has been stressed by scholars both in innovation studies and in economic development. In the innovation literature it has been argued that although traditional industries such as textiles may play an important role in early stages of industrialization, thereafter fast growth is linked to pervasive technologies. In the case of the USA and Germany in the late nineteenth and early twentieth centuries, this was electrical machinery and chemicals and, in the case of Japan, Korea, and Taiwan in the post-war period, it was electronic capital goods, electronic components, and telecommunications equipment (Perez 1985; Soete 1985).

Development economists also agree that machinery and capital goods sectors are critical for economic development because of the interdependence and linkages along the production process (Hirschman 1958; Fransman and King 1984). Without a domestic capability in the production of capital goods—machinery, machine tools, etc.—every other sector is dependent on imported goods and technology. Machinery and capital goods require broad skills, which provide the conditions necessary to adapt and improve products and processes on the shop floor. This enables learning from foreign technology and the development of indigenous technological capability (Amsden 1989).

However, specialization in the production of machinery is difficult. One indication of this is a particular version of the Leontieff paradox—that labour productivity differentials in comparable plants in less developed countries and developed countries tend to be smaller in machine-paced or process-centred sectors than in operator-controlled or product-centred sectors, even when similar techniques are used in both countries (Hirschman 1958). This is because the advantage of process-centred industries for less developed countries is that (although they tend to be more capital intensive) there are basic processes around which work is organized almost naturally (as in smelting, petroleum refining, and brewing). On the other hand, in product-centred sectors such as machinery, work is not organized around one or several key technical processes. It depends rather on the assembly of a hierarchy of components, and coordination between firms.

The technological imperatives in the case of process-centred industries are an aid to the coordination of the production process and to management in order to evaluate plant performance. In product-centred sectors, sequences are less rigid and there is a greater need for organizational and management coordination of plant and office and interfirm operations, being more vulnerable to institutional shortcomings in less developed countries (Hirschman 1958). In the next section, we will explore the differential development in machinery and capital goods in explaining divergent economic growth between East Asia and Latin America.

Why did Latin American countries fall behind (or fail to catch up with) East Asian countries?

East Asia and Latin America have diverged widely since the 1970s in terms of production and trade patterns. East Asian countries have been successful at catching-up with the advanced economies, specializing in machinery and transport equipment sectors, which have become the fastest growing categories in world exports. In contrast, Latin American countries have 'fallen behind' and liberalization and privatization have accelerated their structural change process, reinforcing a pattern of specialization towards 'natural' comparative advantages (the production of industrial inputs that exploit natural resources) (see Chapter 8 for a discussion of comparative advantage theory).[3] These sectors have grown at the expense of final labour-intensive goods and technology-intensive goods (see Table 5.1 for main indicators of all countries considered).

Elsewhere, one of us (Miozzo 2002) compares the divergent specialization in machinery and transport equipment between two East Asian countries— South Korea and Taiwan—and three Latin American countries—Brazil, Argentina, and Mexico—and argues that the degree of success in industrial-

Table 5.1 Main indicators of less developed countries considered

Indicators	Korea	Taiwan	Argentina	Mexico	Brazil
GDP per capita (PPP US$) 2002	16,950	12,884	10,880	8,970	7,770
Population (millions) 2002	47.9	22.5	38.0	102.0	176.3
GDP per capita annual growth rate (%) 1975–2002	6.1	8.1	0.4	0.9	0.8
GDP per capita annual growth rate (%) 1990–2002	4.7	6.1	1.7	1.4	1.3
Gini index (year)	31.6 (1998)	32.6 (2000)	52.2 (2001)2	54.6 (2000)	59.1 (1998)
Adult literacy rates (% of people 15 and above) 2002	97.9	96.3	97	90.5	86.4
Net secondary enrolment ratio (%) 2001–2	89	n.a.	81	60	72
Tertiary students in science, maths, and engineering (% of all tertiary students) 1994–7	34	n.a.	30	31	23
Patents granted to residents (per million people) 2000	490	174	4	1	0
Receipts of royalties and licence fees (US$ per person) 2002	17.4	n.a.	0.5	0.5	0.6
Research and development (R&D) expenditures (% of GDP) 1996–2002	3.0	2.21*	0.4	0.4	1.1
Researchers in R&D (per million people) 1990–2001	2,880	3,265*	684	225	323
Manufactured exports (% of merchandise exports) 2002	92	n.a.	31	84	54

Note: * = Data for 1999–2003.

Source: UNDP (2004), data from Taiwan from MOEA, MOI, and National Science Council. Available at http:// 2k3dmz2.moea.gov.tw/gnweb/statistics/statistics01/reports/A02.xls, http://www.moi.gov.tw.stat/, http://www.gov.tw/ EBOOKS/TWANNUAL/show_book.php?path=2_005_027

ization is interlinked with diverging paths of sectoral specialization, which, as we will see, in turn, reflects specific features of the differences in firm capabilities and national institutions. The institutional structures in which firms and markets are embedded make a difference to the development of certain industrial sectors. In particular, differences in competences and strategies of leading business firms, and other institutions in which agents are embedded and which constrain and guide microeconomic coordination and change will all affect the development of certain industries.

Figures 5.1 to 5.4 show the changes in industrial structure between 1980, 1985 and 1990 in Korea, Argentina, Brazil, and Mexico. Each figure portrays the level of output (in 1980 US$ millions) across eight industrial sectors for each of the years above. Over the period considered, Korea deepened considerably its specialization in machinery and equipment, especially electrical machinery. In contrast, Argentina specialized in resource-intensive sectors, especially petroleum refineries (the exception to specialization in resource-intensive sectors is the specialization in transport equipment, given that the auto industry has been the object of special regimes since its development in the post-war period, see Miozzo (2000)). Brazil has a less pointed specialization in resource-intensive sectors than Argentina, combining a specialization in machinery and transport with resource-based sectors. Mexico has deepened its specialization in resource-intensive sectors such as petroleum refineries and in transport equipment. Much of these developments in transport equipment are related to the foreign-assembly factories or 'maquiladoras' on the Mexican–US border.

Figures 5.5 to 5.9 show the changes in export structure for all six countries in selected industrial sectors from 1970 to 1980, to 1990, and to 1996. Korea

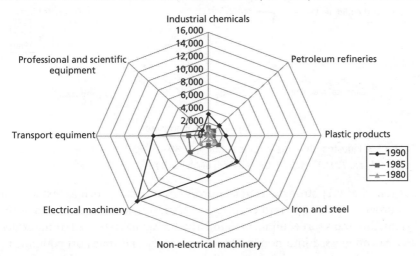

Figure 5.1 Industrial structure change in Korea, 1980–85–90
(*source*: Miozzo 2002: Figure 1, p. 52; data from UNIDO 1992)

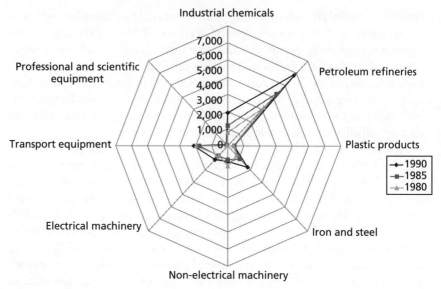

Figure 5.2 Industrial structure change in Argentina, 1980–85–90
(*source*: Miozzo 2002: Figure 2, p. 52; data from UNIDO 1992)

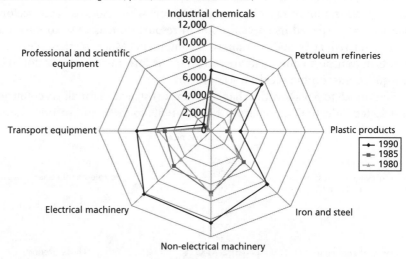

Figure 5.3 Industrial structure change in Brazil, 1980–85–90
(*source*: Miozzo 2002: Figure 3, p. 53; data from UNIDO 1992)

has retreated very strongly from labour-intensive sectors such as textiles and has progressed strongly into exports of electrical machinery and, to a lesser extent, into transport equipment. Similarly, Taiwan has retreated from textiles and has progressed into non-electrical machinery and transport equipment. In contrast, Argentina has retreated from cereals and, to a lesser extent, textiles, and has progressed into crude petroleum. The increase in exports

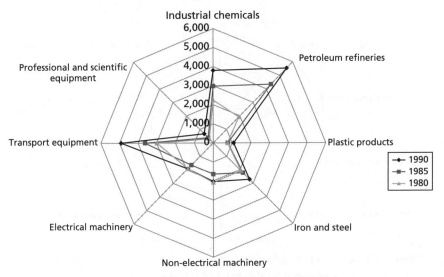

Figure 5.4 Industrial structure change in Mexico, 1980–85–90
(*source*: Miozzo 2002: Figure 4, p. 53; data from UNIDO 1992)

in the only non-resource-based sectors, such as transport equipment, as argued earlier, responds to a special incentive. Brazil has retreated from textiles and metals and progressed into non-electrical machinery and transport equipment. Mexico has retreated from crude petroleum and has progressed into electrical machinery and transport equipment.

Indeed, there is a growing specialization in production and trade in machinery sectors in East Asia and a declining specialization in these sectors in Latin

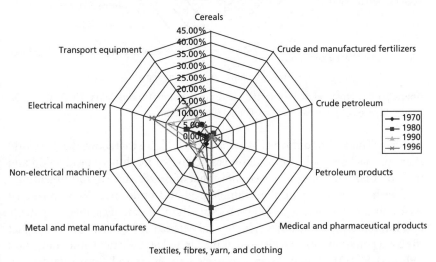

Figure 5.5 Export structure by selected sectors (percentage) in Korea, 1970–80–90–96
(*source*: Miozzo 2002: Figure 5, p. 54; data from UNCTAD 1999)

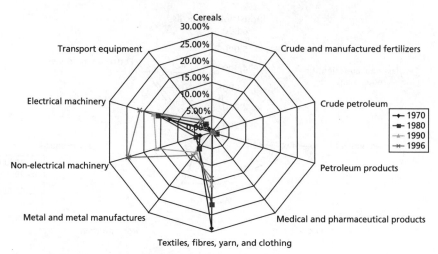

Figure 5.6 Export structure by selected sectors (percentage) in Taiwan, 1970–80–90–96
(*source*: Miozzo 2002, Figure 6, p. 54; data from UNCTAD 1999)

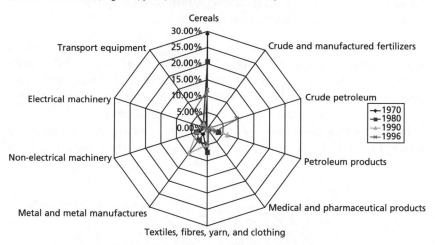

Figure 5.7 Export structure by selected sectors (percentage) in Argentina, 1970–80–90–96
(*source*: Miozzo 2002: Figure 8, p. 55; data from UNCTAD 1999)

America. This is also confirmed by evidence in Table 5.2 that shows that the world share of machine tool consumption (indicative of machinery production and use) in Korea and Taiwan are well above that of Brazil, Mexico, and Argentina.

Elsewhere, we compare the technological and trade specialization of East Asia and Latin America through an evaluation of data available on patents and international trade flows (Huang and Miozzo 2004). They point out that the total patent numbers registered at the United States Patent and Trademark Office (USPTO) of East Asian countries have increased from one-digit to four-digit figures in the past thirty years and have left those of Latin American

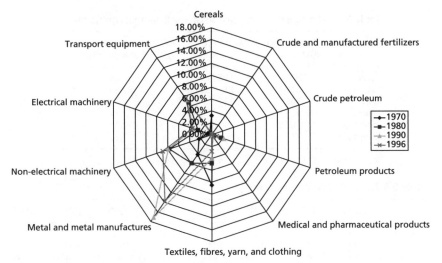

Figure 5.8 Export structure by selected sectors (percentage) in Brazil, 1970–80–90–96
(*source*: Miozzo 2002: Figure 9, p. 56; data from UNCTAD 1999)

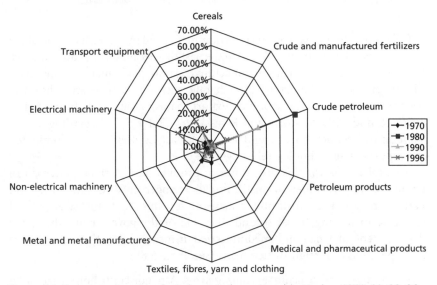

Figure 5.9 Export structure by selected sectors (percentage) in Mexico, 1970–80–90–96
(*source*: Miozzo 2002: Figure 10, p. 56; data from UNCTAD 1999)

countries far behind (see Table 5.3). The results are even more marked when considering the type and quality of technological specialization as reflected by patents, with East Asia showing comparative strength in computers and communications and electrical and electronic sectors compared to Latin American countries (Huang and Miozzo 2004).

Table 5.2 Latin American and East Asian machine-tool consumption

Country by world share	Consumption (US$ million)	World share	Machine-tool consumption (US$ million)/population (millions)
Korea	1,581.4	3.85	39.09
Taiwan	615.8	1.5	32.50
Brazil	356	0.87	2.94
Mexico	255	0.62	3.14
Argentina	82.8	0.2	2.54
Hong Kong	12.2	0.03	2.26

Source: Miozzo (2002, Table 1, p. 57; data from UNIDO 1992).

Table 5.3 Number of patents by country

Country	1965	1970	1975	1980	1985	1990	1995	1999
Argentina	18	23	24	18	11	17	31	44
Brazil	11	17	17	24	30	41	63	91
Mexico	87	43	67	41	32	32	40	76
S. Korea	2	3	13	8	41	225	1,161	3,526
Taiwan	0	0	23	65	174	732	1,620	3,693

Source: Huang and Miozzo (2004, Table AII, p. 639; data from NBER US Patent Citation Data File).

Lall (2000) shows that East Asia has dominated and increased its export share in the less developed countries' total in the past two decades while Latin America has shown stagnation in its manufactured export performance (Table 5.4). The divergence in the export growth rate between the two areas has also been reflected in the change of their export shares to the OECD from the late 1970s to mid-1990s (Alcorta and Peres 1998) (Table 5.5). Regarding export share in the less developed countries' total, East Asia has almost dominated the exports of all technological categories.

An explanation for this divergence in production and trade patterns can be found in the different institutional arrangements in East Asia and Latin America. Four institutions account for this: first, the strategy and structure of leading firms; second, the role of the government; third, the development of small-and medium-sized firms; and fourth, the presence and operation of foreign-owned firms (see Table 5.6).

1. *Strategy and structure of leading firms.* A major contributory factor to these divergences has been differences in the organization of leading business firms. While there are striking similarities, since in both East Asia and Latin America the main agent of industrialization has been technologically diversified business groups, these have operated in very different ways in both regions. In Korea, the banking system (state run until 1981–83 and thereafter under state control) lent long term, at low interest rates and in large amounts to selected 'chaebol'[4] for approved investments. This meant that the transition between sectors and products could be rather abrupt and not depend heavily

Table 5.4 Regional share of developing countries' manufactured export (percentage of developing world total)

	Year	East Asia	Latin America (including Mexico)	Latin America (excluding Mexico)
All manufactures	1985	56.9	23.1	16.9
	1998	69.0	19.3	8.9
Resource based	1985	34.6	32.9	30.7
	1998	47.5	28.0	24.0
Agro based	1985	55.1	32.0	30.4
	1998	55.1	33.1	28.3
Other resource based	1985	25.6	33.3	30.8
	1998	41.4	23.1	20.6
Low technology	1985	71.7	11.9	10.2
	1998	70.2	12.6	5.4
Textile cluster	1985	69.9	9.5	8.5
	1998	67.3	10.4	4.9
Other low technology	1985	75.2	16.6	13.5
	1998	74.9	16.0	6.3
Medium technology	1985	63.4	25.8	17.5
	1998	63.8	28.1	10.2
Auto	1985	40.6	50.3	32.9
	1998	39.8	54.2	16.9
Process	1985	53.4	28.2	25.2
	1998	65.6	19.9	13.0
Engineering	1985	73.0	20.1	10.4
	1998	72.5	22.4	5.8
High technology	1985	81.0	14.8	6.6
	1998	85.5	12.9	2.1
Electronic	1985	84.7	14.0	5.1
	1998	87.2	11.8	1.2
Other high technology	1985	60.3	19.2	15.2
	1998	66.9	25.0	12.2

Source: Lall (2000, Table 4).

on the profitability and efficiency of existing investments. It was therefore possible for the Korean business groups or chaebol to target scale-intensive, mid-technology areas.

Industrial groups in Latin America also have privileged access to capital and advantageous connections with government. However, the relation between industrial groups and banks is not aimed at forming structures to back long-term investments but is rather a way of maximizing financial returns on idle monetary resources or working capital (Miozzo 2002).

Table 5.5 Index of technological specialization in East Asia and Latin America, 1977–95

Country	1977	1983	1989	1995
East Asia	0.74	0.98	1.05	1.80
Latin America and Caribbean	0.16	0.23	0.35	0.48
Argentina	0.12	0.13	0.08	0.07
Brazil	0.22	0.29	0.32	0.23
Mexico	0.50	0.49	1.13	1.62

Source: Alcorta and Peres (1998; Table 9, p. 877).

Table 5.6 East Asian and Latin American institutions explaining the sectoral specialization in machinery

	East Asia	Latin America
Strategy and structure of leading firms	Diversified business groups compete with one another across a range of medium-technology industry with large-scale, long-term state support	Business groups diversify for financial reasons, retracting towards 'non tradeable' and intermediate industries
Industrial promotion by the state	State promotion of industrialization through subsidies and 'disciplining' of recipient firms through strict and monitorable performance standards encourage firms into 'difficult' technologies	State promotion through protection and subsidies with no 'sticks' to encourage entry into 'difficult' technologies
Support of small- and medium-sized firms	Building of network of small- and medium-sized firms for export trade in consumer goods through e.g. land reform	Low political influence of industry in early post-war and liberalization led to contraction of SMES
Presence and relation with foreign-owned firms	Domestic firms used Japanese minority capital for technological upgrading	Multinationals of low efficiency dominated in technologically dynamic sectors

Source: Adapted from Miozzo (2002).

Indeed, differences are evident when in the late 1980s and early 1990s the traditional mechanisms of industrial policy and financial regulation were dismantled in Korea. The response of Korean industrial groups was utterly unlike what would have been expected in Latin America. The chaebol responded to the new situation of freedom and uncertainty by overborrowing massively from domestic and foreign banks in their competitive struggle against one another—running risks of bankruptcy that became apparent in the 1997–99 crisis (Chang et al. 1998). Indeed, some commentators (Henderson 1998) blame the effects of the crisis in Korea on deregulation and dismantling of the 'East Asian model' of development rather than on any intrinsic problems with this model:

In the case of Korea, there emerged between 1961 and the early 1990s a classic developmental state. While corruption of political elites was evident there, it was not oriented towards rent seeking, but indeed towards the enhancement of productive investment. It was one of the best examples of 'developmental corruption'. Subsequently to 1992, however, the state's developmental capacities began to be dissipated. It abandoned long term strategic planning and became increasingly unable to mediate the relation (particularly the financial relation) between the domestic and international economies. The Wall Street-IMF-US treasury view notwithstanding, the internal origins of the Korean crisis lay not in too much regulation, but ultimately, when confronted with deregulationist pressures and ideologies, in too little (Henderson 1998: 34).

Indeed, while in Korea large business groups have invested in internationally competitive sectors such as electronics, business groups in Latin America have receded into 'non tradable' sectors or sectors where there are rents based on the exploitation of natural resources, bureaucratic lobbying, and opportunistic behaviour. Most now concentrate on sluggish or traditional activities such as foodstuffs and beverages, ferrous metals, textiles and clothing, and non-ferrous metals. Within foodstuffs, firms shifted their production to industries such as soy beans and soy products, meat and poultry, and concentrated juices, which make intensive use of natural resources and involve little industrial processing. Only a few groups in Brazil (Cofap, Weg, Dedini, and Machline) maintained a presence in dynamic technology-intensive activities, and specifically in machinery sectors (Garrido 1994; Ruiz 1997). In Argentina, the expansion in the economic influence of twenty-five large, closely held, vertically and horizontally integrated groups is the most marked characteristic of the 1980s and 1990s. These large groups (especially Perez Companc, Techint, Citicorp, and Astra) expanded through the purchase of state firms, through preferential treatment in utilities such as electricity or natural gas and through the ease of transfer of resources and cross-subsidies between firms and vertical and horizontal integration. This resulted in an increase in economic concentration with one-third of the top firms accounting for two-thirds of aggregate sales. Firms in trade (supermarket chains, primary product exporters) have increased their participation from 5.6 to 15.9 per cent in the top 2,000 firms in the 1990s (Azpiazu 1997). Input producers recovered their economic position in the mid-1990s (Aluar, Ipako, PASA, Loma Negra, Indupa, Petroquimica Bahia Blanca, Siderca, Polisur, and Petroken). A growth in tradable but naturally protected goods, such as cement, and a notable growth in exports of intermediate inputs, such as petrochemicals and steel, explain most manufacturing production (Azpiazu et al. 1986; Azpiazu 1997).

2. *Industrial promotion by the state.* The second major contributory factor to these divergences has been the nature of state promotion of industrial activity. While in both East Asia and Latin America, firms and business groups have received state support, only in the former did they have to meet monitorable performance standards or otherwise experience a withdrawal of this support (Amsden 1989; Wade 1990) while there has been no such performance standards and 'discipline' of Latin American business groups.

In Latin America, the state assumed an important role between the 1950s and the mid-1970s, in promoting import substitution industrialization.[5] In Argentina, this was through subsidies to private domestic investment (especially through the Industrial Bank created in 1944), the promotion of foreign investment (especially from the USA), the creation of state enterprises, and as arbiter of social struggles over the distribution of income. In Brazil, tax breaks, credits, investment licences, import facilities, and export promotion were important elements of industrial policy. The state budget (through the inflationary tax and government bonds) and foreign borrowing in the 1970s and 1980s funded industrialization. In all Latin American countries, the government allowed large domestic firms to appropriate important rents, through high levels of protection and subsidies, but imposed no 'sticks'. In Brazil, the few exceptions to this rule were the procurement policy of Petrobras, the state oil company, which subjected suppliers to quality controls and the BEFIEX export subsidy based on quantitative export obligations (Meyer-Stamer 1997). As such, government policies did not succeed in promoting entry into activities with 'difficult' technologies and encourage the undertaking of complex, new technological functions as in East Asia (Lall and Teubal 1998). In particular, this operated in detriment of the development of an internationally competitive machinery and capital goods sectors at the time when industrialized countries where experiencing a transition from electromechanical to electronic production. In Latin America, machinery and transport equipment sectors, which are institutionally complex, requiring careful management of relationships with other firms and with workers, and attention to technological detail, have been left to the weak and undercapitalized small and medium enterprises, and to multinationals.

3. *Development and support of small- and medium-sized firms.* East Asian countries have managed to build a dense network of small businesses which ensures their survival and interfirm cooperation needed in the machinery sectors. There have been no comparable developments in Latin America. During the 1950s, Korea and Taiwan carried out a land reform programme, which enabled the development of smaller firms set up with family and cooperative savings and supported by bank credit. Taiwan, in particular, saw the development of a flexible decentralized network of small- and medium-sized firms focusing on export trade in consumer goods (Castells 1992; Whitley 1992). This picture contrasts heavily with that of Latin America. In Argentina, in the late nineteenth and early twentieth centuries, it is immigrants and large foreign firms turning from exporters to manufacturers who led in the development of manufacturing industry in Latin America. However, the naturalization and political participation of immigrants was low (Cornbilt 1967) (unlike the Chinese in East Asia) and they lacked political weight due to the continued political influence of land-owning interest and the dependence on exports of primary products for the foreign exchange required for imports (Hirschman 1971).

Deregulation and liberalization of the economy in Latin America increased economic concentration. Medium and small-sized firms fell by 10 per cent between 1974 and 1985. These firms, which were suppliers and producers of components for the machinery and transport equipment, were heavily affected by the deterioration of general economic infrastructure in the 1980s and by the entry of foreign suppliers in the 1990s.

Brazil may be considered an exception in that it has important industry clusters which include smaller firms (women's shoes in Sinos valley in Rio

Grande do Sul, men's and children's shoes in the interior of the state of São Paulo, ceramic tiles in the south of Santa Catarina, automotive and capital goods industry around the city of São Paulo, consumer electronics industry in Manaus, and petrochemical industry in Cubatao, Camacari, and Triunfo). Nevertheless, clientelism and the lack of defined local and national responsibility threaten these regional clusters (Meyer-Stamer 1997).

4. *Presence and relations with foreign-owned firms.* Another major contributory factor to these differences is the role of FDI in East Asia and Latin America and the nature of the relations between foreign and domestic firms. While these relations have led to the upgrading of technological capability in East Asian domestic firms, in Latin America these relations have had the opposite effect, leading to a reduction in the contribution and quality of domestic subcontractors and suppliers.

The presence of foreign-owned firms has been and remains stronger in Latin America than in Taiwan or Korea (see Table 5.7) (Amsden and Hikino 1994). This is not to say that multinational corporations have not played an important role in the favourable economic performance of East Asian countries. Some equity capital entered Korea and Taiwan but FDI accounted for very low percentage of gross fixed capital formation (see Table 5.8).

Table 5.7 FDI inflows by area and period, 1970–99 (average annual inflows in millions of US$ and per cent world FDI inflows)

Period	Korea		Taiwan		Argentina		Brazil		Mexico	
	US$	(%)	US$	(%)	US$	(%)	US$	(%)	US$	(%)
1970–74	77	0.5	57	0.4	10	0.1	852	5.8	413	2.8
1975–79	71	0.3	79	0.3	120	0.4	1,823	6.7	790	2.9
1980–84	71	0.2	154	0.4	439	1.1	2,088	5.4	1,500	3.8
1985–89	688	0.5	788	0.6	730	0.5	1,425	1.1	2,178	1.6
1990–94	840	0.4	1,154	0.6	3,026	1.5	1,590	0.8	5,895	2.9
1995–99	4,462	0.8	1,764	0.3	10,599	1.9	18,918	3.5	10,603	1.9

Source: Lopez and Miozzo (2004: Table 1; data from UNCTAD 2000).

Table 5.8 Ratio of FDI inflows to gross fixed capital formation for different periods, 1971–98 (in per cent)

Country	1971–5	1976–80	1981–5	1986–90	1991–5	1996–8
Korea	1.9	0.4	0.5	1.2	0.7	2.8
Taiwan	1.4	1.2	1.5	3.7	2.3	2.3
Argentina	0.1	2.1	5.0	11.1	12.9	13.2
Brazil	4.2	3.9	4.3	1.7	2.4	12.4
Mexico	3.5	3.6	5.0	7.5	11.6	14.5

Source: Lopez and Miozzo (2004: Table 4.2, p. 66; data from UNCTAD 2000).

In East Asia, business groups have forged links with firms in sectors that generate new technologies (such as microelectronics and electrical equipment) and use new technologies (such as motor vehicles, chemicals, and telecommunications). While domestic firms have been the agents of industrialization, they have done so largely as suppliers to Japanese firms. Japanese minority capital or non-equity participation in domestic firms

---

Box 5.3 Strategies of East Asian firms to use foreign connections in electronics

East Asian firms utilized foreign connections to overcome technology and market barriers in electronics. Foreign buyers, multinationals, OEM arrangements and joint ventures and licenses where exploited by domestic firms to progress from simple assembly tasks to more sophisticated product design and development capabilities. East Asian firms travel backwards along the product life cycle, from the standardized market and technology stages to the more uncertain, early design-intensive complex innovation stages.

In Korea, large vertically integrated firms used the needs of demanding export customers as a focusing device to upgrade their technology. During the mid-1960s US multinationals entered into Korea to assemble products using cheap labour, while importing most inputs. As Korean firms acquired sufficient skills, leading Japanese multinationals formed joint ventures in the late 1960s and early 1970s with Korean firms. OEM was used as an alternative to joint ventures. Under OEM, multinationals helped train engineers, select equipment and supply materials and capital goods to domestic Korean firms. OEM enabled Korean firms to export large volumes of goods under foreign brand names and distribution channels, but it was also a training school for Korean firms that learned skills from Japanese and American multinationals. Hence, Korean firms were able to expand into more sectors, to overcome barriers to entry and to access Japanese control channels of distribution into Western markets. OEM and licensing were important for products that were new to Korea (advanced computer terminals, large telecommunications exchanges and semiconductors). As products matured and capabilities were learned, OEM became less important (such as in audio equipment and televisions). However, the lack of high-quality international brand images was felt by many Korean firms to be a long-term constraint on growth. The strategy of larger firms was to invest heavily in R&D and brand awareness campaigns. The results of these strategies are still unfolding, with some firms retreating to OEM and own-design manufacture (ODM) in the early 1990s after sustaining heavy losses in own-brand investments.

By the late 1980s, many of the goods purchased were designed and specified, as well as manufactured, by the local firm, while the foreign buyers simply branded the ready-made product (called ODM in Taiwan). Korean firms carried out some or all of the product and process tasks, according to a general design layout provided by the multinationals. This signified more advanced design skills and often new production technologies. As large firms approached the technology frontier, other learning mechanisms became important, particularly in-house R&D efforts to develop new products and to assimilate advanced foreign technologies. Also, strategic partnership with foreign firms, with Korean firms bringing technological and other assets to bargain for leading edge technologies, access to markets, in areas sectors such as consumer electronics and telecommunications, became important. Also, during the 1980s, Korean firms began investing heavily in overseas high-tech firms.

The story is similar in Taiwan, with industry benefiting considerably from investment by multinationals, joint ventures and foreign buyers. In contrast to Korea, however, industrial development relied on a multitude of small and medium-sized firms and foreign direct

Box 5.3 (*Continued*)

investment continued to play a central role through the 1980s and 1990s. Under OEM and ODM, exports focused domestic learning efforts and help to pull Taiwan's competitive capabilities forward. The Taiwanese case shows how hundreds of tiny latecomer firms clustered together behind the electronics frontier to exploit market opportunities, indicating that the large-scale mass market approach followed by the chaebol is not the only route for less developed countries. In electronics, sewing machines, footwear, bicycles and other fast-growing export industries, small firms made themselves indispensable for foreign buyers and multinationals and forged backward linkages to other industries. In sectors of low capital intensity such as electronics assembly and textile manufacture, the government intervened less than in large-scale complex technological fields and intermediate goods. In the latter, direct intervention and financial support from the government, state-owned enterprises prospered (in petrochemicals, shipbuilding, automobiles) in 1960s.

As firms became internationally competitive, they found joint ventures and licenses insufficient. The latest vintage of technology was not available from the innovators. They had to import technology by going into new arrangements (franchising or OEM) and/or by investing in their own R&D to build upon foreign technology. Some firms became outward investors to engage in alliances to take over innovative firms abroad.

Source: Hobday (1994, 1995).

has ensured technological upgrading. These selected foreign investments created initially low-cost sourcing centres and subcontracting with export orientation.

The chaebol and the Korean state, have managed their relationships with foreign industrial capital very carefully (see Box 5.3). The chaebol refused equity participation of foreign enterprises until the 1970s but even then with strong restrictions. In the 1980s, Korea formed partnerships with Japanese industry and used original equipment manufacture[6] (OEM) agreements to supply electronic products and equipment to Japanese firms, making rapid technological advances possible (Hobday 1994, 1995; Etzkowitz and Brisolla 1999).

Taiwanese firms initially concentrated on production, depending on US and Japanese partners for technology and marketing, including brand names. They became subcontractors of American multinationals or medium-sized Japanese firms, and suppliers of international commercial networks (through Japanese trading companies and American department stores) (Castells 1992). It is the IT industry in Taiwan which has received much attention, with semiconductors (and integrated circuit design) as the most famously successful subsector of the industry, where Taiwanese science and technology policy, based on large public research institutions, and the activities of a flexible decentralized network of small firms created a world-leading industry. Saxenian and colleagues have discussed Silicon Valley-type clusters in Taiwan and other countries (e.g., Bresnahan et al. 2001; Saxenian and Hsu 2001; Saxenian 2002). Taiwan developed the biggest and most advanced pureplay foundries and some of the largest

OEM or ODM subcontractors such as Quanta or BenQ producing for leading US or Japan multinationals such as HP or Dell.

In Latin America, instead, during the post-war period, US multinationals dominated the more technologically dynamic sectors such as machinery and chemicals. This was in the form of subsidiaries or majority-owned affiliates.

Box 5.4 Multinationals and technology development in Latin America and East Asia

The different approaches towards multinationals in East Asia and Latin America can be compared across four dimensions:

- **Openness towards multinationals.** East Asia imposed greater restrictions on multinationals than Latin America. East Asia encouraged mainly 'new forms of investment' from Japan (and especially Korea preferred foreign loans to foreign direct investment), including majority locally owned joint ventures, licensing, subcontracting and other contractual arrangements between local and foreign firms as a means to build up local firms' manufacturing export capabilities. In contrast, in Latin America, mainly US and also European multinationals played a key role during the import substitution industrialization period, mainly as wholly-owned subsidiaries. They invested to exploit domestic markets protected by high tariff and non-tariff barriers and mainly concentrated in capital intensive sectors as well as in consumer goods sectors where oligopolistic competition prevailed. The operation of multinationals in Latin America tended to contribute to trade and current account deficits.

- **Multinationals as enabling or hindering the direction of national industrialization.** In sectors where multinationals have played an important role in East Asia, for example, in textiles and electronics, government policy has been a major influence, promoting joint ventures, screening imported technologies and bargaining over local content agreements. Such practices have firmly embedded foreign firms within a national industrialization strategy. In Korea (and to a lesser extent in Taiwan) this meant tight control and selectivity towards multinationals. In these countries, domestic business groups and networks of small firms respectively, were the agents of industrialization, encouraged by subsidies and performance targets. In contrast, in Latin America, multinationals played a more significant role in industrial output and exports. The limited efficiency and scale of their operations acted as an obstacle against them serving as a competitive stimulus for domestic firms.

- **Contribution of multinationals to the absorption of modern technology.** East Asia has put in place mechanisms to ensure the acquisition and assimilation of foreign technology (such as information by purchasers of their exports; non-proprietary technology; returning nationals; and partnering with foreign firms). In contrast, little emphasis was placed in Latin America on developing absorption capabilities aimed not only at adapting and using efficiently the imported technologies, but also as a basis for the development of a process of endogenous technological learning.

- **Strategy of domestic firms to utilize multinationals to overcome technology and market barriers.** Domestic firms in East Asia used their relations with multinationals, OEM and licences to develop technology and marketing capabilities in contrast to Latin American firms. As they become internationally competitive, they are investing in their in-house R&D and marketing efforts. In Latin America, the extent to which domestic groups utilized multinationals to secure technology and market access has been much lower than in East Asia.

Source: Lopez and Miozzo (2004).

The limited efficiency of their operations acted as an obstacle against them serving as a competitive stimulus for domestic firms, especially in terms of exports (Mortimore 1993). More recently, Latin American countries are undergoing a process of international integration that reduces the contribution of domestic subcontractors and suppliers to scale intensive operations led by large business groups and multinational firms (Cimoli et al. 1998; Miozzo 2000).

In East Asia, therefore, FDI was managed to ensure technological and organizational improvements. In Latin America, instead, the private business interests of multinational corporations have superseded national interests—they make limited investment in R&D and there is a lack of attention to linkages with local suppliers. Increasing dependence on imported components has led to a neglect of previous domestic experience in machinery production and accumulated levels of engineering skills and know-how (see Box 5.4).

Conclusion

The divergence since the 1970s in specialization in machinery and transport equipment can be explained by different institutional arrangements prevailing in East Asia and Latin America. In East Asia, domestic firms exploited their relations with multinationals, OEM agreements and licences to their advantage, learning production methods, reverse engineering products and machinery, and accumulating design skills and technology and marketing capabilities in high-tech sectors such as electronics. While in Korea this relied on the scale and financial power of the large chaebol, in Taiwan, the key was the speed and agility of hundreds of small local entrepreneurs, in both cases implementing incremental process and product improvements on borrowed technology on the shop floor in mid-technology sectors.

In Latin America, large domestically owned business groups and a small number of subsidiaries of multinationals have established modern plants producing capital-intensive, intermediate, resource-intensive goods, with up-to-date process technology, exporting in competitive markets, where Latin American countries are price-takers. The production of these goods, such as iron and steel, petrochemicals, vegetable oils, and papers, and of non-tradables (telecommunications, energy, financial sectors) has grown at the expense of final labour-intensive goods and technology-intensive goods. An exception in Latin America has been the auto industry, the object of an ad hoc industrial policy in Argentina (Miozzo 2002), Brazil, and Mexico. Another exception is the Mexican 'maquila'—an enclave of foreign firms producing computer equipment and televisions—protecting them from liberalization and the generalized deregulation of the economy. These processes have led to increasing dependence on imported capital goods, accentuated by the disappearance of certain sectors (metalworking and specialized suppliers) traditionally associated with the production of incremental knowledge and believed to be a first step in the accumulation of technological capability.

The role of countries in the international division of labour, as reflected in technological specialization patterns may be of increasing relevance in the context of globalization. This is because of the effect of specialization patterns on the terms of exchange, international trade vulnerability, and the impact on the economy in terms of the development of technological capabilities. Countries which manage to specialize in higher value-added products may have better prospects for future growth because these products tend to grow faster in trade (they tend to be highly income elastic, create new demand, and substitute faster for older products); they are less vulnerable to easy entry by lower wage competitors or to technology and market shifts; they have greater potential for further learning (offering more scope for the application of scientific knowledge); and have larger spillover effects in terms of creating new skills and generic knowledge that can be used in other activities (Lall 2000).

Though some believe that the trend of globalization will mitigate the impact of national specificities in shaping the national trade or export structure, government policy, and industrial strategy in East Asia and Latin America (institutional upgrading, better education and training, and industrial promotion or protection) appear to have a decisive influence on national technological specialization. It is also clear that the international distribution of production is increasingly sectorally differentiated. Although technology may have become more internationally mobile, domestic production and innovation activities are still a major determinant of specialization and competitiveness.

It can be argued that the challenges facing less developed countries have never been greater than at present. While all countries find it difficult to cope with the current pace of technological change, globalization, and liberalization, it is the less developed countries that face the greatest challenges. Less developed countries face three main challenges. First, technological change means that competition takes new and rapidly changing forms. As argued in Chapter 4, competition is changing towards forms of organization and technology capable of high-throughput efficiency, and the production of semi-customized products with sophisticated flexible machinery and high skills. While technologies become increasingly mobile, the ability to adopt and use high technologies at best practice levels is highly and increasingly concentrated in a small number of successful industrialized countries.

Second, globalization, which implies a functional integration between internationally dispersed economic activities, may be accompanied by geographical fragmentation. As we see in Chapter 8, the main engines of internationalization and transfer of technology are multinationals (these account for two-thirds of world trade and about half of this is between their own affiliates). Multinationals tend to specialize and contract out more activities and forge stronger linkages with first-tier suppliers and customers. Their international production systems become more tightly integrated and specialized, with different processes spreading over different locations to take advantage of cost, skill, and logistical advantage. Participation in these multinationals' integrated production systems is becoming a condition for international competitiveness in a number of technologically advanced activities (UNIDO 2002).

Third, there have been dramatic regulatory changes affecting investment and trade patterns with important effects for less developed countries. As we see in Chapter 8, the WTO including the Agreement on Trade-Related Aspects of Intellectual Property Rights (TRIPS) and the General Agreement on Trade in Services (GATS) and other pressures for liberalization and deregulation means that less developed countries are now more open to trade, investment, and finance but have little strategy to cope with these changes. They can no longer apply the traditional instruments of industrial policies (e.g. screening FDI, local content, and infant industry protection) used by the advanced countries (Chang 2002) and the East Asian newly industrialized countries when they themselves were industrializing. The only tools they have left are those also used today by developed countries (such as skill creation, FDI promotion, and R&D investment). Some of these challenges will be dealt with in Part IV.

Notes

1 Although the English revolution and civil war, which paved the way for industrialization by removing the essential features of feudalism (not replaced with the Restoration), were inspired by Protestant (and Puritan) Christian ideology (Hill 1958).

2 The idea that less developed economies need to develop different institutions and challenges, and that the existence and interest of developed economies may be a barrier to their development is well developed in development economics. Development economics has two main strands: structuralism (which developed as a critique of neo-classical theory) and dependency (which involved a critique of modernization theory, and included a Marxist strand that is critical of orthodox Marxism as well as of structuralism). The structuralist authors (Paul Rosenstein-Rodan, Ragnar Nurkse, Gunnar Myrdal, W. Arthur Lewis, and Hans Singer) saw the economy in less developed countries as inflexible and facing major constraints and bottlenecks. They therefore distrusted the price mechanism and justified government intervention to accelerate economic development. In Latin America, a particular group of structuralist authors working in the Economic Commission for Latin America (ECLA) (established in 1947) developed their own version under Raul Prebisch, exploring the integration of Latin American economies into the dominant capitalist system from colonial times as producers of primary products, and advocating import-substitution industrialization as an inward development strategy for peripheral economies. The dependency theory originated in Latin America in the late 1960s and early 1970s and viewed underdevelopment as the particular form capitalist development assumes as dependent countries are integrated forcefully into the world capitalist system, and called for national control over the

development process and investment of foreign capital through reform (Henrique Cardoso, Enzo Faletto, Osvaldo Sunkel, Celso Furtado, Helio Jaguaribe, Aldo Ferrer, and Anibal Pinto) or socialist revolution (Ruy Mauro Marini, Theotonio Dos Santos, Andre Gunder Frank, Oscar Braun, Vania Bambirra, Anibal Quijano, Edelberto Torres-Rivas, Tomas Amadeo Vasconi, Alonso Agilar, and Antonio Garcia) to overcome dependence and enable economic development. (For further discussion see Kay 1989.)

3 This does not mean that Latin American countries have not had a number of impressive technological achievements recently. Argentine scientists have earned three Nobel prizes in medicine and the natural sciences. Also, two impressive developments in engineering and technology: the development of nuclear reactors in Argentina and commuter aircraft in Brazil are evidence of the existence of highly trained human resources, leadership of the institutions involved, and appropriate supportive public policies. However, as argued by Teitel (2004), these achievements cannot be adequately interpreted as the result of the working of a well-integrated national system (see Chapter 6).

4 The Korean government intentionally selected large firms or 'chaebol' as an instrument to enable scale economies in mature technologies, develop 'strategic sectors', and lead in exports, helping them with capital formation and diversification and providing loans in 'import substitution projects' (see note 3) (Kim 1993).

5 The import substitution industrialization (ISI) approach has been triggered in different economies by different motives (balance of payment difficulties, wars, gradual growth of income, and deliberate development policies) and has adopted different characteristics according to different motives. However, in most cases, it starts with the production of consumer goods for the home market as a substitute for imports, then moves on to the 'higher stages' of manufacture of intermediate and capital goods. It relies on the use of import and exchange controls, and other forms of state intervention in production, distribution, and exchange (Hirschman 1971). The main intellectual source of the ISI approach was the Economic Commission for Latin America and the Caribbean (ECLAC). The protection of native industries was thought of as a response to slackening demand from developed countries for LDC's primary exports, the trend for the terms of trade to deteriorate and the inability to develop domestic manufactures. In 1949, Prebisch and Singer formulated, simultaneously and independently, the famous 'thesis' on the secular trend for the terms of trade to turn against countries exporting primary products and importing manufactures. They attributed this to the power of trade unions in developed countries and to the conditions of underemployment in the periphery. This argument was put forward to justify a sustained policy of industrialization. The argument was also supported by Lewis in 1954 who claimed that as long as 'unlimited supplies of labour' in the subsistence sector depresses the real wage throughout the economy, any gains from productivity increases in the export sector are likely to accrue to the importing countries, prices in this situation constituting a wrong signal for resource allocation. ISI strategies were not only widely adopted in most Latin American economies in the 1950s, but also in much of Asia, including South Korea, Taiwan, and the Philippines, as well as India, Pakistan, and China. These strategies were also applied in the 1960s in some African countries including Ghana, Zambia, Kenya, and Nigeria.

6 Hobday defines OEM as a specific form of subcontracting. Like a joint venture, it requires a close connection with the foreign partner. Under OEM deals, the local firm produces a good to the exact specification of the foreign company. The foreign firm then markets the product through its own distribution channels, under its own brand name. OEM often involves the foreign partner in the selection of equipment, training of managers, engineers, and workers. It is to be contrasted with own-design manufacture (ODM), where the local firm designs the product to be sold by the multinational (Hobday 1995).

Part III

Systems of Innovation: A Comparative Perspective

Part III examines 'innovation systems'. An important feature of innovation is that firms do not produce innovations in isolation, but through interactions with customers, suppliers, competitors, sources of funding, universities, and other public and private organizations.

The term 'national innovation system' was coined more than twenty years ago, diffused surprisingly rapidly, and is widely used today in academic circles all over the world. It is also widely utilized by regional authorities and national governments, as well as by international organizations such as OCED, the European Union, and United Nations organizations, such as UNCTAD and UNIDO. The basis for analysing national innovation systems is that an important part of knowledge is localized in routines of firms and other organizations, and in the interactions among these. There is also an assumption that the different elements of the national systems are interrelated and that interdependencies are important for innovation performance, resulting in differences in terms of specialization both in production and trade.

Innovation greatly differs across sectors in terms of the sources, nature, and organizations involved. A rich tradition of sectoral studies have shown that sectors differ in terms of knowledge base, the actors and organizations involved in innovation, the links and relations among them, the relevant institutions, and that these differences matter for an understanding and explanation of innovation and its differences among sectors. These studies have highlighted the diversity in the sources of innovation: the role of basic science, government procurement, the inputs of suppliers and users, the importance of technological collaboration, and the significance of small and large firms.

Chapter 6 examines the concept of national innovation systems. It analyses why national innovation systems are important. It discusses some of the institutions which can be considered to form the national innovation system: business firms, educational institutions, public sector research establishments, public policy, financial institutions, legal institutions, trade unions and political organizations, and ethos, culture and attitude towards entrepreneurship and risk taking.

Chapter 7 explores sectoral patterns of technological change. The chapter examines a number of attempts to classify the sources, nature, and characteristics of innovation in different sectors. We examine the peculiar sources and characteristics of innovation in a number of sectors: services, construction, pharmaceuticals, agrofood, and chemicals.

6 National Innovation Systems

A number of innovation scholars in the past twenty years have focused their attention on analysis of technological change at the level of the national economy rather than the industrial sector or firm (Dosi et al. 1988; Lundvall 1992; Nelson 1993; Freeman 1995; Edquist 1997; Laredo and Mustar 2001). 'System' in this context is historically contingent and dynamic rather than deterministic, and certainly does not imply that any national stereotypes are valid.[1] This focus on the national level reflects the fact that national economies differ regarding the structure of the production system and the general institutional set-up, as a result of differences in their historical experiences, and that these differences may affect the rate or the style of innovative activity in the country concerned. The focus on national systems is both different from microeconomic analyses of firm strategies towards technological change and new product development, and different from analysis of global trends, as in the globalization of trade, production, and sources of finance and knowledge, discussed in Chapters 8 and 10. In some senses globalization might be seen as a trend which is counter to the influence of the national system, and therefore the possibility of national government policymaking activities making a difference. Conversely, the choice of the nation state as the critical unit of analysis might be said to overstate the distinction of national institutions and downplay the impact of global networks, and the global impact on national economic processes. There has been a lot of debate in the innovation literature about the relative influence of the national innovation system (NIS) and globalization on innovative activity (Patel and Pavitt 1992; Cantwell 1995; Patel and Vega 1997) to which we return in Chapter 10. There is also debate in the literature about 'varieties of capitalism' and the extent to which national distinctions are being eroded (especially by 'Americanization') (Boyer 2005).

However, we think it is useful to focus on the national system because the historical differences in institutions and approaches are still important. This is particularly so in emerging countries, such as China, where there were many years of relative isolation of the economy in the recent past, and the country's very distinct institutions have had an important impact on the rapid rate of economic, organizational, and technological change in the past decade.

There are a number of definitions of the NIS. Very broadly, it can refer to the distinct characteristics of the process of R&D, production, and diffusion of economic goods (including but not restricted to technology) as it operates within a nation state. Freeman, however, chooses a slightly narrower definition (Freeman 1987): 'The network of institutions in public and private sectors whose activities and interactions initiate, import, modify and diffuse new technologies.'

This definition emphasizes the *institutions* involved and in addition stresses the *network* aspect of their interaction. Patel and Pavitt also have a definition, which underlines these institutions, but in this case emphasizes the *learning and competence* aspect (Patel and Pavitt 1993):

National institutions, their incentive structures and their competencies, that determine the rate and direction of technological learning in a country.

These definitions are not mutually exclusive, and we would adopt a combination of both Freeman's and Patel and Pavitt's definitions, that is to focus on the institutions which make up the NIS, their linkages and their contribution to learning. Lundvall also emphasizes learning in defining the NIS, reminding us that an NIS is a *social* and a *dynamic* system, in which the elements may 'reinforce each other in promoting processes of learning', or alternatively 'combine into constellations blocking such processes' (Lundvall 1992: 2). Larédo and Mustar recall the importance of history in understanding an NIS, that is 'the processes leading to current organizational arrangements .... the history and the trajectories, the interactions between actors, and the roles of institutions and organizations' (Larédo and Mustar 2001: 3).

This chapter examines the concept of NIS. The first section explores the importance of the concept. The second section discusses some of the institutions which can be considered to form the NIS and illustrates the relevance and variations of these institutions in different countries.

Why are national innovation systems important?

A great deal of the work that has been done on NISs is based around the idea that the rate of technological change in any country, and firms' effectiveness in competitive international trade in goods and services, depends on:

1. The scale of R&D and other technological activities.
2. The way in which the available resources are *managed and organized* both at the level of the *enterprise* and at the *national* level.

So, as Freeman (1987) argues, the NIS may enable a country with rather limited resources to nevertheless make very rapid progress for example through appropriate combinations of imported technology and local adaptation and development. On the other hand, a weakness in the NIS may lead to more abundant resources being squandered by the pursuit of inappropriate objectives or the use of ineffective methods. A relatively low level of spending on R&D, as is found in less developed and emerging economies, thus clearly makes the effectiveness of the NIS even more important for the future innovative performance of the country.[2]

The idea of the NIS was developed by a number of evolutionary or neo-Schumpeterian economists to explain the competitive success of certain national economies in certain historical periods, and the way economic gaps can be opened up by certain countries outstripping others at certain times. These scholars included Christopher Freeman in the UK, Carlota Perez in Venezuela, Bengt-Åke Lundvall in Denmark, Richard Nelson in the USA, Charles Edquist in Sweden, Giovanni Dosi in Italy, Luc Soete in the Netherlands, and Phillipe Larédo, Philippe Mustar, and Robert Boyer in France (Freeman 1987, 1995; Dosi et al. 1988; Lundvall 1992; Nelson 1993; Edquist 1997; Laredo and Mustar 2001), though they would not all necessarily use the term 'national innovation system'. Some of them underlined the proposition that the roots of these ideas lay in much earlier work, including that of Friedrich List in Germany in 1841 (List 1841 cited by Freeman 1995) and J. Weiller in France in 1949 (Weiller 1949 cited by Larédo and Mustar 2001).

The central premise of the NIS approach is that major economic upturns are based on the take-off of a new techno-economic paradigm (see Chapter 1, Green et al. 1999)—that is, a constellation of related product or process innovations together with changes in institutional paradigms which define the way a particular society encourages or reacts to change. The combination of new technology and appropriate institutions can lead to changes in industrial dominance of firms and the industrial leadership of countries. The industrial leadership of Britain in the Industrial Revolution, Germany and the USA at the end of the nineteenth century, and Japan after the Second World War are all examples of this.

During the First Industrial Revolution, Britain opened up a technological and economic gap with other countries based on the exploitation of the potential of the steam engine and the many related product and process innovations that allowed it to power manufacture (e.g. textile production), establish a railway system, and give rise to the heavy engineering industries that produced the machinery that was powered by steam. Britain's success was due to a number of factors including: an increase in scientific and inventive activities (e.g. in spinning cotton); novel ways of organizing production, distribution, investment, and marketing (e.g. the factory system, Wedgwood's showrooms, and traveling salesmen); and novel ways of combing invention and entrepreneurship (e.g. the legal business partnership such as that of Boulton and Watt) (Freeman and Soete 1997).

But, as argued in Chapter 3, Germany and the USA overtook Britain in the late nineteenth and early twentieth century with the establishment of a new techno-economic paradigm based on steel, electrification and chemicals, and a new economic upswing which was felt far more by the economies of those countries (and the then 'newly industrializing countries' such as the Netherlands, Japan, Sweden, Switzerland, and Italy) than elsewhere. This was despite the fact that most of the important scientific discoveries and many of the early innovations were made in Britain.[3] The national innovation systems in Germany and the USA, each in their different ways, were far more suited to the innovation and *especially the diffusion* of the new technologies (Ergas 1987), and the exploitation of *new applications* in other areas of the economy (e.g. in precision engineering, street and domestic lighting, transport [electric trains], or buildings [skyscrapers]), in other words they were more suited to the take-off of the new technology system. The main institutional advantages of Germany and the USA were: the professionalization of engineering and management (and, as argued in Chapter 3, the introduction of full time, salaried managers); new management structures, especially the shift from the U-form or functionally departmentalized firm, with multi-site operation, and subsequently the M-form or multidivisional firm; new forms of ownership, for example, the limited liability company; specialized management functions, for example accounting and marketing; in-house R&D, first in the German chemical industry, then the US electrical industry; the introduction of changes in production organization such as the standardization of parts, division of labour, and automation, all of which increased the flow of products through the system (Fordism); and important developments in education, especially in science and technology, with new institutions such as the Technische Hochschulen in Germany and the Institutes of Technology in the USA.

Similarly Japan was responsible in the post-Second World War period for the more successful diffusion of electronics technology in many sectors and applications than the USA, even though much of the original science and technology and some innovation had been carried out in the USA. It was also applied in Japan to more efficient methods of production in many other industries, notably cars. Japan opened up a technological gap with other countries and had a more rapid rate of economic growth in this period (Freeman 1987). As argued in Chapter 4, institutional changes which were key features of the Japanese NIS in this period were: a particular form of government promotion of innovation and strategic industrial policy—the important role of the Ministry of International Trade and Industry;[4] mass education and training for all 18 years olds, giving a skilled workforce capable of fixing as well as operating machines, identifying good and bad quality, and suggesting improvements; the network structure of firms, or keiretsu; flatter management structures and fewer levels of hierarchy; and a close relationship between suppliers and customers, and other new production practices such as the JIT system which saved space in warehouses for keeping stock and fast die changes bringing economies of time in process and product design.

Some of the institutions that form the national innovation system

In the following sections, we discuss some of the institutions which can be considered to form the NIS (summarized in Table 6.1). This is not an exhaustive list, and different authors focus on different institutional arrangements as significant in the NIS, depending, for example, on how broad or narrow an approach is required for their purposes, or whether the focus is prescriptive (as in policy) or analytical (as in social science). Thus, general industrial policy has an impact on innovativeness, even though it is not specifically oriented to technological capabilities. A broad approach to the

Table 6.1 Main institutions that form the national innovation systems

	Main features and comparison between countries
Business firms	Major spenders on R&D in the economy (relatively more in Germany, the USA and Japan than France and the UK). Largest share of national business enterprise R&D: pharmaceuticals in the UK, electronics in Japan and Korea; high tech services in the USA. Historical importance of in-house R&D (Germany and the USA nineteenth century)
Educational institutions	Sums invested in education. Investment in status of engineering (relatively better in Germany and Japan and worse in the UK)
Public sector research establishments	Relatively high percentage of research carried out in government institutions in France and Italy
Public policy	Importance of public procurement (e.g. early US microelectronics and computer industry). Direct support for science and technology (e.g. US support for health double that in Europe, Japan, and Canada combined): link to take-off of biotechnology via start-up firms. Encouragement of linkages between public research and industry (e.g. French Loi de Programmation et d'Orientation). Role of MITI in stimulating innovation in Japan
Financial institutions	Capital versus credit-based national systems. Shareholder pressures in the UK and the USA. Importance of banks in France (state-mediated allocation of loans); Germany (involved in corporate governance of firms); and Japan (involved in keiretsu). Availability of venture capital in the USA, and its importance to start-up firms
Legal institutions	Intellectual property rights (encourages reverse engineering in Japan versus radical innovations in France and the USA). Incentives to commercialize public sector research (e.g. US Bayh-Dole Act, CRADA). Changes in what can be classed as 'property' over past thirty or so years
Trade unions and political organizations	Efforts to counteract negative effects of technological change (e.g. opposition to nuclear research in Germany and France, share of benefits of adoption of IT)
Ethos and entrepreneurship	For example, attitude to taking risks and learning from failure

NIS would include all social, economic, and political institutions that affect learning, searching, and exploring activities (Bozeman and Dietz 2001). Larédo and Mustar (2001), for example, concentrate on the infrastructure which is important for the competitiveness of firms and which falls within the competence of public policies. They have explicitly chosen a set of institutions which each of the authors of the separate national studies included in their book were asked to use as the basis of a comparison.

Some of the institutions which contribute to the NIS are, of course, more important than others at different times in the evolution of a nation. In fact, those that are crucially important at some times may be a hindrance at others.

1. *Business firms.* Most innovations in economically advanced, market economies are developed by business firms, and so this is our first category of institution in the NIS. Table 2.6 gave the OECD's comparative figures for the gross domestic expenditure on R&D, classified according to the source of funds for six of the most economically advanced countries, the USA, Japan, Germany, France, the UK, and Italy, while Table 2.2 gave the expenditure on R&D in the same countries by sector of performance, and Chapter 2 discusses these figures in more detail.

It will be recalled that there are significant differences even among these six most advanced countries. Industry contributes around two-thirds to three-quarters of the funds spent on scientific and technological research in Germany, the USA, and Japan, while it is only about half in France and the UK and less than that in Italy. Chapter 2 indicates that there has been a growth in the share of funds coming from industry in the UK and especially in France in recent years and that the OECD countries in general have seen a reduction in the share of research funds coming from government, which in many of these countries has been accompanied by a corresponding growth in the share coming from industry (often an explicit policy objective). As Chapter 2 noted, Britain has been an exception to this trend with most of the percentage reduction in government share as a result of cutbacks in state funding not having been made up by industry, but by the category 'other sources'. The category 'other sources' consists mainly of charitable organizations like the Wellcome Trust and Cancer Research UK[5] while the share of R&D funds from such 'other sources' is an order of magnitude greater in the UK (23.6 per cent) than in Germany (2.5 per cent), for example, and more than twice that in any of the other countries in the table.

Table 2.2 showed that the majority of scientific and technological research carried out in the advanced countries is done by industry with the implication that the strategies of business firms towards science and technology not only have an important impact on the firms themselves, but on the rate and direction of technological change in the nation as a whole.

There are a number of important factors to be considered in assessing the role of firms in the NIS, including their internal organization and the way in which R&D fits into the structure of the firm. One of the major trends of the twentieth century was a shift in the centre of gravity of the R&D function into the business units from, for example, centralized research centres in order to encourage increased responsiveness to the needs of customers and feedback from the market (Coombs and Richards 1993). In an earlier period, Freeman and Soete (1997) argued that the in-house R&D laboratory was one of the most important organizational innovations in the take-off of the German and US innovation systems at the end of nineteenth century. Elsewhere, Freeman (1987) writes about the way in which 'using the factory as a laboratory' and reverse engineering of imported technology in Japan encouraged a process of learning-by-doing how to innovate as discussed in Chapter 4, which was a key feature of that country's success in opening up a technological and economic gap with the rest of the world after Second World War, and that of newly industrializing countries more recently.

Both successful aspects of the infrastructure for innovation at different times and in different countries, the in-house R&D lab and using the factory as a laboratory represent two opposite trends: the first separates the research activity from other functions in the firm, while the second reintegrates them. This illustrates the point above that a certain feature at different times may be a facilitator or an inhibitor of innovative success. The company laboratory gave firms increased control over the rate and direction of technical change, reducing some of its risks. It allowed firms to make links more easily with other institutions producing and developing science and technology, to appropriate new areas of knowledge, to revolutionize the way they competed and changed their technological bases, and it increased the firm-specific and cumulative nature of technology (Coombs et al. 1987). The disadvantage of the in-house laboratory was the separation of the R&D staff from the rest of the firm, emphasizing their differences in culture and orientation, and representing the potential for conflict (rather than complementarity) in the goals and aims of different staff in the firm. In post-Second World War Japan, a key feature of lean production and design was that the work of the R&D department was very closely related to and sometimes almost indistinguishable from the work of production and process engineers, which meant that the whole enterprise was closely involved in the learning and development process and many ideas for improvement came from the shop floor. The result was a huge reduction in lead times (Womack et al. 1990; Freeman and Soete 1997). Similarly, as argued in Chapter 4, instead of stand alone R&D labs, Intel in the USA today carries out development research through integrated teams in the manufacturing facility through the construction of full-scale experimentation plants and in collaboration with universities.

Table 2.9 showed that a very small proportion of the total number of industrial sectors do the majority of the industrial R&D in any country. The most research intensive sectors are pharmaceuticals, aerospace, electronics, scientific instruments, computers, and (certain) services. Chapter 7 discusses sectoral differences and patterns of inventive and innovative activity. There is often more difference in research intensity between sectors than firms (at least of a similar size) within a sector. R&D intensity clearly varies enormously between high- and low-technology industries, and in the most technologically advanced industries the level of R&D spending necessary to compete, and its cumulative effect, can represent a barrier to new entrants.

There are also strong national differences in the research intensity of the high-tech sectors, as we discussed in Chapter 2. The individual manufacturing sector with the largest share of national business enterprise R&D spending is pharmaceuticals in the UK, services in the USA and Italy, and electronics in the other countries in the table. Germany has a strong pharmaceutical sector: the lower percentage of R&D in pharmaceuticals in Germany reflects the strengths of other sectors in Germany and relative weaknesses of other sectors in the UK. Aerospace has a very small share in Japan. 'Other' accounts for more than half the total only in Japan and Germany, where various sectors based on engineering are particularly strong and innovative. Certain relatively strong and innovative service sectors in Italy, the UK, and the USA are reflected in the share of over 20 per cent going to services in those countries. The share of R&D funding going to basic research also differs from country to country. Rosenberg (1990) discusses reasons why firms pay for basic research, although this has become conventionally an area of public expenditure. Again there are significant differences between countries as well as sectors in the share of R&D spending that goes on basic research.

Another feature of national differences at the level of the business firm is in the balance between small and large firms in the economy. Rothwell (1989) describes small firms as having behavioural advantages (creativity, flexibility, propensity to take risks, and good internal communications) while large firms have resource advantages (finance for investment, range of staff with different skills and experience, size of R&D, and range of products). They can play a complementary role in innovative activity, and alliances between large and small firms can be the key to the take-off of new industrial activities, as exemplified by the alliances in biotechnology between large established firms in pharmaceuticals or agrofood and small specialist firms in genetic engineering, bioinformatics, and other emerging technologies.

Interfirm and interorganizational relationships, the network firm, or 'alliance capitalism' (Dunning 1997), including those linkages which cross national borders, are discussed more fully in Chapter 9. Suffice it to say here that this is another aspect of the important role of the business firm in the NIS. Indeed, Freeman's definition of the NIS (see earlier in this chapter) emphasizes the importance of linkages between institutions as much as the institutions themselves.

The techno-economic paradigms mentioned earlier indicate that the take-off of innovations with the most potential to power an economic upswing are those in infrastructural sectors, such as transport, communications, energy, or materials. Innovations not only have an economic effect, if successful, on the innovating organization itself, and the sector in which it emerges and which grows as a consequence. They can also have an impact on any other sectors which adopt them and thereby improve their efficiency. The innovations with the most power to have this kind of impact are those in infrastructural areas which can sometimes increase the efficiency of most of the industries and firms in an economy.

At various times, key features of the NIS have been the organization of production, such as Fordism in the USA or Toyotism also known as the Japanese Management System in Japan (Womack et al. 1990). This is discussed further in Chapters 3 and 4. Firm-based training systems are an asset of the business firm which is also a feature of the NIS; one of the features of the Japanese Management System is the in-firm training which produces manual workers with a level of skill that enables them to mend faults in the production line and carry out quality control; and which provides polyvalent staff with a background in the various functions of the firm rather than a specialism in just one. This was another key factor in Japanese flexible specialization (Womack et al. 1990). We now turn to the question of education and training more generally.

2. *Educational institutions.* These include institutions for higher education, vocational training, and general education. The ability to learn, adapt to new situations, to adapt and not just adopt, to be flexible in the face of new opportunities, and to continue to learn-by-doing, in short the capacity to be innovative, depends crucially on the level and quality of education of the workforce. Freeman (1989) argues that the two most important institutional innovations of the turn of the century in the take-off of the US and German NISs, were the in-house R&D laboratory, already discussed, and technological universities such as the German Technische Hochschulen and the US Institutes of Technology. When Germany overtook Britain in innovation and production of dyes and subsequently other chemicals, there were nearly ten times as many students studying science and technology at German as at British universities (Beer 1959). Many of these scientists and engineers went on to become managers in German industry, while management in the UK continued for decades to be carried out to a much larger degree either by practical entrepreneurs without specific training or by those with a classical education (see Chapter 3).

There are big differences between countries in the sums invested in education, the investment in skilled workers, and the number of students enrolled on science and engineering courses (see Table 6.2). Lundvall's work emphasizes learning as the essential feature of a successful NIS (Lundvall 1992).

Table 6.2 Education indicators

Country	Percentage of the population of 25–34-year olds who have attained tertiary education, 2001			Expenditure per student in public and private institutions of higher education (current US$, converted using purchasing power parities)	
	Men	Women	Total	1995	1998
Canada	45	56	51	11.5	14.6
France	32	37	34	6.6	7.2
Germany	23	20	22	8.9	9.5
Italy	10	13	12	5.0	6.3
Japan	46	49	48	8.8	9.9
UK	30	29	29	7.2	9.7
USA	36	42	39	16.3	19.8

Source: OECD (2003b).

The specialization of firms in a national economy is the result of an accumulation of competencies, which reflects to a large extent aspects of the public infrastructure of education, such as the subjects that are given more or less emphasis; the focus on craft or vocational training relative to academic education; and the relative status of science and engineering, and also management, as desirable courses. The status of the resulting professions also reflects the status of these subjects in the education system. For years the decline of Britain relative to countries such as the USA, Germany, and Japan has been related to the poor status of engineering as a profession and as a subject for study.[6] In both the USA and the UK the best medical and management schools are very difficult to get into; but while the US engineering schools are also in this category, it is still the case that engineering is a subject in UK universities with relatively low entry requirements. In France the engineering schools are among the country's most elite institutions, requiring extra years of study after the school leaving exams at age 18 to pass the national competitive examination for the limited places in top schools with names such as the Polytechnic, the School of Mining, the School of Bridges and Highways, which in the UK would (from the names alone) be seen as second rate. In Japan and Germany engineering is equally highly regarded. The education system also reproduces social norms and values, which together with the degree of egalitarianism or elitism in the system affects the capacity of the whole workforce to contribute to innovation.

3. *Public sector research establishments.* Public research establishments, which also offer related postgraduate training in research, differ among countries. In most countries some research is carried out in universities, but in some countries there are also important organizations, both independent and government non-profit making bodies, which receive public funding for research and may receive private funding too. The balance between the higher education sector and public research establishments such as these, as centres for research, varies greatly among countries. Examples of

non-university public sector and independent non-profit research organizations include in France the National Centre for Scientific Research (CNRS), the National Institute for Health and Medical Research (INSERM) and the National Institute for Agrofood Research (INRA); in Italy the National Centre for Research (CNR); in Germany the Max Planck Instioues and Fraunhofer Institutes; in the Netherlands the TNO; and in Spain the National Council for Scientific Research (CSIC). The relatively high percentage of research carried out in government institutions in France and Italy, shown in Table 2.2, reflects the importance of such organizations in public sector research in those countries, even though CNRS research in France is classified under the heading 'academic' research (OECD 2003a).

In some countries, therefore, public sector researchers are civil servants with job security, while in others they are not employed directly by government agencies but by independent universities and receive short-term contracts from government agencies (such as the UK research councils or the US National Science Foundation and National Institutes of Health). It might be argued that job security discourages entrepreneurial activity, for example in commercializing the discoveries made in public sector research, and especially in setting up new firms. Good linkages between public research and industry, or between public research and education, may equally be affected by the institutional arrangements for employment of researchers in the public sector. There are certainly national differences in the type and closeness of linkages between public sector research and industry, and in the propensity of researchers to establish new firms to commercialize their discoveries. These are, however, influenced by diverse factors, including intellectual property arrangements and the general cultural environment, both of which are issues to which we will return. Several countries have introduced policy initiatives designed to increase the cooperation between public sector research and industry, and the commercialization of the output of public research, which we discuss in the following section.

4. *Public policy.* Government bodies at local, regional, and national levels have adopted policies to promote and regulate technological change. There are also a growing number of supranational organizations which may also influence innovativeness, from the EU with a parliament and law-making apparatus, to common market agreements such as Mercosur in Latin America and NAFTA in North America.

First of all, a government can be the single most important user of innovations in its country. Procurement policies can decisively affect the rate and direction of technological change, as was the case with the US Department of Defense contracts, which were significant in the take-off of the early US microelectronics/computer industry, which subsequently adopted innovations to civilian applications (Langlois and Mowery 1986). This was discussed in Chapter 2. The welfare state established after the Second World War, with state-funded medical care, provided a growing and reliable level of market demand for the products of the pharmaceutical industry in Europe.

Governments also provide direct support for science and technology, education, and R&D. US government support for basic research related to health via the NIH has been at least double that in Europe, Japan, and Canada combined, whether in absolute terms or as a percentage of the population or GDP. The level of spending on the life sciences was particularly high in the wake of President Nixon's declaration of 'war on cancer' in 1971 (see Chapter 2). The resulting breakthroughs in molecular biology represented an important basis on which the wave of biotechnology firms was created, typically by public sector researchers seeking to commercialize their research output.

Other ways in which public policy affects the NIS include governments' provision of tax and other incentives to firms to invest in R&D, to invest in certain regions, and to encourage certain industries. Governments provide support for the establishment of new, high technology small firm formation via a variety of policies, and by the establishment of Science Parks and Technopoles. Government funding can act as a trigger for private funds, a point to which we return in the next section (Mustar 1993). Policies have been established to encourage transfer of technology from academia/public sector research to industry, as discussed in the last section and again in section 6.

Governments encourage cooperative alliances between firms and other firms or other establishments, as a result of which firms pool resources, take advantage of each others' complementary skills and assets, and reduce the costs and risks of innovation. Policy initiatives have been taken in many countries to encourage closer links between public sector research and industry. For example, in France the Loi de Programmation et d'Orientation 1982 was intended to increase the interaction between CNRS and industry, encourage the commercialization of public sector research, and promote the establishment of new high-tech firms (Mustar 1993). Britain has also introduced a series of policy initiatives designed to encourage the linkages between public research and industry, including the establishment of small firms (Dodgson and Rothwell 1988; Walsh et al. 1995; Storey and Tether 1998; Walsh 1998). The US Federal Transfer of Technology Act 1986, with a similar goal, will be discussed in section 6. Networks and alliances are also the subject of Chapter 9.

Regulations and standards influence the rate and direction of innovation. Broader policy shifts may also shape technological change, for example, the post-Cold War defence conversion, and the application of military technology to civilian uses (see Chapter 2). In some countries and at certain periods of history, industries and firms have been publicly owned in capitalist, market economies, and therefore subject to government policy rather more directly. Emerging countries, such as China, are particularly affected by public policy in the form of nationalized or recently privatized industry and the involvement of public institutions and government agencies directly in business. The latter has been an important part of the approach to market reform in China in particular, while the private sector was still quite small, but the sector of 'quasi-public' firms affiliated with government agencies and institutions has been very important: military-owned companies trade in a broad range of economic sectors, including transport, shipping, pharmaceutical production, vehicle production, electronics, satellites, and telecommunications. Examples are the China Xinxing Corporation and the 999 Enterprises Group operated by the General Logistics Department of the People's Liberation Army.

As argued in Chapter 4, in Japan, government agencies such as the Ministry of International Trade and Industry played an important role in that country's NIS and in its post-Second World War recovery and growth, initially by using its control of quotas of foreign exchange and raw material imports to promote industrial and technological development in areas considered strategically important for future industrial and economic growth. Subsequently, it influenced firms via the collection and diffusion of information, for example on overseas markets and technological developments (Odagiri and Goto 1993), and by the organization of meetings between experts in government, industry, and academia to develop a consensus about appropriate industrial goals. Japanese technology policy is based on the government's close cooperation with industry and its reliance on the private sector to achieve those goals collectively decided to be important (Vittas and Kawaura 1995): at one and the same time an active interventionist approach and an indirect one, that is one which relies relatively little on direct subsidies or funding for industry.

5. *Financial institutions.* Financial institutions can play a crucial enabling role in the innovative process, and affect how firms survive, grow, organize, and form networks. Zysman (1983) introduced a typology of capital- and credit-based capitalisms which indicates that one of the most significant differences[7] between advanced capitalist nations in the period from 1945 to the present has been the sources of investment funds for industry (Albert 1991; Amable et al. 1997; Rhodes and Apeldoorn 1998; Maclean 1999; Coates 2000; Boyer 2005). Thus the French and German stock exchanges have played a far less significant role in those countries than the City of London or Wall Street in the UK and USA. The French and German system has worked more on credit than capital, and firms have been more likely to raise money by medium- and long-term bank loans rather than by floatation of shares or bonds raised on capital markets. In France the state mediated in the allocation of loans: indeed France was said to have a system of 'capitalism without capital' (Bauer 1988).[8]

There are also differences between the French and German systems. For example, in France the state mediated in the allocation of loans, and indeed the major banks and insurance companies were nationalized for a large part of the post-Second World War period. In Germany banks loaned to firms directly and were involved in corporate governance of those firms and, starting in the late 1950s, workers' representatives were also involved in corporate governance. However, from the point of view of support for innovation, in both cases the financial systems encouraged *long-termism*—support for strategies of growth and investment in science and technology, which cannot be achieved in the short term. In the USA and UK, on the other hand, with a greater degree of share trading, there is increasing pressure from shareholders for short-term returns, or shares will be sold. O'Sullivan (1998) argues that shareholders, especially portfolio investors, of all stakeholders in the modern industrial corporation are the ones with least stake in the particular company as an ongoing entity, the least likely to support long term and risky investment that is necessary for innovation and learning.

Japan has had a different financial system from those of France or Germany, but again one which has supported long-termism. Tylecote and Demirag (1992) have compared Germany and Japan with the UK in relation to short versus long-termism. Post-war growth in Japan was supported by a financial structure in which risk was bank-based rather than market-based. A report on the Japanese financial sector by the World Bank (Vittas and Kawaura 1995) indicated that one of the key features was the main bank system and the keiretsu groups (networks of manufacturing, trading, banks, and supplier firms, discussed in Chapter 4). A main bank would normally be a member of a keiretsu, the largest lender, one of the largest shareholders, and would take the lead in organizing loan syndications. It would monitor the performance of the borrower firm on behalf of the other lenders and would work out a rescue plan if a member of the group was in difficulty. Consequently, the relationship between banks and industry was close. Investment tended to be concentrated towards industrial firms rather than other economic sectors. The keiretsu acted as intermediaries in channeling funds towards small firms at their periphery. Different roles were played by debt and equity, compared for example to the US system. Securities markets and institutional investment were underdeveloped compared to the US system. Interest rates were low—artificially low according to many commentators. The main bank system was consistent with government policy for the role of the financial system in promoting industrialization and growth, and various government measures supported the emergence of the main bank system, even if it was not deliberately created by the state. For example, in the early 1950s banks were allowed to own up to 10 per cent of the equity of a firm, as a means of preventing foreign ownership of Japanese firms.

Globalization, deregulation of finance markets, and shortages of public funds for investment have been making inroads into the differences in the various financial systems, and the Anglo-Saxon or market-based system is becoming more dominant, with a significant increase in shareholding in the more capital-oriented countries. In France, for example, an article in *Le Monde* (*Le Monde*, 16 March 1999) argued that by 1999 France had become one of the countries most open to foreign investment in the world, with 35 per cent of capital in the hands of foreign investors. The Japanese financial system also appears to be in a period of transition, with a shift in focus from the banking sector to the stock market, although according to the CEO of a Japanese securities firm, the change was evidently taking place more slowly than he would like.[9] Meanwhile, recent trends in the USA are that shareholders' organizations intervene increasingly in the decision-making process of firms, requiring strategic information in a highly standardized form, including progress and evaluation of ongoing R&D projects, on a month to month and even week to week basis. Staff in the HQs of Pension and Mutual funds are in regular contact with the firms in which their funds are invested, asking for such information in as much detail as possible. The pressure on short-term performance creates a very unstable environment for firms (Chesnais 1997; Chesnais and Serfati 2000).

The market-based financial system also means that successful small firms may be quickly bought up (Walker 1993), often by overseas firms, while other small firms with long-term potential cannot get financial support. Small firms may be able to secure financial stability and access to markets by means of collaboration with a larger firm, but relations between the large and the small firm may be very unequal in favour of the larger one, the larger firm may also be in another country, and collaboration may prove to be a precursor to acquisition.

Another aspect of the finance system of particular importance to innovation is the availability of venture capital, which is the main source of funding for new technology-based businesses (in the creation of start-ups and support for their ongoing viability) in most OECD countries, especially in the USA (Mulder 1991; *OECD Observer*, 17 December 1999), but is very underdeveloped in Japan. The USA is generally held to have the most readily available sources of venture capital for the establishment of new firms, and this was an important factor in the commercialization of innovations in microelectronics, computer-aided design (CAD), and biotechnology (Florida and Kenney 1988). The US Venture Capitalist organization typically has a hands-on-role, nominating directors with otherwise missing skills (e.g. in finance, marketing). Most of the US venture capital funds go into investment in the expansion stage, although funding of seed capital is over a third of the total (*OECD Observer*, 17 December 1999). European venture capital markets have grown quite fast since the early 1980s and the venture-capital-funded boom in biotechnology start-ups in the USA. The total EU venture-capital market was half that of the USA in 1997 (*OECD Observer*, 17 December 1999), a total which had doubled in three years (Rausch 1998). The UK has the largest European venture capital market in terms of amount invested and number of investments made, but only a small proportion of that is seed funding or start-up capital. Venture capital is not used uniquely to fund high-tech start-ups—firms attracting venture capital in Europe tend to be less research intensive than those in the USA. More than 30 per cent of European venture capital in 1995 and 1996 went to machine tools, pollution control and recycling equipment, and high-fashion clothing and other consumer products (*OECD Observer*, 17 December 1999). In 1997 only a quarter of European venture capital funds went to firms in information technology, communications, health and biotechnology, compared with 78 per cent in the USA.

Canada has the largest venture capital market relative the size of its GDP. After the UK the largest venture capital markets in Europe are France, Germany, and the Netherlands. Typically venture capital companies in Europe focus on later-stage investments, such as management buy-outs, which come to fruition over a shorter time period; and they rarely became involved in the management of the company receiving funds, in contrast to US venture capital organizations (Wilson 1992, 1995; *OECD Observer*, 17 December 1999).

An article in the *OECD Observer* in 1998 (O'Shea and Stevens 1998) stated that OECD governments were acting as venture capitalists by providing funding to small high-risk firms with the aim of stimulating innovation and increasing employment, to fill the gaps left by the private sector (see also last section). A variety of schemes exist among OECD governments, see Table 6.3. The general aim is that government schemes should leverage private funds, for example by matching the funds invested by the public sector. One

Table 6.3 Typology of government venture capital programmes

Type	Purpose	Example
Direct supply of capital		
Government equity investment	To make direct investments in venture-capital firms or small firms	Belgium—investment company for Flanders (GIMV)
Government loans	To make low-interest long-term and/or non-refundable loans to venture-capital firms or small firms	Denmark—VækstFonden (business development finance) loan programme
Financial incentives		
Loan guarantees	To guarantee a proportion of institutional loans to qualified small businesses	France—Sociètè Française de Garantie des Financements des Petites et Moyennes Entreprises (SOFARIS)
Equity guarantees	To guarantee a proportion of the losses of high-risk venture-capital investments	Finland—Finnish guarantee board
Tax incentives	To provide tax incentives, particularly tax credits, to those investing in small firms or venture-capital funds	The UK—enterprise investment scheme and venture capital trust scheme
Investor regulations		
	To allow institutions such as pension funds or insurance companies to invest in venture capital	The USA—modifications of employment retirement income security Act

Source: O'Shea and Stevens (1998).

particularly successful scheme in this respect was Yozma in Israel (Avnimelech and Teubal 2003). Mustar (1993) reports that government funds and under-wiriting of new firms acted as a 'trigger' to encourage private funds in France while Germany's biotechnology sector has recently emerged on the basis of funding by the venture capital industry stimulated by government (Broetz 2001). Large established firms may supply finance to small ones on the basis of an alliance in which knowledge and the rights to use technology are acquired in exchange (Walsh et al. 1995).

Perez (2002) examines the interaction between financial capital and the upsurge and subsequent life cycles of new technologies. As a way of ordering and examining the historical processes at work, she characterizes the following phases. The early upsurge of new technology is a period of explosive growth, but also turbulence and uncertainty in the economy. Venture capitalists rush to invest but many early expectations are disappointed and the bubbles created by financial speculation or technological euphoria burst. The explosive upsurge of new industries and firms occurs in a context in which the well-established institutions are still dominant, and this stimulates a phase of structural adjustment. Financial capital encourages investment in the new industries so intensely that they grow and strengthen and generate the need for a new regime of regulation. Political and social change accumulates, the new technology becomes accepted as the new common sense, and a period of more harmonious growth follows, in which there is a good match between technology and the institutional framework. High levels of employment make this phase seem to be a 'golden age' or 'belle époque'. Maturity follows with diminishing returns to the technologies that are now older and more mature. Eventually, attention is switched to a new generation of radical innovations with more potential.

6. *Legal institutions.* One of the most important legal institutions affecting innovation is the intellectual property rights (IPR) system, which includes patents, trademarks and copyrights, and allows inventors and entrepreneurs to make money from the implementation of their scientific and technological knowledge as goods and services, while enabling the knowledge to be available to subsequent inventors who are then able to build upon it. The aim is to achieve the optimum balance between encouraging the inventor to invent (which means strong protection, broad patents, and a long period of protection) and encouraging the maximum diffusion of knowledge and encouragement to subsequent inventors (which means weaker protection of original invention, narrow patents, licensing, and a shorter period of protection) (Merges and Nelson 1994; Foray 1995; Mazzoleni and Nelson 1998; and, referring specifically to changes in US law, Eisenberg 1996). From an economic point of view the purpose of the monopoly is to give enough scope and duration to protect the inventor and thus encourage innovation, but not so much that it causes economic inefficiency (Mazzoleni and Nelson 1998).

Patenting the output of public sector research, while justified by policymakers as a means of encouraging the commercialization and hence adoption into practice of discoveries funded by the government, has a number of disadvantages (see Eisenberg 1996; Mazzoleni and Nelson 1998). These are that the public pays twice for the same invention; private appropriation of publicly sponsored research calls into question the rationale for the state to fund it in the first place; and restriction of access to discoveries made in basic science is to the detriment of both public and private sectors. Coombe (1998: 7) criticizes intellectual property regimes as incentive structures aimed at producing a socially optimal supply of intellectual creations, without considering what is owned or how rights of possession are exercised. The legal focus is on those who own the intellectual property, without regard to the contributions or interests of others in whose lives it figures (Coombe 1998: 8).

Foray discusses the differences between IPR regimes in different national innovation systems from this point of view, underlining the differences particularly between the US and French systems on the one hand and the Japanese system on the other, as intellectual property regimes which respectively encourage radical inventions relative to incremental ones, and vice versa (Foray 1995). The Japanese IPRs system encourages reverse engineering and modifications rather than radical innovations, compared to both France and the USA. The latter two countries achieve a greater emphasis on radical innovations but in different ways, France relying more on the administrative powers of the state and the USA on the legal system and the right to sue for infringement.

A great many countries have made attempts of various kinds to increase the implementation, which usually means the commercial exploitation, of research funded by the government (see also sections 3 and 4). Some of these approaches have involved the IPR system. Thus, in the USA the Bayh-Dole and Stevenson-Wydler Acts of 1980 encouraged public sector researchers and small firms (later any size firms) to take out patents on discoveries made with government finance. The Federal Transfer of Technology Act (1986) was another intellectual property based approach to the encouragement of the commercialization of public sector research, especially in areas sponsored (heavily) by the Department of Defence and the NIH. Under this act, CRADAs are a mechanism whereby the state agency and the firm enter into a partnership to exploit the research output. One of the goals of the CRADA is to stimulate commercialization by private firms of investions which may not have been patented, by providing for exclusive use in some other way; another goal is to encourage US and not foreign industry to profit from discoveries funded by the US government (Eisenberg 1996 and personal communication). However, concern about the benefit to the public if a multinational gets a monopoly has been expressed in a series of Congressional Hearings (Walsh and Goodman 1999).

In the recent past, debates about whether patenting living things should be allowed have had an important impact on biotechnology (and hence the pharmaceutical, food, and other sectors which use it) and the possibility of commercial exploitation of genetically modified organisms (GMOs). In fact the concept of what may be considered to be property is not static, but has evolved considerably over the past century and especially rapidly over the past thirty to forty years. Early in the twentieth century patent laws were changed to permit the patenting of novel chemicals, where before only the processes by which they might be obtained could be patented. In 1970 in the USA the Plant Variety Protection Act was introduced to give patent-like protection to the developers of novel, sexually reproduced plants. Internationally, plant breeders' rights were established under the Union for the Protection of New Varieties of Plants (UPOV) Convention of 1961. In 1980 the Chakrabarty vs. Diamond decision in the US Supreme Court permitted an oil-degrading genetically engineered microorganism to be patented, which opened the door to patenting of GMOs more generally (Kloppenberg 1988: 131, 261). In 1987, the USPTO issued a statement to the effect that it 'now considers non-naturally occurring, non-human, multicellular living organisms, including animals, to be patentable subject matter'. In 1988 a patent was allowed on the 'oncomouse', a mouse which had been genetically engineered for a predisposition to develop cancer, and by 1999 over 200 patents in the 'plant biotechnology' category had been granted by the USPTO (Nuffield Council on Bioethics 1999).

However, European developments have been slower: Article 53b of the European Patent Convention stated that patents should not be granted in respect of plant or animal varieties, or essentially biological processes for the production of plants or animals, and plant varieties were only protected under the UPOV Convention. The 1999 judgement in a test case appealed by Novartis was that plants were *not* excluded from patentability (Roberts 2000), and the European Patent Office has now granted several patents on seeds and plant varieties, although the patent convention itself has not been changed. Opponents of 'patents on life' such as Greenpeace continue to campaign for member states to stop the practice (Greenpeace 2000).

To be granted a patent, an invention must be novel (and non-obvious), useful (or industrially applicable), and the result of human labour or human ingenuity. That means that, in principle, chemical substances which occur naturally are not patentable, since they are not made by human labour but by (say) a plant. A genetic sequence is not, in and of itself, useful—it is only useful when used for example together with other data to preduct a predisposition to an inherited disease. However, what patent offices allow to be patented has changed by custom and practice and not necessarily explicitly by changes in the law, which is likely to open the way to a large rise in the number of challenges in the courts in the view of the Nuffield Council on Bioethics

(1999). The distinction between nature and human labour has been continually re-negotiated so that what was once natural and therefore unpatentable has since become patentable, even though the novelty or human ingenuity involved may simply be purification or isolation from a plant or animal raw material (Hayden 1998). DNA and other biological molecules are treated like other chemical molecules for the purpose of patenting. In the area of human reproductive technology, stored embryos have been ruled to be 'neither property nor people'[10] (Strathern 1996; Rabinow 1992).

Trademark law has also changed its focus over the course of the twentieth century. The initial rationale of the trademark, to prevent consumer confusion and protect the public, has given way to a focus on the commodity value of design associated with particular brands and the protection of the owner of the trademark. Indeed, Coombe suggests that nowadays 'protecting consumers from confusion has become a ruse by which corporations protect themselves from competition' (Coombe 1998: 60, 64–6). Trademark law was used for example in the appropriation of the unpatented natural product anti-cancer drug, Taxol, by giving the manufacturer ownership over the name Taxol®, even though it had been introduced into the literature some twenty years earlier by a chemist in the public sector and widely used since (Goodman and Walsh 2001). Cassier (2002) has surveyed the expansion in methods of appropriation used to protect knowledge or resources which were once non-patentable, such as collections of genealogical or medical data used as resources in identification of genes, or used as intermediate research data for locating and characterizing them (e.g. Myriad Genetics' collection of data on the population of Utah and DeCode Genetics' collection of data on the population of Iceland, Pálsson and Hardardóttir [2001]). Such methods of appropriation include exclusive-use contracts, private databases protected by commercial confidentiality (which may or may not be traded), the extension of patentability to include genetic sequences, and government-industry collaboration within the CRADA. The USPTO has come to interpret a gene as equivalent to a chemical formula for a product, invention as human intervention in nature, and utility (of partial sequences) as clues for future discovery (of the whole gene) (Cassier 2002).

As innovation becomes more and more evidently the result of *networks* of inventive and innovative activity (see Chapter 9), where it becomes increasingly difficult to identify one or two individuals who can be named on a patent, either it becomes difficult to invoke the IPR system or the latter is used in a way that fails to reward all the contributors. A slightly different but related case is the *cumulativeness* of inventive and innovative activity, in which subsequent inventors increasingly build on previous inventions. Indeed, Foray suggests that conventional IPR regimes are experiencing a crisis, especially in certain sectors such as biotechnology, software and consumer electronics, because they discourage later inventors or improvers. An appropriate IPR regime, he argues, should take this into account and act as an essential coordinating mechanism for innovation within the market system (Foray 1995). This is an area of the social science literature which economists, sociologists, and anthropologists have all considered from their very different disciplinary perspectives (Strathern 1996; Coombe 1998; Strathern et al. 1998) and which one of us discusses further elsewhere (Walsh 2002; Walsh and Goodman 2002). Writings on biotechnology and IPR by economists of innovation concentrate on ownership by industry or at least ownership within industrial society: cultural property and indigenous knowledge in non-industrial societies and communities are outside their scope. But human genetic diversity and biodiversity among plant and animal species, the use of human tissue for therapeutic and diagnostic purposes, the propagation of plant species by cell culture, and the genetic modification of plants to enable cultivation in previously hostile climates, have all raised concerns about appropriation of indigenous and traditional knowledge,[11] which will increasingly impact on the industrial societies which use them.

Following the WTO agreement on Trade Related Aspects of Intellectual Property Rights in 2000 (see Chapter 8), many countries, which are poor in conventional terms but rich in biological and cultural resources, have faced international pressure to introduce intellectual property legislation to protect outside investment, and national pressure to protect local resources. For example, a model law for the Pacific region is in the process of being drafted by WIPO/UNESCO.[12] Firms in Western, industrialized countries will experience the impact of these changes if they have not already modified their practices, while Western biologists seeking to conduct research (especially botanical expeditions) in less developed countries are already having to respond to demands for the compensation of traditional communities for use of their knowledge.[13]

Another area in which the legal system is an important institution in the NIS is in determining the nature of contracts between firms, which can affect their innovative capacity. Anti-trust law in the USA was modified in the early 1980s to permit interfirm cooperation. Legal partnership was important in the take-off of the UK NIS during the Industrial Revolution. Limited liability companies and the encouragement of risk-taking were important in the take-off of the US NIS.

Environmental and product safety regulations affect innovation by requiring a certain level of funding for compliance (e.g. toxicity testing of drugs), which might otherwise be spent discovering new products. On the other hand, regulations also stimulate innovation in greener products and processes, measuring equipment and safer products, and in ways of conserving resources and energy, or recycling materials.

7. *Trade unions and political organizations.* Trade unions and political organizations may try to achieve changes in policy, or promote or oppose technological change more directly. Trade unions may protest about technological change that threatens jobs security or health, and campaign for changes that protect their interests, or to make sure the benefit of the technological change is felt by the workforce and/or the population at large and not just shareholders.

In Germany the relative success of the greens and environmentalists in the 1980s had an important effect on regulations about pollution. There is much lower spending on nuclear research in Germany than France, as a result of green campaigns in the former, and while France has the overwhelming majority of its electricity generated by nuclear power stations, the proportion in Germany is small and not increasing. The ethics of biotechnology were also widely discussed in the public arena, and some of the work done by German companies was outside Germany.[14] Indeed, it is relatively recently that German government agencies have adopted policies aimed at encouraging biotechnology start-up firms.

8. *Ethos, culture, and attitude towards entrepreneurship and risk taking.* The culture of a society as far as it affects entrepreneurship, risk taking, money making, or inventiveness is not really an institution, is certainly far from universally felt within a country and has the risk of being seen either as a 'residual' category for explaining developments that are not easily linked to specific other features of the NIS, or indeed of becoming a stereotype. We have included it as we think, nevertheless, it can be a powerful factor in the national innovation system, just as something almost as difficult to pin down, firm culture, can have an important influence on the innovativeness of an individual firm.

It is often said that the USA has a more entrepreneurial culture than Europe, meaning that people are more prepared to take risks, failure is seen as a lesson to be learnt, not a personal fault; it is more likely that researchers will set up their own firms; and there is a very widely held view that anyone can 'make it' if they work hard enough (the 'Log Cabin in White House' philosophy). Similarly there was some discussion in China as it began to embrace market forces as to whether Chinese culture was entrepreneurial. Given years of central planning there was concern in the People's Republic that entrepreneurship was alien: and yet hard work, motivation, and entrepreneurship are widely seen outside China as typical characteristics of Chinese communities abroad.

Of course, it is a moot point as to whether culture or institutions have more influence. Institutions do after all encourage or discourage entrepreneurial behaviour—via readily available venture capital, terms for university staff that encourage part-time work for industry, and in the case of some of the 'emergent' capitalist economies, a legacy of central planning.

Conclusion

This chapter examined the concept of national innovation systems and attempted to illustrate some of the elements that are included in analyses of the NIS. The NIS concept has been used as an heuristic device to offer a framework to understand how national systems of innovation create diversity, reproduce routines, and select certain firms, products, and sectors. National systems differ in terms of specialization both in production and in trade, and in terms of knowledge base. The NIS concept has been useful for policy-makers as it combines a particular view of the economy with a certain flexibility in terms of what parts of the economy should be included in the analysis. This is important, as the components of the economy related to innovation with the most important impact on economic growth and competitiveness differ over tine and space. The literature on NIS also underlines the importance of technology policy for economic growth. In re-evaluating the effectiveness of a NIS, policymakers may well make plans to change some of the institutions that make it up. However, borrowing ideas from other countries is not necessarily efficient. What works elsewhere may not transplant well—institutions need to be appropriate to national history and goals. And changes in one kind of institution are likely to have knock-on effects elsewhere. The connections and linkages between institutions are as important a part of the NIS as the institutions themselves. One of the advantages the Nordic countries have, even though their small size is in some ways a disadvantage, is the connections that exist between individuals in different institutions, and between the institutions themselves (Walsh 1988). Thus relationship between funding and industrial firms; between the education system and industrial firms; between public research and industrial firms; between firms and other firms are all important aspects of the NIS, although we discuss them more fully in Chapter 9 on networks and strategic alliances. An entrepreneurial spirit can pervade the whole NIS; and government policy and legal institutions can encourage or discourage these links.

Perez (1988) argues that 'catching up' may not be so much about overtaking the leading countries, as running in a new direction altogether. Thus Germany and the USA did not overtake Britain in the sense of running faster along a fixed trajectory, but in adopting the organizational and managerial innovations that enabled them to make the best use of new technologies and new industries, notably steel, electrification and chemicals, and enabled those industries to fuel an economic upswing more efficiently than was the case in Britain. In re-thinking the national innovation system today, identifying the opportunities for 'running in a new direction altogether' is an attractive proposition, especially when combined with the adoption of some of the best practices that might be observed elsewhere, while carefully considering how they fit with the country's national history and chosen goals, and taking into account which national features and characteristics might best be exploited to give the country a unique competitive position in the world.

The examination of NIS is all the more important as globalization becomes a major theme (Chapter 10). To cope with the problems connected with globalization, the EU and other trading blocks call for an understanding of the historical role and characteristics of national systems.

Notes

1 The word 'system' is also used, in a different context (e.g. in systems theory), to refer to something formalized, abstracted, and controllable. Consequently, some authors have sought different terms, for example 'styles' of innovation, to avoid this implication, though this term, too is not unproblematic. See Green et al. (1998) and the collection of papers in the same issue.

2 A quite different illustration of the importance of the NIS is given by Joseph Needham's major work *Science and Civilization in China* published by Cambridge University Press in seven volumes, several of which have three parts, over the period 1954–2004. This work shows that Chinese science and technology were far in advance of those in the West in the era before capitalism took off in the latter countries, but that economic development was held back because at that time the new capitalist system in the West (and one might say the then-NIS) was more efficient than the feudal-type system then in place in China.

3 The USA was dependent on imported Sheffield steel in the first half of the nineteenth century; when Carnegie built his first Bessemer plant for steel rails in 1875 it was on the basis of technology he had observed during a visit to Britain. Similarly, Faraday (in Britain) established the principle of the electric motor in the 1820s, and announced the discovery of electromagnetic induction in 1831 (Freeman and Soete 1997, Chapter 3).

4 Which promoted the idea of Japan's adopting and then developing the latest technology in world terms rather than having a strategy of exploiting its 'comparative advantages' in traditional industries with large numbers of low-paid workers, as conventional economic theory would have suggested.

5 Formed from a merger between the Imperial Cancer Research Fund and the Cancer Research Campaign.

6 See, for example, the Finiston Report *Engineering Our Future* prepared by a government committee chaired by Lord Finniston, and which reported in 1980, HMSO.

7 Other differences include conflictual versus cooperative management of labour markets and industrial relations, and different funding principles and management mechanisms for welfare provision.

8 The French state had a great deal of control over the funds lent to industry via nationalization of main banks and insurance companies after the Second World War, followed by a second wave of nationalization during President Mitterrand's first term of office during 1981–8. These banks started to be privatized in 1988, a process that was still ongoing more than ten years later, for example, Crédit Lyonnais offered shares to account holders in July 2000. The total value of shares held publicly was still small until the mid-1990s; for example, debt was the main form of financing. Even after privatization, core shareholders and key

decision-makers are still chosen by the state as part of its master-minding of a web of cross-ownership of major firms. These shares are not tradable in the same way as shares on the stock exchanges, and the nomination of CEO remains with the state.

9 'Shift to a market-focused financial structure: Japanese economic revival through active market participation of individuals', Noriko Maki (TV Tokyo) interview with Junichi Ujiie (CEO and President of Nomura Holdings), reported on the company's website http://www.nomuraholdings.com/news/group/020929.html 29.09.92, accessed 15.5.03.

10 This was the conclusion of the Tennessee Supreme Court concerning frozen embryos stored in a fertility clinic (Strathern 1996). There has also been debate about whether genetically modified human tissue, for example, for therapeutic purposes should be the property of the original owner of the tissue or the firm that modified it. Paul Rabinow refers to the case of Moore vs Regents of the University of Califonia, the key point of which was the question of whether Moore could claim property rights over tissue taken from his body during an operation and subsequently modified to generate a commercial product. The claim that the resulting product relied on human ingenuity (and was patentable by the modifiers) was upheld, and Moore criticized by the judge for his 'commercial motives' (Rabinow 1992).

11 Strathern (1999), for example, writes about a seminar convened in 1997 in Port Moresby, Papua New Guinea on IPRs in the context of policy discussions over biodiversity protection.

12 This was one of the topics of discussion at the conference Innovation, Creation and New Economic Forum: approaches to intellectual and cultural property, University of Cambridge 13–15 December 2001.

13 Interview with Douglas Daly, Botanist at New York Botanical Gardens, 29.8.96., in the context of a study of Taxol, the anti-cancer drug found in the bark of *Taxus brevifolia*, the Pacific Yew (Goodman and Walsh 2001).

14 Not only because of ethical concern, however, but also to tap into the science and technology infrastructure in other countries more advanced in the technology such as the USA.

7 Sectoral Patterns of Technological Change

Introduction

Two characteristics of innovation suggest it may be useful to attempt to classify sectoral patterns of technical change. First, most of the knowledge applied by firms in innovation is not general-purpose or easily transmitted and reproduced. Knowledge and innovation activities tend to be appropriate for specific applications (differentiated and localized), largely firm-specific and industry-specific, tacit and cumulative in development over time, and appropriable by specific firms (Polanyi 1967; Atkinson and Stiglitz 1969; Nelson and Winter 1977; David 1985; Teece 1986; Arthur 1988; Pavitt 1991).

Second, sectors vary in the relative importance of product and process innovation, and both in the sources of process technology and in the size and patterns of diversification of innovating firms (Pavitt 1984; Dodgson and Rothwell 1994). Pavitt (1984) was the first to point out, however, some regularities. For example, in some categories of sectors (such as textiles or construction), the sources of technology are the suppliers of equipment, while others (such as chemicals) contribute directly to their own process or product technology. Also, while firms in assembly and continuous process industries (such as automobiles and steel) concentrate more on process innovations, those in mechanical and electrical engineering (such as machinery) concentrate on product innovations. In chemicals and related products, there is a spectrum of strategies so that the sectors producing the higher value-added products (such as pharmaceuticals, agrochemicals, food additives and catalysts) are the more likely to focus on product innovation, while producers of bulk commodity chemicals can usually be categorized with continuous process industries.

The 'sectoral systems' literature (Malerba and Orsenigo 1996; Breschi et al. 2000; Malerba 2002) seeks to understand and compare the sources and patterns of technological change in different industries, focusing especially on learning processes and technological opportunities, appropriability conditions, cumulativeness in knowledge, and the relevant knowledge base in an industry. Also, drawing on case studies and surveys, a number of contributions have highlighted the diversity in the sources of innovation in different sectors and the integrated nature of innovation, demonstrating the interdependence of numerous organizations in the innovation process (see the edited collection by Dodgson and Rothwell 1994). That is, there are considerable variations among industrial sectors in the relative contributions of elements of the supply and demand sides. Among others, these include the significance of small and large firms, the inputs of suppliers and users, the importance of collaboration, the role of basic science, and the importance of government procurement.

Contributions to the understanding of particular sectors have led to wider lessons regarding the relation between innovation and the economy. For example, the work by Mowery (1996) on software has identified the importance of defence-related R&D funding and procurement in innovation, the importance of IPRs, and the effect of 'first mover advantages', particularly for the US packaged software industry. Our own work has emphasized the importance of high levels of basic health-related research (on the supply side) in the US pharmaceutical industry, the establishment of publicly funded health care (on the demand side) as a stimulus to the European pharmaceutical industry, and the importance of collaboration with new entrants and of IPRs to both (Walsh et al. 2000; Walsh and Le Roux 2004).

Research on sectors characterized by complex, high-value capital goods produced by firms working together in projects, raises new innovation issues previously unexplored for mass-produced goods. This emerging literature on 'innovation in complex products and systems' (Davies and Brady 2000; Gann and Salter 2000; Hobday 2000; Prencipe 2000) includes the study of telecommunication exchanges, aircraft engine control systems, and 'intelligent buildings'. The authors point to the role of tacit knowledge and other intangible assets in innovation in this sector. And, more importantly, because the span of managerial control may be outside the boundaries of the individual firm, they show that collaboration is an important element of innovation in complex products and systems. Knowledge boundaries may be different from production boundaries defined by make-or-buy decisions, and knowledge and organizational coordination in these complex products and systems demand interactive management, in many cases through 'systems integrator' firms which coordinate the work (R&D, design, and manufacturing) outsourced to suppliers (Brusoni et al. 2001).

This chapter explores the similarities and differences amongst sectors in the sources, nature, and impact of innovation. A first section describes the taxonomy of patterns of technological change developed by Pavitt (1984). A second section presents a taxonomy of patterns of innovation in services. A third section examines innovation in construction. A fourth section is concerned with innovation in pharmaceuticals. A fifth section considers innovation in the agrofood industry. A final section examines innovation in chemicals.

A taxonomy of sectoral patterns of innovation

Drawing on data collected at the Science Policy Research Unit (SPRU, University of Sussex) on 2000 significant innovations and of innovating firms in Britain from 1945 to 1979, Pavitt (1984) suggests a taxonomy of sectoral patterns of innovation (see Box 7.1 for definitions). He argues that the rate and direction of technical change in any sector depends on the sources of technology, the nature of users' needs, the possibility of appropriation by innovators of their activities, the technological trajectories, and the size and diversification of innovating firms.

Pavitt (1984) suggests a taxonomy including three categories (see Table 7.1):

1. *Supplier-dominated firms.* Supplier-dominated firms can be found mainly in traditional sectors of manufacturing such as textiles and housebuilding and in many services (see the next section for a more detailed classification of services). They are generally small and have weak in-house R&D and engineering capabilities. They appropriate less on the basis of a technological advantage than on the basis of professional skills, aesthetic design, trademarks, and advertising. Their technological trajectories involve cutting costs. They make only a minor contribution to their process or product technology. Most innovations come from suppliers of

---

Box 7.1 Key definitions in Pavitt's sectoral taxonomy

Innovation: a new or better product or production process commercialized in the UK, whether first developed in the UK or in any other country.

Nature of the technology produced in the sector: the importance of process and product innovation may vary. Process innovations are defined as innovations that are used in the same sectors as those in which they are produced. Product innovations are defined as innovations that are used in different sectors from those in which they are produced or sold direct to final users.

Sources of technology used in the sector: the technology used in a sector can come from inside firms (R&D labs and production engineering departments) or from outside (suppliers of production equipment and materials, users, and government financed research and advice).

The nature of users' needs: the nature of users' needs vary. For standard structural or mechanical materials, price is of major importance; for machinery and equipment, performance and reliability will be given more importance relative to purchase price. In other cases, safety, quality, ergonomics, standardization may be also important user needs.

Means of appropriation of the benefits of innovation: this refers to how innovators appropriate a sufficient proportion of the benefits of their innovative activities to justify expenditure on them (e.g. secrecy for process innovations, technical lags in imitation for product innovations such as aircraft and, patent protection for pharmaceuticals).

Technological diversification of innovating firms: this can be vertical (as in equipment, materials and components) or concentric (in related and unrelated product markets).

Source: Pavitt (1984).

Table 7.1 Sectoral technological trajectories

Category of firm	Typical core sectors	Determinants of technological trajectories			Technological trajectories		Measured characteristics		
		Sources of technology	Type of user	Means of appropriation		Source of process technology	Relative balance between product and process innovation	Relative size of innovating firms	Intensity and direction of technological diversification
(1)	(2)	(3)	(4)	(5)	(6)	(7)	(8)	(9)	(10)
Supplier dominated	Agriculture; housing; private services traditional manufacture	Suppliers; research extension services; big users	Price sensitive	Non-technical (e.g. trade-marks, marketing, advertising, aesthetic design)	Cost-cutting	Suppliers	Process	Small	Low vertical
Production intensive — Scale intensive	Bulk materials (steel, glass); assembly (consumer durables and autos)	PE suppliers; R&D	Price sensitive	Process secrecy and know-how; technical lags; patents; dynamic learning economies; design know-how	Cost-cutting (product design)	In-house; suppliers	Process	Large	High vertical
Production intensive — Specialized suppliers	Machinery; instruments	Design and development users	Performance sensitive	knowledge of users; patents	Product design	In-house; customers	Product	Small	Low concentric
Science based	Electronics/ electrical; chemicals	R&D public science; PE	Mixed	R&D know-how; patents; process secrecy and know-how; dynamic learning economies	Mixed	In-house; suppliers	Mixed	Large	High concentric

Note: PE = Production engineering department.

Source: Pavitt (1984: 354).

equipment and materials. A relatively high proportion of the process innovations used in the sector are produced by other sectors (e.g. information-intensive design, retailing, marketing, and logistics processes in textiles), even though a relatively high proportion of innovative activities are directed to process innovations (e.g. developments in spinning, weaving, and knitting are all processes to which textile firms pay much attention and that can contribute to faster production and lower employment).

2. *Production-intensive firms.* Production-intensive firms include those producing standard materials and those producing durable consumer goods and vehicles. Technological skills are used to exploit scale economies. Since it is difficult to make scale-intensive processes work up to full capacity, production engineering departments—one important source of process technology in production-intensive firms—identify and solve technical imbalances and bottlenecks. The other important source of process innovations in production-intensive firms is small and specialized firms that supply them with equipment and instrumentation, and with which they have a close relationship. The way in which innovating firms appropriate technological advantage varies considerably between the large-scale producers and the small, specialized firms. For large-scale producers, technological leads are reflected in know-how or secrecy in their capacity to design and operate continuous process or assembly systems, such as the float glass process developed by Pilkington in the late 1950s. Instead, specialized suppliers such as mechanical engineering and specialized industrial machinery, where learning and interaction between users and producers is the most important source of knowledge, concentrate instead on continuous improvements in design, product reliability, and on the ability to respond quickly to users' needs.

3. *Science-based firms.* Science-based firms are found in sectors such as chemicals/pharmaceuticals and electronics. The main source of technology is the R&D activities of firms in the sector, based on the rapid development of the underlying sciences in universities. There are barriers to entry due to the sophistication of the technologies and underlying sciences and dynamic learning economies in production. Firms appropriate technological advantage through a variety of methods (e.g. patents in fine chemicals and natural technical lags in electronic components).

Pavitt (1991) revised this taxonomy and attempted to map the variety in the nature of sources of technology, technological trajectory, and their implications for management (see Table 7.2). In this revised taxonomy, he added an 'information intensive' category, the key strategic opportunity for which (together with production-intensive sectors) is the progressive integration of radical technological advances into products and production systems, and

Table 7.2 Basic technological trajectories

Definition	Source of technology	Trajectory	Typical product groups	Strategic problems for management
Science-based	R & D laboratory	Synergetic new products; applications engineering	Electronics; chemicals	Complementary assets; integration to exploit synergies; patient money
Scale intensive	Production engineering and specialized suppliers	Efficient and complex production and related products	Basic materials; durable consumer goods	Balance and choice in production technology among *appropriation* (secrecy and patients); *vertical disintegration* (co-operation with supplier); and *profit centre* 'Fusion' with fast-moving technologies
Information intensive	Software/systems dept. and specialized suppliers	Efficient (and complex) information processing, and related products	Financial services; retailing	Diffusion of production; technology amongst divisions; exploiting product opportunities; patient money
Specialized suppliers	Small-firm design and large-scale users	Improved specialized producers goods (reliability and performance)	Machinery; instruments; speciality chemicals; software	Matching technological opportunities with user; absorbing user experience; finding stable or new product 'niches'

Source: Pavitt (1991: 44).

in diversification vertically upstream into potentially productive production technologies (e.g. CAD and CAM, robots, and software). The key strategic tasks are ensuring the diffusion of best practice technology within the firm and choices about the degree of internalization of production technology.

Thus, Pavitt shows that firms have constraints on choices regarding process or product innovation and the breadth or specialization of their production. This is because of the requirements of the particular technologies in each sector. As argued by Pavitt (1991: 43)

the patterns of innovative activities described above can be seen as the result of cumulative and differentiated diffusion amongst firms of four pervasive technological systems, each with its distinctive skills and sources of technological competence: (1) mechanical (design and production engineering); (2) chemical (R&D laboratories); (3) electrical-electronic (R&D laboratories); and (4) software (systems departments).

Innovation in services

Services innovation is a topic of growing interest for innovation researchers and policymakers. Services account for more than 70 per cent of value added and employment in the industrialized countries. Despite the economic significance of services and the strategic importance of some services, the innovation literature is dominated by studies of manufacturing and the production of tangible goods. Services are a 'residual' category which includes all activities that are neither engaged in the extraction of materials (primary sector) nor the production of goods (secondary sector). Indeed, services are involved in a variety of transformations including physical transformations (e.g. transportation of goods and building services), transformations of information (e.g. banking and telecommunications), transformations of knowledge (e.g. R&D services and consultancies), and transformations of people (e.g. education and health care) (Miles 1995; Coombs 1999).

Services have been neglected in studies of innovation because they have been regarded as lagging behind other sectors in terms of innovation, capital accumulation, and economies of scale (Baumol 1967). They are regarded as slow in their uptake of new technology and as 'supplier dominated' (Pavitt 1984). Barras (1986a, 1986b), however, shows that productivity growth is boosted by investments in capital equipment embodying new technologies, particularly IT, suitable for application in services. There is evidence that services are heavy users of new technology, though the levels of uptake vary dramatically across different subsectors. About three quarters of all expenditure on IT hardware in the UK and the USA stems from services (Coombs 1999), with financial services at the vanguard of IT expenditure. As well as being users of new technology, some services are innovators, producing innovations for their own use in new systems configurations and applications, and for other sectors in cases such as computer or software services (services account for 25 per cent of private business expenditure on R&D in the UK and the USA) (Coombs 1999).

It is the growth of a particular segment of the services sector—knowledge-intensive business services (KIBS)—which has captured the attention of the media, the research community, and policymakers (EC 1998, 2003; OECD 1999; Miles 2003; Peneder et al. 2003). For Miles (2001), KIBS encompass all those business services founded upon technical knowledge and/or professional knowledge. This broad definition captures both the social and institutional knowledge involved in many of the traditional professional services (such as management consultancy and legal services) and the emerging technological and technical knowledge involved in high-tech services (such as computer and R&D services) (Miles 2001; EC 1998). However, many sectors are inevitably difficult to classify reliably since firms undertake a range of activities. For example, a logistics services firm may provide business with high-tech services, but in many cases its main activity may in fact be transport and ought not to be defined as KIBS (Miles 2001: 5). Similarly, data on KIBS do not encompass the full range of knowledge-intensive business *activities*, some of which are sold as business services while others are coordinated within the organization (Miles 2003).

Pavitt (1984) located all services in one of the four types of sectors that he identified, namely, 'supplier dominated' firms. This is, however, a simplification of the complexity of their innovative activities and potential. Elsewhere, one of us has reclassified services into three groups to reflect the variety of innovating services firms (Soete and Miozzo 1989; Miozzo and Soete 2001) (see Table 7.3):

1. *Supplier-dominated firms.* Supplier-dominated firms can be found mainly in personal services (restaurants and hotels, laundry, repair services, barber and beauty services) and in public and social services (education, health care, and public administration). Firms in the first sub-sector are generally small, and their in-house R&D, engineering capability, and in-house software expertise are weak. They appropriate less on the basis of a technological advantage than on the basis of professional skills, aesthetic design, trademarks, and advertising. On the other hand, firms in the second sub-sector are large organizations (which often are, or have been, at some time provided by public sector organizations). Overall, supplier-dominated firms make only a minor contribution to their process technology. Most innovations come from suppliers of equipment, information, and materials.

2. *Scale-intensive physical networks sectors and information networks sectors.* A second group consists of two sectors comprising what can be called

Table 7.3 Sectoral technological taxonomy of services: Determinants, directions, and measured characteristics

Category firm	Typical core sectors	Sources of technology manuf./serv.	Type of user	Means of appropriation	Technological trajectory	Source of technology	Relative size of innovating firms
Supplier dominated	*Personal services:* restaurants, laundry, beauty	Manuf.	Performance sensitive	Non-technical	Product design	Suppliers	Small
	Public and social services: health, education	Both	Quality sensitive	Not allowed, public	Improving performance	Suppliers	Large
Physical networks	Transport, wholesale	Manuf.	Price sensitive	Standards, norms	Cost-cutting, networking	In-house, suppliers	Large
Information networks	Finance, insurance, communications	Both					
Scale-intensive							
Specialized suppliers/ science-based	Software, specialized business services	Serv.	Performance sensitive	R & D, know-how, skills, copyright, product differentiation	System design	In-house, customers, suppliers	Small

Source: Miozzo and Soete (2001: 161).

'scale-intensive' (or production-intensive) 'physical networks' and 'infor-mation networks' firms. The first subsector involves large-scale processes with considerable division of labour, simplification of tasks, and the substitution of machines for labour. Its development is closely related to the application of modern ICT, initially, at least, with the aim of reducing costs. Firms heavily dependent on scale-intensive physical networks can be found in transport and travel, and wholesale trade and distribution. The second subsector includes firms dependent on information networks (finance, insurance, and communications). In both, while technological innovations may well originate in manufacturing firms (such as ATMs used in banking), the nature of these innovations will be strongly deter-mined by service use. Such 'service dependent' suppliers in turn might provide their large service customers with specialized knowledge and experience as a result of designing and building equipment for a variety of users, often spread across a number of service activities.

3. *Science-based and specialized supplier firms.* Science-based firms are no longer confined to the handful of manufacturing sectors such as pharma-ceuticals and electronics. The last couple of decades have seen the emer-gence of an increasing number of business services closely linked to R&D, software, and the development and application of information technolo-gies. In all these sectors, the main sources of technology are the research, development, and software activities of firms in the sector itself.

Services have a number of peculiarities: in terms of their product (their product is intangible, hard to store and/or transport, and its quality is difficult to demonstrate in advance to potential clients); in terms of their delivery (greater reliance on interaction between clients and services suppliers than is the case for traditional mass-production sectors and, in general, they have to be produced and consumed in the same location and point in time); and in terms of production (most services firms tend to be small, low-technology and many services firms employ unskilled workers—this does not apply to the above scale-intensive and many science based services sectors). The two central features: intangibility and client intensity (meaning that the uncer-tainty regarding the quality of services often requires close and continuous interaction between buyers and sellers) have influenced efforts to develop theories of innovation in services.

One of the earliest attempts to develop a theory of innovation in services was the 'reverse product cycle' developed by Barras (1986c) to describe the innovation process in what he calls 'user' industries. The standard product cycle theory suggests three phases of development: first, the introduction phase, characterized by product innovation; second, the growth phase, char-acterized by process innovations designed to improve the quality of a de-creasing range of products; and third, the maturity phase, shifting to a more incremental process improvements designed to reduce the unit costs of a relatively narrow range of products in markets near saturation (Kuznets 1953; Utterback 1979). In contrast, Barras argues that in services, the transmission of new technology, such as IT, from the capital goods sector in which it is produced to the 'user' sector in which it is applied, the cycle starts with (back office) process improvements to increase the efficiency of delivery of existing services, moves on to process innovations which improve service quality, and then leads to product innovations through the generation of new services (see the example in Box 7.2).

However, Barras' approach has limitations. First, the conclusions are specific to IT. Second, services are seen as passive recipients of innovations acquired from other sectors (Miles 1995). Although these criticisms of Barras' framework are important, Barras' work suggests two important characteristics of innovation in services. First, the level of IT diffusion in services is very high. Second, the organization of innovation in services rarely takes the form that is typical in manufacturing. Indeed, the role of organizational innovation

---

Box 7.2 Innovation in financial and business services

As the reverse product cycle progresses towards its next stage, firms in the adopting industry become more active in pursuing the R&D function as to 'expand technological possibilities' for themselves . . . . Typically in service industries this has initially involved a mixture of technology monitoring and market research, in order that firms can better appreciate their changing technological possibilities and market conditions. Increasingly, however, firms in vanguard sectors, such as financial and business services, have been investing substantial resources directly into development, particularly software development. Such activities are either pursued by special departments within the major firms in the industry, or alternatively by subcontracting to small specialist consultancies which grow up to service these major firms. By this means the innovation process begins significantly to affect the organizational structure of the industry, in those areas of activity subject to the most rapid growth and change.

It is through the impetus generated by this development activity that the adopting industry is driven to the third stage of the reverse product cycle—the generation of new products . . . . These are typified by interactive network-based services, such as home banking and shopping, which are likely to become established once the current technological, economic, and social barriers to their adoption are overcome . . . .

By this stage, the technological trajectory in vanguard industries can be described as being 'user dominated' rather than 'supplier dominated'. For the gathering momentum of innovation among leading firms will impose increasingly far-reaching demands upon the technology supply industries, as well as upon the institutional structures of adopting industries, while at the same time opening up wholly new product markets for the new services. It is through these accelerating processes of technological, market, and institutional change that the vanguard industries do so much to determine the character of the new techno-economic paradigm, creating opportunities for the much wider spread of product innovations among other, lagging sectors of the economy. Such is the stage now being reached as the financial and business services sector sets the parameters of the emerging Service Revolution.

Source: Excerpt from Barras (1990: 226–7).

in services is important. Miles (1994) notes the trajectory of self-servicing in organizational change in services, those organizational changes brought by changes in regulation (privatization of banking and telecommunications, and externalization of public services), and those in the search for quality assurance and improvements. Service firms rarely have R&D departments (of course, there are important exceptions such as large telecommunications firms and computer services firms). In general, services firms set up product or project development teams on an ad hoc basis (Sundbo 1988). Many of the innovations are developed in the course of specific projects for clients, and are therefore not always easy to distinguish from the 'customization' of the usual service. This may have an advantage for the types of near-market innovations that are often adopted, but it often means that there is limited coordination of learning experiences and that innovations that are made may often not be reproduced in subsequent projects (Miles 2001).

High customer intensity may have the consequence that it may make it difficult to locate the organization responsible for the innovative effort (see example on Box 7.3 on innovation in airports). In addition, there is some confusion as to what is a new service, as distinct from an improved version of an existing service (Barras 1986c). Because services tend to be simultaneously consumed as they are produced, the product and its process of delivery are inextricably interlinked.

A problem with services firms is that they tend to be poorly integrated into innovation systems and make little use of innovation-related facilities offered by institutions such as universities, research institutes, government

---

Box 7.3 Innovation in services: The dual approach glideslopes at Frankfurt airport

... faced with a level of demand in excess of that available with its existing infrastructure (for example, runways and taxiways), air traffic control procedures and equipment, Frankfurt airport (like other congested airports, such as London Heathrow) has sought ways of increasing its capacity. A significant difficulty is that Frankfurt's two main runways are too close together to allow independent operations, instead how one is used is dependent on the use of the other. This reduces capacity. To alleviate this, and to increase capacity, Frankfurt has recently begun experimenting with a dual glideslope approach procedure. Conventionally, aircraft line up one after the other—converging on the runway using the same final approach glideslope (akin to a road in the sky). With Frankfurt's dual glideslope alternative there are two roads leading to the same physical runway. By making smaller aircraft use the upper glideslope on one runway, whilst large aircraft use the lower glideslope, on the other, smaller aircraft are able to fly above the turbulent wakes of the large aircraft, and therefore closer behind the large aircraft. This reduction in separation between aircraft allows an increase in the capacity of the system to handle flights. This experiment in procedure requires the involvement and cooperation of the airlines (especially Lufthansa), air traffic control, and the airport operator. It is clearly an innovation that is distributed between the three agents involved. Indeed, it is one that relies upon their co-operation.

Source: Excerpt from Coombs et al. (2003: 1133–4).

laboratories, and few of these institutions are tailored to the requirements of services (Miles 2001; Tether et al. 2001). Indeed, the field of innovation studies has been slow in examining innovation in services because organizational changes are difficult to survey (for an example of the organizational changes see Box 7.4 on the telecommunications sector). Moreover, the main way to quantify innovation, patents, is biased against services: although patent data is the longest running historical record of technological activity, it does not cover many aspects of the evolution of new services. The patent system is based on protecting technological advances that can be incorporated into products. Much of the innovative output generated by service firms cannot be protected under the patent system, although the system was relaxed in some developed countries in the 1970s and 1980s to allow certain types of computer software to be protected by patent clauses (in addition to the inclusion of software in copyright law in the USA in 1976 and in the UK in 1985).

This interactivity and customization has often meant the provision of services on a small scale and local basis. However, many services have been standardized for a long time (such as railways, communication, broadcasting services). Also, fast food chains (such as McDonald's) provide affordable food at predictable quality to a large number of consumers. There has been a trend towards 'industrialization of services' (Levitt 1976) with services emulating industrial practice (mass production of standardized products, higher division of labour, and levels of technology). However, newer evolution towards semi-customization and flexible specialization may also apply to services. Also, as argued by Miles (1995), the 'convergence' between manufacturing and services means not only that manufacturing is becoming more like services but services more like manufacturing.

Outsourcing of services activities previously carried out in-house has increased the demand for specialized services provision. Outsourcing is a practice found across all sectors of economic activity. In the public sector, privatization and 'marketization'—in response to political imperatives (and to some extent changing macroeconomic constraints on governments)—have been especially important in driving growth in outsourcing. In the private sector pressures to downsize and cut costs, as well as opportunities to externalize groups of highly unionized workers, or workers whose strong professional identity (and strong wage demands) may be at odds with the firm's human resources strategy have been important. As argued by one of us elsewhere, outsourcing has been a major driver of KIBS such as computer services and R&D that were once provided in-house and therefore classified as manufacturing (Miozzo and Grimshaw 2006a). Table 7.4 illustrates the links between different management functions that have been traditionally administered in-house and the range of markets for business services that have grown as a result of outsourcing these functions. For completeness, the list includes both knowledge-intensive and operational business services. There

Box 7.4 Technology, skills, and organization in the telecommunications industry

There are a number of challenges facing the UK telecommunications industry: technological changes (digitalization), organizational changes (breakup of bureaucratic organizational forms) and changes in industry structure (liberalization and alliances). These have important implications for the strategies of UK telecommunications firms and for skill patterns and work organization. First, at the heart of the current ICT revolution is the process of digitalization, the move from analogue signals in continuous wave form to digital signals in the on/off, 0/1 language of the computer. Digital transmission means that many more calls can be carried on a single cable, that signals have to be re-generated at much less frequent intervals, and that, overall, the systems are much more reliable. Digital switching requires much smaller and considerably more reliable exchanges and, since they are essentially elaborate computers, they can be re-configured or repaired remotely .... Because of digitalization, the range of alternative telecommunications technology equipment incumbents can choose from for the provision of advanced services has diversified enormously. The same services (voice, internet, video) can also be provided through several different technologies, including mobile, optical fibre, co-axial cable TV, fixed radio and satellite. Newer entrants are therefore able to enter the market on the basis of the latest transmission technology or the one that most clearly fits its strategy.

Second, in contrast to manufacturing, where the main challenge was to overcome the rigidities and waste associated with mass production, the main problem for the large public telephone operators has been to overcome the bureaucratic nature of the former large monopolies, created under a particular technological and regulatory paradigm, beginning by AT&T in the USA, and imitated by many countries, including the UK. These were required to uphold detailed operational protocols to ensure quality and universal service (Batt, 1995). A rigorous system of performance measurement and expanded managerial hierarchy was developed to supervise hard-to-monitor tasks (Batt 1995). As a consequence, the dominant firms within the industry developed stable and efficient but highly bureaucratized routines. In the context of a new technological paradigm characterized by flexibility and fast product innovation, the formerly public telephone operators are faced with high labour costs and slow response times against new smaller more nimble entrants.

Thirdly, until the 1980s the conventional wisdom was that the telecommunications industry should be regarded as a 'natural monopoly' mainly because of economies of scale. Thus, the real cost and price of calls fell and the public nature of the service ensured universal access in most countries (Keefe and Batt, 1997). Deregulation and/or privatization of the incumbents in the 1980s was carried out under the assumption that new technologies would have a decentralizing thrust and were therefore best met by a less monopolistic market structure ....

These technological and institutional developments have interacted with crucial changes in labour markets. Digital exchanges have not only increased the reliability of equipment, but have also allowed automatic fault testing, fixing and remote monitoring. Digitalization has therefore increased network economies of scale and created opportunities for centralization and labour shedding. Some of the tasks have become simplified to the point that low skilled operator services can check for basic faults. The result has been the relative obsolescence of engineering skills and second line management and an attempt to outsource functions that are regarded as 'non-core' such as reprographics. On the other hand, by diversifying the range of services that they are able to provide with new technologies, firms have increased 'front-end' employment to meet data traffic in areas such as sales, solutions, helpdesk, product development, design, media and marketing.

Source: Exerpt from Miozzo and Ramirez (2003: 65–6).

Table 7.4 Linkages between internal management functions and markets for business services

Internal management function	Related market for business services
Administration	Management consultancy; legal services; auditing and accountancy
Human resources	Temporary work agencies; personnel recruitment; professional training.
Finance	Banking; insurance; renting and leasing
Production and technical function	Engineering and technical services; tests and quality control; R&D services; industrial design; maintenance and repair of equipment
Information systems	Software and IT services; telecommunications
Marketing and sales	Advertising; distributive trade; public relations; fairs and exhibitions; after-sales services
Transport and logistics	Logistics; transport services; express courier
Facility management	Security services; cleaning services; catering; environmental services/waste disposal; energy and water services; real estate (warehouses)

Source: Adapted from EC (2003: Annex 1, Box 1).

are obvious difficulties in putting a figure on the size of the overall outsourcing market; one study estimates a value for 2003 of Euros26.4 billion in Europe and Euros38 billion in the USA (http://www.tpi.net).

As shown by our own work, an important area of research is the role of a number of knowledge-intensive services in the diffusion of new modes of business organization and the way in which the increasing internationalization of services, including the operation of multinationals in this sector, interacts with the process of innovation in services (Miozzo and Grimshaw 2006*a*). The traditional non-tradability of services has been changed by IT. By collapsing time and space at decreasing costs, IT makes it possible for services to be produced in one place and consumed simultaneously in another. For example, ATMs reduce the need for the physical presence of customers in the bank. Also, specialized international computer networks make possible the decentralization of a growing volume of services such as the processing of data and financial management within transnational corporations (Miozzo and Soete 2001). On the other hand, intangibility gives a particular character to this increased transportability. Due to the intangibility of services, much of the new trade enabled by new information technologies is in the form of intrafirm rather than arm's-length transactions (Miozzo and Miles 2002).

Indeed, in a number of industries, we see the deepening of capabilities and increase in scale in a handful of very large supplier-independent services providers in telecommunications (AT&T, Cable & Wireless), engineering/ construction (WS Atkins), personnel (Manpower Inc.) (Quinn 1999). One consequence of the concentration of the supply base is an emerging potential for supplier firms to actively shape the outsourcing market. Observations of a similar nature have been made in studies of management consulting (McKenna et al. 2002) and investment banking (De Long 1991). This is the case of computer services firms such as Electronic Data Systems (EDS), IBM, Fujitsu, and Accenture that have expanded with the IT outsourcing market. Though some of these firms initially established a reputation as manufacturers of computer hardware, today they specialize in developing novel combinations of KIBS which they provide to clients around the world. In particular, they have expanded on the basis of selling bundles of services in the form of IT outsourcing contracts, characterized by long-term contracts (typically three years or more), the takeover by the supplier of the client's assets (infrastructure and, in most cases, staff), and the adoption of responsibility for service delivery, as specified contractually in a service level agreement. These services include IT infrastructure (hardware and operating systems), software applications development, and support and helpdesk. These firms develop special capabilities in the form of a corporate 'methodology' or set of 'processes'. These are systematic procedures used by all employees for carrying out the activities in the firm (Miozzo and Grimshaw 2006*b*). IT outsourcing is not an all-or-nothing affair. IT outsourcing agreements involve a complex mix of standard formal contracts, informal trusting relations and, crucially, the transfer of IT staff (from the client to the IT supplier) (Grimshaw and Miozzo 2006*b*). Client organization managers generally expect IT outsourcing to enhance performance and innovation—through economies of scale, production efficiencies, and access to specialized knowledge and new technologies. However, quite unexpectedly, managing this process demands a great deal of management input (from both client and supplier) and client investment in retaining relevant expertise. Moreover, given the ubiquitous penetration of IT in all business functions and the inseparability of information from production technology, IT outsourcing tends to be accompanied by significant changes in the wider production technologies of the client organisation (Miozzo and Grimshaw 2005).

Innovation in construction

The peculiar characteristics of the construction industry are regarded as a barrier to large-scale innovation and dissemination of technological and organizational advances. These 'peculiarities' include the physical characteristics of the product (buildings are large and designed to be long-lasting), the one-off designs and lack of prototyping (lack of continuity in its 'production function'), the fact that production and innovation activities take place at clients' premises, the fragmentation and traditional separation between the design process and production (exacerbated by the standard contracting system), and the informal nature of many of its management practices. These peculiarities have been the cause of concern for academics and policymakers since they have been the basis of conflictual relations between contracting parties that cause delays, productivity and quality problems, and failure to attract and retain skilled and motivated staff.

Although the sector is classified by Pavitt (1984) as supplier dominated, there has been no absence of major technological developments in construction since the 1950s. These include new materials, prefabrication of modular components, industrialization of buildings, on-site mechanization, improved building services, application of electronic data interchange (EDI), CAM, computer integrated manufacturing, and new structural solutions (see Box 7.5 for a typology of construction innovation). Also, our own work has explored recent developments in project management and procurement (namely, Design and Build and Partnering between contractors and clients) (Miozzo and Ivory 2000). The beneficial effects of these changes, however, have been limited for two reasons. First, new management practices place greater demands on the interface between different organizations and new technologies require enhanced precision in assembly. Together, these pressures contribute to increased complexity in an institutional environment already characterized by fragmentation in responsibility, adversarial labour relations, safety considerations and a range of regulations, standards, and codes. Second, these problems may, in turn, be exacerbated by the specific nature of the skills profile and employment conditions of the construction workforce (e.g. high level of self-employment) (Clarke and Wall 1998).

Construction facilities are large, complex, and long-lasting, and they are created and built by a temporary alliance of disparate organizations concentrated temporarily on a single project and affected by standards, codes, tests, and provisions for consumer protection, safety, and environmental awareness

---

Box 7.5 A typology of construction innovations

... a reinforced steel bar with a raised profile represents an incremental innovation to a general contractor, with a modest expected improvement in performance from increased interaction surfaces with the concrete, but no significant change in concept or links to other systems. In contrast, fibre reinforced plastic reinforcing bars with a traditional profile for cast-in-place concrete slabs is a modular innovation, with a change in the core concept (from steel to FRP) but no changes in links to other systems. Self-compacting concrete, which eliminates the vibration and consolidation stage of placing concrete ..., is an architectural innovation, since it uses available materials in a modified mixture but causes significant changes in related processes. A new bridge design, which might use FRP sheets as tensile members and as the stay-in-place forms for a high performance self-compacting concrete slab and incorporate small active dampers to absorb dynamic load impacts would be an example of a system innovation, coordinating the set of complementary innovations to achieve new levels of performance. The use of advanced composite materials to make a whole bridge is an example of a radical innovation, with changes in the core concepts as well as the links to other systems and with the potential to render current technologies obsolete.

Source: Excerpt from Slaughter (2000: 3–4).

(Tatum 1986, 1987; Laborde and Sandivo 1994; Rosenfeld 1994; Arditi et al. 1997; Slaughter 1998). It has been suggested that the description of construction as an 'industry' is unsuitable (Groak 1994) and that more attention has to be given to the construction project (Allinson 1993; Winch 1998). Different sectors of construction (those building sophisticated urban offices, bridge building, or housing maintenance) use fundamentally distinct technologies, resources, and skills. Others argue that construction is better viewed as a process rather than an industry (Tatum 1987; Gann 1994), which includes designing, constructing, maintaining, and adapting the built environment. All agree that these activities involve a multitude of organizations from a range of different industrial sectors, working together in temporary coalitions on project-specific tasks. The project-based nature of these activities is important when considering innovation because this creates discontinuities in the development of knowledge and its transfer within and between firms and from one project to the next (Winch 1998; Gann and Salter 2000).

The majority of R&D is carried out by materials and components producers who develop products aimed at improving the performance of buildings and structures (Quigley 1982; Pries and Janszen 1995). Very little R&D is carried out with the aim of improving construction processes (Table 7.5 shows that business expenditure on R&D as a percentage of total construction output is smaller than 0.1). It is becoming increasingly recognized by industry and government that this adversely affects the performance in use of technologies developed 'up-stream' of the integration, assembly and installation work carried out by the project-based construction organization (Gann 1997). Moreover, some large materials and components producers may be the source of major innovations for construction, but they may not regard construction as their primary market in terms of the focus of their R&D efforts (e.g. chemicals, synthetic materials, and glazing products). Firms with technical capabilities (of which there are only a handful in the construction sector) must 'intercept' or 'tap' technologies developed elsewhere in other industries or other countries and reconfigure them for specific purposes within their projects (Gann 1997; Toole 1998).

Table 7.5 Business expenditure on R&D expressed as a percentage of total construction output

Country	1991	1992	1993	1994	1995	1996	1997	1998
Denmark	0.0076	0.0065	0.0057	0.004	0.0025	0.0026	0.0023	0.0007
France	0.0201	0.0212	0.0217	0.02	0.0213	0.0214	0.0280	—
Germany	—	—	—	—	0.0142	0.0164	0.0188	0.0206
Sweden	—	—	—	—	0.0123	—	0.0166	—
UK	0.0586	0.0519	0.0368	0.0346	0.0239	0.0225	0.1006	0.0953

Source: OECD (2000), FIEC (1999).

The study of construction innovation brings to light two issues that have general applicability to studies in other sectors. First, our own study of the sector reveals the importance of issues of corporate strategy and structure. Although the 'systems of innovation' literature (see Chapter 6) includes the internal organization of the firm and financial institutions as factors that shape learning and innovation, there is little elaboration on how differences in patterns of ownership, finance and management, and organizational structures contribute to the generation of process and product innovation. One of us has collected international comparative evidence on the effect of the structure of ownership and management on innovation in the construction industry (Miozzo and Dewick 2002). Our research shows that particular structures of ownership and management, namely concentration of ownership, cross-holdings, and decentralization of management, which characterizes the Germanic as opposed to the Anglo-Saxon corporate governance system, may generate more appropriate institutional conditions to support the commitment to irreversible investments in (firm-specific) innovation in construction firms.

Second, construction innovation reveals the importance of the relations between agents in the process of innovation. The construction process may be regarded as an archetypal network system (see Chapter 9), since construction

---

Box 7.6 Interorganizational relations in construction

In the construction industry, the interactions and interdependencies between organizations (including contractors, government, clients, designers, sub-contractors, suppliers and tenants) have an important role in shaping the process of production and innovation. The successful adoption of innovations depends, in part, on the efficient and cooperative functioning of the whole network. However, the evidence from the Scottish Homes policy of promoting sustainable technologies reveal factors that enabled and hindered innovation. On the one hand, the Scottish Homes Agency was very proactive in driving policy initiatives to promote sustainable products and processes. As such, all the conditions for the successful introduction and diffusion of innovation appear to be present—an industry characterized by a network form, backed up by funding from a body with a strong strategic focus. On the other hand, a number of factors conspired against innovation—factors that in fact lie at the heart of the particular network form characteristic of the construction industry. Relations between housing associations and contractors were marred by conflicting profit and non-profit motives, which led to differences in the willingness to develop alternative procurement forms. Representatives from the design teams (architects and consulting engineers) added an additional element of conflict due to their favouring traditional procurement as a better condition for innovation. Finally, the importance of relations with tenants means that innovation must also be accompanied by education packs if the technologies are to be applied effectively.

In conclusion, therefore despite the strong adherence of a major Housing Agency (Scottish Homes) to a policy of promoting sustainable technologies, in fact it was the very characteristics of the network form of the construction industry that appears to conspire against innovation.

Source: Excerpt from Miozzo and Dewick (2004: 122–3).

projects are planned and executed in the context of interorganizational decisions, activities, and relations. Organizations of varied forms exchange information and know-how, sometimes on an episodic and sometimes on a continuous basis. Although some attention has been paid to particular organizational forms in the construction industry such as the 'quasi-firm', based on a set of stable relations between a general contractor and special trade subcontractors (Eccles 1981), and to the comparative effects of different national contractual systems in the construction industry (Winch and Campagnac 1995; Winch 1996), little attention has been paid to interorganizational relations supporting innovation (see Box 7.6). Our own research compares the relations of contractors with subcontractors and suppliers, government, universities, clients, and their international collaborations in five European countries. Our research shows that in countries where interorganizational relations are strong, such as Denmark and Sweden, the productivity of the construction industry is higher, despite high labour and material costs and tighter safety regulations (Miozzo and Dewick 2004).

Innovation in pharmaceuticals

The pharmaceutical industry is an example of a science-based sector in Pavitt's taxonomy, with more than 15 per cent of sales typically spent on R&D. Figure 7.1 shows the annual rate of appearance of new chemical entities approved as pharmaceutical products over sixty years. The sector has a very

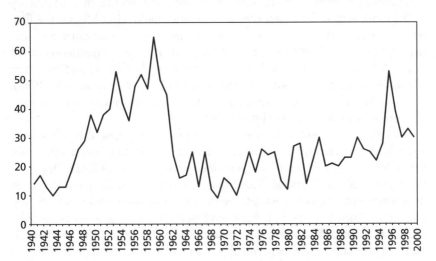

Figure 7.1 Annual approval of new chemical entities
(*source*: OTA 1981; Walsh 1984; Kaitin 2000)

complex selection environment (see Chapter 1); it has experienced major organizational changes in recent years; the way it appropriates technological advantage has become considerably modified; and it has faced a revolution in the technologies it uses in both the discovery and production of new products.

The pharmaceutical industry is one of Europe's best performing high-tech sectors and represents a large proportion of some European countries' total industrial R&D (EFPIA 2003). In the UK and France, 28.7 and 13.3 per cent of total industrial R&D funds were spent on pharmaceuticals (see Table 2.9 in Chapter 2). The European industry is still important in world terms, in contrast to electronics and other high-tech sectors where US and Japanese firms have long dominated their industries worldwide, but it has begun to be overtaken by US firms in innovation: 24 of the top 50 New Chemical Entities (NCEs) introduced during 1995–9 originated in the USA and only 16 in the EU (Gambardella et al. 2000). Between 1990 and 2000, US R&D investment grew fivefold, while in Europe it only doubled; European firms are spending increasing proportions of their R&D budgets in the USA. In biotechnology, the dominance of the USA is even greater: the pharmaceutical industry has 3.5 times as many employees working on biotechnology in the USA as in Europe (EFPIA 2001).

The sector is made up of a very large number of small firms together with a small number of global oligopolies which dominate the sector. The industry's R&D is concentrated in these large firms, which compete within therapeutic categories. In the whole sector, no firm accounts for more than a quite modest percentage of the world market for drugs but in particular therapeutic categories, there are often as few as two large firms which account for the vast majority of the sales in that category. Table 7.6 shows that by 2001, the top 20 firms accounted for 66 per cent of the world market, but Pfizer—the firm with the largest share of the world drugs market—accounted for no more than 7.5 per cent. Firms can be highly dependent on just one or two major drugs: for example, in 1994, just before it bought Wellcome, just one drug (Zantac) accounted for 40 per cent of Glaxo's sales[1] (de Aenelle 1998). Prilosec, AstraZeneca's ulcer drug, alone accounted for nearly 40 per cent of the company's sales in 2001 (Pilling 2001).

Over the past twenty years, the search process for new drugs has been strongly influenced by advances in biotechnology and IT, and a shift from dependence on chemistry to an increasing 'biologization' of R&D. One of us has argued elsewhere (Walsh 2004) that there have been three paradigms in drug discovery, associated with three different organizational forms for the innovating firm. The first paradigm was based on the extraction of alkaloids[2] and other active substances from natural products, which were commercialized by pharmacies—the new entrants of the nineteenth century. Innovation was carried out almost exclusively by European firms. During much of the twentieth century the second paradigm involved the synthesis of chemicals,

Table 7.6 Leading pharmaceutical corporations, 2001

Firm	Country	Sales £	Growth* (%)	Share of world market** (%)
Pfizer	USA	18.275	13	7.5
GlaxoSmithKline	UK	17.066	12	7.0
Merck & Co	USA	12.916	12	5.3
AstraZeneca	UK	11.147	12	4.6
Johnson & Johnson	USA	10.828	21	4.4
Bristol-Myers Squibb	USA	10.422	7	4.3
Novartis	SWI	9.767	9	4.0
Aventis	FRA	8.501	11	3.5
Pharmacia Corp	USA	8.265	15	3.4
Abbott	USA	7.507	10	3.1
Leading 10 firms		**114.694**	**12**	**47.0**
American Home Products	USA	7.45	12	3.1
Lilly	USA	7.105	9	2.9
Roche	SWI	6.757	3	2.8
Schering-Plough	USA	5.733	6	2.4
Takeda	JAP	4.395	13	1.8
Bayer	GER	4.269	−1	1.8
Boehringer Ingelheim	GER	3.428	11	1.4
Sanofi-Synthélabo	FRA	2.766	9	1.1
Amgen	USA	2.565	22	1.1
Eisai	JAP	2.197	15	0.9
Leading 20 firms		**161.36**	**11**	**66.1**

Note: *calculated in US$; ** IMS Health audited markets. IMS Health was the source of ABPI's data. IMS = International Marketing Services; ABPI = Association of the British Pharmaceutical Industry.
Source: http://www.abpi.org.uk/statistics (accessed 8 March 2004).

most of which did not already exist in nature, by large multidivisional and multinational chemical firms with extensive resources, R&D labs, and a skill base in chemistry and chemical engineering. The USA began to play a role in drug discovery with the wartime commercialization of penicillin, a collaborative project between major firms which established mass screening as an important method of drug discovery.

The third paradigm was based on the exploitation of an interdisciplinary combination of biotechnology, genomics, proteomics, mathematics, software design, computer engineering, and bioinformatics for the design of therapeutic products. These technological changes allow a more systematic approach to drug discovery at the same time as speeding up the process of producing and screening a large number of potential drugs. The organizational form associated with their development and commercialization in the late twentieth and early twenty-first century is a series of complex networks which involve a variety of profit-making and not-for-profit organizations working in collaboration. The output of these networks may be available via marketplace transactions or freely available to those who have made the necessary investment in the skills and knowledge needed to make use of it, or indeed restricted for use within the network, perhaps leading to the further adding of value for later commercial output (McMeekin and Harvey 2002).

The third paradigm, which we have called 'molecular design', is thus a constellation of related innovations brought to market by heterogeneous networks of organizations characterized by their complexity, density, and the number of different organizations involved at the same time. These networks are made up of permutations and combinations of: organizations managing the public databases established by the Human Genome Project in the USA, Japan, and Europe[3] (and which regularly exchange data with each other); a variety of other public sector research institutions; private firms trading proprietary databases assembled by adding value to the publicly available data; multinational drug firms (which may have assembled private databases for their own use by adding value to publicly available and purchased data); software providers; computer firms; and a variety of specialist firms (e.g. in genomics, bioinformatics, proteomics, combinatorial chemistry, molecular simulation modeling, computer-aided drug design, high-throughput screening, cell and tissue banking, and data mining and visualization). Meanwhile, what was once exceptional behaviour—academic scientists active in a hands-on relationship with industry—has become expected practice, indeed an activity necessary to generate sufficient funds for future research.

Box 7.7 gives as an example the SNP consortium, a non-profit foundation financed by the Wellcome Trust and a number of (otherwise competing or potentially competing) multinational firms in the life sciences and IT, which produces publicly available knowledge free of charge.[4]

In the analyses of Kuhn (1962)—on scientific paradigms—and Dosi (1982)—on technological paradigms—new paradigms replaced the old ones. Our paradigms of drug discovery have not done this, but have coexisted, side by side, in the toolkits of the pharmaceutical companies. Indeed, some significant new products appeared as a result of 'semi-synthesis'; from natural products, a hybrid of the first two paradigms;[5] while even the sophisticated computerized methods of designing and testing molecules, based on knowledge of the molecular structure of protein and gene targets, still result in promising molecules being made using traditional 'wet chemistry', a combination of the second two paradigms.

Intellectual property rights (discussed in more detail in Chapter 6) are an important part of the infrastructure for innovation, associated with both the demand and supply sides. Thus they are designed to encourage inventors by ensuring that they can benefit from their discoveries and their investments; at the same time, they allow a firm to have a monopoly and therefore charge monopoly prices (if only temporarily) and thus encourage the establishment of a market for the invention. They may also encourage a market in the patents themselves, in the form of licensing and various cross-licensing arrangements. And freely available technology may not be implemented at all, if a firm cannot protect its ability to generate a revenue from its discoveries, for example, by patenting them. Tylecote and Ramirez (2004) argue that

---

Box 7.7 The SNP consortium

The SNP Consortium was formed in April 1999. It is a collaboration of pharmaceutical and IT firms (each of which contributed $3 million), the Wellcome Trust (a charitable trust which funds research in the life sciences and contributed $14 million), and several academic centres.

It was established as a non-profit making entity, and a condition of the Wellcome Trust's funding was that information generated by the consortium's research would be made freely available.

Single Nucleotide Polymorphisms (SNPs) are common DNA sequence variations among individuals. The SNP Consortium's mission was to identify the 300,000 or so SNPs distributed through the human genome, and make the information available. By the end of 2002, 1.8 million had been characterized.

The firms in the consortium were AP Biotech, AstraZeneca, Aventis, Bayer, Bristol-Myers Squibb, F. Hoffman-La Roche, Glaxo Wellcome, IBM, Motorola, Novartis, Pfizer, Searle, and SmithKline Beecham. Some of these have since changed their names and/or merged with others.[1]

The work is performed by four research centres: The Whitehead Institute/MIT's Center for Genome Research; The Sanger Centre; Washington University in St. Louis School of Medicine, SHGC.

All the resulting data were stored and accessed in databased maintained by Cold Spring Harbour Laboratory.

Source: Company websites.

1 Just to give Pharmacia as an example, SNP Consortium member AP Biotech (initially Amersham Pharmacia Biotech) is described variously as a joint venture of Nycomed Amersham (55 per cent) and Pharmacia Corporation (45 per cent) or a merger of Amersham Life Science and Pharmacia Biotech. AP Biotech became Amersham Biosciences in 2001, while one parent, Nycomed Amersham, became Amersham PLC the same year. Then in 2002, Amersham PLC acquired Pharmacia Corporation's 45 per cent of Amersham Biosciences. Pharmacia still remains a pat of the SNP Consortium, however, having acquired Monsanto's drug business, G. D. Searle, (by first acquiring the whole of Monsanto and then reselling Monsanto as an agro-food business without Searle). In December 2002, Pharmacia shareholders voted to approve the proposed merger with Pfizer, another consortium member.

---

appropriability, or the ability of intellectual property and other frameworks to ensure that the profit from innovation accrues mainly to the shareholders of the firm, is one of three major challenges for financial and corporate governance systems. They suggest that patenting is an effective means of intellectual property protection in pharmaceuticals. Other research suggests, however, that pharmaceutical firms have had to rely on a variety of other means of appropriating knowledge, some of which we discuss in Chapter 6.

In that chapter we outlined the recent expansion of what can be considered intellectual property, and therefore subject to protection via patents, trademarks, and copyrights. Of particular relevance to pharmaceuticals and agrofood are the rapid changes over the past twenty-five years in what the public expects and accepts in IPRs, especially covering biotechnology. It will be recalled that these have been extended to cover life forms such as novel plants, GMOs, and genetic sequences, despite opposition especially to the latter. And that trademark law has evolved from an emphasis on protecting consumers from 'fakes' to the protection of manufacturers from competition, while new methods of appropriation of resources or knowledge have been adopted, including exclusive-use contracts, private databases covered by the terms of commercial confidentiality, and the CRADA introduced in the USA under the Federal Transfer of Technology Act (1986). The first two have been used to appropriate collections of genealogical and medical data, then used to add value to gene sequence information in the development of diagnostics and therapies. Chapter 6 has already discussed the problems of IPR where the innovation process is cumulative over time and/or distributed over multiple actors. Establishing IPRs and extending their scope (both geographically and in terms of what constitutes 'property') is one way of privatizing what was once in the public domain, or the property of a community, and of creating markets in those areas.

The evolutionary economics concept of a selection environment (Nelson and Winter 1977) captures the idea of the environment into which an innovation is launched, and which determines whether or not it will be a success (Chapter 1). The selection environment comprises the market plus a variety of institutions which determine whether or not a market *can* exist, or its extent. It is quite complex in the case of pharmaceuticals, and includes doctors who test new drugs and prescribe licensed ones, and the regulatory system, compliance with which is necessary for the innovation to be sold. Pharmaceuticals firms have to prove their new products' safety and efficacy, and sometimes that they represent significant improvements over products already available, in order to get a license to sell them from a national licensing authority or the European Medicines Evaluation Agency.

The structure of demand for pharmaceuticals is unusual in that the end-user plays very little part in the purchase decision: it is the doctor who writes a prescription and thereby determines the drugs that will be sold, although two recent trends have made some inroads into this position. First, it is no longer uncommon for drugs, which have been available only on prescription for a period of time, to become available over the counter. Glaxo SmithKline's Zantac (a histamine receptor antagonist to treat ulcers in the stomach and intestines) is an example. Second, since 1997, when the FDA relaxed its broadcast advertising regulations in the USA, it has become much more common for manufacturers to promote medicines directly to the public, encouraging patients to ask their doctors for branded products by name. Thirty-three products were advertised on US radio or TV in the first two years of the new policy[6] (Lexchin and Mintzes 2002).

Until then, drug firms' very high level of promotional and marketing activity was largely invisible to the general public: it was aimed at doctors, in the form of regular visits by company representatives, and tons of promotional material through the post, including a huge array of products bearing company logos and product brand names. In the 1960s, The Sainsbury Report (1967) found that the UK industry spent more on marketing than on research, while in the USA the Kefauver hearings reported spending on marketing well over 20 per cent of sales and four times as much as R&D (Goodman 2000). By the 1990s marketing represented 25 per cent of sales (Tarabusi and Vickery 1998).

Not only do patients rarely decide which drug to buy, they typically do not pay for their medicines, either. In most countries, private or public health insurance schemes (or a mixture of both) reimburse patients for the cost of their medicines, although where insurance is private or partly private, there are substantial sections of the public who are not covered by insurance, typically the poorest. The pattern of separating payment from consumption, as well as the removal of product choice from the consumer, has been widespread enough to affect decisively the pattern of competitiveness in the sector. Price competition has traditionally been rather unimportant in pharmaceuticals, and firms have tended to compete almost entirely on the basis of new and improved products (reflected in the number of new products launched each year shown in Figure 7.1).

Although drug firms have always produced minor variations on existing medicines (chemical variants of active ingredients or different formulations of dosage forms), a focus on price reduction through process innovation has not characterized the competitive strategy of firms in this industry. The strong emphasis on product innovation has been one of the reasons why the industry was always heavily dependent upon its R&D activity—to keep the flow of new products arriving—and on its marketing activity to persuade doctors to prescribe the new brands. In order to keep their profits high and recoup the costs of R&D, firms have been under pressure to introduce new products onto the market regularly. High prices are charged for patented and branded drugs, but once the patent has expired, other firms may make the drugs and sell them under their generic name at a much lower price.

Pisano (1997), however, has argued that radical changes in the market and technological environments of the pharmaceutical industry since the 1980s have now begun to emphasize the important strategic role of process development and manufacturing capabilities for an industry which had traditionally competed on the basis of introducing new products alone.

Given that public or private insurance pays for most drugs, the structure of the market is oligopsonistic or even monopsonistic. This is increasingly the case even in the USA, where health care and health insurance is largely in the private sector, as a result of the increased importance since the mid-1990s of Health Management Organizations, which are linked to health insurance firms and provide health care for about half the US population (and 70 per cent of employer health plans). Many of them have generated prescription management firms as subsidiaries, and these are in a strong position to negotiate discounts from pharmaceutical firms competing for their products to be included in the prescription management firms' formulary lists (*Scrip*, May 1996). In most OECD countries, the price of drugs is strongly controlled or even set by national authorities.

Public opinion and political pressure are very important in matters concerning health, and firms in the pharmaceutical industry have tried to participate in the political process through the influence and lobbying of their various industry associations. Even though consumers rarely make the decision about which drug they will use, or pay for them, they have managed to play an increasing role in shaping innovation. They are increasingly active in patients' organizations which not only provide support for others with similar conditions, but fund—and therefore shape the direction of—research, and they lobby public authorities over ethical aspects of health care or access to treatment, in some cases achieving changes in evaluation protocols. Epstein (1995, 1996, 1997) showed that lay AIDS activists challenged the way in which clinical trials were carried out, and by insisting on their rights and claims as patients, were able to change them. Richards (1988, 1991) analysed non-experts' participation in biomedical assessment and decision-making in the controversy over vitamin C as an anti-cancer agent. Callon and Rabeharisoa (2003) and Rabeharisoa and Callon (2001) demonstrated that patients and their families play an active role in the direction of research and the coproduction of knowledge in a study of AFM, the French Muscular Dystrophy Association.[7] The birth control movement—more of a political or pressure group than a patients' organization, but claiming to represent the interests of potential users—played an important part in funding and managing research on oral contraceptives as well as campaigning for legalization of birth control (Marks 2001: 3–59). Table 2.6 in Chapter 2 gave the percentage of R&D funding coming from sources that were neither government nor industry, which was as much as 23.6 per cent in the UK. This is the category that includes charitable trusts and patients' organizations, and indicates that the level of funding, and therefore of innovation shaping, from such organizations is not trivial.

Innovation in the agrofood sector

The agrofood industry is not one industry but several, with activities in primary products (agriculture and fishing), manufacturing (food and drink processing and manufacturing) and services (wholesaling, retailing, and catering). Tansey and Worsley (1995) call it a food *system*. The agrofood 'industry' or system thus contains a long supply chain in which some parts of the chain are suppliers or clients to some of the others. In addition, in recent years, the agrofood industry can be considered to have expanded to include producers of agrochemicals (fertilizers and pesticides) and food additives. Some of these latter firms (notably Monsanto, ICI, Ciba, and Sandoz), part of the chemical industry, began during the 1970s to buy seeds firms, to do R&D in conventional plant breeding,[8] and to produce seeds that were compatible with the use of their pesticides. These firms (together with some of the specialist biotechnology firms established for the purpose such as Calgene[9]) were also involved in plant biotechnology R&D from the 1980s,[10] and in the 1990s began to produce genetically modified (GM) foods and other crops, and now can be considered part of the agrofood industry.

The agrofood industry thus includes a range of activities from the traditional to the high tech. Some techniques for making beer and wine, for milling and bread-making, for the extraction of oil and the preserving of meat, fish, fruit and vegetables, date back thousands of years. These sections of the industry are still strongly influenced by cultural traditions and the huge variety of local specialities. They transform raw foods using techniques specific to each product (e.g. bakery, cheese-making, and winemaking). At the same time, the modern food processing industry is, in contrast, based on the industrial production of standard products at minimal cost and which are easily marketable, using generic techniques not specific to particular products (e.g. fermentation, sterilization, or deep-freezing) (Byé 1999). Finally, the production of GM foods is an activity within the high-tech and science-based field of biotechnology.

Food is the largest manufacturing industry in Europe, and the European industry is larger than its US or Japanese counterparts, both in terms of turnover and employment. Another area of contrast is the role played by small and large firms. The hundred largest food manufacturing firms are responsible for 80 per cent of all value added (Lang 2003a). Table 7.7 shows the

Table 7.7 World's ten largest food manufacturing firms

Company (ranked by size*)	2002 sales (US$bn)	2002 net income (US$bn)	Brands
Nestlé	64.3	5.5	Nescafé, Crosse & Blackwell, Branston, Coffee Mate, Shredded Wheat, Findus, Buitoni, KitKat, Perrier
Unilever	50.7	2.2	Hellman's, Bird's Eye, PG Tips, Flora, Carte d'Or, Ben & Jerry's, Colman's, Wall's, Pot Noodle, Marmite, Knorr
Sara Lee	17.6	1.0	Ballpark, Bryan, Hillshire Farms, Sara Lee
Frito-Lay	14.3	n/a	(Owned by PepsiCo) Cheetos, Doritos, Frito's, Lay's
Kraft Foods	29.7	3.4	(Owned by Altria, formerly Philip Morris tobacco) Kraft cheese, Birds, Jacobs Suchard, Lyons, Cote d'Or, Maxwell House, Philadelphia, Nabisco, Oreo, Ritz
Tyson Foods	23.4	0.4	Tyson chicken
Groupe Danone	14.2	1.3	Danone yogurt, Jacob's cookies
ConAgra Foods	27.6	0.8	Banquet, Chef Boyardee, Healthy Choice
H. J. Heinz	9.4	0.8	Heinz ketchup, Heinz beans, Star-Kist, Farley's, John West, Linda McCartney Meals, Weight Watchers' Foods
General Mills	10.5#	0.9#	Cheerios, Chex, Go-gurt, flour, and baking mixes

Note:*=no. of employees, #=2003 figure.

Source: Adapted from firms' websites and Burnson (2003).

world's largest ten. However, more than 90 per cent of firms in the industry are small (fewer than 100 employees), and such firms account for nearly half the turnover of the industry (Byé 1999).

Many writers have noted the historical shift in dominance over the food supply chain since the Second World War, from farmers and food producers to retailers, in particular the large (increasingly globalized) supermarkets (e.g. Harvey 2002; Wilkinson, 2002; Lang 2003a, 2003b). Retailers decide what to stock and what to promote to the public, and consequently make a crucial contribution to market demand. They are sufficiently powerful that they can specify tight delivery times (and even JIT delivery), prices, margins (Lang 2003b), and quality (Byé 1999), while they are able to induce manufacturers to produce in the retailers' brand names and take on the responsibility for packaging and labelling (Byé 1999). Table 7.8 shows the world's largest food retailers and the extent of their global activity. At the same time, small firms can still find new openings by meeting demand for product diversity.

Patterns of demand for food products and services have been widely studied from a sociological and anthropological as well as marketing perspective. These are largely outside the scope of this brief account, except to give a few examples. Warde, for instance, has written widely on the sociology of food and consumption (Warde 1997, 2000; Warde and Martens 2000). Anthropologist Mintz (1996) shows the significance of what we eat and how we eat it in expressing who we are, while our choices about food are shaped by an

Table 7.8 World's largest food retailers and their global activity, 2002

Company	Home base	No. of stores	Sales (US$bn)	No. of countries of operation
Wal-Mart	USA	5,164	244.5	12
Carrefour	France	10,704	64.7	33
Royal Ahold	Netherlands	9,407	59.2	27
Kroger	USA	3,667	51.8	1
Metro AG	Germany	2,411	48.5	28
Tesco	UK	2,294	39.5	11
Costco	USA	400	38.0	7
Albertstons	USA	1,688	35.6	1
Rewe Zentrale	Germany	12,077	35.2	12
Aldi	Germany	6,609	33.7e	12
Safeway	USA	1,887	32.4	2
ITM Enterprises	France	12,863	31.5e	8
Ito-Yokado	Japan	23,700	27.2e	12*
Edeka	Germany	14,374	27e	6
Auchan	France	1,120	25.9	15
Sainsbury	UK	681	25.9e	2
Aeon	Japan	8,120	24.6e	9
Tenglemann	Germany	7,015	24.4e	13
Schwartz Group	Germany	5,342	21.6e	23
Casino	France	9,056	21.5e	21

Note: *=plus franchise operations in five other countries; e = estimate.

Source: http://www.supermarketnews.com/sntop25.htm (accessed 28 June 2004).

increasingly complex global economy. His book *Sweetness and Power* (Mintz 1986) shows, for example, that the spread of Islam was a determining factor in the establishment of sugar consumption, and uses sugar as a case study in the social shaping of demand and new norms of consumption. Méadel and Rabeharisoa (2001) have examined the role played by taste and tasting in the construction and renewal of agrofood markets, while Tomlinson and McMeekin (2002) use household survey data to argue that social class is a stronger determinant of food consumption behaviour than income.

Byé (1999) identifies strongly contrasting patterns of demand for food. In one case[11] he relates urbanization and the break-up of the extended family to the large market for snacks, fast food, and cook-chill and frozen prepared meals, and to food manufacturing firms' strategies of internationalized marketing, product standardization, economies of scale, and keeping down prices. In another case,[12] where meals are more commonly produced and shared in a family setting and the market is influenced strongly by taste and quality, the survival of small producers with close links to agriculture and local craft networks is encouraged, together with competition based on diversity, freshness and tradition, and less emphasis on standardization or price, and more on economies of competence (see also Chapter 4 on this point in relation to the 'Third Italy').

However, there are further contrasts in the demand patterns to be found, including the growth in demand for processed food among urbanized consumers in newly industrializing countries, especially as industrialized production contributes to price reduction. And in the economically most advanced countries, in addition (or in reaction) to the growth of fast food, an increasing fashion for 'natural food' (e.g. cheese made with unpasteurized milk) has promoted the revival of traditional and craft-based food sectors, and a renewed demand for fresh products, for food which retains characteristics normally taken out by industrial processing (e.g. wholemeal bread), and for organic foods, especially among wealthier consumers for whom quality is more important than price. Furthermore, new market opportunities have been identified for new ranges of food products to be developed to meet consumer needs in beauty care, nutrition, or health, such as neutraceuticals and special food for niche markets among the young, the elderly, or the athletic. Neutraceuticals are foods with beneficial health effects, such as grapes that help to reduce heart disease, tomatoes that help control prostate problems, broccoli that helps protect against cancer, and alfafa to resist tooth decay (Radford 1997). Since these are foods which, in some senses, compete with pharmaceuticals, similarly high prices can be charged for them.

In a series of papers, Rama and colleagues (Rama 1996, 1999; Alfranca, et al. 2001, 2003*a*, 2003*b*) observe that demand in the food industry is widely seen as conservative, with little potential for technological change. R&D expenditures in the industry are less than 1 per cent of turnover, and few patents are generated. However, the authors challenge this picture on the basis of a number of long-term studies of patents granted to food and beverage multinationals, pointing out that since turnovers are high, R&D budgets are quite large in absolute terms, especially in the large industrial groups. The authors conclude: 'While the food and beverages industry is usually considered a low-tech industry, profitability and growth seem to depend on the food firm's ability to continually innovate' and to apply a range of scientific advances (Alfranca et al. 2001). Furthermore, they argue that gains in average productivity are comparable with those of other manufacturing sectors. They find that innovation strategy plays an important role in competition among food firms, while advertising and product differentiation (the other main contributors to competitiveness in the industry) also depend on design innovations (minor improvements in packaging and presentation of products). Some food and beverage multinationals patent an invention and then do not innovate again. Innovation is concentrated in a small group of persistent innovators who benefit from the cumulative effects of innovation and learning. Finally, the authors show that past innovation is a much stronger indicator of future innovation than exogenous causes of technical change such as regulatory or market changes.

Some parts of the industry are supplier dominated, use the output of a great deal of public sector agricultural R&D, and have a broad interface with non-food supplier industries which, for some firms, are more important contributors of innovation than internal R&D. The industry's capacity to apply acquired knowledge also depends on innovative activity in adjusting and adapting acquired innovations and in learning-by-doing. Sometimes food companies collaborate with innovation suppliers in order to acquire customized products or techniques such as in packaging, logistics, quality control, or control of pathogens.

Table 7.9 shows some of the recent innovations in the food supply chain. Some important innovations adopted by the food industry from other industries have included new methods of transporting and preserving perishable goods or reducing the time in storage or distribution, in management of the supply chain, and innovations in the foodstuffs themselves. Developments in agricultural biotechnology are among the most recent innovations initially generated outside the industry, and a counterexample to the demand-led picture of innovation in certain other parts of the food industry. In addition to GM crops, they include genetically engineered animals, or products that come from them (such as milk); diagnostic methods for crop or animal diseases; and new search methods in R&D. The main features genetically engineered into crops include resistance to herbicides (often but not always the herbicides produced by the agrochemical firms which developed the GM crops), resistance to insect pests, and enhanced nutritional properties (e.g. high-polyunsaturated oil content) or properties that increase shelf life,

Table 7.9 Twentieth century revolution in food supply chain

Innovations	Examples
How food is grown	Mass use of agrochemicals, hybrid plant breeding
Animal rearing	Factory farms, intensive livestock rearing, prophylactic use of pharmaceuticals to increase weight gain
Biotechnology	GM plants, animals, animal products (e.g. milk), diagnostics and processing
Food sourcing	Local ⇒ regional ⇒ global supply points; seasons transcended; monoculture encouraged in farming (in contrast to diversity in supermarket)
Processing	Extrusion technology, fermentation, additives
Quality shaped by technology	Mass production to deliver consistency and regularity, niche products with 'difference'
Workforce	Employment reduction on farms in developed world; pools of cheap (often immigrant) labour for manual tasks, e.g. grading and picking; moves to 24 hour working
Marketing	New emphasis on product development, branding and selling; dazzling display of apparent choice
Retailing	Main gateways to consumers; contracts and specifications allow retailers (large supermarkets) to become gatekeepers between primary producers and consumers
Distribution	Use of airfreight, regional distribution systems, heavy lorry networks, satellite tracking
Supply chain management	Centralization of ordering, computerization, bar-codes, electronic point of sale, loyalty cards, flexible specialization, JIT distribution
Shaping of consumer tastes and markets	Mass marketing of brands, product placement, investment in advertising, targeting of consumer types
Market shaping	Rapid regionalization, moves towards globalization, emergence of cross-border concentration

Source: Adapted from Lang (2003*b*).

automatic handling, and value to weight ratio (e.g. low water content). Neutraceuticals can also be produced by genetically engineering desired properties into food (Walsh 2002).

By the mid-1990s all the leading agrochemicals producers, Bayer, Novartis (now Syngenta),[13] DuPont, Hoechst (now Aventis),[14] Monsanto, Rhône-Poulenc (now Aventis) and Zeneca (now Syngenta), with 60 per cent of the world market between them, were producing genetically engineered crops (Nottingham 1998). Figure 7.2 shows that the take-off in the number of field trials of GM crops worldwide began in 1992, the year in which China planted more than 2 million acres of virus-resistant tobacco (Tampubolon 2003). By 1998 more than 5,000 field trials were being held involving 60 GM crops, more than 60 countries and about 75 million acres (Tampubolon 2003). GM crops are produced more widely throughout the world than other biotechnology products (such as drugs). For example, Argentina and China are among the top 10 growers of transgenic seeds, while 70 per cent of soya grown in Argentina is transgenic (Tampubolon 2003).

The non-market parts of the selection environment are particularly relevant in understanding the success and failure of food products and services, and especially those based on biotechnology. Regulations covering food safety

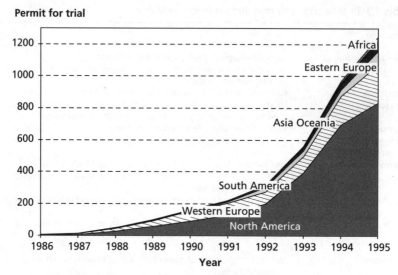

Figure 7.2 Worldwide GM crops field trials
(*source*: Tampubolon 2003)

and environmental protection affect the market, while professional experts in the fields of nutrition, agriculture, and ecology carry out trials and prescribe or recommend products. Firms consider it necessary—and worthwhile—to lobby law and policymakers and to direct promotional material at the professionals and experts as well as advertising and propaganda at the public. In the area of food safety and environmental risk, Steward (2001) uses the case of bovine spongiform encephalopathy (BSE) to focus on outcomes of the innovation process, and role played by networks and narratives during the process of innovation. The drive to commercialize genetically engineered foodstuffs involved heavy lobbying of trade organizations, regulatory bodies, lawmakers, the media, and consumers, all market-creating activities (Vidal and Milner 1997). The introduction in the USA in 1993 (and elsewhere soon after) of a fast-track system for granting release permits for field trials and commercial planting of GM crops, was a consequence of public policy in this area which considerably speeded up the process of take-off of innovation in GM crops and affected the rate of growth of the market for the products.

Multinationals such as Monsanto expected that the application of genetic engineering to food would be welcomed by the public for their beneficial effects for crop production and the environment. In the USA, GM food was accepted fairly readily, but in Europe many consumers regarded it as contaminated (*Guardian*, 15 December 1997). Monsanto launched an advertising campaign in the summer of 1998, on the assumption that they only needed to supply the public with the necessary facts and logic to convince them otherwise. Advertising is a traditional method of creating markets, but this time promotion had the opposite effect: people became more resistant to the new technology as they became more aware of it. Retailers, too, criticized Monsanto for denying consumers a choice by mixing GM crops with traditional varieties before they entered the processing and export pipeline, and then leaving them (the retailers) to reassure the public (Morse 1996; Wrong 1999*a*). In 1996, European food retailers campaigned with Greenpeace against non-labelled imports, and consumer organizations advised caution towards GM foods, fearing that scientific, ethical, and social concerns were being swept aside, and that decisions had been made on behalf of consumers with minimal public debate (Maitland 1996). The result was that the Monsanto advertising campaign, which had cost the firm £1 million, 'was overwhelmed by the society-wide collapse of support for genetic engineering in foods' in 1998, especially in Germany and Britain (Greenberg 1998*a*, 1998*b*).

Innovators, even established firms with a great deal of experience, can sometimes wildly misjudge potential markets. In an area where ethical issues are important it is even easier to misjudge public opinion, and the agrofood industry, especially Monsanto, seems to have succeeded in the late 1990s in what would normally be a nearly impossible task: it unified (in opposition) the various stakeholders or elements of the selection environment. End users, farmers, retailers, wholesalers, government bodies, consumer organizations, environmental organizations, the press, and even prestigious chefs[15] were all drawn, to a greater or lesser extent and some only temporarily, into the network of opposition to the new technology. From early 1998 no new GM crops were authorized for planting or use in the EU, an unofficial moratorium made official by the EU Environment Ministers' Council in 1999 (FOE 2004). Monsanto finally admitted that it had lost the public relations war by appearing arrogant and condescending (Wrong 1999*b*). The following year, in a further move towards improved public relations, Monsanto placed in the public domain the data it had assembled on the rice genome (Monsanto 2000). In the UK, following a widespread public debate 'GM Nation?' and reports in 2003–4 from the GM Science Review chaired by the Government Chief Scientific Advisor (GM Science Review Panel 2003, 2004), the Secretary of State for the Environment proposed in 2004 limited commercial planting subject to various restrictions (*New Scientist*, 9 March 2004). Public policy has thus defined the boundaries of the market.

Innovation in chemicals

The chemicals industry is an example of a science-based industry in Pavitt's taxonomy, but since 1984 when he proposed it, a great deal has changed in the chemical industry and its approach to innovation. Even in 1984, some parts of the industry (such as bulk commodity chemicals and commodity plastics) were more like production-intensive than science-based firms. Synthetic materials had once been a science based activity in the days of the discovery and innovation of a range of new materials, but many of these (e.g. nylon, polyethylene, polypropylene, PVC) had become, with maturity, production-intensive, with only a few new materials (such as carbon fibres) still the result of science-based innovative activity.

We have described these changes in the 1980s as the chemical industry 'reinventing itself' (Walsh and Lodorfos 2002: 278). The industry in the 1980s was faced by declining returns to effort in discovering new molecules using the knowledge and methods available on the supply side. But the new opportunities posed by new technology in the form of biotechnology and information technology were not always perceived initially as opportunities but as threats: first commercialized by new entrants or firms outside the chemical industry, they had the potential of destroying the chemical firms' competencies and pushing them aside in forming a new industry based on automation of molecular design, discovery, and testing plus a whole range of new products and processes. On the demand side the markets for the industry's core businesses were levelling off or declining. The increased stringency of environmental protection, product safety, and occupational health and safety regulations, could be seen as difficulties in the selection environment for new products, or—since the result was increased costs, and greater opportunity costs in R&D—as problems on the supply side.

Many chemical firms were conglomerates with a huge spectrum of products and markets, and before 1990 the sector could be defined as the complex of industries related to the exploitation of chemical knowledge or which have grown around a chemical base (Chesnais and Walsh 1994). This definition included synthetic materials, pharmaceuticals, dyes, paint, bulk chemicals and intermediates, food additives, speciality chemicals, photographic chemicals and agrochemicals. If we were to include firms which had ownership links to chemical companies, or which were based on chemical reactions and flow processes, then the definition widened further and the boundaries of the industry became even more blurred, including activities which are normally classified in other industrial sectors. For example, glass (part of building materials) or oil refining and petrochemicals (part of mining and petroleum). Meanwhile, the move by some agrochemicals firms into seeds and plant breeding placed them in an area traditionally defined either as part of agriculture or of food, drink, and tobacco (see earlier section). Even earlier, Unilever was a firm classified as part of the food industry and is now the world's second largest food manufacturing firm (see Table 7.7), but also makes household and personal cleaning materials, which are classified in the chemical industry.

The first thing firms in the chemical and related products industry did in response to the increased challenges on both the supply and demand side, was to shift the focus of their activities into higher value-added production, not only by changing the emphasis of their R&D but also by buying firms with desired specialisms. Several chemical firms bought pharmaceutical firms either to strengthen their existing business in the area or to move into it. Agrochemicals firms moved into plant breeding and production of seeds. Fine chemicals, catalysts, and high-specification synthetic materials were other high value-added areas in which chemicals firms increased their focus and their efforts, while at the same time some of them moved out of their lower value-added petrochemicals and bulk commodity chemicals activities by selling their interests in those areas. An increased emphasis began to be placed on R&D in the life sciences, initially in the form of exploratory basic research.

The commercialization of biotechnology was typically carried out by collaborative alliances of established chemicals, pharmaceuticals, agrochemicals, and other firms with the specialist biotechnology firms which had developed the new technology but did not have the necessary complementary skills and assets to commercialize it (see Chapter 9 for more on alliances). The established firms lacked the new technology but did have the production, distribution, and marketing skills and capacity necessary, and had experience of steering

---

Box 7.8 The emergence and evolution of Aventis

1990	Rhône-Poulenc pharmaceuticals acquires Rorer to form Rhône-Poulenc Rorer
1990	Institut Mérieux merges with Connaught to form Pasteur Mérieux Connaught
1993 and 1995	Rhône-Poulenc Rorer acquires Applied Immune Sciences
1994	Hoechst (60 per cent) and Schering (40 per cent) form Joint Venture, AgrEvo
1995	Rhône-Poulenc Rorer acquires Fisons
1995	Hoechst pharmaceuticals division buys Marion Merrell Dow from Dow chemicals and acquires Roussel-Uclaf to form Hoechst Marion Roussel
1996	Hoechst buys Plant Genetics Systems
1998	Rhône-Poulenc Rorer acquires Pasteur Mérieux Connaught and Centeon to form Rhône-Poulenc Pharma
1998	Rhône-Poulenc demerges Rhodia (chemicals)
1998	AgrEvo acquires part of Cargill Seeds (another part goes to Monsanto)
1998–9	Hoechst sells Vianova synthetic resins and Herberts coatings and demerges Celanese (synthetic materials)
1999	Rhône-Poulenc Rorer merges with Hoechst Marion Roussel to form Aventis
2001	Aventis sells Crop Science to Bayer to form Bayer Crop Protection (including remaining 26 per cent owned by Schering); Aventis retains its core competence in pharmaceuticals

new products through regulatory procedures as well as a network of contacts with doctors and other professional specialists who would do tests and recommend products. The first successful products of biotechnology were diagnostics, followed by pharmaceuticals and then (from the mid-1990s) agrofood products.

During the 1990s, many of the conglomerate chemicals firms demerged their life sciences businesses, and these in turn divided into separate pharmaceuticals and agrobusiness activities in the 2000s so that the latter firms can be considered to have migrated from the chemicals to the food industry. For example, Syngenta was formed in 2000 from the agrofood businesses of the life-sciences firms Novartis and AstraZeneca, which in turn had their origins in chemical firms Ciba-Geigy, Sandoz, and ICI. Box 7.8 shows the emergence and evolution of Aventis as a way of illustrating the merger and demerger activity which allowed chemical firms to reinvent themselves. A third example is Monsanto, once a very ordinary and not particularly high-tech chemical firm, but which by the end of the 1990s had become one of the best known producers of GM foods (and the only one which members of the public could name) (Walsh 2002; Walsh and Lodorfos 2002). The strategic reorientation taken by Monsanto is illustrated by the sharp decline in their chemicals patents followed by an increase first in pharmaceuticals and then the beginning of the growth in their agrofood patents (see Figure 7.3, though it only contains data up to 1994 and therefore only the beginning of Monsanto's move into innovation (chiefly genetic modification) in food).

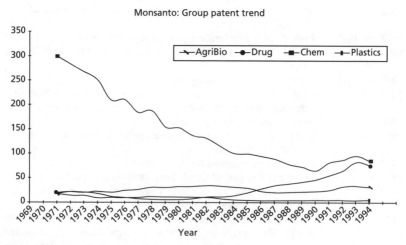

Figure 7.3 Monsanto: Group patent trend, 1970–94

(*source*: Tampubolon 2003)

Conclusion

This chapter has shown some of the wide range of sectoral patterns of innovation, much of which is based on our own research in the sectors which we have used as case studies. We have shown that innovation differs across sectors in terms of the sources, nature, organizations, and actors involved in innovation. Differences across countries in sectoral systems are important and have affected the economic performance of difference countries (Malerba 2002). There is some evidence that countries that do not have effective sectoral systems characteristics do not perform well in those sectors in international markets. The same holds for countries that attempt to replicate the success of leaders by copying some features of sectoral systems of leading countries, without having the appropriate organizations and linkages. By contrast, countries that have tried to specialize in subsectors with knowledge base and institutional requirements that match their institutional framework have been successful in those sectors.

Notes

1 This was an important factor in the acquisition, since Wellcome offered strength in several complementary areas with the possibility of adding new drugs to the new firm's product range.

2 The alkaloids are a series of highly complex organic bases found in plants, which often have a powerful action on the human or animal system, as poisons or medicines. The first one discovered was morphine (1817); other examples include strychnine, nicotine, and quinine.

3 The public databases associated with the Human Genome Project are GenBank at the National Center for Biotechnology Information (NCBI) in the USA, the European Molecular Biology Laboratory (EMBL) database at the European Bioinformatics Institute (EBI), and the DNA Databank of Japan (DDBJ).

4 Though as McMeekin and Harvey (2002) point out, the participant firms are likely to have a comparative advantage in applying the new knowledge.

5 In 1960, the year when the greatest number—ever—of new chemical entities (NCEs) were approved as drugs (see Figure 7.1), 18 per cent of new prescriptions in the USA were still for drugs derived from plants (Goodman and Walsh 1998), while during the period 1959–80, natural products accounted for 50 per cent of prescriptions. In the period 1983–94, 39 per cent of the NCEs introduced worldwide continued to be derived from natural sources, while 61 per cent of those introduced for oncology treatments came from natural products (Quinn et al. 2002).

6 Of which it was found that 17 violated the Food, Drug and Cosmetic Act, typically by inadequate communication of risks. Just under 20 per cent of 320 advertisements analysed offered a monetary incentive to the reader for using the promoted drug (Lexchin and Mintzes 2002).

7 They have identified three kinds of patient organization: those who recognize a difference between expert know-how and lay experience and either encourage cooperation between professionals and patients or try to acquire comparable expertise to that of the specialists; those who reject the scientific or medical community's defining of their state and potential threat to their identity (e.g. deaf people who refuse cochlear implants); and those who try to establish parity between specialists and patients.

8 While agrochemicals firms moved into seeds and conventional plant-breeding as well as plant biotechnology, large conventional seed firms, such as Pioneer and DeKalb, moved into biotechnology R&D, though spending much less on it than the agrochemicals firms (Walsh and Lodorfos 2002: Table 3).

9 Set up in 1980. These firms produced GM plants, designed molecules for specific end uses (e.g. agrochemicals designed to kill specific pests, see for example, AstraZeneca 2000) and often commercialized their output in collaboration with established agrochemical firms. In the 1990s, several of them were also subsequently acquired by agrochemicals firms (e.g. Calgene by Monsanto).

10 Despite its subsequent strong position in agrobiotechnology, Monsanto's research in this area was more of a monitoring activity until the 1990s, when the firm's patenting in the field began to take-off (Walsh and Lodorfos 2002).

11 Byé writes about Northern Europe but this could equally apply to North America.

12 He writes about Southern Europe but again his observations apply more widely.

13 Syngenta was formed in 2000 from the agribusiness division of Novartis (Switzerland) and the agrochemicals business of AstraZeneca. AstraZeneca, in turn, had been formed in 1999 by a merger between Zeneca (UK) and Astra (Sweden). AstraZeneca and Novartis refocused on their core competences in pharmaceuticals after the spin-off of Syngenta.

14 Hoechst merged with Rhône-Poulenc to form Aventis in 1999.

15 Most of the UK chefs rated 8 out of 10 or more in the 1999 *Michelin Good Food Guide* backed the Friends of the Earth campaign for a 5-year ban on GM food (Brown 1998).

Part IV
Globalization and Innovation

The globalization debate is both complex and contested. Commentators from across disciplines as diverse as political economy, economics, management sciences, and geography are polarized. At one extreme there are those who see a new 'world order' comprising placeless, global reach oligopolies, devoid of territorial loyalties whose activities are facilitated by the newly liberalized and rapid movement of finance and credit across national frontiers and a common consumer culture. At the other extreme, there are commentators who deny that globalization forces are giving rise to new economic forms and structures. These commentators see the retention, and indeed increased importance of, territorial heterogeneity, particularly at the scale of the nation state. Another position, adopted in this book, sees problems in both positions and uses the term globalization to describe a process, which stresses ongoing qualitative changes. It also acknowledges that the idea of 'global' activity is rather loosely used, since most of the flows of overseas trade and investment are concentrated within the Triad (North America, Japan, and Europe) (though with effects for the rest of the world); that globalization is a process which is more noticeable in some sectors than others; and that it is one that proceeds in ebbs and flows. In brief, this process is seen as one where there is increased centrality and mobility of credit capital (with foreign direct investment growing at three times the rate of growth of international trade, internal investment, or national economies of the OECD areas since the 1980s) and the development of new forms of business organizations (manifest in a wave of international mergers and acquisitions, intrafirm trade within multinationals and networks of interfirm and interorganizational cooperative alliances). This process has important effects on innovation and the prevalence of national innovation systems.

Chapter 8 examines the ways in which trade and the operation of multinationals have influenced the operation of national production systems, and how this has changed between the period of 'classic multinationalization' and the period called 'globalization'. The chapter discusses the relevance of different theories of international business and trade (product cycle, new trade theory, eclectic theory, global commodity chains, geography and knowledge creation, and globalization of innovation) to understand the relation between technology and changing international division of labour. The chapter gives a background of the changes in international trade negotiations (World Trade Organization) and framework for policy, which have important implications for innovation.

Chapter 9 explores networks and strategic alliances as a qualitative change accompanying globalization. It analyses the reasons for the growth in alliances, the databases complied by researchers to analyse them, and different approaches to study alliances and networks (complementary assets, actor-network theory, and transaction cost economics). A number of networks and alliances are examined (including US CRADAs, Benetton network, linkages between small and large firms in biotechnology, and the case of the Maastricht region).

Chapter 10 examines in detail what is meant by globalization and the debates surrounding the concept. The effects of globalization on the international division of labour and the integration of strategy and management within multinationals is explored. The chapter considers the implications of globalization for national governments and for innovation. The evidence regarding the globalization of innovative activity is assessed.

8 Technology, International Investment, and Trade

Introduction

This chapter explores the changes in the ways in which trade and the operation of multinationals have influenced the structure and organization of national production systems. We describe two distinct phases: a period of 'classic multinationalization' (1955–75) and a period that has been termed 'globalization' (after the late 1980s). Globalization is discussed more fully in Chapter 10, but to summarize, globalization is characterized by several features: FDI has been driving internationalization more strongly than trade; there have been substantial qualitative changes in the organization and management of multinationals with increasing concentration of production in the worldwide intracorporate networks of multinationals (and networks of multinationals with small firms and public sector research), increasing mergers and acquisitions across national borders, and the development by these multinational firms of integrated strategies and management systems on a global basis. Furthermore, there is much debate in the popular media and academic literature as to whether, or to what extent, a loss of many of the attributes related to the economic sovereignty of nations might be taking place. These developments have brought changes in the national production and innovation systems, with some countries attracting multinationals in high value-added and R&D-intensive activities and upgrading their industrial structures, while others failing to attract high value-added operations of multinationals, failing to upgrade their industry, and further losing international competitiveness.

We survey a number of international business and trade theories that can offer us an insight into the complicated relation between technology, international investment, and trade, and we then assess how certain recent events have challenged these theories. We also examine international agreements governing trade and international investment that affect the international division of production and innovation, and national production and innovation systems. We explore the changes in the world economic system brought by the WTO, with special attention to the two new agreements it oversees: the TRIPS and the GATS.

The first section examines the shift from classic multinationalization to globalization. The second section reviews international business and trade theories developed to explain recent changes in the international economy. The third section presents the new international negotiations governing trade, investment, and innovation. A final section draws conclusions from the analysis.

From classic multinationalization to globalization

The influence of trade and the operation of multinationals on the structure and organization of national production and innovation systems has changed dramatically from the 'classical' period of multinationals' expansion (1955–75) to what is often referred to as the period of globalization (after the late 1980s) (see Chapter 10 for a further development of these ideas). These changes are taking place in the context of increasingly close interdependencies between countries by means of international trade, FDI, and financial globalization. The latter is characterized by the global character of monetary markets and the worldwide impact of the level of interest rates prevailing in dominant economies, along with their limiting effects on the autonomy of domestic macroeconomic management in other countries. In addition, these changes have occurred in the context of a turn in policies in the 1980s and 1990s, with the Thatcher/Major and Reagan/Bush governments in the UK and USA initiating the dismantling of many of the policy instruments used to regulate social, economic, and technological change (Chesnais 1992).

While Chapter 10 discusses globalization in more detail, this section will focus on the changing effect of trade and the operation of multinationals on national production and innovation systems. International trade has generally received more attention than the operation of multinationals in the economic literature. These two processes are usually treated separately since they come from two different traditions of economic thought (Chesnais 1992). Although the two processes have become more and more closely intertwined and are harder and harder to disentangle in their effects, we can point out some differences between them. The study of international trade has its origins in Adam Smith's work on the division of labour as dependent on the extent of the market. This regards countries as separate national economies. Trade may call for adjustments in the domestic industrial structure but does not threaten the cohesion of national production systems (Chesnais 1992). The study of multinationals, however, has its origin in the work by Karl Marx on long-term capital accumulation. The first serious attempt at economic analysis of the multinational was Hymer (1976). There have been several interpretations of his contribution as well as extensions of this work (Pitelis 1994). The most widely held interpretation suggests that multinationals exploit 'ownership advantages' (access to capital, product differentiation, and managerial skills) that help offset the natural disadvantages they face vis-à-vis host country rivals. A second interpretation suggests multinationals collude with rivals to increase profits. Hymer also refers to the ability of multinationals to 'divide and rule' workers, to locational factors and to product cycle reasons to explain their existence. Many of the theories of multinationals such as 'market power' (Kindleberger 1969), 'internalization' (Buckley and Casson 1976), the 'eclectic' theory (Dunning 1988), and divide and rule (Cowling and Sugden 1987), build on Hymer's work. Hymer's views moved in favour of the Marxist tradition, giving rise to theories in which multinationals are seen as an aspect of a more general inherent tendency towards the self-expansion of capital and its internationalization (Palloix 1973) and where demand-starved firms due to 'wasteful expenditure' by governments and firms (armaments and advertising) look for overseas expansion (Baran and Sweezy 1960).

Following Chesnais (1992), we argue that there are two distinct phases in terms of the effects of trade and international investment on national production and innovation systems. First, there was the phase of classic multinationalization (1955–75). During the period of classic multinationalization, international trade still grew faster than FDI. FDI was guided by the characteristics of host economies or 'locational advantage' (this includes natural resources, labour costs, skills, market protection, and external economies). Up to the beginning of the 1980s, government policies could act effectively to increase some of these locational advantages by providing incentives and/or constraints on firms to resort to FDI (e.g. through import substitution industrialization (ISI), see Chapter 5). FDI was dominated by strong flows of outward US investment especially in the manufacturing sector and smaller investment flows within Europe. Japanese FDI in the USA and Europe was very small. FDI was driven by product cycle considerations (Vernon 1966) (see below). US firms established production on a 'multi-domestic' basis, adapting their operations to the characteristics of host economies. During this period, international trade and the operation of multinationals did not impair the cohesion of most national production and innovation systems (especially in Northern and Western Europe), and in many cases had beneficial effects, forcing domestic industrial restructuring and the adoption of more efficient technologies and forms of organization and reducing the level of monopoly in domestic markets (Chesnais 1992).

During the new phase, the so-called globalization phase, international trade and the operation of multinationals have a more dramatic impact on the national systems of production and innovation. Globalization is a popular term coined by journalists and politicians. Some researchers rejected it as a catchword and argue that the globalization hypothesis has been overstated

(Hirst and Thompson 1999).[1] Others struggled to give it a scientific meaning (e.g. Chesnais 1992, 1997; OECD 1992; Chesnais and Simonetti 2000). Drawing on the work of Chesnais, we argue in this book that the term globalization refers to two related processes. The first concerns some important changes in the organization, scope and effects of international production, technology sourcing, and marketing by multinationals. The second concerns the loss by an increasing number of OECD countries (probably all except Japan, Germany, and the USA) of much economic sovereignty. It is hard to date very precisely the moment at which these two parallel and partially related processes reached full maturity, but by the mid to late 1980s the elements of the new phase had emerged.

Since the late 1980s, FDI in manufacturing and services has been driving internationalization more strongly than trade and is determining international location patterns for the production and exchange of goods and services (see Figure 8.1). The role of FDI and multinational activity in the world economy continues to grow, as reflected in the sales, assets, value added (gross product), employment, and exports of foreign asset (see Table 8.1). With respect to multinationals, globalization refers to the increased production and distribution in worldwide intracorporate networks and increased concentration in key manufacturing and services, leading to world oligopolies. With respect to countries, globalization is marked by a loss of sovereignty in the area of macroeconomic policy, in particular, the subordination to levels of interest rates fixed independently of their own needs. It is also

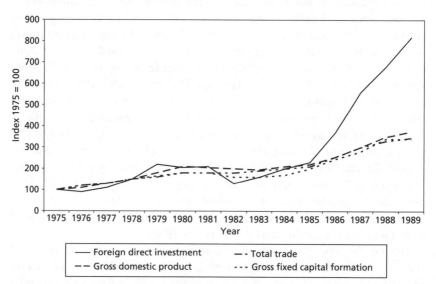

Figure 8.1 Trends in foreign direct investment, gross domestic product, trade and gross fixed capital formation in the OECD area 1975–90, current prices
(*source*: Chesnais 1992: 281)

Table 8.1 Selected indicators of FDI and international production, 1982–2003 (in billions of dollars and per cent)

Item	Value at current prices ($ billion)			Annual growth rate (%)						
	1982	1990	2003	1986–90	1991–95	1996–2000	2000	2001	2002	2003
FDI flows	59	209	560	22.9	21.5	39.7	27.7	−41.1	−17.0	−17.6
FDI outflows	28	242	612	25.6	16.6	35.1	8.7	−39.2	−17.3	2.6
FDI inward stock	796	1,950	8,245	14.7	9.3	16.9	19.1	7.4	12.7	11.8
FDI outward stock	590	1,758	8,197	18.1	10.7	17.1	18.5	5.9	13.8	13.7
Cross-border M&As[a]	—	151	297	25.9[b]	24.0	51.5	49.3	−48.1	−37.7	−19.7
Sales of foreign affiliates	2,717	5,660	17,580[c]	16.0	10.2	9.7	16.7	−3.8	23.7[c]	10.7[c]
Gross product of foreign affiliates	636	1,454	3,706[d]	17.4	6.8	8.2	15.1	−4.7	25.8[d]	10.1[d]
Total assets of foreign affiliates	2,076	5,883	30,362[e]	18.2	13.9	20.0	28.4	−5.4	19.6[e]	12.5[e]
Exports of foreign affiliates	717	11,194	3,077[f]	13.5	7.6	9.9	11.4	−3.3	4.7[f]	16.6[f]
Employment of foreign affiliates (thousands)	19,232	24,197	54,170[g]	5.6	3.9	10.8	13.3	−3.2	12.3[g]	8.3[g]
GDP (in current prices)[h]	11,737	22,588	36,163	10.1	5.1	1.3	2.7	−0.9	3.7	12.1
Gross fixed capital formation	2,285	4,815	7,294	13.4	4.2	2.4	3.8	−3.6	−0.6	9.9
Royalties and licence fee receipts	9	30	77[i]	21.3	14.3	7.7	9.5	−2.5	6.7	—
Exports of goods and non-factor services[h]	2,246	4,260	9,228	12.7	8.7	3.6	11.4	−3.3	4.7	16.6

Note: Not included in this table are the values of worldwide sales by foreign affiliates associated with their parent firms through non-equity relationships and the sales of parent firms themselves. Worldwide sales, gross product, total assets, exports, and employment of foreign affiliates are estimated by extrapolating the worldwide data of foreign affiliates of TNCs from Austria, Estonia, Finland, France, Germany, Hungary, Italy, Japan, Portugal, Sweden, Switzerland, and the USA (for employment); those from Austria, Finland, France, Germany, Hungary, Italy, Japan, Portugal, and the USA (for sales); those from Japan and the USA (for exports); those from the USA (for gross product), and those from Austria, Germany, Japan, and the USA (for assets) on the basis of the shares of those countries in worldwide outward FDI stock.

Source: UNCTAD (2004, Table 1.3, p. 9).

[a] Data are available only from 1987 onward.

[b] 1987–90 only.

[c] Based on the following regression result of sales against FDI inward stock (in US$ million) for the period 1980–2001: Sales = 1542.5036+945042*FDI inward stock.

[d] Based on the following regression result of gross product against FDI inward stock (in US$ million) for the period 1982–2001: Gross product = 493.8792+0.39537*FDI inward stock.

[e] Based on the following regression result of assets against FDI inward stock (in US$ million) for the period 1980–2001: Assets = − 1389.4785+3.850915*FDI inward stock.

[f] For 1995–8, based on the regression result of exports of foreign affiliates against FDI inward stock (in US$ million) for the period 1982–94: Exports = 288.4750+0.454011*FDI inward stock. For 1999–2003, the share of exports of foreign affiliates in world exports in 1998 (33.3 percent) was applied to obtain the values.

[g] Based on the following regression result of employment (in thousands) against FDI inward stock (in US$ million) for the period 1980–2001: Employment = 1,5162.6220+4.731003*FDI inward stock.

[h] Based on data from the International Monetary Fund, *World Economic Outlook*, April 2004.

[i] 2002.

marked by a need to attract FDI, but also a change in location advantages which countries can offer to multinationals, weakening the capacity of individual governments to strike 'hard bargains' with multinationals (Chesnais 1992). Today countries compete with each other to attract and keep multinationals (including their own) in order to maintain their industrial employment and the cohesion of their production and innovation system. In the last three decades, locational advantages have changed and are increasingly shaped by investment, education, and technological capacity. In contrast to the phase of classic multinationalization in which multinationals from the OECD were attracted by natural resources, labour costs, skills, and protected markets, during globalization, multinationals from the OECD are increasingly concerned with supply-side features of countries, especially the potential for 'science-based' types of developments on which multinationals can build. Multinationals are shifting to 'global' as distinct from multi-domestic strategies through IT, which facilitates world-based intracorporate networks. Globalization thus involves qualitative changes in the opportunity offered to large firms to distribute their R&D, manufacturing, and marketing facilities worldwide in a number of different national locations, to source key technological and intermediate inputs internationally and to manage their value and profit-creating activities on a global basis (see Chapter 10 and Chesnais 1992).

Thus, since the 1980s, there has been a concentration of FDI within the Triad (the USA has changed from being a 'home' country to being a 'host' country for multinationals and Japan has become an important 'home') (Chesnais 1992, 1988). The Triad—the European Union, the USA, and Japan—accounted for 71 per cent of world inflows and 82 per cent of outflows in 2000 (UN 2001). OECD trade increasingly involves products characterized by significant economies of scale in production, extensive product differentiation, or close links to the science base. While some countries/regions are attracting multinational investment in R&D intensive activities, other regions can only expect to attract subsidiaries concentrated in assembly and low value-added activities. Cantwell (1989) argues that these processes are likely to reinforce patterns of cumulative causation. By this he means that countries that are still experiencing growth through upgrading their industrial structures, and devoting more resources to support indigenous technological capability, are likely to attract inward multinational investment in R&D-intensive activities. They are also likely to benefit from technological accumulation in the associated affiliates and some technological dissemination outside them. By contrast, countries losing international competitiveness can only expect to attract subsidiaries concentrated in assembly and low value-added activities. Similarly with respect to outward foreign investment, in industries where domestic multinationals hold an internationally strong competitive position—they can usually afford to invest more in technology creation, which through upstream linkages may benefit their domestic suppliers. This will strengthen the latter's competitive capacity to supply the affiliates of foreign firms requiring their products. More subcontracting work is then given to domestic suppliers by foreign affiliates which further strengthens their technological capability.

What can international business and trade theories tell us about technology, international investment, and trade?

This section explores the different theories of international business and trade and discusses their relevance to the understanding of the relation between technology and the changing international division of labour. We review the following theories: product cycle, new trade theory, the eclectic paradigm, global commodity chains, the views adopted within economic geography on knowledge creation and international division of labour, and the debates on the globalization of production and innovation. These contributions have been selected because they have addressed the key role played by technological changes in shaping the international economy. They can contribute to our understanding of the new international distribution of production and innovation activities.

Much of international trade and investment orthodoxy is grounded in very well-developed models of the economic process from traditional trade theory to the more modern strategic trade theory. In common to all these intellectual perspectives is a central concern with whatever inhibits the free flow of goods, services and capital, and this is ultimately grounded in a particular view of market competition. This view of competition is very different from the dynamic viewpoints expressed by evolutionary and innovation scholars. Conventional economic theory of trade is based on the concept of 'comparative advantage'. Drawing on David Ricardo, the Hecksher–Ohlin theorem argues that a country has a comparative advantage in products containing a high proportion of inputs that are abundantly available to local industry, and a low proportion of input that are comparatively scarce. Thus, because some countries have particular natural resources, cheap labour, certain skills, easily available capital, or prevailing weather, according to the theory we would expect to find that those countries have a comparative advantage in production and export of goods taking advantage of such endowments. The comparative advantage essentially amounts to an opportunity to produce certain goods *more cheaply* than other countries. For example, Canada has mountains and therefore relatively cheap hydroelectricity for making an energy-intensive product like aluminium. It is, therefore, logical that Canada would be the home base for a multinational with a substantial share of the world market in aluminium and aluminium products (Alcan).

However, international trade theory underwent a profound change in the 1960s, beginning with Posner's development of a set of concepts (1961) that explained a large part of foreign trade from the starting point that a country which first introduces a *new product* may export it at least until imitators come into the market, and may then maintain the technology gap that has been created by means of continued innovation. It was Posner who first spoke of 'non-price' factors, including innovation, the product cycle, the operations of multinational enterprises, delivery dates, and sales efforts, in competitiveness. This contrasted with the price and cost factors which had previously tended to dominate trade theory. By 1979, in Britain for instance, concern with the problem of 'de-industrialization' had led to the publication of a book with that title by the National Institute of Economic and Social Research (Blackaby 1979), the majority of leading economists and policymakers contributing having concluded that a variety of non-price factors were the major cause of a lack of competitiveness and consequently of slow growth in output and declining share of world manufacturing exports in Britain.

Further developments of trade theory, some of which we consider in more detail later, explored the importance, not of a comparative advantage which allowed a country to produce goods more *cheaply* than another, but a competitive advantage that allowed it to produce goods that were *qualitatively* different in some way, for example, more technically sophisticated, better designed for ease of use, longer lasting, safer, ergonomically better, easier to repair or maintain, and so on. Dosi et al. (1988) and Dosi and Soete (1988) pointed out that what appeared to be a comparative advantage was in those cases not the result of any 'endowment', but the result of what was essentially a *learning process*. That is, innovative advantages are established by the gradual accumulation of capital and technology, which are not freely available but firm-specific, and which are both the result and the cause of technological specialization in certain areas. During the same period (1970s–1980s), empirical evidence that indicated that more expensive products sometimes outsold cheaper alternatives if they were qualitatively better in some way was also accumulating (e.g. the various contributions to the book edited by Pavitt in 1980, mentioned in Chapter 1). More generally, empirical research was demonstrating a correlation between economic growth and the growth of national technological activities (e.g. Pavitt and Soete 1980; Fagerberg 1985, 1988). 'Contrary to popular belief', said Fagerberg (1985), 'neither growth of relative unit labour costs nor differences in welfare state activity seem to have strong effects on the balance of payments constraint and growth', and technological innovativeness makes an important contribution to economic performance.

VERNON'S PRODUCT CYCLE

The first contribution to integrating trade and FDI with explicit reference to technological change was the product cycle theory developed by Vernon. Vernon (1966) was the first to integrate trade and FDI and a view of technology as part of a wider set of market structure factors, including entry, product differentiation and standardization, and the nature of demand. Vernon explained what factor endowment theory could not—the so-called Leontieff paradox of the 1950s. Leontieff pointed out that the USA specialized in exports with high labour content despite the high wages in that country (see Chapter 1). Vernon argued that, to begin with, products would be manufactured and consumed solely in the USA, where producers were more aware of the possibility of introducing new products due to internal market characteristics such as the existence of consumers with relatively higher average income and the availability of relatively unrationed capital, and because there is a need for swift communication between the market and the firm. With the passage of time, demand expands and products become standardized; concern over production costs begins to take the place of concern over product characteristics. If overseas demand is large, it would first be met with US exports, but if scale advantages of manufacturing in a single location (especially if this has high labour costs) are exhausted, US producers will establish production units in other advanced countries where there markets are. Demand would also appear in less developed countries and would be met by European or US exports. Ultimately, as products mature, the location of production might shift to less developed countries, which might then export to the USA and to other advanced countries (see Figure 8.2).

The product cycle model led to an important conclusion regarding the relation between technology and international investment and trade. The model showed that different types of geographical location are relevant to different stages of the product cycle. There are two problems with this model, however. First, it was developed to explain international production during the classic multinationalization period before the mid-1970s, in which access to large and/or high income markets, still partially protected by trade barriers, occupied a major place in the strategies of multinationals and in which the USA was the main home country of those multinationals. Second, the model may not be applicable to products whose design does not become 'standardized' or for which there is no 'dominant design' (such as pharmaceuticals— see Chapter 7).

Implications of the product cycle have been derived for less developed countries. For example, analysis of Asia Pacific as an integrated region began with the idea of 'flying geese' (Akamatsu 1956), with Japan at the front and, as Japanese wages increased and the yen appreciated, production facilities and technology flowing outwards from Japan to the more successful

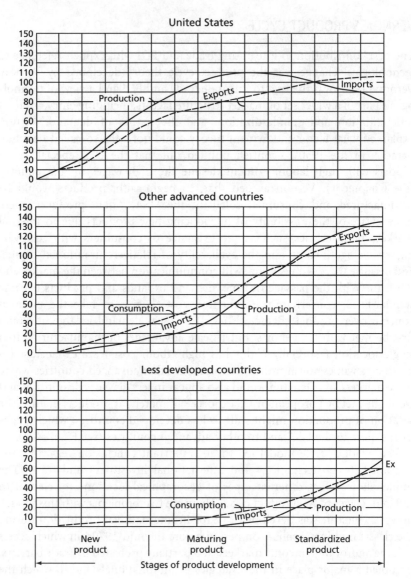

Figure 8.2 Product cycle model
(*source*: Vernon 1966: 199)

East Asian newly industrializing countries, and then to the second-tier Association of South East Asian Nations (ASEAN) economies and to China. Also, it has been argued that firms from newly industrializing countries tend to enter at the mature, standardized end of the product life cycle and gradually assimilate technology and learning, travelling backwards along the product life cycle to new technologies (Hobday 1995).

NEW TRADE THEORY

The product cycle hypothesis was largely ignored by mainstream economists due to the difficulties both in thinking about and in formalizing the introduction of an ever-growing number of goods, until 'new' trade theory (Helpman and Krugman 1985; Krugman 1995). New trade theorists argue that conventional models of comparative advantage do not give an adequate account of world trade because much of the world's trade in manufactures is trade between industrialized countries with similar factor endowments. Also, much of the trade between these countries involves two-way exchanges of goods with similar factor proportions.[2] New trade theory draws from industrial organization theory and incorporates the concept of imperfect competition as a form of market structure, the role of economies of scale to explain intraindustry trade in particular, and the arbitrariness of capital and technological accumulation in particular locations.[3] New trade theorists distinguish between interindustry trade based on comparative advantage and intraindustry trade based on economies of scale. They argue that the industrial structure of a country's production will be determined by its factor endowments. Within each industry, there are assumed to be a range of potential products, each produced under conditions of increasing returns. Because of these scale economies, each country will produce only a limited subset of products in each industry. This intraindustry specialization is arbitrary. Each country will import products even in industries in which it is a net exporter. The more similar the countries are in factor endowment, the less different their industrial structures, and the more their trade will have an intraindustry character. New trade theorists suggest that trade in manufactured goods among industrial countries is 'benign' that is, something, less likely to cause adjustment problems than trade between countries at different stages of development and hence easier to liberalize (e.g. by eliminating trade quotas and tariffs).

New trade theorists suggest that, in some manufacturing sectors, specifically those where R&D plays a crucial role, there may be a strong temptation to engage in protectionist or interventionist policies. However, Krugman (1996) argues that the prospects of 'strategic trade policy' are not very good for three reasons. First, he argues that there is no evidence that aggressive strategic trade policy can produce large gains. Second, reaching a practical consensus on which sectors are really strategic is difficult. Third, attempts at implementing strategic trade policy turn into thinly disguised interest-group politics.

There are problems, however, with new trade theory. Although this theory may account for intraindustry trade by factors associated with product differentiation and increasing returns, it does not fully explain the causes behind these factors (Aoki 1995). Nevertheless there are a number of issues highlighted by new trade theories that may have important implications for the relation between technology and the international division of labour. These issues include:

- A rise in intraindustry trade (trade in similar goods between similar countries—especially within Europe).

- The emergence of 'supertraders', countries with extremely high ratios of trade to GDP. (e.g. exports as percentage of GDP in 1990 was 174 for Singapore, 144 for Hong Kong, 78 for Malaysia, 70 for Belgium, 64 for Ireland, 52 for the Netherlands). Semi-finished products are sent to have labour-intensive operations on them and then shipped on.

- The emergence of large exports of manufactured goods from low-wage to high-wage countries (for instance, Malaysia may assemble notebook computers, the microprocessors for which are developed in the USA—but this will appear as a 'high tech' export from Malaysia).

These developments distort conventional indicators of trade and economic growth and force us to examine the created advantages regarding innovation and rethink traditional perspectives on trade (especially comparative advantage).

THE 'ECLECTIC' THEORY

Dunning developed the eclectic theory (Dunning 1977, 1980), which relies on the Ownership Location and Internalization (OLI) paradigm. This model has been, for more than two decades, the dominant analytical framework to explain international trade and international production. It argues that the extent and location of foreign production by multinationals is determined by the interaction of three sets of variables. First, ownership-specific advantages are competitive advantages relative to those of other firms (and particularly those in the country in which they are seeking to make their investment). Second, locational advantages are those advantages of alternative countries which firms need to use jointly with their own competitive advantages. Third, as argued by internalization theory (Buckley and Casson 1976), the greater the net benefit of internalizing cross-border intermediate product markets, the more likely it is that the firm will prefer to engage in foreign production itself rather than license the right to do so. Also, depending on the economic and political features of the country, multinationals may pursue different objectives: market-seeking; resource-seeking; rationalized or efficiency-seeking; and strategic asset-seeking FDI.

In brief, the eclectic theory argues that a firm will engage in foreign value-adding activity if:

1. It possesses ownership advantages vis-à-vis firms of other nationalities in serving particular markets (e.g. possession of intangible assets (such as

know-how), advantages of common governance, i.e. the advantages of activities being internalized in a firm).

2. Assuming it possesses ownership advantages, it must be more beneficial to the enterprise possessing these advantages to use them (or their output) itself rather than to sell or lease them to foreign firms (internalization advantages).

3. Assuming it possesses ownership and internalization advantages, it must be in the global interests of the enterprise to utilize these advantages in conjunction with at least some factor inputs (including natural resources) outside its home country, otherwise foreign markets would be served entirely by exports and domestic markets and domestic production (location advantages) (see Box 8.1 for a fuller explanation).

Although the framework may be helpful as a descriptive and taxonomic device, doubts have been raised about the capacity of this model to explain and to predict the behaviour of multinationals (Buckley 1989). Its forecasting power may be impaired not just because of the concentration on classification but by the excessive number of variables emerging from the three OLI classes of advantages and used to explain international involvement (Ietto-Gillies 1992). However, implications may be drawn about the sectors that are likely to generate more international production, the countries that are likely to generate greater outward investment, and the importance of new markets (e.g. China) for the expansion of various kinds of market-seeking investment.

GLOBAL COMMODITY CHAINS

The literature on global commodity chains and global production networks (GPNs) seeks to explain the impressive magnitude of increases in foreign economic presence in certain less developed countries and in peripheral regions of the developed countries (Gereffi and Korzeniewicz 1994). These contributions combine an analysis of core–periphery relations within the framework of multinationals and their networks of production relationships. Since production steps can be separated, it is common for the sourcing of labour-intensive components and stages of production to be from low-wage countries, especially for products that are subject to intense price competition. Gereffi (1994) uses the idea of alternative governance structures within commodity chains to differentiate between 'producer-driven' and 'buyer-driven' commodity chains. The former are associated with capital- and technology-intensive industries (e.g. cars, computers, and semiconductors) where power is concentrated in the headquarters and flows downward through the dispersed subsidiaries and value-added flows back up the commodity chain. The latter refer to chains within which central services (such as

---

Box 8.1 The eclectic paradigm of international production

---

1. **Ownership-Specific Advantages** (of enterprises of one nationality (or affiliates of same) over those of another)

   a. Property rights and/or intangible asset advantages Product innovations, production management, organizational and marketing systems, innovatory capacity; non-codifiable knowledge; 'bank' of human capital experience; marketing, finance, know-how, etc.
   b. Advantages of common governance

      (i) Which those branch plants of established enterprises may enjoy over *de novo* firms. Those due mainly to size and established position of enterprise, for example, economies of scope and specialization; monopoly power, better resource capacity and usage. Exclusive or favoured access to inputs, for example, labour, natural resources, finance, information. Ability to obtain inputs on favoured terms (due for example, to size or monopsonistic influence). Exclusive or favoured access to product markets. Access to resources of parent company at marginal cost. Economies of joint supply (not only in production), but in purchasing, marketing, finance, etc. arrangements).
      (ii) Which specifically arise because of multinationality. Multinationality enhances above advantages by offering wider opportunities. More favoured access to and/ or better knowledge about international markets, for example, for information, finance, labour etc. Ability to take advantage of geographic differences in factor endowments, markets. Ability to diversify or reduce risks, for example, in different currency areas, and/or political scenarios.

2. **Internalization-Incentive Advantages** (i.e. to protect against or exploit market failure)
   Avoidance of search and negotiating costs.
   To avoid costs of enforcing property rights.
   Buyer uncertainty (about nature and value of inputs (for example, technology) being sold).
   Where market does not permit price discrimination.
   Need of seller to protect quality of intermediate or final products.
   To capture economies of interdependent activities (see b. above).
   To compensate for absence of future markets.
   To avoid or exploit government intervention (for example, quotas, tariffs, price controls, tax differences, etc.).
   To control supplies and conditions of sale of inputs (including technology).
   To control market outlets (including those which might be used by competitors).
   To be able to engage in practices, for example, cross-subsidization, predatory pricings, leads and lags, transfer pricing, as a competitive (or anti-competitive) strategy.

3. **Location-Specific Variables** (these may favour home or host countries)
   Spacial distribution of natural and created resource endowments and markets.
   Input prices, quality and productivity, for example, labour, energy, materials, components, semi-finished goods.
   International transport and communications costs.
   Investment incentives and disincentives (including performance requirements, etc.).
   Artificial barriers (for example, import controls) to trade in goods.
   Infrastructure provisions (commercial, legal, educational, transport and communication).
   Psychic distance (language, cultural, business, customs, etc., differences).
   Economies of centralization of R&D production and marketing.
   Economic system and policies of government; the institutional framework for research allocation.

Source: Excerpt from Dunning (1988: 27).

product specification, purchase orders, and marketing) are separated from production conducted by dispersed independent manufacturers (e.g. large retailers or brand name merchandisers in footwear). Corporate power originates with the retailer/brand holder and although it can be dispersed by independent ownership of manufacturers, value-added stems from the branding and marketing functions. Further work along these lines by Henderson et al. (2002a) considers how GPNs of firms (e.g. involved in design, production, and marketing of a given product) are organized globally and regionally, identifying the lead firm and the distribution of corporate power within the networks, and the influence that institutions have on the networks. We discuss this work further in Chapter 10.

There are some problems with this analysis in that, even though a good proportion of the exports of, for example, the East Asian newly industrialized countries are caught up in global commodity chains; it is the local ownership of production which is responsible for the greater increases in output (Storper 2000, and for illustrations of this evidence for South Korea, see Amsden 1989, and for Taiwan, see Wade 1990). This framework, however, helps trace the international relocation of production processes through networks of firms and the geographic concentration at a global or regional level.

GEOGRAPHY AND KNOWLEDGE CREATION

While the above strands of literature may provide some explanation of the international division of labour, they are less comfortable in explaining the distribution of knowledge-based activities, particularly those between and within advanced countries and under the governance of multinationals. One contribution from geography to explain the organization of production and its relation to the creation of knowledge is Storper (1995). He suggests a typology of four basic kinds of production system based on the different kinds of interaction around the tasks of technology or knowledge development, each of which is characterized by a particular tendency in the dispersion or concentration of this development. The first includes non-durable consumer goods heavily affected by fashion and/or design, which are concentrated in particular geographical areas where informal processes of communication are central. Examples of these include the fashion centres of the world, high-quality machinery production and metalworking districts (as in southern Germany, Japan, or Italy), and customized advanced service-delivery networks in London, Tokyo, or New York. The second includes large-scale R&D-oriented high-tech industries which are tied to geographically concentrated entrepreneurial networks of innovators (such as Silicon Valley), even though their other innovative activities are not highly localized. The third category includes the case where economies of scale and long production runs dominate. Here, products are typically made by large oligopolistic firms that are capable of operating production systems on a national and international scale such as those in the automobile industry. The fourth includes the recent transformation towards flexible specialization that requires, even in mature industries, regional cores that facilitate such organizational developments as JIT production and other organizational innovations (discussed in Chapter 4 and shown, by Womack et al. (1990) for the automobile industry and by Piore and Sabel (1984) for more traditional craft sectors in the Third Italy). Storper (1995) argues that, first, many industries have an early stage where technologies 'pop up' in many different places. Second, in most industries, production is consolidated around one or just a few places (such as Detroit for automobiles, Silicon Valley for semiconductors). Subsequently, knowledge required for routine production diffuses to many other places and the industry's production units tend to spread out (see attempts to copy Silicon Valley in Cambridge, the UK, and Taiwan in Saxenian 2002 and Chapter 10). Nevertheless, much of the most advanced technology development stays at the industry's initial centre.

GLOBALIZATION OF PRODUCTION AND INNOVATION

While in the first section of this chapter we argued that the structure and organization of national production systems has changed since the mid-1970s towards the globalization of production and distribution, more relevant to students of technology is the debate as to whether there has been a globalization in the production and commercialization of knowledge (Cantwell 1995; Patel 1995; Dunning 1997; Dunning and Wymbs 1999; Pavitt and Patel 1999). On the one hand, contributors to this debate argue that countries are very specialized in terms of what kinds of technology their firms patent (Patel and Pavitt 1991). The big firms of the world generate a high percentage of their worldwide patents in their home countries, and these are quite consistent with the overall profiles of export specialization of the home country's economy. This is because even large firms are embedded in wider institutional contexts and systems of externalities which enable them to generate new commercializable knowledge (systems of innovation, see Chapters 6 and 7) and these are highly specific to particular countries and regions. Pavitt and Patel thus argue that globalized firms produce most of their patents in their country of origin; that is, that the national system of innovation is still the most important influence in the production of knowledge and organization of innovation. Others argue that the conclusions drawn by Patel and Pavitt are problematic because their argument relies on patent statistics and these do not account fully for the sourcing of technological knowledge. We discuss these debates in more detail in Chapter 10.

International negotiations, the new world economic system and innovation

The WTO, established on 1 January 1995, is the umbrella organization governing the international trading system. Its three main pillars are a revised General Agreement on Tariffs and Trade (GATT)[4] for cross-border merchandise trade, the Agreement on TRIPS and the GATS. The new world economic system is not one of truly integrated world markets but one based on the powerful influence of the Triad, as evidenced by the participants of major trade disputes (see Box 8.2). It has also been argued that the WTO may be condemned to failure because it is a technical body lacking in political power, political understanding, and political skill (Rugman 2001) unable to deal with the economic and social integration issues posed by the operation of multinationals and with the matters that involve environmental regulations, labour standards, and human rights. In what follows, we will focus on the TRIPS and the GATS.

TRIPS

Protection of IPR was one of the three new issues, along with trade in services and trade-related investment measures (TRIMs) on the agenda for the Uruguay Round Negotiations[5] (1986–94), the inclusion of which was a requirement for US participation in the talks (Stegemann 2000). US corporations with an interest in strengthening patent and copyright protection shaped the intellectual property related trade diplomacy of the USA during the Uruguay Round. While the patent interests were led by research-based pharmaceutical producers, the copyright interests included the publishing, motion picture, recording, and software-design sectors (Stegemann 2000). What these industries had in common was that their products could be copied at relatively low cost and therefore they had the most to gain from strengthening the protection of IPRs internationally. The groups lobbied energetically for support from US trade diplomacy but pursued different strategies. While the patent interests sought minimum standards for patent protection worldwide (including pharmaceutical patents) and were opposed by the World Intellectual Property Organization (WIPO) (a UN agency with a one-nation, one-vote decision-making), especially by less developed countries, the copyright interests sought to enforce existing national standards of copyright protection. Also, while the patent interests concentrated on achieving a multilateral solution through GATT, the copyright interests favoured bilateral diplomacy, which usually meant unilateral use of US leverage and trade sanctions through 'section 301' of the Trade Act of 1974 and amended in

---

Box 8.2 EU and US trade wars

---

1. **Bananas**. The dispute is about free access to the EU banana market. The US food multinationals Chiquita Brands (formerly the United Fruit Company) and Dole successfully lobbied the US government to take the EU's banana regime to the courts of the WTO. Bananas produced by US companies in Central and South America can be up to 60 per cent cheaper than those produced in the Caribbean, but have faced tariffs, quotas, and distribution barriers in Europe (which gives preferential treatment to bananas originating from ex-colonies and to EU producers). Europe is acting to protect one of its most important international development programmes and the interests of domestic distributors through its licensing system. The EU's banana regime had created trade tensions for decades before it was disputed under the GATT and eventually the WTO has ruled against the EU twice but the EU has been reluctant to comply fully (Rugman 2001).

2. **Beef**. The dispute between the USA and the EU over hormone-treated beef turned into a trade war when the EU failed to comply with the findings of the WTO's dispute settlement body. In 1966, the EU consolidated a series of regulations that prohibited the use of six hormones for growth promotion purposes, claiming that these were hazardous to human health. EU citizens support the European Parliament in what appears to be a health and safety regulation. WTO proceedings found against the EU arguing it must change its regulation and allow imports of hormone-treated beef. The EU made no changes to its regulations (Rugman 2001).

3. **Foreign sales corporations**. The USA has appealed against a 1999 decision by the WTO that its foreign sales corporations tax scheme is an illegal export subsidy. Foreign sales corporations are offshore subsidiaries of large US corporations, mostly located in tax havens such as the US Virgin Islands and the former British colony of Barbados. They carry out export transactions on behalf of their parent corporations (this includes firms such as Boeing, General Motors, Eastman Kodak, Microsoft and Caterpillar, and US affiliates of foreign corporations such as Daimler-Chrysler). The USA exempts 15 per cent of a foreign sales corporation's profits from corporate income tax. Firms set up skeleton companies in tax havens to fill the requirements for a foreign sales corporations. Originally, to claim tax exemption on profits, the goods had to be 50 per cent manufactured in the USA. Whether or not exports increase as a direct result of tax relief, US firms are better off through the foreign sales corporation tax scheme. The foreign sales corporations also provide an incentive for foreign companies to set up affiliates in the USA. WTO found against the USA and the USA will appeal (Rugman 2001).

4. **Genetically modified crops**. The USA has filed a complaint to the WTO (together with Canada and Argentina), challenging EU's ban on genetically modified (GM) crops. The USA argues that the EU's claims regarding the health effects of GM crops are scientifically unfounded. The USA claims genetically modified crops would boost agricultural productivity in less developed countries. Others claim small farmers in less developed countries would be ruined by dependence on seeds from US multinationals like Monsanto Egypt, which was originally going to be a complainant, withdrew its support for the case before the WTO. The EU is exercising pressure on Argentina[1] to reconsider its support for the case (*Financial Times*, 29 May 2003, p. 8).

1 Argentina's corn exports to the EU, for instance, have tripled since 1995 during the period when US corn growers were blocked from Europe because of the GM moratorium (*Financial Times*, 29 May 2003).

1984. However, their interests converged in the Uruguay Round (Stegemann 2000). The adoption of the TRIPS Agreement in the Uruguay Round was a trade-off across issues: the less developed countries granted greater protection of IPR in exchange for more secure access to the import markets of industrialized countries. However, the benefits for less developed countries are still to be demonstrated.

The TRIPS covers seven main areas of intellectual property: copyrights, trademarks, geographical indications (a sign used on goods that have a specific geographical origin and possess qualities or a reputation that are due to that place of origin, for example, Tuscany olive oil or Roquefort cheese), industrial designs, patents, layout designs of integrated circuits, and undisclosed information including trade secrets. In each area, the agreement specifies minimum standards of protection that governments must provide, requires governments to put in place procedures to enforce them, and provides means of dispute settlement. In practice, the TRIPS put in place a universal set of IPR protection standards that satisfied the demands of industrialized countries. The benefits to firms in developed countries (in promoting innovation though increased potential returns and though the diffusion of knowledge through the publication of patent application) of high levels of IPR protection have been explored theoretically and empirically. More clear, however, are the benefits to be accrued by multinationals in the 'life sciences' and information sectors. On the other side, the argument made by industrialized countries is questionable: they suggest that higher levels of IPR protection would also benefit less developed countries by encouraging local innovation and by attracting foreign firms that would be more willing to invest and transfer technology.

Although there has been a long tradition of studies of IPR (starting with the work of Machlup, Arrow, Scherer and Nordhaus) many aspects remain misunderstood. It has been argued that debates regarding the effect of IPR in economic development suffer from incomplete understanding of the nature of intellectual property and measurement problems. Furthermore, the impact of IPR is 'case sensitive'—different for different industries and countries (Abbott 1998).[6]

In the future, two things seem certain. First, an increase in the number and scope of TRIPS Agreement complaints brought by industrialized countries against developing countries might reasonably be foreseen (if we use as a predictor the number of countries cited in the US Trade Representative in its annual Special 301 report on IPR) (Abbott 1998). Second, important future negotiations will focus on areas in which less developed countries have a major stake, such as defining rights over genetic resources, biotechnology inventions, plant varieties, and the development of the legal framework for the digital environment.

The TRIPS agreement could affect investment, technology transfer, and innovation. Stricter IPR can have negative effects on less developed countries. Such rights may not stimulate local innovation and may not promote overseas innovation relevant to these countries' needs. They are also likely to raise the cost of technology imports—through higher licensing fees and product prices, more advanced skills needed to manage the new regimes and greater scope for monopolistic practices by holders of IPRs. Finally, stricter IPRs can constrain technology development through copying, and reverse engineering—activities used to great effect by newly industrializing economies and, earlier, by many industrialized countries (UNIDO 2002, see Box 8.3).

In the eyes of some developing countries' analysts, less developed countries are being harried into adopting intellectual property protection that would guarantee the proprietary interests of multinationals in information hardware

---

Box 8.3 The case against strong protection of intellectual property rights

Protection of intellectual property rights has played an ambiguous role in technological and industrial development. Many of today's industrialized economies relied on slack intellectual property rights to promote the technological development of their enterprises, shifting to stricter rules only when they had achieved technological parity with the leaders. The most technologically dynamic East Asian Tigers—the Republic of Korea and Taiwan Province of China—used copying and reverse engineering to promote local enterprises, only recently adopting stricter intellectual property rights.

Protection of intellectual property rights is based on the premise that innovative activity is seriously constrained if innovators cannot reap the fruits of innovation. Thus copyrights protect the rights of authors (book, music, software), trademark registration protects unique trade logos and symbols, and patents protect the rights of inventions with industrial applicability (products as well as processes). For technology development, patents are most relevant.

Patents are supposed to spur innovation. They grant exclusive rights of use, sale and manufacture to owners of intellectual property, compensating them for undertaking expensive and risky innovative activities. But in exchange, owners must disclose the invention on the patent document for 'anyone skilled in the art' to be able to replicate. Thus patents are a trade-off a market distortion is created in exchange for disclosing the information on the technology. This disclosure is intended to benefit society by disseminating new technologies and encouraging competitors to invent around it, encouraging a second round of innovation.

Advocacy of strong intellectual property right presumes that the benefits of appropriation for innovators and disclosure for competitors outweigh the drawbacks of market distortions, making intellectual property rights beneficial to society. This presumption, almost impossible to test empirically, remains the subject of debate. Most less developed countries, seeing themselves as users of existing technologies rather than makers of new ones, consider it premature to adopt Western models of intellectual property right protection. Indeed, technological catch-up could be constrained if developing countries enforced stronger intellectual property rights. Stricter rights could raise the cost of technology imports and restrict the ability to learn from reverse engineering . . . .

Two developments may change the shape of things to come. First, investment flows are seeking global destinations, and enterprises' ability to protect their knowledge assets is a critical determinant in choosing destinations. Second, all WTO members that are signatories of the TRIPS agreement have agreed to reform their intellectual property rights regimes by 2004. Though the eventual benefits of this universal protection remain to be seen, for now such reform is a bitter pill for domestic industry and consumers to swallow.

Source: Excerpt from UNIDO (2002: 24).

and software and 'life sciences' at the expense of biodiversity, the 'social' needs of innovation and the every day rights of consumers and users (Box 8.4). The countries that will benefit from the harmonization of patents and copyrights laws are those whose economies produce and export pharmaceuticals and software (especially the US, followed by Japan and the EU), in which market consolidation has become an objective of key players and every perceived barrier—from piracy to protectionism—a matter of concern in multilateral trade negotiations. These are followed by a second tier of countries (China and India) that have information capacity in certain areas but are weak in others, and would have preferred to have a stake in the international information market before agreeing to intellectual property rules (Thomas 1999). Countries that did not have adequate protection for product or process patents have been given the option to develop a regime by 2000 or 2005. Countries that opted for the later date, however, were required to accept patent applications from 1995 (on the 'pipeline' principle) and exclusive marketing rights (EMRs) respectively for pharmaceuticals and agrochemicals. These mechanisms invalidate the concessions ostensibly given to less developed countries during the transitional period (Thomas 1999). IPR is also discussed in Chapter 6.

GATS

One of the Uruguay Round's three 'new' trade issues, alongside TRIMs and TRIPs, is services, which made their way to the global trade policy agenda at the end of 1993 largely against the vocal opposition of an influential group of less developed countries' GATT members. Brazil and India led the resistance, arguing that services were primarily a matter of domestic regulation. Accordingly, services were seen as having little to do with international trade and, thus, were best left out of the trading system's purview. It was strongly felt in less developed countries that the advent of a multilateral framework of rules and disciplines for services was largely inimical to their development prospects and fledgling service sectors. Less developed countries do not have much of a comparative advantage in the production and exchange of services. They also feared that a full-scale negotiation would afford developed countries (and especially the USA), a back-door way of achieving greater investment regime liberalization than under the considerably watered-down negotiating mandate that was agreed for TRIMs (Sauve 2000). Less developed countries were not alone, receiving the support of the EU before it recognized the crucial role that services trade and investment liberalization (e.g. elimination of FDI screening and local content requirements) would need to play in fulfilling the ambitions of the Single Market programme.

Box 8.4 TRIPS and the less developed countries

---

1. **The case of India**. In India, the issue of seed patents has received attention from national and international farmers coalitions and NGOs. The farmers demonstrations in the early 1990s against the multinational seed firm Cargill, and the contemporary struggles against the introduction of genetically modified 'terminator' cotton seeds by the multinational Monsanto have been widely discussed. The shift to hybrid seeds have transformed regions from mixed farming to a monoculture of hybrid cotton, making farmers dependent for their livelihood on the success or failure of the cotton crop. Despite strong pressures from the WTO, the lobby against seed patenting in India has prevented the passage of the Patent Amendment Act in the Indian Parliament. It has also been argued that the 'pipeline' principle (also called mailbox) encourages patent applications which will surely be declined for being anti-national (e.g. 'basmati' rice, 'turmeric', 'neem'). Also, EMRs allow easy entry of multinationals such as the British pharmaceutical multinational GlaxoSmithKline and the American agricultural and pharmaceutical multinational Monsanto. The German pharma-ceutical and agricultural multinational Hoechst holds patents on compounds extracted from Indian indigenous medicinal plants. Despite the Biodiversity Convention, there are no mechanisms to tackle 'bio-piracy'. The lack of policing in the protection of biodiversity and 'cultural heritage' stands in marked contrast to many efforts launched to safeguard patents on biogenetic resources and acquire and protect copyrights for products from 'sunrise' industries (Thomas 1999). Unlike patents, the issue of copyrights has not elicited the same level of sympathy at national levels or from NGOs. For some researchers, the lack of popular lobby impedes debates on the future of copyrights in India (Thomas 1999). This has led to a fast accommodation with global, TRIMS-friendly, copyright laws. An example of the neglect in this area is the lack of indigenization of software in India. While, for example, the Windows NT platform has been adapted and translated the major Latin languages and 'enabled' for many languages such as Catalan and Icelandic and the Mackintosh operating system has been localized for many languages, including that spoken in the Faeroe islands, neither firms offer programmes in Hindi—one of the most widely spoken languages in the world (Thomas 1999).

2 **The case of Latin America**. The process of reform of IPRs legislation in Latin America is driven by the need to comply with the TRIPS Agreement and to respond to the demands of the USA, rather than local private or technocratic groups (with the possible exception of breeders' rights) (Correa 2000). Contrary to expectations, the TRIPS has not eliminated tensions with USA, which insisted on using unilateral mechanisms rather than the multi-lateral procedures established under the WTO. The changes in patent laws, particularly in the pharmaceutical field, has been the most contentious area in the current process of reform of IPRs regimes in Latin America. The majority of countries excluded the protection of pharmaceutical products until TRIPS. The US government and the American pharma-ceutical industry applied pressures to get not only an immediate recognition of pharma-ceutical product patents, but also a retroactive protection under the so-called 'pipeline' principle. The USA placed Argentina on the 'priority watch list' and retaliated against Argentina (Correa 2000). Regarding copyrights, foreign software firms implemented (not-ably through the 'Business Software Alliance') an aggressive campaign in Latin America to combat piracy, including the multiple use of individual licences. Regarding geographical indications, the main demandeur in this area is EU. The adoption of new laws has led to significant increase in patent applications, for the consideration of which many national offices are poorly staffed and lack sufficient resources. In particular, this has led, as in India, to an increase in applications for trivial or nonpatentable developments. Also, this has led to an increase in litigation, especially 'strategic litigation' against small- and medium-sized

Box 8.4 (*Continued*)

firms to suppress local competitors (Correa 2000). Serious concerns have been raised about the impact of pharmaceutical patents on prices of medicines and affordability to the public (there are a number of studies showing welfare losses and income gains to patent owners for different countries). There is no evidence that this might be compensated by foreign direct investment. On the contrary, Latin America has experienced de-investment and the only investment it has witnessed is that designed to acquire local firms.

The GATS, which came into effect in 1995, was the first multilateral agreement to cover trade in services. The GATS defines trade in services as the supply of a service through any of four modes of supply (Chang et al. 1999; Mukherjee 1999):

1. Cross-border trade (e.g. exporting software on a computer disc/CD-ROM, sending business reports, or architectural blueprints by fax and computer-to-computer transfer);

2. Trade by consumption abroad (the movement of consumers from one country to another to avail of foreign services, as in tourist services or medical services; although it also includes activities such as ship repair abroad, where only the property of the consumer moves);

3. Trade through commercial presence (the setting up of an establishment in a foreign country, including corporations, joint ventures, partnerships, representative offices, and branches); and

4. Trade by temporary presence of people (movement of service providers from one country to another, as in the case of lawyers travelling abroad to provide legal services or intracorporate transferees).

The development of communication and transportation infrastructures has favoured the growth of cross-border supply even in sectors where it was hardly considered an option until recently (see Miozzo and Soete 2001; Miozzo and Miles 2002). Each country has scheduled its commitments in individual sectors with respect to each mode, with the level and nature of commitment generally differing across modes. Like the GATT, the GATS provides a legal basis on which to negotiate the multilateral elimination of barriers that discriminate against foreign service providers and otherwise deny them market access. Unlike the GATT, in which the principles of national treatment (e.g. non-discrimination) and market access (e.g. freedom of entry and exit) are provided automatically, in the GATS they are negotiated rights and obligations. The negotiations on national treatment and market access for services in the GATS constitute the equivalent of tariff negotiations for goods in the GATT (Broadman 1994). The approach by the USA and EU is to eliminate 'barriers' to trade in services, including restrictions to the number of service suppliers, limits on foreign ownership or shareholding, restrictions on the type of legal entity, and compulsory joint venture or numerical quotas.

The GATS has come under heavy criticism, especially because it does not have a pro-development agenda (*The Guardian*, 25 February 2003). The USA proposed the GATS because it thought it would not have to offer concessions but on the contrary expected to receive concessions (Lazar 1990). The USA and now the EU requests market access on 'backbone' or 'enabling' sectors such as telecommunications, financial services, transport, and certain business services in less developed countries (http://europa.eu.int/comm/trade/services/). The EU is seeking gains for its banking, telecommunication, and business services firms, linking these to the reform of the common agricultural policy (export subsidies which depress global food prices and impoverish farmers in less developed countries). This includes the much-criticized initiatives for the provision of water in poor countries such as Bolivia, Panama, and Trinidad (*Guardian*, 25 February 2003).

Export interests of less developed countries have not been included in the GATS rules and regulations. The specific commitments of member countries as contained in the GATS clearly indicate that it is essentially a trade deal for multinationals from the industrial countries (Mukherjee 1999). Analysts point out that the USA pushed labour services and immigration issues off the bargaining table but, nevertheless, had no qualms about forcing its views on fair labour standards on less developed countries (e.g. Lazar 1990). Indeed, the area with fewest commitments in the GATS is low-skilled labour-intensive activities (quotas, migration, qualifications) (Rugman and Boyd 2001). The participation of less developed countries is more as importers of services rather than exporters of services. There are, however, a handful of successful export services from less developed and newly industrialized countries— South Korean and Brazilian construction firms, Singapore airlines, Indian computer software (Athreye 2005; Kagliwal 2004), and health services in Cuba (which receives both patients for treatment and students for training). For the rest of the less developed countries and their services, the economic sustainability issues in the context of importing large quantities of services without appropriate openings in exports are quite important, given the precarious foreign exchange position of most less developed countries and the mounting trade and fiscal deficits (Mukherjee 1999). Despite the growing importance of cross-border electronic delivery of software services, the movement of people remains a crucial form of delivery. About 60 per cent of Indian exports in computer software are supplied through the temporary movement of programmers. However, the US and other countries' governments have introduced quotas and other restrictions on visas hindering these exports (Mattoo 2000).

The US proposals for the GATS supposedly focused on trade-related issues, not investment issues, but in addition to advocating the principle of national treatment, the USA also called for the right of commercial presence. Commercial presence in most cases would necessitate an establishment in the trading partner country and so it is unclear how implicitly incorporating a right of establishment together with the principle of national treatment could not be anything other than allowing foreign investment in all service sectors covered by the agreement. Therefore, while supposedly an agreement on trade-related issues, not investment-related issues, the right of commercial presence requires establishment and therefore investment (Lazar 1990). Indeed, the mode of supply against which the greatest number of bound commitments were undertaken relates to commercial presence ('establishment-related' trade in services). The GATS is therefore as much an investment agreement as one concerned with cross-border trade. In the case of less developed countries, such an outcome is problematic, given their initial misgivings over the treatment of FDI under a services cover (Sauve 2000).

While some (e.g. Sauve 2000) argue that the quickest way to promote service sector efficiency is to continue unilateral dismantling of discriminatory and non-discriminatory barriers to services trade and investment, others (e.g. Koekkoek 1988) argue that infant-industry considerations (limited in scope or time), designed to give less developed countries the opportunity to catch up with the developed countries are best. The paradox of GATS, and of less developed countries' attitudes towards it, is that during the period of its development far-reaching changes in less developed countries policies towards trade and investment in services have taken place, especially in the key infrastructural areas of basic telecommunications and financial services (Sauve 2000). Since the mid-1980s, under various lending programmes of the World Bank and the IMF, comprehensive macroeconomic and structural reform programmes were introduced across less developed countries. Trade policy reforms were critical components of the reform package, with many non-tariff barriers being swept away, tariffs being rationalized, and measures being introduced to facilitate trade. Some argue that less developed countries' 'autonomous' liberalization efforts have not received credit from other countries (or reciprocal or comparable liberalization from their trading partners) (for the case of Korea see Choi 2001).

In addition to the above, the USA's attitude towards the GATS has been severely questioned. It has been argued that if the USA's intention was to liberalize trade in services in order to produce global economic benefits and to restore the pre-eminent role of the GATT as a regulator of international commerce, it would not have strengthened the protectionist potential of section 301 with the Trade and Tariff Act of 1984 and the Omnibus Trade and Competitiveness Act of 1988. Indeed, in 1986 for example, the USA, with the threat of sanctions (under section 301) was able to secure access for its insurance companies into the Korean market (Lazar 1990).

Liberalization in trade in services is a controversial issue. Mattoo (2000) argues that services and goods liberalization differ. In services, attaining efficiency is not just a matter of liberalizing trade barriers but of instituting an appropriate domestic regulatory framework. Policy choices under negotiating pressure may be inadequate, leading to market access concessions that allow increased foreign ownership of existing firms rather than new entry, and guarantee the privileged status of foreign incumbents. Indeed, little concern in the literature and in the policy discussion is given to the types of reform of less developed countries in response to the GATS and the implications or desirability of these outcomes.

Conclusion

This chapter reviews a number of different theories of international business and trade that can offer us an explanation of the complex relation between technology and internationalization. We seem to have entered a new phase of internationalization, 'globalization', characterized by qualitative changes in the operation and management of multinationals and concentration of investment. Also, there have been important changes in international trade negotiations and the framework for policy. In Chapters 9 and 10 we explore further the impact, the relation between innovation and globalization by analyzing networks and strategic alliances for the development of innovations, and the changes in the international location of innovation.

Notes

1 The arguments of Hirst and Thompson (1999) are discussed in detail in Chapter 10.

2 There are other critiques of the Hecksher-Ohlin model, including the neglect of the specific nature of the internal problems of capital accumulation in less developed countries. This model assumes identical production function in the same industry in all countries, but, in fact, more advanced economies may be more cost effective even in industries with high labour content due to superior infrastructure and better management and workforce skills.

3 Two ways of formalizing the international product cycle in a dynamic framework, the 'product variety' model (notably Krugman 1979) and the 'quality ladder' model (notably Segerstrom et al. 1990; Grossman and Elhanan 1991) have been developed. These models determine the rate of investment and the resulting pace of innovation in a general equilibrium model of ever-rising product qualities. Long-run growth rates depend positively on the extent of product differentiation, on the stock of fixed resources (an implication of dynamic increasing returns), and on the productivity of resources in the research laboratories, but depend negatively on the subjective discount rate. These models include a 'seesaw' product cycle (Krugman 1995)—when an improved variant is introduced, it would first be exported

by the high-wage North; when the technology diffuses, the industry would move south; but the North would reclaim the industry when a better variant was introduced.

4 There has been a rivalry between the GATT and the United Nations Conference on Trade and Development (UNCTAD) throughout the 1970s, with most less developing countries opposing the GATT in their approach of promoting less developed countries' trade opening and export promotion (Finger 1991).

5 The Uruguay Round is the largest trade organization in history, spanning seven and half years (twice the original schedule) and, by the end, including 123 countries. The trigger for the Uruguay Round was a November 1982 ministerial meeting of GATT members in Geneva. After many debates, oppositions, and negotiations, the round of negotiations was launched in September 1986 in Punta de Este, Uruguay. The agenda covered most trade policy issues and talks were going to extend the trading system into several new areas, notably trade in services and intellectual property, and to reform trade in the sensitive sectors of agriculture and textile. Some negotiations were completed quickly (e.g. telecommunications and financial services), other need further negotiation and a number of issues are now part of the Doha Development Agenda. Critics argue that the majority of less developed countries would lose from agricultural and textile liberalization being negotiated in the Doha round while the book is being written. As argued by Robert Wade in an article in *The Guardian.*

Developing countries should be prepared for the Doha round to fail and then support a new trade round on terms fairer to them. They should insist on changing the terms away from 'you open your markets to our manufactures and services and we promise to open ours to your agricultural exports'.... In the new round they should insist on the right to use an array of industrial policy instruments of the kind that most of the developed countries used when they were in their development phase, which they gave up in the agreements from the Uruguay round (*Guardian*, 13 November 2005).

6 Some writers in economics and law have approached intellectual property rights critically (see Chapter 6), but few economists have addressed the more fundamental assumptions on which intellectual property rights systems are based, such as the possibility of identifying inventors or other owners of intellectual property which is produced in distributed innovation processes or networks. Anthropologists and sociologists, however, have considered questions of intellectual and cultural property produced as a result of the cumulative skills of whole communities, possibly over several generations (e.g. Strathern 1996, 1999; Coombe 1998; Harvey 1998). Indigenous knowledge about plants, for example, belongs to a whole community rather than to identifiable individuals, and is based on tacit knowledge of complex local ecologies and on subtle skills in selection and breeding (Harvey 1998). Current intellectual property rights, however, tend to protect more rigorously the property rights of Western biotechnology companies in reproducing new plant strains by cell culture (as well as creating new ones by genetic engineering), rather than protect the ownership rights of whole communities in non-industrialized societies over the new strains and new species they have developed over generations. Similarly in the area of music, the use of traditional tunes or copyrighted musical themes in new arrangements and new combinations, provides a problem for international agreements on copyright law (Andersen 2004). As Harvey (1998) points out, re-contextualization is part of the creative process, and is more than simply abstracting and adopting pats of existing work. Contemporary use by a community may be quite different from earlier uses (which may be patented or copyrighted). In Chapter 6 we discuss the expansion in recent years of the definition of what constitutes 'property', and in the variety of ways in which ownership rights can be exercised. Patent law has changed its scope over the

twentieth century while a variety of other instruments have also been mobilized, including copyright, trademarks, and exclusive rights to databanks. On balance there has been a gradual convergence of different intellectual property rights systems (though they are based largely on Western visions and legislation), even though the extension of patent and copyright law into new areas, such as business process methods, or new areas of software and web design, means that there will always be 'administrative lag' in covering newly emerging fields associated with commerce and innovation. Related to these changes in what constitutes 'property', is the extension of markets into areas where they did not previously exist, and the privatization of material and intellectual property previously in the public domain (see Chapter 6).

9 Networks and Alliances

Introduction

In Chapters 8 and 10 we discuss globalization, the current phase in the internationalization of economic activities, as being characterized by a number of qualitative changes which are much more important than quantitative changes like the extent of overseas compared to home investment or the amount of world trade compared to domestic trade. These qualitative changes include the increased importance of FDI from the mid-1980s, compared to world trade as a mechanism for international activity; increased levels of intrafirm trade within multinationals, and important changes in the structures of the organizations in which innovation takes place. These structural changes include the increasing concentration of global oligopolies, following successive waves of mergers and acquisitions across national borders; and the development of a complex of international networks of interfirm and interorganizational cooperative alliances, joint ventures, and technological agreements (see also Chesnais 1997; Chesnais and Simonetti 2000; OECD 1992).

This chapter focuses on some of these qualitative changes in the forms of organization and the management structures of innovating firms. Multinationals are orchestrating activities within and external to the firm which make them the central nervous system of a much larger group. Dunning (1997) has called this 'alliance capitalism'. He suggests that the tendency of firms to enter into alliances is a key feature of late twentieth century capitalism, with the 'network firm'—meaning a cluster of firms and other organizations linked together in a variety of collaborative alliances—as this period's characteristic organizational form.

In some senses, however, agreements, collaboration and cooperation involving technology have been around a long time. Examples are the trusts of the late nineteenth century and international cross-licensing, for example, in the chemical and electrical machinery industries of the 1920s and 1930s. Cartel agreements on prices and who makes what are another example of collaboration, while the research consortia between the major oil companies of different countries, again in the 1930s, are further cases. More recently there are customer–supplier arrangements for joint development or technical assistance in the post-Second World War period. Two examples of cartels are the German chemical and dye cartel, out of which the conglomerate firm IG Farben was formed in 1926 and disbanded at the end of the Second World War (e.g., Hayes

1987); and the very strong European cartel in sex hormones formed by drug firms Schering, Roussell, Boehringer, Ciba, and Organon in the 1930s and 1940s (Gaudillière 2005; Gaudillière forthcoming). US firms such as Parke Davis sought to break those firms' monopoly positions by finding alternative routes to sex hormones which had not already been patented by members of the cartel. Success was only achieved with the establishment of the new firm Syntex in Mexico in 1944 to make progesterone from various species of *Dioscorea*, a plant source to replace the animal sources hitherto used. User–supplier networks are discussed by Lundvall (1985, 1992), while Freeman and Soete (1997) refer to user–supplier links in the application of computers and Walsh et al. (1980) refer to them in the adoption of synthetic materials.

If networks have existed for some time what, then, has given rise to such a growth in publications on collaborative alliances, joint ventures, and other linkages among innovators in the last twenty years? First of all there has been a considerable growth in numbers of agreements since the 1980s (see Figure 9.1). Second, there has been an increase in the range of industrial sectors involved in agreements. Third, the numbers of agreements which cross national borders has grown particularly in recent years. And fourth, the number of agreements involving technology, that is, collaborative production of new technology, or sharing of technology, had grown by the early 1980s. In a study conducted at the International Business School, INSEAD, Morris (1984) for example, reported that 64 percent of alliances and joint ventures involved production of scientific

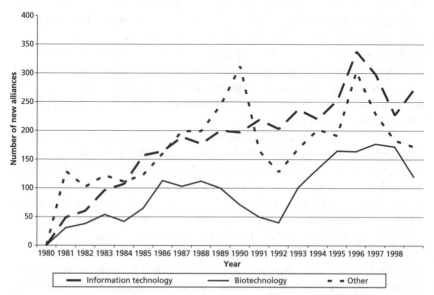

Figure 9.1 International interfirm alliances in high-tech industry. 'Other' includes new materials, aerospace and defence, automotive, chemicals (non-biotech).

(*source*: Tampubolon 2003, data from MERIT-CATI database)

and technological knowledge and were not just joint ventures in marketing and/ or production, which had been more common in earlier agreements.

ICTs have promoted collaboration, permitting easier contact among researchers in the same firm and their collaborators elsewhere, sometimes in different countries, by means of intrafirm communication devices such as the firm intranet, videophone, or teleconferencing. CAD and testing of products from large complex engineering projects to molecules, plus design of manufacturing processes, services and advertising, can all be linked by computer so that different members of the team at a distance can see and interact with the same image on the screens of a network of computers (computer assisted collaborative work).

There has been an increased variety of types of agreements. The OECD (1992) classified nine types of competitive and pre-competitive agreement, for example (see Table 9.1). These were:

a) University-based collaborations with industry, financed by the firm.

b) National and international government–industry projects, such as those within the European Union's various Framework Programmes. ESPRIT, for example, the European Strategic Programme of Research on Information Technology, ran from 1984 to 1998 in four phases within the first four Framework Programmes. BRIDGE, (Biotechnology Research for Innovation, Development and Growth in Europe) ran from 1990 to 1994 within the second Framework Programme. The seventh Framework Programme is due to run from 2007 to 2013 and will support cooperative research in key scientific and technological areas between universities, industrial firms, research centres, and public authorities. The key areas in question include food and health (and biotechnology related to these), ICTs, nanotechnologies, new materials, new production technologies, energy, and the environment (including climate change).

c) Research corporations in the private sector, financed by several firms who are shareholders. An example was the European Computer Research Centre formed by ICL, Bull, and Siemens in 1987; this later formed the basis for the ESPRIT programme, so started as an example of '*c*' and became an example of '*b*' (Mytelka 1995). Another example was the Microelectronics and Computer Technology Corporation formed by twenty-one US firms in 1982 once the antitrust legislation had been modified to allow this to happen by the National Cooperative Research Act 1984 (Nelson 1993).

d) Large firms give venture capital to smaller ones to keep a window of opportunity open without making the commitment of an investment in developing in-house capabilities until they know whether they want to pursue them further. For example, Hoffmann La Roche provided continuing venture capital money to the biotechnology firm Genentech. Later, in

Table 9.1 Research, technology, and manufacturing cooperation agreements and the R&D, production, and marketing spectrum

Pre-competitive stage			Competitive stage			Manufacturing and marketing cooperation		
Research and development cooperation			Technological cooperation					
A	B	C	D	E	F	G	H	I
University-based cooperation research financed by associated firms (with or without public support)	Government-industry cooperative R&D projects with universities and public research institute development	Research and development corporations on a private joint-venture basis	Corporate venture capital in small high-tech firms (by one or by several firms otherwise competitors)	Non-equity cooperative research and development agreements between two firms in selected areas	Technical agreements between firms concerning completed technology, including among others technology-sharing agreements; second-sourcing agreements; complex two-way licensing; cross-licensing in separate product markets	Industrial joint-venture firms and comprehensive R&D, manufacturing, and marketing consortia	Consumer-supplier agreements, notably partnerships	One-way licensing and/or marketing agreements (including OEM sales agreements)
Many partners		Several partners	Few or very few partners					

Source: OECD (1992).

1990, the Swiss drug firm took a controlling interest of 51 percent of Genentech, and then in 1999 bought the remaining shares so that it became a wholly owned subsidiary. Monsanto made a venture capital investment in the agrobiotechnology firm Calgene, and again, bought it later, in 1997.

e) Non-equity cooperation: when two or more firms make a commitment to fund a specific research project of specified duration.

f) Technology agreements based on technology already existing for example, sharing of US design capabilities and Japanese fabrication competencies in semiconductors (cross-licensing).

g) Comprehensive R&D, manufacturing, and marketing consortia. This category includes joint ventures, in which the consortium exists as a legal entity whose shares are owned by two or more other firms. AgrEvo was a joint venture in agrobiotechnology between Schering AG and Hoechst, which has since been bought by Aventis, the merged firm formed from Hoechst and Rhône-Poulenc. Airbus is an example in aircraft of a joint venture of 20 percent BAe Systems (formed from a merger of British Aerospace and Marconi Electronic Systems) and 80 percent European Aeronautical Defence (EADS) (formed from Daimler-Benz Aerospace or DASA (Germany), Aerospatiale (France), and Construcciones Aeronauticas SA or CASA (Spain)). Box 9.1 summarizes the evolution of the Airbus consortium, Box 9.2 and Figure 9.2 show the collaborative activities between European aerospace manufacturers to build and market Airbus aircraft. Aerospatiale is responsible for developing and manufacturing the

---

Box 9.1 The evolution of the Airbus consortium

Formed in 1970 as a consortium of France's Aerospatiale and Deutsche Airbus to make the first twin-engine wide body airliner A300

- Spain's CASA joined in 1971;

- Airbus Industrie Group d'Interet Economique (Airbus GIE or consortium) transferred headquarters from Paris to Toulouse in 1974;

- British Aerospace joined in 1979;

- The four partners—Airbus France, Airbus Deutschland, Airbus UK, and Airbus Espana operated as national companies, each with distinct responsibilities for producing various parts of the aircraft, which would be transported to Toulouse for final assembly. The sales, marketing, and customer support was conducted by Airbus GIE.

- The Airbus Consortium transferred holdings into a new company established in 2000, a joint venture 80 percent owned by the European Aeronautic Defense and Space Company (EADS) (formed by a merger of Aerospatiale Matra of France, Daimler-Chrysler Aerospace of Germany (DASA) and Construcciones Aeronauticas of Spain (CASA), ownership retained by the French and Spanish governments), and 20 percent owned by BAE Systems (formed by a merger between British Aerospace and Marconi Electronic Systems).

Source: http://www.airbus.com (accessed 27 September 2005).

Box 9.2 The Airbus joint venture

The Airbus joint venture coordinates collaborative activities between European aeronautics manufacturers to build and market Airbus aircraft. The joint venture involves four partners: Aerospatiale (France), DASA (Daimler-Benz Aerospace, Germany), British Aerospace (UK), and CASA (Construcciones Aeronauticas SA, Spain). Research, development, and production tasks have between distributed among the partners. Aerospatiale is mainly responsible for developing and manufacturing the cockpit of the aircraft and for systems integration. DASA develops and manufactures the fuselage, British Aerospace the wings, and CASA the tail unit. Final assembly is carried out in Toulouse (France) by Aerospatiale. Unlike production, commercial and decision-making activities have not been split between partners. All strategy, marketing, sales, and after-sales operations are carried out by the Airbus Industrie joint venture, which interfaces with external stakeholders, such as customers. To buy an Airbus, or to maintain their fleet, customer airlines cannot approach the partner firms directly, but have to deal with Airbus Industrie. Airbus Industrie defines the alliance's product policy and elaborates the specifications of each new aircraft model. Airbus defends the point of view and interests of the alliance as a whole, even against the partner companies themselves should the individual goals of the latter enter into conflict with the collective goals of the alliance.

In the business environment of the Airbus joint venture are competing aircraft manufacturers, and the suppliers of components, sub-assemblies and engines, which can be seen as a producers' pyramid, with hierarchical tiers, progressively less detailed in terms of aerospace components from 1 to 3 (see Figure 9.3):

1. Aircraft assemblers—Airbus and Boeing duopoly for planes over 100 seats, plus Bombardier and Embraer (regional jets), Bell and Eurocopter (helicopters).
2. Manufacturers of propulsion systems (engines)—General Electric, Pratt & Whitney, Rolls Royce
   On-board avionics—Honeywell (USA), Sextant Avionique (France).
   Airframe structures and subassemblies such as landing gear—Messier-Dowty (France), Héroux-Devtek (Canada)
   Nacelles (outer casings)
   Hydraulic systems
3. Electronic subassemblies and fuselage parts. The aircraft industry is high-value added and strongly affected by scale and timing. It depends on rapid technological progress, government R&D and supply chain management (strategic alliances, product co-development, certification of suppliers, delivery times, sharing of risk and costs). It is highly concentrated, has high barriers to entry, and increasing returns, requiring very large capital commitments to design and produce aircraft. It is one of the industries with the highest international R&D partnering index.

   The industry is characterized by geographical clusters of prime contractors surrounded by hundreds of small and medium suppliers of components and parts, e.g., in Seattle (around Boeing), Toulouse (around Airbus) and around General Electric engine plants in Cincinnati, Ohio, and Lynn, Massachusetts. These aerospace producing regions are very specialized, with international spillovers (components can be shipped from one region to another as transportation costs are only a small proportion of total costs).

Source: Do et al. (2003); Niosi and Zhegou (2005); Hagedoorn (2002).

---

cockpit and for systems integration, DASA the fuselage, British Aerospace the wings and CASA the tail unit. Final assembly takes place in Toulouse by Aerspatiale. (Figure 9.3 shows the aircraft producers' pyramid.)

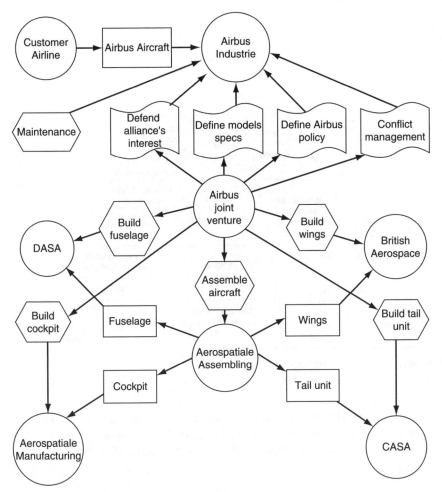

Figure 9.2 Collaboration in the Airbus consortium
(*Source*: Do et al. 2003: 4)

h) Customer supplier agreements, which are longer term than market transactions.

i) One-way license agreements with transfer of technology. These might involve medium-term interaction to ensure transfer of technology, not just market transactions.

This chapter considers alliances and networks as a qualitative organizational change accompanying globalization. The first section explores the existing databases on interfirm agreements. The second section examines the reason for the growth in alliances since the 1980s. The third section explores different disciplinary approaches to the study of networks. The fourth section explores US policy to encourage collaboration between firms and public sector research

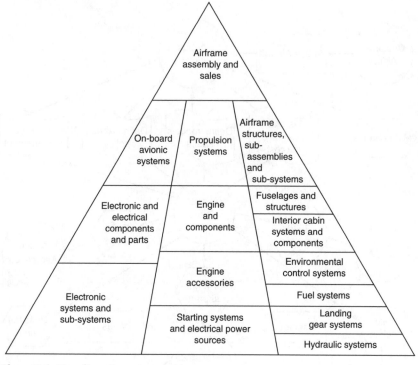

Figure 9.3 Aircraft producers' pyramid
(*source*: Niosi and Zhegy 2005: 12)

organizations. The fifth section examines the linkages between small and large firms in biotechnology. The final section considers the tensions between networks and national innovation systems in the case of the Maastricht region.

How do we know about agreements?

In the 1980s several groups of researchers began to compile databases of interfirm agreements. For example the MERIT/CATI database at the University of Maastricht contained information on several thousand agreements between firms from 1980 (Hagedoorn 2002) and is the original source of the data used in Figure 9.1. These databases have been used to indicate the growth of agreements over time in various high- and medium-technology areas, and the numbers of agreements by region (e.g. US–Japanese agreements, US–European agreements). The LAREA/CEREM database (LAREA/CEREM 1992) at the Université de Paris X at Nanterre focused mainly on biotechnology. A database mainly of agreements between firms in ICT was constructed at Bocconi University, Milan. The earliest database was the one constructed by researchers at INSEAD, the international business school at Fontainebleau, mentioned above. Not all of these research databases have been kept up to date. For example, the LAREA/CEREM one was considered too much work to maintain, and not really a worthwhile use of research resources, once similar data became available from businesses,[1] though the MERIT database has continued to be maintained, and is now publicly traded. A variety of commercial databases is available via the Internet: for example, recap.com provides to subscribers a database on biotechnology alliances and agreements.

The original databases were constructed on the basis of information published in the business press (such as the *Financial Times*) and various trade journals (such as *Scrip* for alliances in pharmaceuticals). Chesnais (1988) has discussed the limitations of data from these sources, which may be summarized as follows: the data and their accuracy and completeness depend on organizations such as those mentioned wishing to publish the information, and depend on the firms making the agreements providing the details in the first place. Firms in some industries may be less inclined to make their alliances public than others. A majority of the source journals are in English, which may reflect a bias towards agreements in English-speaking countries, and is likely to focus on those by firms in the advanced countries. There may be a tendency to underestimate the number of agreements in early years, before the topic became fashionable. However, most experts on the phenomenon of alliances concur that there has definitely been a substantial growth in the number and variety of agreements since the 1980s.

Why has there been such a growth in alliances since the 1980s?

Alliances are risky, and are not without disadvantages. The alliance partner might be a competitor, and might be expected to act opportunistically. A certain level of trust between the partners is necessary, and this might prove to be misplaced. Potential partners might be expected to give as little and get as much as possible from the arrangement. There are, however, several reasons why forming an alliance with another firm has nevertheless become an attractive proposition. First, the number of technologies and specialist fields contributing to any innovation or industry has increased dramatically, so innovating firms need to keep up to date in a wider and wider range of activities. Few firms have the resources to be constantly at the cutting edge of such a wide range of disciplines and fields. In principle, they could buy in some of the expertise they need, but there is a substantial amount of evidence from the innovation literature that indicates how important it is to be doing R&D in a field oneself, in order to benefit from knowledge bought in from elsewhere (Cohen and Levinthal 1989).

A researcher in a field will understand the significance for their work of new advances in that field, and whether a particular area of knowledge is worth licensing from someone else. Related to this is the importance of tacit knowledge in adopting a new technique or technology—an innovating firm which buys in techniques developed elsewhere will have to go through a learning process before becoming as efficient at using the new knowledge as the developers of it.

Research and development now costs a lot more than it once did, in real as well as relative terms, because the cost of specialist equipment, materials, and highly trained staff has increased more rapidly than the average costs of staff and production inputs, and there is more specialist equipment, materials and expertise to buy, aside from buying in outside knowledge as such. The increased range of activities needed for any successful innovation, mentioned earlier, will also increase the cost of innovation. Continuing innovation by supplier firms will further increase the costs of materials and equipment by generating completely new tools and inputs that a firm will need in order to keep up with its competitors.

Another source of increased costs and additional areas of expertise for the firm is the changes in the regulatory environment, generating, for example, the need for compliance with standards, pollution controls, product safety, proof of efficacy (drugs), requirements for recyclability, or use of energy. There has also been an increasing science content in technology over the past few years, so that car manufacture, for example, is as high-tech as aircraft manufacture was a couple of decades ago, while aircraft manufacture is of course even more high-tech (Walsh 1988). This means that many more areas of technology require inputs from basic science, which again adds to the costs and the breadth of competencies in innovation. Development work is usually more costly than basic science, but the latter adds to the costs if it is an additional expenditure, and—more important—it adds to the uncertainty of a project.

Lastly, the increased levels of international competitiveness add further pressures on the innovating firm. To recoup their additional costs they need to move into more markets (both in terms of geographical area and new applications). The further a market is from the firm's core competencies, the more risky the venture; and the more players in the market, the greater will be the competition over market share. Shortening product cycles increases the pressure on firms to launch a product quicker, and to move into new markets more speedily, too. This increases levels of risk, and the likelihood of launching a product before all the troubleshooting has been done, with consequent damage to the firm's reputation.

There is a tension between the need for flexibility—where smaller firms have the advantages—and the need for the critical mass necessary in R&D, production, and distribution for the 'take off' of an activity—which is where the resource advantages of larger firms are significant (Rothwell 1989). Also, there is a tension between the need for economies of scope and economies of scale.

High-tech areas in particular need a lot of investment in research, development, and design just for a firm to be able to be a player in their chosen field, which can be a barrier to innovation for smaller firms and new entrants.

Arm's-length relationships, or buying and selling in the marketplace between producer and user of knowledge, involve costs and risks, while internalization, for example via merger or acquisition of a small firm with the desired technological capability, could mean increased inertia—the problem of the larger firm. So a trade-off between these two might be achieved by collaboration, which involves neither an arm's-length transaction, because a longer-term relationship requiring a degree of trust between the partners is involved, nor is it a hierarchical relationship such as may be found where all the activities are managed in-house, because the firms have not merged. There will also be a trade-off between the short-term financial advantages of an arm's-length relationship (where one firm is not committed to longer term investment in a technological specialism) and the longer-term advantages of being in a strong position to build a good technological base, to move into new markets, and to exploit discoveries (which might come from a merger) (Mytelka 1995).

Agreements, therefore, are a compromise between the advantages of flexibility and the reduction in uncertainty, with the possibility of sharing costs, risks, and skills. The advantage of a cooperative research agreement is that the firm that wishes to access a new area of technology can work with the one that produces it, thus gaining tacit knowledge and the experience to understand the significance to their project of what their partner is contributing but without bearing all the costs, including the opportunity costs, of developing everything they need in-house. We return to consider these issues more fully in the theoretical discussion.

The reasons for collaboration so far considered are supply side issues: they contribute to firms' abilities to produce innovations in an increasingly competitive situation. Our own research also suggests a demand side factor in firms' strategic thinking: that is, they hope that by forming alliances with other organizations overseas (and sometimes eventually taking over firms or setting up subsidiaries in the overseas location) they can also influence demand side conditions. For example, they can influence the regulatory environment and the attitude of professional intermediaries who recommend (or do not recommend) innovative products (Walsh et al. 2000). Monsanto's advertising campaign to promote the safety and environmental friendliness of genetically modified crops, discussed in Chapter 7, is an example of an unsuccessful attempt to influence consumer demand and the regulatory environment. The Senior Advisory Group on Biotechnology (SAGB) was set up in the early 1990s by the largest chemical firms worldwide which had an interest in biotechnology and branches in Europe. The job of SAGB was also to influence the demand side by providing material to convince the European Parliament and administration that the industry's points of view concerning intellectual property and regulatory issues were in fact in line with the interests of the EU as a whole (e.g. SAGB 1990). That is, they sought to enlist the European authorities' support of their project.

Different approaches to alliances and networks

Agreements and collaboration between actors in the innovation process have been studied from a variety of disciplinary perspectives, especially during the 1980s and 1990s. Just as the theoretical bases have been different from one to the other, so has the type of empirical work carried out. It would be a stereotype to say that much of the economics work has focused on formal agreements between firms, while much of the sociological work has been concerned with informal networks of individuals, since there are studies in both disciplines that fit the other category, or neither, while there has also been some convergence or interdisciplinarity in the empirical studies, if not the theoretical frameworks (e.g. Senker and Faulkner 1996). Indeed, many of the studies of interfirm or interinstitutional alliances have not been analysed as *networks* at all. Pisano (1989, 1990), for example, in a study of biotechnology in the pharmaceutical industry, did not consider networks of multiple linkages but a set of individual agreements in which choices were made in each case between in-house R&D, outsourcing, and collaboration involving ownership of some of one firm's equity by the other, each choice being analysed using transaction cost economies (discussed later). Hagedoorn's work, in contrast, not only used a different disciplinary perspective (still economics, but neo-Schumpeterian or evolutionary economics) but also mapped a network of interfirm agreements in IT, biotech, and other areas, showing clusters of interactions, strong and weak links, and geographical closeness (e.g., Hagedoorn 2002).

Many of the economists' studies of alliances focused on formal links between firms because they used the databases mentioned earlier, which are compilations of just such links. However, sociologists also use data sets of individual linkages, compiling information on the motivations of the partners or the benefits and problems the partners expect from the relationship. They may examine issues involved when a partner from a business culture works with someone from a public research culture, or when partner from a different national or regional culture collaborates. Questions of decision-making, control, power and hierarchy are also the subject of sociological studies of collaborative agreements. Powell, at Stanford University, has written extensively about organizational behaviour and the structure of organizations (notably networks) and draws on the work of economists such as Schumpeter, Nelson, Winter, and Mowery (Powell et al. 1999; Powell 2000).

1. *A strategic management approach to networks: complementary assets.* Complementary assets were originally a concept of Teece (1986), although it has since grown wings, being adopted and adapted by many other scholars. The idea is that the benefits of exploiting a new technological opportunity do not necessarily go to the owner of the technology. Exploitation—which might be implementation in practice in a variety of ways as well as commercial exploitation—requires in addition to the technological knowledge, a variety of competencies and other assets, such as management skills, manufacturing skills, marketing skills, accumulated knowledge in all these areas, distribution networks, finance, and networks of linkages with professionals or lead users to test and try out new products, feed back to the innovators, and later recommend the products to new users. In some cases an important complementary asset may be the relationship established with a regulatory body and the experience of steering a product through the regulatory system: another may be the ability to lobby and campaign to change the regulations, especially where products and services with a controversial or ethical dimension are concerned—like oral contraceptives in the 1960s[2], in vitro fertilization in the 1970s[3] and food or drugs based on GMO in the 1980s.[4]

2. *A sociological approach to networks: actor-network theory.* The concept of actor-networks was developed by Callon, Akrich, and Latour at the Centre de Sociologie de l'Innovation at the Ecole des Mines in Paris, and Law in Keele and then Lancaster University (see, Callon 1986; Law 1992; Latour 1993; Law and Hassard 1999). One of most important things to do in commercializing an innovation is not just getting it to work and developing an efficient production process (if it is a product). It is building *a network of interests* in the success of the innovation, making sure a range of actors, all with their own different goals and interests, identify the success of the innovation as being the way to reach their own goals, or equivalent to them. As Akrich et al. (2002) say, the 'classical' analyst of innovation explains the success or failure of an innovation in terms of its intrinsic qualities, which persuades more and more users by its infectious quality (or fails to do so). They, however, remind the reader that the adoption of an innovation goes through a series of decisions which depend on the particular context in which the innovation will be used so that success or failure depend on the expectations of the users and the particular problems which they hope the innovation will solve, and therefore on the alliances which the innovator can mobilize in support of the innovation, and the active participation of all those who have decided to develop it. The interests of all the participants then become bound up with those of the innovator so that all the actors are aiming for the same objective.

The networks in actor-network theory are different from those studied by economists such as Hagedoorn or sociologists such as Powell, in that not only are both formal and informal linkages, between individuals and organizations, part of the network, but things as well as humans play an important part in the actor-network. Furthermore, the actors are unable to exist independently of the networks which they create in the course of their social existence, and which define who they are and how they function, just as the networks cannot exist without the actors which make them up. As argued by Callon:

The actor-network should not ... be confused with a network linking in some predictable fashion elements that are perfectly well defined and stable, for the entities it is composed of, whether natural or social, could at any moment redefine their identity and mutual relationships in some new way and bring new elements into the network. An actor-network is simultaneously an *actor* whose activity is networking heterogeneous elements, and a *network* that is able to redefine and transform what it is made of (Callon 1987: 93).

A person can only play the role of a researcher, for example, by being linked to other researchers, through conferences, publishers, journals, libraries, and emails for the exchange of knowledge and research material, as well as being linked to sources of primary information, for example experimental methods and laboratories, samples of material to be studied, or archives and interviews, as appropriate. They are likely also to be linked to sources of research funds and users of their research output (which might be firms or policy-makers). Their connections to other people will often take place via inter-mediaries (papers, patents, samples, equipment, money, and the complex socio-electronic networks of the Internet). With other linkages and other networks the person concerned might play additional roles (e.g. parent, political campaigner, DIY enthusiast, or patient) or might have alternative occupations altogether.

Mustar's case study of the adaptation of microwave technology for industrial uses (rather than domestic uses, as in microwave ovens) illustrates this approach (Mustar 1991). The main event described in the case study was the creation of a small firm by researchers from the public sector. The technological innovation was the industrial application of microwaves for drying a range of items including manuscripts, chemical compounds, and biscuits. The organizational innovation was the establishment of the firm to commercialize the work of a government science laboratory. To succeed, the entrepreneurs enlisted the support of a variety of people and organizations with very different goals. One was Electricité de France (EDF)—the public utility firm whose goal was to exploit new uses of electricity, and to find ways in which customers would use more electricity, in order to increase sales. Another was the CNRS (National Science Research Centre), which is not a single centre as the name suggests, but the main employer of public sector researchers in the sciences and social sciences in France. It is somewhat like the UK's Research Councils or the USA's National Science Foundation (NSF), which are also government agencies, except that in addition to funding research, CNRS also employs (typically on long-term contracts) the scientists who carry out that research, whereas the UK Research Councils and NSF allocate research funds to organizations which are independently managed (though they may be dependent for finance on public funds) to carry out the research (typically on short-term contracts). Like other public sector research organizations (whether considered part of the civil service or independent) the goals of the CNRS were, and are, the pursuit of knowledge, the dissemination of knowledge via the publication of books and papers, and increasingly the demonstration that the research they fund is a useful way of spending public money (e.g. by providing inputs to innovation, decision-making or policymaking activities).

Another actor in the story was the French Ministry of Industry, whose goal was national independence in energy, and yet another was AFME—l'Agence Française du Management de l'Energie, the French energy management agency—whose goal was energy saving. Various lead users, customers and potential customers played a role in the story, including the food industry, and in particular the biscuit manufacturer which sought a way to produce crisper biscuits. Another example of a lead user was a museum whose goal was to preserve and restore the manuscripts and documents in its collections. There were also various investors: banks, venture capitalists, and firms, whose goals were to make profits and gain other financial benefits. The various individuals who were employed by the new firm, whether they were the researchers from CNRS who created the enterprise as a way of commercializing their discoveries, or other staff recruited from elsewhere, had an assortment of personal goals, including a successful career (however defined), rewarding work, a good standard of living, an interesting life, and so on.

All these actors not only had very different goals, but in some cases their goals conflicted (e.g. Electricité de France wanted to increase the use of electricity in France, while AFME wanted to economize on it). However they were all led to believe that their individual goals could be met by achieving the common goals of the successful creation of a new small firm, and the commercialization of the innovation. Mustar's analysis describes a network of interests expanding like ripples on a lake, so that new participants are drawn in by one or more of the existing ones, the commitment of each one built on that of each of the others. Actor-network theory uses a number of concepts (or the terminology for them) which come originally from semiotics, and which we now discuss. The concept of 'translation' is used to describe the way in which innovators or network builders present their own objectives in such a way that they represent an opportunity to someone else with different goals, just as a translator will represent something in a foreign language or in professional or technical jargon in such a way that it means something to someone from a different language or cultural group. An entrepreneur will thus translate a scientific or technological discovery into a business or investment opportunity, as the founders of the microwave firm did. Callon, for example, writes about a translation process which first reduces the macrocosm of the 'world' to the microcosm of the laboratory by formulating complex problems into ones that are easier to treat and solve; then second, the world of the laboratory submits these to a questioning process that can be written about and discussed; and then third, the outcome of this is disseminated back to the 'world' so it can in some senses be reconfigured (Callon 2003).

A related concept used by actor-network theory is the 'obligatory passage point', which captures the idea that the innovator makes support for the innovation or some other goal indispensable to other actors in such a way that their interests become bound up together, and their goals are translated into the common one. The founders of the microwave firm convinced a number of organizations that their goal of making money would be reached by investment in the firm, and persuaded the museum that its goal of restoring manuscripts could be achieved by drying them using microwave technology in the form supplied by the firm as part of the process, while the biscuit manufacturing firm came to believe that it would achieve a competitive edge by selling crisper biscuits, which in turn could be done by using the new technology. Support for the innovation or for the success of the firm became an intermediate goal or obligatory passage point, and the actors concerned were enrolled or enlisted into the network.

Actor-network theory also uses the term 'intéressement' which means 'interest' in the sense of profit sharing, or workers' participation, and is used to refer to the way in which the enlistment or enrolment of new actors into the network takes place—they are 'interested' by the translation. The normal French word for interest is 'intérêt' which is used to mean intellectual interest, return on investment, material interest, or advantage, and we do not find it very helpful to translate intéressement as 'interest' though English language publications by the proponents of actor-network theory do in fact use the words 'interest' and 'intéressement'. We prefer to translate it as the enlistment of other actors. Akrich, Callon and Latour have recently republished in English a two-part paper which originally came out in French in 1988 (Akrich et al. 2002), and which illustrates some of these points with reference to a series of cases from the innovation literature. As the title suggests, two of the key elements in the success of innovation according to their analysis are the art of 'intéressement' and the art of choosing the right spokesmen and women.[5]

The anti-cancer drug, Taxol, mentioned in Chapter 2, has a number of networks, and the cutting as well as building of several networks as the story unfolds (Strathern 1997; Goodman and Walsh 2001). Just to take one example, the Environmental Defense Fund, a Washington-based activist group who were concerned about the fate of the old growth forests, petitioned the US Fish and Wildlife Service in 1990 to list the pacific yew tree, *Taxus brevifolia*, as a threatened species. Taxol was extracted from the bark of the pacific yew, which in turn was harvested in the old growth forests of the Pacific Northwest, and the Environmental Defense Fund used the fate of the tree as a symbol of the fate of the forest as a whole. The significance for us is that they were able to enlist the support of a number of actors, some of whom might have been expected to be opponents, including William McGuire, the oncologist in charge of the clinical trials of Taxol with ovarian cancer, and Susan Horwitz, the biologist who had discovered Taxol's unusual mechanism of action. The American Cancer Society also sent a letter of support. The press portrayed a confrontation between those who had an interest in harvesting the yew tree and processing the bark to obtain Taxol (including women with ovarian cancer as well as the various cancer charities, the NCI, and the doctors and scientists doing research on cancer) and the environmental campaigners who wanted to save the forest and thus prevent or at least restrict the harvesting of the yew. The Environmental Defense Fund, however, were able to enlist the support of all these actors, because their petition, if successful, would have led to the sustainable management of the yew harvest, as well as research into the tree and its habitat, which was in everybody's interests. Box 9.3 and Figure 9.4 illustrate the wider Taxol network.

As we have seen, links between humans are often defined by the movement of non-humans such as money, publications, scientific instruments, and biological/chemical/geological specimens between them. It is an important role because the skills and knowledge of a human actor can be incorporated in the object or inscribed on it: in the design of an artifact, the programming of computer, the chemical compound that no one else has synthesized, or the analytical technique developed as a result of original research. It is also important because objects can have a substantial effect on other actors. So in actor-network theory, things are allowed to be actors though 'by themselves, things don't act. Indeed ... there *are* no things "by themselves" ... instead there are *relations*, relations which sometimes make things' (Callon and Law 1995). Thus, a banknote is more than a piece of paper. It represents the conventions of commerce, the relationships of banking and investment. It links people, causing them to act in certain ways (Strathern 1999: 194). Studying the interaction of actors and the movement of non-humans at the same time, giving each equal weight in their descriptions, is also a way of overcoming the constant over-emphasis, de-emphasis and re-emphasis of 'natural' versus 'technical' or 'discovery-push' versus 'market demand-pull' forces in describing an innovation, or 'social shaping' versus 'technological determinism' and the similar dichotomy of nature versus nurture in education and psychology in other disciplines.

During the 1930s, an important aspect of the work of research scientists investigating steroid hormones was the passage through the network which linked them, of samples of material such as progesterone and

Box 9.3 The Taxol network

The Plant Screening Program was an interagency cooperative research programme to screen plants from all over the world for anticancer activity. It was coordinated by the US National Cancer Institute (NCI) and the US Department of Agriculture (USDA), whose jobs were to collect plant samples, to screen them for anticancer activity, to organize the extraction of active plant materials and their transfer to the clinic as medicines, and to organize the transfer of the plants from which they were derived to crop status in the USA. The (mainly) botanists at the USDA collected the plant materials and studied promising plants and their habitats; the (mainly) chemists at the NCI organized the screening process and oversaw the progress of promising compounds through its own and the Food and Drug Administration's testing, clinical trial and decision procedures.

Figure 9.2 illustrates the network of organizations and individuals involved. The list below indicates their interests, and their role in the taxol network.

1. **Chemists**: interested in understanding more about the structure of complex molecules and the relationship between structure and biological activity. Extracted, isolated, and purified active ingredients of yew bark; determined structure of Taxol, investigated chemical properties and named it Taxol in 1969. Later sought synthetic alternative to extraction from bark.
2. **Botanists**: interested in plants and their habitats, especially where the plants had economic potential. Collected plant samples worldwide and sent them back to Washington, DC, to be redistributed to subcontractors for screening.
3. **Cell biologists**: to understand the mechanism of action of cells in the presence or absence of outside materials, e.g., chemicals. Discovered taxol's unique mechanism of action 1979.
4. **Clinical oncologists**: new ways of treating cancer, improving the quality of life and survival rate of people with cancer. Carried out clinical trials of Taxol, beginning 1984.
5. **Public sector researchers** in general: pursuit of knowledge, publishing papers.
6. **NCI**: coordination of search for natural product that would be active against cancer. Justification of huge level of government spending on cancer projects in general and plant programme in particular. Oversaw progress of Taxol from tree to clinic.
7. **USDA**: coordination of plant collection, and collection of knowledge about promising plants and their habitats. Owned yew trees on Forestry Commission land.
8. **US Department of the Interior**: owned yew trees on public land managed by the Bureau of Land Management.
9. **Loggers and bark collectors**: from multinational timber companies to independent individuals—to make a living from the trees in the forest. As subcontractors to USDA then NCI cut trees, stripped bark and shipped it to chemical firms for extraction of Taxol in bulk.
10. **Environmental campaigners**: to achieve the sustainable management of the forest
11. **People with cancer**: to get better, or prolong life, or reduce discomfort. Treated with Taxol or other drugs.
12. **Pressure groups** of cancer activists concerned about perceived lack of investment in breast cancer (e.g., compared with AIDS) and concerned about price of drugs.
13. **Bulk chemical suppliers (SMEs)**: to make money by acting as intermediaries between raw material suppliers and the drug industry, using their 'good manufacturing practice' status. Produced Taxol in bulk from yew bark and supplied it to Drug firm to manufacture dosage form.
14. **Drug firm**: to get to product to the clinic, make a profit, gain market share, retain good reputation, etc. (profits not often possible in the cancer business (hence the public sector involvement)). Commercialized Taxol.

Box 9.3 (*Continued*)

15. **Food and Drug Administration (FDA)**: regulated clinical trials and market launch. Gave clearance for Taxol to be used in ovarian cancer (1992) and breast cancer (1994).
16. **Investors**: to gain financial benefits.
17. **Individuals**: to achieve a successful career, rewarding work, good standards of living, an interesting life, etc.

Some of these actors were led to believe that their individual goals could be met by supporting the goal of the Plant Screening Program and the commercialization of the chemical discovered as a result. Later all of the actors were encouraged to believe that their individual goals could be met by supporting the development and commercialization of Taxol (including the way in which it was managed and carried out).

androsterone, extracted from animal tissue and body fluids. It was important because these samples were extremely expensive when obtained from these sources, and the academic scientists benefited from the donation of material by the industrial firms with which they were collaborating (see Walsh 1998). However, it was more than the equivalent of a donation of resources from industry to public sector science: and indeed some of the researchers who supplied samples were in the public sector themselves, such as Tsukamoto and Ueno in Japan, who supplied Russell Marker (at Pennsylvania State College), with diosgenin which they had extracted from the root of a species of yam, *Dioscorea tokoro*, in 1936 (Tsukamoto and Ueno 1936). These samples embodied important advances in knowledge made earlier, often by the researcher who made the donation, which the recipients would otherwise have had to acquire in some other way, for example by obtaining a license to a patent. In the case of the diosgenin from *Dioscorea*, Marker was able to use it as a starting material for making progesterone, the whole process published jointly with Tsukamoto and Ueno shortly before their respective countries declared war with each other (Marker et al. 1940). It was a process of enormous significance for the take-off of further research in the field, and subsequently for the production of steroid drugs (anti-inflammatories, contraceptives), not to mention the development of the pharmaceutical industry in Mexico, as a result of a major drop in costs due to the replacement of animal by vegetable raw materials, once new sources of *Dioscorea* in Mexico had been exploited.

3. *Economic approach to networks: transaction cost economics*. Actor-network theory is primarily a sociological approach to the understanding of networks, although it is not a conventional sociological approach, and it is strongly influenced by evolutionary economics. We turn now to a more clearly economic approach to networks. To economists, the price system is the key mode of coordinating resource allocation. The alternative is to coordinate it hierarchically within the firm, in which case the firm by means

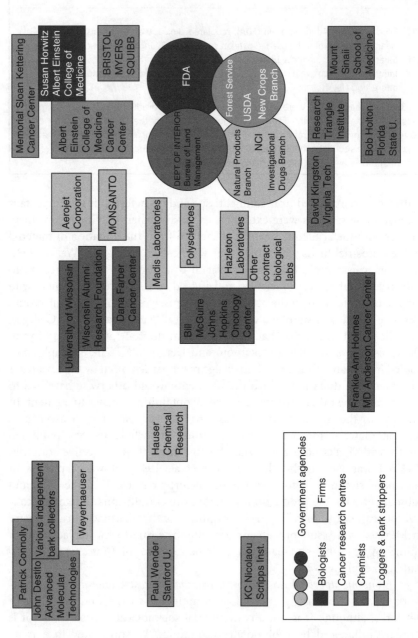

Figure 9.4 The Taxol network

of entrepreneurial decision or command will have replaced the market. This it is considered to do in certain circumstances, notably when the cost of using the price mechanism is too great. Williamson (1975, 1985) calls this cost a transaction cost and argues that when the cost of a market transaction is high (in his words, when there is high uncertainty, asset specificity, and transaction frequency), then a hierarchy is desirable, otherwise the market mechanism is the most efficient one. And markets are likely to be less efficient in particular exchanges, especially in R&D and knowledge.

This means there is a *market failure* in arm's-length transactions involving knowledge. Market failure in this sense is not the same as failure (for example of an innovation) on the market, but the failure of market forces (or market forces alone) to achieve the necessary allocation of resources. Market failure is also an argument used to justify government intervention (even by governments which are generally against intervention). For our argument here, the question is one of market failure of arm's-length transactions in intangible assets (such as selling know-how). The costs of transactions will be particularly high for this kind of transaction because:

1. Knowledge has some features of public goods (e.g. does not get used up when it is used, so it is hard to arrive at a 'correct' price) (but see Callon 1994).
2. Information impactedness and the expectation of opportunism means that in the case of a market in knowledge, buyers do not pay without knowing what they are getting, but once they do know, they have already got it, cannot give it back, and so do not have to pay. This is an argument used to justify the creation of knowledge created in-house by R&D departments rather than buying it, with some exceptions for example licenses to patents. However there has been a great increase in markets in knowledge in recent years (see Athreye 1998).

A network is neither a market nor a hierarchy (see Table 9.2) The firms are still separate entities, and autonomously managed. But on the other hand they have a long-term relationship involving trust—which is more than just a single transaction. Williamson did not initially write about networks, though he did put a footnote about the keiretsu as an exception to his theory, describing it as neither market nor hierarchy. It has been principally supporters of transaction cost economics following Williamson who have developed his ideas to apply them to networks, describing them as an intermediate form between network and hierarchy.

This is a view which many economists have criticized (Chesnais 1996). His main point is that the firm plays a more central role than Williamson allows for, and he describes the market vs hierarchy approach as a sterile dichotomy. His argument is that firms are not islands of planning and coordination in a sea of market relations, but that planned coordination extends beyond the

Table 9.2 Forms of economic organization

Parameters	Forms		
	Market	Hierarchy	Network
Normative basis	Contract, property rights	Employment relationship	Complementary strengths
Means of communication	Prices	Routines	Relations
Degree of flexibility	High	Low	Med–high
Amount of commitment among parties	Low	Med–high	Med–high
Tone and climate	Precision and/or suspicion	Formal, bureaucratic	Open-ended, mutual benefits
Relations between economic agents	Independence	Hierarchical	Interdependence

Source: OECD (1992: 78), Powell (1990), Kaneko and Imai (1987).

boundaries of the firm. We might add that, on the other hand, market relations are increasingly adopted within firms in the form of cost centres. Williamson, says Chesnais, sees the firm as an alternative to the market, rather than recognizing it as *the* main institution in capitalist for example market economies for creating value by transforming resources (see Chapter 1). The capacity of firms to reduce the transaction costs of markets is only one of the sources of corporate viability. Firms also depend on their capacity to maximize labour productivity by a range of decisions about the organization of production; by their capacity to innovate; and by their capacity to manage organizational change, all of which are of central importance in the profitability and growth of the firm. In short, transaction cost economics leaves no place for a dynamic approach to innovation and production, and it excludes an active role for managerial strategy. Networks are a way for firms to bring together their strengths and increase capacity so as to create value by pooling innovative and productive abilities. Chesnais believes that networks should be analysed using economic concepts such as their resource, value and surplus creating potential, not as an intermediate between market and hierarchy but as a phenomenon in its own right.

We can offer the possibility of some kind of rapprochement between sociological and economic approaches, since Chesnais argues that networks should be analysed as a phenomenon in their own right, not as something which is neither one thing nor the other—neither market nor hierarchy. And Larédo and Mustar, Callon and colleagues argue that the network is a new form of economic actor or entity requiring its own analysis (Larédo and Mustar 1996). We now turn to some case studies of networks and alliances. In addition the keiretsu or network form of Japanese industrial structure, and Italian industrial districts involving networks of SMEs, are discussed in Chapter 4, while global production networks are discussed in Chapters 8 and 10.

US CRADAs

This example of a network is a government policy instrument for encouraging collaboration between firms and public sector research organizations or state agencies. Antitrust legislation was for a long time an important feature of the American national innovation system which is associated with support for competition, encouragement of small units, and backing for the small firm. Interfirm collaborative alliances were strongly discouraged under this legislation until the National Cooperative Research Act 1984 reduced antitrust penalties for collaboration among firms involved in pre-commercial research. It has since been extended beyond the pre-competitive stage (Mowery and Rosenberg 1993, Mowery 2001). The change in legislation enabled the foundation of the Microelectronics and Computer Technology Corporation (mentioned earlier) and the growth of research consortia in general.

This was part of a raft of new legislation which permitted collaborative research and which was aimed at encouraging the better exploitation by US firms of discoveries made in the USA. Several new acts covered IPR and were intended to address concern, given the level of government funding in defence related projects and on health in particular, about the practical implementation of the output. They included the Bayh-Dole Act in 1980, the Stevenson-Wydler Act in 1980, and the Federal Transfer of Technology Act in 1986. Eisenberg (1996) analyses in detail this 'sea change' in government legislation, while the effects of the Bayh-Dole Act in particular, which permitted patenting of government-funded research, have been discussed by economists of innovation such as Mowery and Nelson (Mazzoleni and Nelson 1998, Mowery et al. 2001), see Chapter 6.

Influenced by the success of Japanese cooperative research and technological development, the CRADAs are a mechanism for encouraging the transfer of technology from the public sector to industry, introduced in the USA under the terms of the Federal Transfer of Technology Act. CRADAs are agreements which can be signed by agencies of the US state with private sector organizations in order to commercialize the results of research funded by government. One of the explicit statements in the legislation was that it should encourage American firms in commercializing research output funded by the US government, instead of it going abroad.

For example, the anti-cancer drug, Taxol, discussed earlier, was commercialized using a series of CRADAs signed between the drug company Brisol Myers Squibb and three state agencies: the NIH (NCI), the Department of the Interior and the Department of Agriculture. Taxol was a natural product extracted from the bark of *taxus brevifolia*, the Pacific yew tree, native to the northwest of North America. It was not patented, and the CRADA can be seen as a new way of assigning intellectual property to the company commercializing it. Commercial development of an unpatented chemical as a pharmaceutical product would not otherwise have been an attractive business proposition.

Under the CRADA, the NCI agreed to collaborate with Brisol Myers Squibb on ongoing and future clinical studies to obtain FDA approval for the marketing of Taxol, and the NCI would make available exclusively to the company the data and results of all Taxol studies. Two further CRADAs gave the firm exclusive access to the bark (or other parts) of all yew trees on Federal land (which was managed either by the USDA (Forest Service) or the Department of the Interior (Bureau of Land Management). The firm, for its part, agreed to make available free of charge the necessary amounts of Taxol for further clinical trials, and provide funds to pay for a comprehensive inventory of the quantity and quality of *taxus brevifolia* on public lands. These arrangements did not go unchallenged, and Taxol and *taxus brevifolia* were the subjects of a number of Congressional Hearings. Concern was expressed (among other things) about whether giving a monopoly to a private firm was the best way of commercializing Taxol from the point of view of the public interest. It was suggested that the public could be paying twice for the innovation: once through the taxes which supported the research, and once by paying monopoly prices for the production (which are normally justified as a means of recovering the costs of research).[6]

The Benetton network

Belussi (1989) and Belussi and Arcangeli (1998) discuss in detail the case of Benetton, which is also mentioned as an example of a network firm by Chesnais (1997) and OECD (1992). It is also an example of the networks in Italian industrial districts, discussed in Chapter 4. One of the key features of network firms like Benetton is the IT-intensive management techniques they use for a range of vertical transactions up and down the value chain, with smaller manufacturing subcontractors and with retailers. The firm introduced computer-aided design of garments, computer-controlled knitting machines and computerized stock-control in the mid-1980s well before the technology was widely diffused. They were able to offer a wide variety of designs, with a high quality to price ratio, to respond rapidly to changes in fashion, and to get their new designs into retail shops very fast.

At the centre of the network were a number of specialist activities in which Benetton had a strong in-house capability, such as overall planning, strategic management and monitoring of the manufacturing functions, fashion and market forecasting, design and advertising. The central management function was not only to develop the strategy for Benetton but to control the critical resources of all the autonomous firms in the network, both manufacturing subcontractors and retailers. In the early 1990s the firm was famous, or infamous, for its advertising, often aiming to shock, certainly to be discussed and noticed, and which did not necessarily have much to do with the products the firm was selling.

At the same time, manufacturing was strongly decentralized, with only seven fully owned factories accounting for less than 20 percent of output, (OECD 1992: 104), while the rest of the firm's products were made by 350–450[7] small and very small firms and artisan shops, almost all of which existed before joining the Benetton network. These small firms were linked by computer to Benetton HQ both for management purposes and for the input of computer-aided design to computer-aided manufacturing.

At the other end of the value chain, a highly decentralized sales network was based on a two-tier structure in which about 70–5 firms acted as agents for the group, gathering orders, collecting market information and information about fashion trends, and supervising and promoting the sales of thousands of retail outlets in dozens of countries. The second tier consisted of some 2,500 independent firms, which owned the 4,500 retail outlets for Benetton products, and again a large number of them existed before joining the network. These shops were required to follow style and display directions from Benetton HQ, disseminated by the agents, from whom they ordered their goods. They were committed to selling only Benetton products.[8]

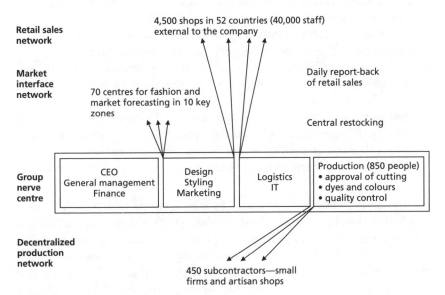

Figure 9.5 Benetton: Example of a network firm

(*source*: Chesnais (1997) (our translation))

Large firm–small firm linkages in biotechnology

Biotechnology grew out of molecular biology, almost exclusively an area of public sector research with no commercial aim in view, the major breakthroughs taking place in the mid-1970s. Profits from commercialization of biotechnology did not begin to be generated until the late 1980s, initially in health diagnostics, then in pharmaceutical products such as genetically engineered human insulin and growth hormone. In the early 1980s when biotechnology was first being commercialized, although several forecasts referred to the potential impact of the new technology in other sectors, the majority of applications were in pharmaceuticals. Agricultural applications such as genetically modified soya, tomatoes and other crops began to take off in the mid-1990s. The main applications of biotechnology are as follows:

1. A paradigm change[9] for the pharmaceutical industry and other sectors generating chemical molecules with biological effects, biotechnology combined with information technology offers *a new way of searching for new products,* reducing reliance on the random synthesis and mass screening that came to be known as molecular roulette, with the aim of automating and speeding up the search process, reducing time to market, and at the same time making the search process more rational. Techniques include combinatorial chemistry, computer-aided molecular design, high throughput screening, bioinformatics (to process and store the amount of data generated) and more recently genomics, proteomics, and other specialist activities. More details are discussed by one of us elsewhere (Walsh 2004).
2. New *processes* such as genetic engineering to produce human insulin, or waste treatment using genetically engineered microorganisms.
3. New *products* such as the flavr savr™ tomato, genetically modified soya, diagnostic kits, 'blue jeans' genetically modified cotton (which is already indigo in colour as it grows).
4. New sources of *energy* such as fuel alcohol, biomass. The commercial viability of these will depend on their cost relative to petroleum, which in turn depends on political events in and affecting petroleum-producing countries. The cost will include the environmental and opportunity cost of using them.

Biotechnology was commercialized by start-up firms, mainly in the USA at first, rather than by drug, agrofood or other established companies. Many of them were inventor-entrepreneurs who had made discoveries in the public sector and set up a firm to commercialize them, in some cases, no doubt, encouraged by the changes in legislation in the USA (discussed earlier). Figure 9.6 indicates the numbers of start-up firms in the USA, UK, France, and Canada. It may be seen that by far the largest number of new firms was

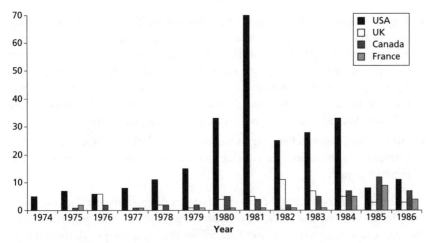

Figure 9.6 New firm start-ups in biotechnology in the USA, UK, Canada, and France (*source*: Walsh et al. 1995)

established in the USA than in the other countries, and the peak year for start-up firms was 1981 in the USA, and somewhat later elsewhere.

The new firms represented a potential challenge to established industries, since they might have grown, challenged established firms, and formed the basis of a new industry just as microelectronics firms, although many of them spun-off from a large established firm (Bell), replaced traditional manufacturers using valves, mechanics and other technology, and grew into a new industry. But in the case of biotechnology established firms, mainly multinationals, had advantages too. They had not developed the new technology but they had strong in-house R&D, and had been at the forefront of successive waves of innovation for decades, building up firm specific competencies and strong market power. They possessed some of the complementary assets (discussed earlier) necessary to commercialize the new technology, many of which involved various kinds of influence over the selection environment:

- Distribution networks, for example among doctors, pharmacies, agricultural institutes, farmers.
- Networks of intermediaries, such as consultants who would carry out clinical trials and later prescribe the drugs, or experts in agricultural institutes who would supervise field trials and later recommend the new crops or agrochemicals.
- Marketing skills and experience.
- Production and formulation skills and experience.

- A good relationship with the regulatory authorities (such as drug safety committees, environmental safety committees, occupational safety committees) who grant licenses for trials and then marketing, and who may have to decide what tests are required in each case. In some cases this includes the resources to lobby government organizations, when new legislation is envisaged, to try and convince decision makers that the interests of the industry coincide with the public interest, as discussed earlier.

- Finance and financial management skills are obviously necessary for investment in innovation, for development work, production, marketing and product launch.

Many of the new small firms in biotechnology had the technological knowledge but not the skills, knowledge, and experience in other areas, or the resources necessary to commercialize the technology. Biotechnology became commercially successful in the first place where it was implemented by the collaborative efforts of a large and a small firm sharing complementary skills, knowledge, and resources. Some of the European and Japanese conglomerate chemical firms and multinational drug firms, for example, formed important linkages with specialist US biotechnology firms as a way of moving into the new area.

Why did the large firms not develop biotechnology in-house? There were a great many costs and risk involved in moving into a new field, taking on new staff with the necessary skills at a time in the development of biotechnology when they were not sure whether they would want to commit themselves in the long term to the new technology, how profitable it would turn out to be, or indeed, which area of biotechnology to pursue. Many areas of knowledge would have been needed to develop and commercialize a discovery at a time when the whole field was very uncertain and the large firms already had major sunk costs in their traditional areas. It was cheaper to use alliances with small firms as a window of opportunity, which they could move into more seriously if it proved worthwhile or exit easily, simply by not renewing the agreement, if it did not. Lastly, it has been suggested that many of the established firms, especially the conglomerate chemical firms, had a 'culture' that was oriented towards chemistry (Galimberti 1993). Not only the research staff but the management of the firm would typically have a background in chemistry or chemical engineering, and would see problems, approaches to finding solutions to the problems, and new product strategies, in chemical terms, making them particularly uncertain about the 'turn back to biology'.

Why, then, were the small firms willing to share their most valuable asset? One of the main reasons was lack of money. The development of biotech products from the discoveries of molecular biology took a lot longer than expected, and after the initial hype around biotechnology encouraged massive investment by venture capital firms in new start-ups, there followed a period of disappointment at the results during which many investors got cold feet. The other main reason was that they lacked the complementary assets needed to commercialize their innovations, especially in such a particular market as that for pharmaceuticals, where clinical trials, regulatory compliance, and marketing activity aimed at doctors all required very specialist experience, not to mention networks of contacts in the appropriate domains. Many of the biotech start-ups lacked one or more management skills, too, and those that had them among the US firms often had acquired them as a condition of receiving venture capital.

The outcome was that some of the small firms did well and grew into manufacturing firms; some became mostly contract research laboratories, having decided they did not have the resources to produce a product for the market; and some were taken over by established firms wishing to acquire their own in-house capabilities and deciding that acquisition of a specialist firm was the easiest way to do it.

An individual network may not be a stable entity–it will last as long as the various partners continue to need the links with each other. But the network firm as a form of innovative organization is likely to continue for much longer. If one or more of the partners finds it more efficient to carry out the important innovative activities in-house, perhaps because they have acquired for themselves the new technological (or organizational) competencies needed to innovate, then the collective agreement is likely to end. Some large firm–small firm collaborations in biotechnology have ended with the acquisition of the small firm by its larger partner. The Roche-Genentech and Monsanto-Calgene cases given earlier are examples. But it is very likely that further collaborative agreements will be signed in new areas of uncertainty. While individual networks may have a finite life, the network firm as a phenomenon continues.

The first wave of biotechnology networks were in diagnostics and drugs, the second wave was in agro-biotechnology, and more recently they have been formed in more specialist areas. Walsh (2004: 210) lists over 50 such specialisms, including:

- Combinatorial chemistry and high throughput screening, the partial automation and speeding up of the molecular discovery process.

- Genomics, involving the identification of gene targets and the design and development of molecules to react with them.

- Proteomics, focusing on the structure and function of proteins in the cell, and the design and development of molecules that can block, modify or enhance a protein's action. Most diseases manifest themselves at the level of protein activity.

- Bioinformatics, or the storage, processing and analysis of molecular biological information–all the data collected in the above specialist activities–including the design and development of software for data 'mining' tools, prediction of structures and simulation of macromolecules.

Some of these developments have been discussed in Chapter 7 in connection with the pharmaceuticals or agrofood sectors.

The influence of networks versus national innovation systems: the case of the Maastricht region of the Netherlands

This example relates to Chapter 6, considering the limitations of the advantages of network firms compared to the influence of the national innovation system. Dankbaar, Corvers and Hassink at MERIT carried out a survey of firms in the Maastricht region of the Netherlands. Maastricht is in a part of the Netherlands almost completely surrounded by Belgium and Germany, near the German city of Aachen and the Belgian city of Liége (see, Corvers et al. 1995; Hassink et al. 1995). They wanted to see what links were made with other firms and other institutions which were geographically close but located across the national frontier, compared with links made with institutions further away but still in the Netherlands. They found that the most important linkages by far were between customers and suppliers. These were the most important partners for the development of new and improved products and processes. And they found that the majority of the firms' suppliers, customers, and competitors were in other parts of the Netherlands, despite the geographical distance and the relative inconvenience of interaction, rather than within the German or Belgian parts of the same region. About 20 percent of the firms surveyed had acquired technological knowledge from public research centres and another 10 percent were planning to do so. Again, however, the research centres chosen were located elsewhere in the Netherlands (for example, TNO or the technological universities at Eindhoven, Delft or Twente, rather than locally but over the border). This is in spite of the fact that Aachen—nearby but in Germany—offers a good supply of publicly available technological knowledge at the largest technological university in Europe.

These findings raised the question of regional versus more remote national linkages. The authors surveyed some of the factors that would have an effect on one or the other. The factors they found in favour of regional linkages included the common industrial heritage of the region. The Maas-Rhine region is a former coal mining area with other declining traditional industries in addition to coal, and levels of unemployment higher, and output per head lower, than the average in each of the three national economies. Second were the EU's policies for promoting development in region, and for removing obstacles caused by national—or natural—borders, so that the region is seen as central in Europe rather than peripheral in each of the nation states. The Maas Rhine region had been designated a Euregion since 1976. Third, the region has several features likely to promote innovativeness, including a substantial number of independent, innovative small firms and a good source of technological knowledge and technologically skilled personnel, although these are somewhat fragmented between the nation states.

They identified a number of factors which acted against regional linkages, including the existence of three nations, four cultures and three languages in the region (or four, counting Flemish and Dutch as separate languages). National policies to foster technology transfer and economic development were different in each of the states and have tended to be oriented towards national goals and resources rather than cross-border cooperation. Different national policies have stimulated developments in different directions in each of the three parts of the region that fall within different national borders.

There is therefore an interesting tension between national and regional systems of innovation, the role of the state, the role of Europe, and the question of culture versus geographical proximity or distance. So far the advantages of networks or network firms have not overcome the barriers of separate national systems of innovation despite increased European integration.

Conclusion

Although networks have existed for some time, there has been considerable growth in networks and alliances since the 1980s and in the range of industrial sectors involved in the networks and alliances. Also, these networks now tend to cross national boundaries and involve collaborative production or sharing of technology. Networks contribute to the innovative capabilities of firms by exposing them to new sources of ideas, enabling faster access to resources and enhancing technology and knowledge transfer. A number of different approaches to networks have emerged in the strategic management, the sociological and economics literature to explain the particular ways in which networks shape innovation.

Notes

1 Personal communication (e-mail from Michel Delapierre 23.06.03).
2 The first birth control pill was commercially launched by G. D. Searle in 1960. Much of the biological testing of the active ingredients by Gregory Pincus and colleagues, and the clinical trials by John Rock and colleagues, were carried out in the state of Massachusetts, where the

sale, advertising, display and even use of contraceptives were still illegal under the Comstock Laws passed in the 1870s. The Supreme Court decision in Griswold vs. Connecticut in 1964 reversed the legislation prohibiting the use of contraceptives (even by married couples) which was still in force in ten remaining US states, including Massachusetts. Campaigns by pressure groups played a very important role, not only in the legalization of birth control, but also in influencing the research that was carried out (Walsh 1980; Marks 2001).

3 Louise Brown was the first baby to be born using in vitro fertilization, in the UK in July 1978, following ten years of research. In Britain, the Warnock Report, or *Report of the Committee on Human Fertilization and Embryology*, chaired by Dame Mary Warnock, (Cmnd 9314, HMSO 1984, London) examined the 'social ethical and legal implications of recent and potential developments in human assisted reproduction'. A white paper based on it was published in 1987, and the Human Fertilization and Embryology Act was passed into legislation in June 1990. In France, similar legislation was passed in 1994.

4 GMOs and in vitro fertilization were not illegal in the way that contraceptives were, but their commercial use or practical application are related to changes in legislation. In the case of GMOs, these were controversial changes in what could be patented, because firms were more willing to commercialize technology over which they could exercise intellectual property rights. The landmark legislation permitting the patenting of genetically modified organisms was Diamond vs. Chakrabarty 1980, see chapter 6. In vitro legislation was the subject of legislation introduced by Governments in response to what they perceived as public concern about the ethical implications of the research and the direction in which it was going, under which IVF and similar techniques, embryo research, and other related activities, came under the scrutiny of officially established independent ethics committees in most countries.

5 A quite different (and non-technological) example to illustrate some of these ideas comes from Ben Pimlott's newspaper review of the memoirs of Tony Benn (the British Labour MP for Chesterfield, who retired at the 2001 general election, and who had been Minister of Technology in the 1964 Labour Government). Benn was a socialist who had the misfortune to inherit a peerage (in the days when peerages could still be inherited), and he campaigned for the right to give it up so he could go on being an elected member of the House of Commons, rather than an unelected member of the House of Lords. (He has also campaigned for an elected Upper House (such as a Senate) to replace the House of Lords, and indeed the abolition of peerages altogether). Pimlott says this campaign by Benn revealed a lot about the latter's political style, which included ' ... irrepressible optimism, never taking no for an answer, a purposeful lust for publicity, plus a stunning ability to convince himself, and others, that his own interests and those of the nation, coincide ... ' Benn's wish to continue being a Member of the House of Commons coincided with his belief in elected representation, and these democratic sentiments were used to enlist the support of enough other MPs, and the public who elect them, to be able to change the law. The possibility of giving up an inherited peerage became one of a number of obligatory passage points in the path towards a more democratic Britain.

6 For more details of networks constructed—and cut—in the course of the taxol story, and of the Congressional Hearings and intellectual property issues see Goodman and Walsh (2001).

7 The numbers have varied over time—OECD (1992) reports 350 subcontractors, while Chesnais (1997) reports 450.

8 Again there is a difference between the two sources in the last reference as to whether the retail outlets are considered to have a franchise from Benetton. OECD (1992: 104) suggests that the relationship is not a normal franchise one since no charge is made for using the brand name, whereas Chesnais (1997: 157) describes the shops as franchises.

9 Whether or not this represents a paradigm change is discussed in Walsh (2004).

10 Globalization of Trade, Production, and Technology

Introduction

When we think about globalization, we may start by thinking about what it is that is being globalized, and the examples that first spring to mind include products which you can get almost everywhere in the world, apparently untouched by the culture and consumer preferences of the country concerned, such as McDonald's hamburgers or Coca-Cola. As long ago as 1996 *The Sunday Telegraph* announced that Belarus and Tahiti had become the 100th and 101st countries to open a McDonald's (*The Sunday Telegraph*, 15 December 1996). Other kinds of examples include Ford cars, which are US owned but made as well as bought all over the world, and recordings of American pop music which are widely consumed throughout the world, to the point that some countries have adopted policies to promote their own national pop music, as many other nations have adopted, or tried to adopt, trade policies to protect national manufacturing.[1] (In France, for example, the *loi Toubon* passed in 1994, among other things, restricts the transmission of English-language music to 40 per cent of daily airplay.)

So far we have given examples of American products bought by customers outside the USA, but there are many others: Japanese cars and consumer electronics are also widely traded throughout the world, while Lego toys from Denmark, Benetton sweaters from Italy, IKEA furniture from Sweden, Swatch watches from Switzerland, and Nokia mobile phones from Finland are examples of products from smaller economies that have a large international market, to the point that Lego, Benetton, and Nokia, at least, are no longer seen as specifically Danish, Italian, or Finnish outside their home markets.[2] This raises the question as to what is being globalized. We explore this question in the first section below. But first, we will outline the structure of the chapter as a whole. The second section examines the concept of globalization. The third section examines the changes in the international division of labour and integration of strategy and management in multinationals. The fourth section examines the different positions on whether globalization is taking place. The fifth section examines the geographical scope of the process of globalization. The sixth section explores the implications of globalization for national governments. The seventh section analyses the implications of globalization for innovation. A final section assesses the evidence on the globalization of innovative activity.

What is being globalized?

Does this mean consumer tastes are becoming globalized? Clearly there are some important changes that have taken place since the Second World War in Europe, and over a longer period in the USA. Movements of population in the form of waves of immigration and emigration have taken with them different patterns of consumption, especially of domestic practices and consumer products such as foodstuffs, cooking equipment and methods, fabrics, clothing, films, and music. During the same period, the spread of supermarkets from the USA, on the one hand, and food stores initially serving immigrant communities and opening longer hours than conventional shops, on the other hand, have both successfully captured different sections of the established markets of traditional, specialist high street shops.[3] Meanwhile, innovations in transport, refrigeration, freezing, canning, freeze-drying and other methods of preserving freshness, mean perishable products such as foods that are 'exotic' to a country can be imported. Cheap holidays abroad mean wider segments of the population, at least in the richer countries, widen their experiences and tastes and increase demand for formerly 'foreign' products.

At the same time, there are still major differences between countries in such areas as:

- patterns of demand, work practices, tastes, celebrations, and feast days
- regulatory regimes (e.g. concerning product safety or emissions of pollutants)
- national or industry standards: for example, in electricity supply (220–40 volts in Europe or 110 volts in USA); in power sockets (small blades in USA, small pins in most of Europe); in the gauge of railway track; in keyboard layout (e.g. anglophone QWERTY; francophone AZERTY); in telephone/modem sockets. We are very aware of different standards in computer operating systems (e.g. Microsoft versus Mackintosh), though these are not national differences[4]
- artisan- or craft-made or customized products versus the purchase of mass-produced equivalents (from food to clothes and furniture)

Perhaps more significantly, there are also huge differences in wealth and poverty and what people can buy.

So, while there are increasing numbers of 'global products' such as those mentioned earlier, from Coca-Cola to Nokia mobiles, the 'global consumer' is still a long way away. National, regional, and local tastes and patterns of consumption are still very dominant, though clearly more dominant in some product markets than others. And within geographical areas, patterns of consumption vary among socio-economic and ethnic groups (Molnár and Lamont 2002; Tomlinson and McMeekin 2002).

Patel (1995) has identified the products which vary rather little from country to country as including consumer electronics, aircraft, electronic control systems, or weapons. Either home demand is the key specifier, even where the output is exported, or a multinational firm based in one particular country may have a monopoly on supply while consumer preferences in overseas markets do not provide market signals for significant product differentiation. On the other hand, products which are more culture-specific include food and drugs (Patel 1995). Despite the prevalence of previously mentioned McDonald's and Coca-Cola, and the acquisition of a taste for 'foreign' and 'exotic' meals in many countries, patterns of food consumption vary strongly between countries, regions, and socio-economic and ethnic groups. Drugs may seem quite standardized, but regulations concerning safety and licensing differ[5] and so do delivery methods. There are quite definite consumer preferences for tablets in some countries where suppositories would be the choice in others, and injections are favoured more in some cultures than others. In some countries certain drugs are available over the counter where a prescription would be required for them in others. Even the concept of what constitutes an illness to be treated with medication differs between countries. For example, although in most countries people with high blood pressure are generally advised to modify their diet or lifestyle and may be prescribed medication, low blood pressure can be considered a treatable condition in some countries (e.g. Eastern Europe) but a desirable state of affairs in others (e.g. Britain) (Blackwell 1976).

However, globalization is not just about products that may or may not be globalized, or whether the 'global consumer' is still more of a myth than a reality despite greater trading of goods on a worldwide scale. Globalization takes place in many ways, including the following:

1. *Products*: the global consumer and the global product (standard products traded worldwide or custom-made for local markets) as discussed earlier.
2. *Trade*: exports of raw materials, services, energy, high-tech products, machinery, plant, components, goods of all kinds. Any of these may be made or generated in the firm's home country and sold abroad.

3. *Production*: involving (multinational) firms with manufacturing subsidiaries in other countries. Overseas production is adopted for many reasons. The firm may need to customize products for local markets. It may seek to avoid tariff barriers, as Japanese car firms manufacturing in UK, or US and Japanese electronics firms manufacturing in Ireland have done to avoid EU tariff barriers or quotas. The firm may also calculate that it is more cost effective to manufacture in or near its overseas markets than export from its home base, if the ratio of value added to volume or weight is high. Foreign direct investment (FDI) may involve either greenfield investments or mergers with and acquisitions of existing firms and plant. Athreye and Keeble (2000) have shown that three-fifths of all intra-Triad FDI has taken the form of acquisitions rather than greenfield investment (see also 'money' below number 4).

4. *Money*: international finance. Deregulation of financial markets liberalized capital flows and gave a big impetus to the expansion of international flows of finance. There is less dispute in the literature about whether financial globalization is a real phenomenon than there is about globalization via trade or production, that is, it is generally agreed that a huge expansion of international financial flows has taken place. (We return later to the question of whether globalization is a real phenomenon.) Financial globalization includes both flows of investment income from FDI and from portfolio investments: foreign financial portfolio investment in shares and government bonds, in particular, has grown spectacularly. By the end of 2001, 37 per cent of UK company equities and 18 per cent of UK government bonds were owned abroad. UK life assurance and pension funds held 22 per cent of their assets in the form of foreign equities and bonds (Sutcliffe and Glyn 2003). (Foreign ownership of French companies is mentioned in the discussion on 'varieties of capitalism', number 10.)

5. *Mergers and acquisitions* across national borders, such as the 1999 merger between Rhône-Poulenc (France) and Hoechst (Germany) to form Aventis, in the chemicals, agrofood, and pharmaceuticals sectors, or that in the same year between Zeneca Group PLC (UK) and Astra AB (Sweden) to form AstraZeneca, also in pharmaceuticals. This wave of international mergers and acquisitions, which has led to the rise of powerful global oligopolies, is described by Chesnais and Simonetti (2000) and Mytelka (1999, 2002) as a key feature of globalization (a point to which we return later). Mergers and acquisitions across national borders pose the question of internationalization of corporate management, globalization of corporate strategy, and the distinction between multi-domestic and global industries (Porter 1986). Multi-domestic industries are those where international strategy collapses into a series of domestic strategies, while global industries exploit the competitive advantage of integrating activities worldwide, a point to which we return under 'international division of labour' (number 8).

6. *International movement of labour* (skilled, unskilled, and professional) and related flows of income. This might appear to be easier nowadays (at least in principle) with international agreements allowing the free movement of labour within, for example, the EU, Mercosur, or the North America Free Trade Agreement areas. In practice, however, the movement of labour has never been so restricted or regulated. Most developed countries have tightened controls against unskilled migrants in particular, although they try to attract certain skilled ones. Immigration has been very important in the history of the USA, and especially during the Belle Epoque or third Kondratieff upswing, but it has been restricted in recent years, while worldwide, the number of people with a country of residence different from their country of birth has grown very slowly (Glyn 2004).

7. *Knowledge and technology*, traded via market relationships or acquired in some other way, for example through collaborative agreements with the owner of the technology, or the establishment of overseas R&D labs (which in turn interact with the local science and technology infrastructure), see for example Hegde and Hicks (2005). This category would include payments and receipts for technology and technical assistance, international data flows and related flows of income, and non-equity technological agreements between corporations and firms. Markets in knowledge are the subject of an increasing literature in the innovation field, see for example Athreye (1998), Arora et al. (2001), Cesaroni (2004), and Hicks and Hegde (2005).

8. *International division of labour*, which is not the same as the international movement of labour, but involves the internationalization of corporate management, the globalization of corporate strategy and, especially, a greater degree of international coordination and integration of facilities by multinational enterprises. Indeed, a firm considered to be 'global' may have no greater geographical dispersion than before, but have more internationally integrated structures (Ramirez 2005). This allows the firm to access nationally differentiated centres of excellence and—where the firm's technology base is characterized by a growing interrelatedness of previously separate technologies—permits the firm to broaden its technological activity (Ramirez 2005). We return to this point later.

9. *Political control*: globalization of political control or government administration, in other words, imperialism or colonialism. Some countries may directly control others, exporting administration systems, infrastructure and culture, while securing preferential terms for trade and manufacturing for their national firms.[6] Former colonial relationships between countries have in some cases given way to substantial economic links after independence has ended direct rule.

10. *Ways of doing things*, culture, styles of management, patterns of leisure activity. In this section we might include different 'models of capitalism'

or 'varieties of capitalism', an indication of globalization being, for example, the extent to which a US or Anglo-Saxon form of capital-dominated capitalism, in which shareholders and share-trading play an important role, is becoming more dominant in countries previously typified by credit-based capitalism in which banks and bank loans play a key role (Coates 2000). As we mentioned in Chapter 6, many French firms have quite recently begun to raise money by issuing shares which have then been traded on the stock exchange, where before they would obtain finance in the form of bank loans, and indeed many of them were partly or wholly owned by the French state. As a consequence more than one-third of the forty largest French companies came to be owned by US pension and mutual funds by the late 1990s (*Le Monde*, 16 March 1999) (see also 'money' number 4).

We might also include here more general shifts within countries towards market-driven systems of production. As argued in Chapter 1, in the ideology of early twenty-first century capitalism, markets have become the best, or even the only efficient, means of organizing and governing an economic system, even though in practice, the market is often an unsatisfactory way of governing and coordinating behaviour or allocating resources (Nelson 2003). Regulations and other non-market elements may be necessary to make market governance work, while for many activities it is socially more desirable or economically more efficient to use other modes of organization and governance. However, since 1989, the market has re-imposed its influence, as illustrated by the collapse of the centrally planned economies, the spectacular growth of the private sector in China, and the privatization of state owned enterprises and service provision in both OECD and less developed countries (Glyn 2004).

What does globalization mean?

Having established that globalization involves, or can involve, a large number of different activities carried out across national borders, including trade, production and the movement of finance, knowledge and labour, it would be helpful to focus on a more precise definition of what we mean by globalization and whether it is different from other international activities in other periods of time. During the 1990s there was a great deal of hype about globalization, and a large number of articles on the subject appeared in a range of media from television, magazines, serious newspapers, and the popular press to academic and scholarly publications.[7] In these articles, there were almost as many meanings given to the term 'globalization' as there were authors. As argued in Chapter 8, we have chosen to define globalization in a similar way to the OECD (1992:

210–13), Chesnais (1997), and Chesnais and Simonetti (2000: 10–11). First of all, we take the view that globalization is a *process*, rather than the outcome of that process, so that what is important in assessing whether or not it is taking place is not the *extent* of (say) the interconnectedness of firms or economies, but the existence of *trends*, even in their early stages, that indicate that an increase in such interconnectedness is taking place. Thus, when it is argued (e.g. Sutcliffe and Glyn 2003) that FDI is very low compared to total investment and that therefore globalization is a very exaggerated phenomenon, we would suggest that what is important is not the low percentage of FDI (compared to domestic investment or GDP), but the *growth* in FDI compared to the *growth* in domestic investment or GDP, especially over the last 30 years. In fact, as we argue later, the increased internationalization of economic activity began during the nineteenth century: what is new about the end of the twentieth and beginning of the twenty-first century is not the extent of international activity, but the changing nature of capitalism on an international scale, and the way in which it is organized and managed.

We also focus for the rest of this chapter on globalization as an *economic* phenomenon, leaving aside for discussion elsewhere such questions as *cultural* globalization—for example the extent of the worldwide adoption of American clothes or popular music, their effect on local styles and forms, and what this signifies—even though there are, of course, important links between these and economic trends.

Firstly, if we take *internationalization* rather generally to be the process of increasing interrelationships and economic interdependence on an international scale of previously separate national economies (via various combinations of trade, FDI, and sourcing of inputs of capital, capital goods, knowledge, information, labour, raw materials, and energy sources) then we define *globalization* as the most recent phase of this process. The various phases of globalization have been as follows.

The first major phase of the internationalization of capitalism was the period of Victorian imperialist expansion which formed the economic background to the Industrial Revolution. The dominant features of nineteenth century imperialism were international trade in manufactured goods from the industrialized countries, in exchange for raw materials from the non-industrialized countries, together with investment in and direct colonial rule of some of the latter by some of the former. The international economy was dominated by the Gold Standard and the idea of Pax Britannica from the mid-nineteenth century until 1914 (Hobsdawm 1968: 111). The economic upswing at the end of the nineteenth and beginning of the twentieth century, known as the Belle Epoque or the third Kondratieff, saw the USA and Germany open up a technological and economic gap with the rest of the world. The newly industrializing countries of the time (e.g. Italy, Japan, Switzerland, Sweden, and the Netherlands) also began to catch up in terms of technology, industrialization, share of markets, and demand for raw materials. The increased competition for export markets, for sources of raw materials and for 'spheres of influence' led to nationalistic and imperialistic policies and to an arms race (facilitated by the great many military applications of the new technologies), all of which culminated in the First World War (Freeman 1989). As early as 1848, Marx and Engels anticipated much of what is said about globalization today:

The bourgeoisie has, through its exploitation of the world market, given a cosmopolitan character to production and consumption in every country. To the great chagrin of reactionaries, it has drawn from under the feet of industry the national ground on which it stood. All old-established national industries have been destroyed or are daily being destroyed. They are dislodged by new industries, whose introduction becomes a life and death question for all civilized nations, by industries that no longer work up indigenous raw material, but raw material drawn from the remotest zones; industries whose products are consumed, not only at home, but in every quarter of the globe. In place of the old wants, satisfied by the production of the country, we find new wants, requiring for their satisfaction the products of distant lands and climes. In place of the old local and national seclusion and self-sufficiency, we have intercourse in every direction, universal interdependence of nations. And as in material, so also in intellectual production. The intellectual creations of individual nations become common property. National one-sidedness and narrow-mindedness become more and more impossible, and from the numerous national and local literatures, there arises a world literature (Marx and Engels 1848, cited by Glyn 2004).

After the depression of the 1930s, accompanied by policies of autarchy or economic self-sufficiency, the period of the post-war boom in the West (the fourth Kondratieff or the Golden Age of capitalism), characterized a new phase of internationalism, whose key features were the economic upswing of the industrialized countries and the struggle for independence of the colonial world. In this period, the prime motor of economic growth and international technological diffusion was international trade (Hagedoorn and Soete 1991), facilitated by international agreements between economically advanced capitalist countries such as the Bretton Woods Agreement, signed in 1944. The latter introduced the international monetary system known as the Bretton Woods system (which lasted until 1971), based on stable but adjustable exchange rates, with the US dollar as the standard to which every other currency was pegged.

In this period, exchanges of manufactured goods among the industrialized countries were far more important international activities than trade between the industrialized countries and the colonial world, which had typified the earlier part of the twentieth and the end of the nineteenth century. This period also saw the increasing marginalization of many of the poorest countries. International trade between the industrialized countries was also more important than FDI, which was to predominate towards the end of the century.

The most recent phase of internationalization, which we call globalization, is characterized by a number of different trends, notably:

1. The increased rate of FDI, which since the mid-1980s has grown three times as fast as international trade (especially in the service sector), or as internal investment (measured by gross fixed capital formation), or as the national economies of the OECD area (measured by GDP) (see Figure 8.1).
2. A wave of international mergers and acquisitions, such as GEC's and Siemens' takeover of Plessey (in telecommunications) to form GPT, which is now called Marconi Communications as a result of GEC's subsequent (1999) buyout of Siemens' share, and merger with GEC's defence and telecoms subsidiary Marconi SpA (acquired earlier). Or the purchase by the Swiss drug multinational Hoffman La Roche of the smaller biotechnology start-up firm Genentech based in California.
3. A growth in intrafirm trade, that is, trade between different branches of the same multinational firm which are based in different countries. A third of world trade now takes place, not between autonomous enterprises and independent countries, but among entities belonging to a single corporation (Chesnais and Simonetti 2000: 11–12).
4. A rise in the establishment of collaborative alliances, joint ventures and technological agreements between separate firms, and between firms and other organizations (for example, universities) often in different countries. This is what Dunning has called 'alliance capitalism', although Chesnais and Simonetti (2000: 12) suggest that this may be no more than a new name for what Baran and Sweezy (1960) called 'global monopoly capitalism' (which is not to say that these authors do not consider alliances to be a significant phenomenon, as earlier work indicates, for example, Chesnais 1988, 1996) (see Chapter 9 for more on alliances and networks).

These trends consist of qualitative as much as or more than quantitative changes: changes in the *nature* of international capitalism, such as changes in organizational structure and management, rather than in the extent of geographical spread. One of the implications of globalization as a consequence of this focus is the international division of labour together with the integration of strategy and management on a worldwide scale.

International division of labour and integration of strategy and management

A global division of labour can exist within an industry, within a multinational firm, or within a network of firms involved in collaborative alliances around one (or more) multinational firm. A multinational firm can put in place a management strategy and structure that enables the coordination and integration of international activities. It can strongly influence such integration across a network of interlinked organizations, to a greater or lesser extent depending on its power in that network; and a small group of multinational firms in an industry, again depending on their power, can bring about a greater or lesser degree of coordination within the industry.

After the merger between Swedish Astra and British Zeneca, AstraZeneca defined itself as a global rather than a British, Swedish, or European company (Ramirez and Tylecote 2004), but using a much looser definition of globalization than we have done in this chapter, or that of Ramirez and Tylecote. Fifty per cent of the firm's business was conducted in the USA, while more than 50 per cent of its profits were the outcome of commercial activities in the USA (Ramirez and Tylecote 2004). Ramirez (2005*b*) also reports that Astra-Zeneca was in the process of shifting towards an international division of labour in R&D in terms of therapeutic areas, but that at the time she conducted her interviews, 1999–2000, this was still work in progress rather than a reality. The firm does, however, have an integrated strategy and approach to management.

Bartlett and Ghoshal (1997) give an example of a single (range of related) innovation(s) to illustrate the idea of global strategy: a series of liquid detergents commercialized by Procter & Gamble (P&G) as liquid Tide in the USA, liquid Ariel in Europe, and liquid Cheer in Japan. They were developed as a result of collaboration and coordination of the firm's European, US, and Japanese research staff responding to particular conditions in the detergent market in each region (e.g. high clay content of dirt in clothes in the US market), different competing products in each regional market (e.g. European powder detergents with superior performance to the liquids because they contained levels of bleach, enzymes and phosphates not permitted in the USA) and different technological opportunities (e.g. a more robust surfactant developed in the company's Japanese subsidiary).

Clairmonte and Cavanagh (1981) wrote long ago about the worldwide division of labour in the textile industry, describing the many activities in the value chain from raw material to final product, including the sourcing of cotton, wool, silk or synthetic fibres, spinning, weaving or knitting, dyeing, printing, finishing, cutting, clothing design, manufacture of clothes, marketing (including the fashion industry and its shows), distribution, and retailing. What they described was a web of interconnected multinationals with the power to dominate production, distribution, and employment, throughout the whole chain of raw fibre preparation, yarn preparation, weaving, knitting, clothing production, wholesaling, retailing, and production and distribution of textile machinery. In this case the division of labour was not so much within one multinational but in the industry, although the most powerful multinationals had a very dominant position in determining the activities of the other firms in the value chain or network.

Dicken (1992) also wrote about the worldwide division of labour in the textiles and clothing industries, and about three other sectors: automobiles, electronics, and services. In contrast to the P&G case, which illustrated the division of labour within the firm, and the firm's global innovation strategy, much of the worldwide divisions of labour he discussed, like that of Clairmonte and Cavanagh, are those within industries rather than individual firms, and thus involve arms length, market-based transactions among customers and suppliers along the value chain. There is little cross-ownership or FDI although a small number of multinationals (e.g. clothing retailers or automobile assembly firms) still hold considerable power.

In his section on electronics, however, Dicken emphasizes not only the operation in global markets by semiconductor and consumer electronics firms, but also their global organization of production within the firm. He indicates a clear geographical separation between the different stages of the production process (Dicken: 330–6), with various activities performed outside the firm's home country, but R&D, design and more complex stages of production remaining either in the firm's home country or established in a smaller number of other countries with the necessary skills. However, the literature that has since developed in this area indicates that the degree of offshore production varies between US, Japanese, and European firms, while the activities along the value chain that are carried out offshore, rather than at home, have changed over time as some newly industrializing countries have gone through a learning process enabling them to carry out more sophisticated value-adding work. Ernst (2004*a*), for example, discusses Japanese production networks in the electronics industry, while in another publication (Ernst 2004*b*) he observes that chip design, despite its high knowledge intensity, has begun both to be outsourced to other firms, and to have begun to move offshore to certain Asian countries (see Box 10.1). Saxenian (2002) has also written about the emergence of Silicon Valley type clustering and networks in Taiwan, China, and India.

We have used the term 'value chain' rather loosely to capture the idea of a series of successive activities each of which involves some addition of value, and the totality of which leads to a final product (or process or service), although in fact Dicken and colleagues are more precise in their terminology, and critical of the concept of 'value chain' (e.g. Henderson et al. 2002*b*). The term 'value chain' was introduced by Porter (1985) to capture a series of discrete value adding stages performed by a firm during a product's movement through design, manufacture, packaging, advertising, and sale. The term global value chain (GVC) analysis is used by Hayter (2005) and others, drawing both on Porter's concept of a value chain and on the industrial organization literature. This approach is used to analyse the way that value-adding stages, carried out in different countries, are integrated into a global

---

Box 10.1 Global design networks in chip design

Chip design is the process which generates the greatest addition of value in the electronics industry. It involves highly complex technological knowledge, uncertainty, and the coordination of experiments across both functional and disciplinary boundaries, with critical bottlenecks in verification and testing. Tacit knowledge is a major feature of the interpretation of chip performance and as a source of ideas about where to search for improved performance. As a result, chip design draws on a wide and increasing range of fields of specialized knowledge, which in turn gives rise to links with the wider knowledge communities and the development of competencies within the firm for experimenting and learning across cognitive and functional boundaries. Chip design, as a consequence, used to be restricted to a few centres of excellence, mainly in the USA, but also in Europe and Japan. However, a massive geographical dispersion of chip design has taken place in recent years, giving rise to the emergence and growth of Taiwan and Korea as leading electronics exporting countries, followed by the rapid growth of electronics exports from China and India as well as Singapore and Malaysia. Chip design is moving to Asia in response to radical changes in design methodology (from 'system-level integration' to 'modular design') and organization (in the form of the automated 'design factory'). At the same time, integrated forms of design organization within one firm are giving way to a form of vertical specialization in which stages of chip design are outsourced to other firms ('*the dis-integration of firm organization*') and relocated across national boundaries ('*geographical dispersion*'). Global multinationals integrate geographically dispersed companies into hierarchical global design networks where knowledge sharing acts as the glue that keeps these networks growing.

Source: Pavitt (1999, 2003*a*, 2003*b*), Ernst (2004*b*)

---

production system. Hayter uses as case studies, a similar set of industries to those discussed by Dicken, namely apparel and footwear, electronics, automobiles, agro-commodities, and financial and IT services.

In criticizing the term 'value chain', Henderson et al. (2002*a*) consider the merits of the 'filière' concept and actor network theory, but choose the term 'global production networks' (GPNs) introduced by Ernst and colleagues (Ernst 2002; Ernst and Kim 2002), (see Chapter 8) as the best way of characterizing networks based around transnational corporations and which operate 'within and across vertically disintegrated agglomerations of economic activity in different countries, rather than through a series of stand-alone overseas investments'. They favour the GPN as a suitable framework for dealing with the global, regional and local economic and social dimensions of the processes involved in many forms of economic globalization. A special issue of *Industry and Innovation* was devoted to GPNs in 2002. However, Ernst and colleagues themselves (e.g. Ernst 2004*b*; Ernst and Kim 2002) do not use the term GPNs as an alternative to 'value chain' but rather as a more precisely defined specific example of a value chain or set of related value chains. Ernst and Kim (2002), for example, describe GPNs as a major organizational innovation in global operations and a catalyst for international knowledge diffusion, 'combining concentrated dispersion of the value chain across the boundaries of the firm and national borders, with a parallel process of integrating hierarchical layers of network participants'. The related concept of global design networks is outlined in Box 10.1.

Some of the examples given here are cases of global division of labour in an industry, where the various activities carried out in different locations are the work of independent firms. This is different from the global division of labour within the boundaries of one company, in which the firm specializes in different technological and other activities in different locations, exploiting the complementary potentials of the different geographical sites, and extending its core competencies through internally coordinated learning and innovation activities (Cantwell 1992; Pearce 1999). In this case, a global strategy optimizes the location of activities from a worldwide perspective (Porter 1986; Dunning 1993; Chesnais et al. 2000).

However, in recent years the emergence of a third form of organization, networks around global corporations, including the GPNs and global design networks discussed earlier, has cut across these distinctions (see also Chapter 9). Langlois (2003) suggested that a shift from the hierarchical organization of R&D, design, and production within vertically integrated multinationals, would involve a greater reliance on arms-length transactions between firms in different countries, and that, therefore, the visible hand of the large global corporation would tend to become invisible, and a resurgence of market forces would take place. However, Ernst (2004*b*) argues, on the contrary, that network integration is the necessary complement to the tendency towards increased outsourcing to other firms with geographical dispersion across national borders. Global corporations, he says, integrate geographically dispersed companies into hierarchical global design networks. They construct networks to gain quick access to skills and capabilities at lower cost overseas locations that complement their core competencies, and they dominate control over network resources and decision-making. Vertical specialization increases the number and variety of network participants and the variety of business models, which in turn increase the organizational complexity of these networks.

Deregulation of finance and innovations in information technology have also enabled globalization to take place more effectively (Howells 1995, 2002). The management of a single firm with divisions which cross national borders and different time zones, or the management of a network with geographically dispersed autonomous components, and the operation of R&D or other functional teams within either, is made possible by information technology. Intranets, e-mail, teleconferencing, computer-supported cooperative work, videophone, and multimedia allow the movement of information, the establishment of social and professional linkages, and the discussion of ideas, plans, results, and strategy. They enable the design and testing of engineering and other physical products, or molecules which might become chemical products, by team members working simultaneously in several locations. We can also observe an interaction here between technological and social/

economic trends. Not only is IT acting as a stimulus or enabling mechanism for globalization, but also conversely globalization disperses technological activity and contributes to the generation of new organizational structures within which the technological innovation takes place.

Is globalization a myth?

As part of the 'hype' of globalization in the 1990s, there was considerable debate about whether or not it was a real phenomenon—was it really taking place, or was it a myth? Arguments that globalization is indeed a myth or at least greatly exaggerated include the following (Hirst and Thompson 1999):

1. Most multinational firms still have a strong national base, making the most of a particular national innovation system.
2. Most international activity, such as FDI, flows of trade, and production of technology are concentrated in the advanced industrial countries, rather than dispersed throughout the globe.
3. Most less developed countries remain marginal in both investment and trade, apart from a small minority of newly industrializing economies.
4. Today's international economy is less open and less integrated than it was during the period 1870–1914. For example, in 1914, 7.3 per cent US investments were overseas, a level reached again only in 1966. FDI still represents a small percentage of total investment, despite its rate of growth.
5. Not only is trade and investment concentrated in the 'Triad' of North America, Japan, and Western Europe (point 2), but also these major economic powers can exert powerful governance pressures over financial markets and other economic trends, especially where they are able to coordinate policy among themselves.

This means that global markets are not beyond regulation and control, and the internationalization of money and capital markets that has taken place since the 1970s are potentially, at least, reversible.

However, not only are the first three of these points indisputable, they can equally be seen as *central features of globalization*, rather than evidence against it (Chesnais 1997: 25). The argument in point 4 about the extent of inter-nationalization, obscures the very important *qualitative* changes that had taken place, especially in the last 20 years, in the ways in which capital is employed in the creation of value, particularly in the organizational structures and ways of managing large firms and groups, and the relationships they establish among themselves at the heart of global oligopoly (Chesnais 1997). These qualitative changes (introduced earlier in this chapter) include:

- Changes in the forms of organization and management structures within multinationals leading to a global division of labour; the distinction between geographical spread of activities and functional integration (discussed earlier).
- Changes in the relationships established by global oligopolies amongst themselves, such as cartels and more recently cooperative alliances and networks.
- The multinationals orchestrating activities within networks internal and external to the firm, so that it acts as the central nervous system of a much larger group, whose main aim is the advancement of the global competitive strategy of the core organization.
- New forms of investment including joint ventures, franchising and similar arrangements, or minority holdings abroad as a protection against expropriation.

Finally, the argument in point 5 can be countered by considering how much the USA, in particular, has to gain from the self-regulating or liberal market economy. And the USA is so influential among the G3 (Triad) nations that the restoration of regulation and control is unlikely (Chesnais 1997: 27).[8] This is not, however, an argument against the continuing importance of government or the need for industrial and technological policies (Chesnais and Simonetti 2000: 3).

Glyn (2004) and Sutcliffe and Glyn (2003) have reviewed the quantitative data used to analyse the extent of globalization, concluding that they would not wish to suggest that globalization is neither large nor important, but that it is a gradual rather than a sudden process and has not in general reached unprecedented levels (as some of the authors whom they criticize would claim). They examine the following indicators:

1. *Exports.* They argue that it is share of exports at current and not constant prices which most closely reflect productivity gains and the share of resources devoted to exporting activity. On this basis they show that shares of exports in GDP exceeded levels of 1913 by a comparatively modest degree. We have argued (above) that the existence of a trend here is more significant than the extent of the phenomenon.
2. *Foreign direct investment.* They consider that comparison of trends in FDI to those in domestic investment is more reliable than a comparison with GDP. They conclude that FDI as a percentage of domestic investment has certainly grown over the last three decades, and especially rapidly in the second half of the 1990s, but is still a good deal smaller than commonly supposed (see Figure 10.1). We use both domestic investment and GDP (as well as track) to compare with FDI (Figure 8.1), although the data are only available to 1990.
3. *Multinational corporations.* The tendency has not so much been that the largest multinationals are now controlling much more of the world

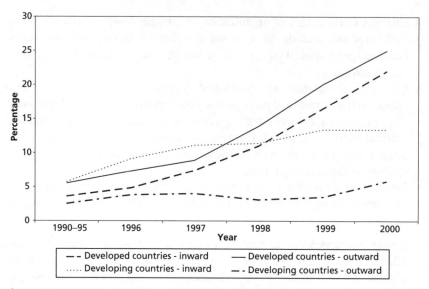

Figure 10.1 FDI as per cent of gross domestic investment
(*source*: Glyn and Sutcliffe 2003)

economy, but that the nature of the firm has been changing—globalization
has meant that a growing number of companies (including small- and
medium-sized firms) have global interests, rather than that a given number of companies directly control more of the globe. And that this is the
continuation of very long-term tendencies towards industrial concentration taking place slowly. Our main argument about globalization also
concerns the changing nature of the firm, specifically, increased concentration via mergers and acquisitions, and the network structures within
which innovation now takes place.

4. *Finance.* There is a general consensus that a huge expansion of international financial flows has taken place; cross-border bank lending
and transactions in bonds and equities have grown spectacularly. However,
this is not necessarily the internationalization of the ownership of financial
assets—many transactions represent the reshuffling of existing portfolios.

5. *Labour.* Where deregulation of finance has contributed to a large growth in
international flows, international movement of labour is highly regulated:
economically advanced countries have increased regulation of immigration in recent years. As a consequence, migration to the USA in the 1990s
(for example) took place at only one-third of the rate seen during 1900–10
(as a proportion of the population), while the proportion of the world's
population resident in countries where they were not born is estimated to
have risen from a little over 2 to a little under 3 per cent during the last 30
years, and is around 10 per cent in both Europe and the USA.

A lot of the debate about whether or not globalization is taking place hinges on what the term 'globalization' actually means, so that different conclusions about exactly what is happening under the heading of 'globalization' can be drawn from different meanings of the term. Hence the possibility, mentioned earlier, that several of the central points made *against* globalization can not only be said to be indisputable, but also *key features* of the present phase of the globalization of capital. While Sutcliffe and Glyn claim to be 'globalosceptics' they advance similar arguments to those we have put forward in characterising the last 30 years of internationalization, which we have called globalization.

Is globalization really *global*?

However, these activities, which together are what we call globalization, are not all taking place to the same extent in all parts of the globe. On the contrary, as Hirst and Thompson (1999) argued, they are very highly concentrated in the three major trading blocs known as the Triad, namely Japan, North America, and Europe. These areas are the focus of most international activity. The OECD (1992) published some data to illustrate this concentration. From 1980 to 1990 intra-Triad FDI stock nearly tripled, from US$142 billion to US$410 billion. In 1980 the stock of inward investment within the Triad was 30 per cent of worldwide inward investment, and by 1988 had gone up to 39 per cent. Less developed countries' share of FDI was 18.6 per cent during the period 1985–9, a figure which increased to 35 per cent in 1995, but was concentrated in the newly industrializing economies with only 1 per cent of this going to the 100 weakest states.

Chesnais and Simonetti (2000) have since updated those figures, showing that 68 per cent of the stock of inward FDI was still held by OECD countries, despite the growth of South East Asia's, and especially China's, inward stock since 1990. OECD countries also account for 90 per cent of the world's outward stock of FDI (Chesnais and Simonetti 2000).

Implications of globalization for national governments

The issue here is the role of the nation state, the national system of innovation, and national economic and science-technology policy, and whether the policy or institutions of any individual nation can have an influence on a global firm which has operations within its borders. The financial resources available to the world's largest firms often exceed the financial incomes of whole countries, including major industrialized countries. They are also greater than the foreign exchange reserves held by most major countries' central banks (Chesnais 1997), for example General Motors' turnover is higher than the GNP of Denmark; Exxon's turnover is bigger than that of Norway, and Toyota's turnover is greater than that of Portugal.

This gives firms a large amount of power and the ability to avoid, ignore, or resist the effects of government policies, national institutions, or cultural practices. Firms can relocate, close down significant productive capacity, and reduce their workforce by hundreds or thousands. In short they affect the livelihoods of large numbers of people. Yet governments are elected and can be removed if their policies are too unpopular (at least in democratic countries), whereas company managements cannot, and may not have any loyalty to the state in which they are based. This raises the question as to whether national borders are becoming obsolete.

In support of the continuing power of the nation state, it has to be noted that there are still few genuinely transnational companies with footloose capital and no specific national identity. Firms are still more likely to be based mainly in one country and trade multinationally on the strengths of their major national location, even if production is carried out elsewhere.

At the time that Rhône-Poulenc health business merged with the small US firm Rorer to form Rhône-Poulenc Rorer, there was a great deal of concern expressed in the French press about the 'defrancization' of Rhône-Poulenc, partly because the headquarters of the firm shifted to Collegeville, Pennsylvania. When Rhône-Poulenc Pharma merged with Hoechst Marion Roussel to form Aventis, press releases were careful to announce that the headquarters would be in Strasbourg (France), and that the merging firms were 'equal partners', the merger reported rather like a marriage, with the Hoechst CEO inviting the Rhône-Poulenc CEO on a family visit to Germany, and being invited in turn to go to the soccer world cup in France with the Rhône-Poulenc CEO.

According to Ramirez (2005b), nearly all the large pharmaceutical firms she interviewed had an integrated strategy and approach to management (one exception being Johnson & Johnson, which was very decentralized), although only the ones with a big international research effort had an international division of labour in research. On the other hand it was still unusual, even in the internationalized pharmaceutical industry, to have a substantially international shareholder base. Shareholders still tend to be mainly of one nationality unless there has been a large cross-border merger or acquisition, as is the case with AstraZeneca or Glaxo SmithKline.

Implications of globalization for innovation

The issue here is whether globalization of innovative activity is happening, or whether R&D mostly stays at home, with the national innovation system still exerting the main influence over its rate and direction. Examples of management of globalized firms given in this chapter, with global R&D and not just production activities or international trade, suggest that it is—but the question is whether these are typical.

There are a number of dimensions to international technological deployment by multinationals, which is not just a question of location of R&D abroad, but can also include global exploitation of technology, sourcing of technology, and technological collaboration (Howells and Wood 1993; Archibugi and Michie 1995; Howells 1997), as follows:

1. Overseas location of R&D in specialist facilities, or in-house R&D in subsidiaries abroad, created specially or acquired by mergers and acquisitions (we return later to the advantages and disadvantages of location of R&D activities in another country);
2. Purchase of technology from other, overseas, firms by licensing and from small firms and public sector research institutions by means of agreements (and which may involve equal or unequal relationships);
3. Strategic alliances between large companies, possibly to construct barriers to entry to other firms or to exploit complementary assets, and which generate new knowledge;
4. A multinational firm taking out a patent abroad, or establishing standards abroad; and
5. Exploitation of technology abroad by means of the sale of licences, by exports, or by production abroad.

A firm might prefer to license another firm, which means selling technology abroad rather than manufacturing overseas itself. There might be a number of reasons summarized below:

1. It does not have enough resources or assets for FDI, so it is cheaper to license another firm;
2. Entry barriers are high for FDI, so it is easier to license another firm;
3. Technology is changing rapidly, so the firm can respond more quickly to new opportunities if it licenses an existing firm rather than sets up its own overseas operations;
4. It is licensing technology in a peripheral not a core business area (and it is more important to the firm to keep control of its core business activities);

5. The technology is not very complex, so it is easy to transfer, involving little tacit knowledge; or
6. The firm is concerned that the host country might appropriate foreign assets.

On the other hand, a firm might prefer to invest abroad rather than license another firm if:

1. Operations are readily transferable overseas;
2. Technology is more economically exploited overseas;
3. Operations can be more profitably exploited by the enterprise than by licensing to an independent firm; or
4. The multinational firm gains a monopolistic advantage by overseas production.

Advantages of overseas R&D include:

1. Access to the host country's science base;
2. Access to the host country market;
3. The need to adapt to local tastes and patterns of demand;
4. The need to be seen as a 'local' firm in the overseas market, for political or marketing reasons;
5. The availability of staff with skills not available or cheaper than at home, perhaps as a result of an increased variety of interrelated technologies providing an input to the innovative process;
6. The need to interact with sophisticated lead users in the overseas market, to get feedback on innovative products and services;
7. A favourable regulatory environment overseas, or the need to do local R&D to comply with local regulations;
8. Other favourable government policies abroad, such as tax breaks, financial incentives, the availability of technological advice and support;
9. The possibility of influencing the selection environment (e.g. by lobbying governments or interacting with expert intermediaries); and
10. A merger or acquisition has given the firm an overseas research facility.

On the other hand there are also disadvantages of doing R&D overseas if:

1. There is a loss of economies of scale in R&D by dispersal abroad;
2. There are a greater variety and quantity of skills in one place;
3. The links with the scientific and technological infrastructure at home are more important;
4. The links with decision-makers at company headquarters are decisive;
5. Government policies are in place which encourage research staying at home; and
6. The firm is producing standard products for world markets and has no need to go abroad.

Globalization of innovative activity: The evidence

A substantial body of literature now exists which provides empirical evidence to contribute to our understanding of whether innovative activity is being globalized (see Chapter 8). A number of indicators have been used.

First, patenting carried out by firms outside their home base may be used as an indicator of globalization of innovative activity. Strictly speaking, patents are an output of the *inventive* rather than innovative process. But US patents taken out by non-US firms generally signify an intention to market the invention in the USA, and may thus be taken as a measure of (intended) *innovative* activity as well. A majority of patents registered in the USA in the 1980s and 1990s by firms worldwide come from inventors with addresses in the firm's home country (Patel 1995; Patel and Pavitt 1997; Patel and Vega 1999). This suggests that globalization of innovation is *not* taking place to any significant degree, although there is a great deal of variation among industrial sectors, and a great deal of variation among home-based countries.

The most internationalized firms are those with principal activities in drink and tobacco, food, pharmaceuticals, and building materials (those requiring the most adaptive R&D to meet the demand of local markets). The least internationalized are aircraft, motor vehicles, scientific instruments, and computers (all sectors where geographical closeness of R&D, design, and production are important in the launching of innovative new products). Dutch and Belgian firms carried out more of their technological activities abroad than in their home country, but Italian, French, German, and especially Japanese firms had the lowest proportion of patents taken out from overseas locations.

However, if patent data are examined over the long-term, and the rise of internationally integrated structures for technological development (such as the networks we have discussed earlier) are taken into account, then leading firms in science-based industries do not necessarily have innovative activity that is a great deal more geographically dispersed than it was in the past, but they do show a greater division of labour and more integrated strategies internationally, including their division of labour in, and strategy towards, innovative activities (Cantwell 1995; Cantwell and Kotecha 1997; Cantwell and Janne 1999).

A second indicator of globalization of innovative activity is the location of R&D laboratories outside the firm's home country. A relatively small but growing percentage of R&D activity takes place abroad, with differences between industries and home countries (e.g. Pearce and Singh 1992; Pearce 1999; Pearce and Papanastassiou 1999). Overseas laboratories are developing distinctive capabilities so they are increasingly able to take on more strategic roles, or carry out original product development, or contribute to pre-competitive research, rather than just adapt existing technology to new markets. Access to basic research and sophisticated customer knowledge abroad is also an important motive for firms' carrying out R&D in other countries (Gerybadze and Reger 1999; Kuemmerle 1999), Cantwell and Pearce show that global R&D strategies are of growing importance.

A third indicator of globalization of innovative activity is the growth in inter-firm and inter-organizational alliances and networks which cross national borders. Firms can source scientific and technological knowledge abroad, which would provide an input to the innovation process, but would not be measurable by looking at the location of a firm's patenting activity or its research laboratories. The global design networks introduced by Ernst (2004b) and discussed earlier, would also be a source of new technological knowledge from abroad, and with the additional feature that some of it might not be patentable in any case (in the home country or overseas). Ramirez (2003, 2005) examined five dimensions of the process of globalization of R&D in the pharmaceutical industry, finding the process to have been rather uneven along these dimensions, and also finding important differences between US and European multinationals. In particular, she examines networks and alliances between the firms and a variety of other organizations (including other firms).

Hagedoorn (2002) has calculated the share of R&D alliances which are made across national borders, and found a slightly downward trend from the mid-1970s to the end of the 1990s, despite a strong growth in absolute numbers. He explains this by the growth in the share of US domestic collaborations out of the total, which were encouraged by the changes in antitrust policy in favour of alliances; and by the Uruguay Round that reduced some non-tariff trade barriers (e.g. in telecommunications equipment or pharmaceuticals) that formerly gave an important motive for R&D-based international collaboration.

Guellec and van Pottelsberghe de la Potterie (2001) have developed three new patent-based indicators of internationalization of technology which are intended to reflect international cooperation in research as well as the location of research facilities of multinational firms. These are:

1. The share for a given country of patents with a domestic inventor and a foreign applicant in the country's total domestic inventions; this is intended to reflect the extent to which foreign firms own domestic inventions;
2. The share for a given country of patents with a foreign inventor and a domestic applicant in the country's total domestic applications; this is intended to reflect the extent to which domestic firms control foreign inventions; and

3. The share for a given country of patents with a foreign resident as coin-ventor in the population of patents with a domestic inventor.

They found that, over the period 1980–95, the degree of international R&D collaboration more than doubled. From 1990 onwards cross-border ownership of inventions grew to a 12 per cent share of OECD patents in 1994. The most internationalized sectors are chemicals, oil refining, pharmaceut-icals, and food and beverages. The countries with the most internationalized technology are the UK, smaller countries such as Belgium, Austria and Ireland, and less developed countries such as Turkey, Mexico, and Poland. Twelve per cent may seem to be a rather small proportion, but first we are talking here of the proportion of inventions authored by collaborators in different countries (rather than the share of R&D carried out abroad or the share of patents coming from overseas subsidiaries), and international col-laboration in R&D is a more difficult as well as more recent phenomenon. And second, what is key here, as in so many other examples of international activities mentioned earlier in the chapter, is that we are observing a phe-nomenon that may be small in magnitude at the moment, but which is a growing trend, and that is what is significant. Once again, the key feature of globalization is not the extent to which it has already happened, but the ongoing upward trend, and the changing nature of the innovative process and the organizational structures within which it is taking place.

Conclusion

Globalization can be regarded as an ongoing complex (and contradictory) process (rather than an end-state), which is realized in institutionally, histor-ically, and geographically specific sites. Multinationals are at the centre of this process, as they organize production and innovation on an international basis. Networks of firms are involved in the production, R&D, design, and marketing of different products, which are organized globally and regionally. The internationalization of production and R&D raises important issues of welfare, since it can provide opportunities for positive effects of the multi-national on the host (and home) economy. However, there are many cases when these positive effects are not realized (Blomstrom and Kokko 1998; Aitken and Harrison 1999; Gorg and Strobl 2001). The changing division of labour and the integration of strategy and management in multinationals have important effects on the systems of production and innovation in different countries and regions.

Notes

1 For example, Ralph Nader and James Love in a letter to President Clinton dated 4 February 1997, asked the US government to reconsider its trade sanctions against Argentina. These had been imposed because the Argentine government had permitted the sale of a generic version of the unpatented drug taxol, the branded and trademarked version of which was manufactured and sold by Bristol Myers Squibb in the USA.

2 For example, in an interview with the design manager of Lego at Billund, Denmark in January 1981, we were told that Lego considered it a sign of their international success that consumers in most overseas markets thought that Lego was a product native to their own country. IKEA, however, deliberately markets itself as Swedish in the UK, with Swedish flags outside and Swedish food in the café (although no particularly Swedish theme in French branches); and watches are traditionally associated with Switzerland.

3 More successfully in some countries than others. Italy and France, for example, still have a thriving sector of artisan food stores specializing in particular products and competing in quite local markets, on the basis of freshness, absence of additives, and individual service, as argued in Chapters 4 and 7. At the same time out-of-town hypermarkets have also seized a substantial share of the market.

4 Though some operating systems have been more widely adopted in some countries—Apple Macs seem to be more widespread in France than Britain.

5 Although increasingly standardized protocols for safety testing are being adopted; for example, Europe-wide licensing by the European Medicines Agency began in 1995 (http://www.emea.eu.int/htms/aboutus/emeaoverview.htm). Meanwhile, approval in certain countries at least short cut approval in others, and various intergovernmental organizations including the World Health Organization have initiated efforts to harmonize drug regulation internationally. The International Conference on Harmonization of Technical Requirements for the Registration of Pharmaceuticals for Human Use started in 1990.

6 **The Times Atlas of World History** (Parker 1993) illustrates the rise and fall of empires from the earliest periods of human history (e.g. Byzantine, Persian, Greek, Roman) to European overseas expansion many centuries later; and equally the rise of nationalism and struggles for independence from colonial rule during the twentieth century.

7 In the words of Hirst and Thompson (1999: 1) 'Globalization has become a fashionable concept in the social sciences, a core dictum in the prescriptions of management gurus, and a catch-phrase for journalists and politicians of every stripe.'

8 Though Chesnais suggests that the 'triumph of the liberal market economy', which is global in nature, is also temporary, since it is at the mercy of future financial crashes.

Appendix Table 1 Gross domestic expenditure on R&D by sector of performance 2001 or nearest year, percentages

OECD country	Industry (%)	Higher education (%)	Government (%)	Other (%)	Total (%)
Australia	47.1	27.1	23.1	2.7	100
Austria	63.6	29.7	6.4	0.3	100
Belgium	71.6	23.9	3.3	1.2	100
Canada	57.5	30.3	11.9	0.3	100
Czech Republic	60.2	15.7	23.7	0.4	100
Denmark	64.9	19.4	14.5	1.2	100
Finland	71.1	18.1	10.2	0.6	100
France	62.4	18.5	17.7	1.4	100
Germany	70.5	16	13.4	0.1	100
Greece	28.5	49.5	21.7	0.3	100
Hungary	40.1	25.7	25.9	8.3	100
Iceland	58.9	18.8	20.1	2.2	100
Ireland	71.8	20.1	8.1	0	100
Italy	50.1	31	18.9	0	100
Japan	73.7	14.5	9.5	2.3	100
Korea	76.2	10.4	12.4	1	100
Mexico	25.5	26.3	45	3.2	100
Netherlands	57.1	29.2	13	0.7	100
New Zealand	29.7	34.3	36	0	100
Norway	59.7	25.7	14.6	0	100
Poland	35.8	32.7	31.3	0.2	100
Portugal	32.6	36.1	21.4	9.9	100
Slovak Republic	67.3	9	23.7	0	100
Spain	52.4	30.9	15.9	0.8	100
Sweden	77.6	19.4	2.8	0.2	100
Switzerland	73.9	22.9	1.3	1.9	100
Turkey	33.4	60.4	6.2	0	100
UK	67.4	21.4	9.7	1.5	100
USA	74.4	14.2	7	4.4	100
OECD Total	69.6	17.3	10.4	2.7	100
of which:					
EU	64.5	21.2	13.5	0.8	100
Non-OECD countries					
Argentina	22.8	35	39.9	2.3	100
China	60.4	9.8	29.7	0.1	100
Israel	73.2	17	6.2	3.6	100
Romania	61.6	11.3	27.1	0	100
Russian Federation	70.3	5.2	24.3	0.2	100
Singapore	63.3	23.6	13.1	0	100
Slovenia	57.8	16.2	24.3	1.7	100
Chinese Taipei	63.6	12.5	23.3	0.6	100

Source: OECD (2003a).

Appendix Table 2 Gross domestic expenditure on R&D by source of funds, 2001, percentages

OECD country	Industry (%)	Government (%)	Other (%)	Total (%)
Australia	45.9	46.1	8	100
Austria	39.4	41.3	19.3	100
Belgium	71.6	23.9	4.5	100
Canada	41.9	31.3	26.8	100
Czech Republic	52.5	43.6	3.9	100
Denmark	59	31.2	9.8	100
Finland	70.8	25.5	3.7	100
France	52.5	38.7	8.8	100
Germany	66	31.5	2.5	100
Greece	24.2	48.7	27.1	100
Hungary	34.8	53.6	11.6	100
Iceland	46.2	34	19.8	100
Ireland	66	22.6	11.4	100
Italy	43	50.8	6.2	100
Japan	73	18.5	8.5	100
Korea	72.5	25	2.5	100
Mexico	23.6	61.3	15.1	100
Netherlands	50.1	35.9	14	100
New Zealand	34.1	50.6	15.3	100
Norway	51.6	39.8	8.6	100
Poland	30.8	64.8	4.4	100
Portugal	32.4	61.2	6.4	100
Slovak Republic	56.1	41.3	2.6	100
Spain	47.2	39.9	12.9	100
Sweden	71.9	21	7.1	100
Switzerland	69.1	23.2	7.7	100
Turkey	42.9	50.6	6.5	100
UK	46.2	30.2	23.6	100
USA	68.3	26.9	4.8	100
OECD Total of which:	63.6	28.9	7.5	100
EU	56.2	34.5	9.3	100
Non-OECD countries				
Argentina	20.8	74.3	4.9	100
China	57.6	33.4	9	100
Israel	63.9	28.8	7.3	100
Romania	47.6	43	9.4	100
Russian Federation	33.6	57.2	9.2	100
Singapore	54.2	38.1	7.7	100
Slovenia	54.7	37.1	8.2	100
Chinese Taipei	64.9	33.3	1.8	100

Source: OECD (2003a).

Appendix Table 3 Government funding of R&D: Defence vs. civil objectives, 2002 or latest year

OECD country	Civil (%)	Defence (%)	As % of civil R&D				
			Economic development	Health and environment	Space programmes	Non-orientated	General university funds
Australia	92.7	7.3	28.8	19.2	0.0	31.8	12.9
Austria	100	0	12.5	8.0	0.1	13.6	65.8
Belgium	99.8	0.2	32.4	10.0	11.4	23.4	18.8
Canada	95.2	4.8	31.3	24.3	7.0	6.3	29.9
Czech Republic	n/a	n/a	n/a	n/a	n/a	n/a	n/a
Denmark	99.4	0.6	19.0	15.2	2.3	20.7	42.9
Finland	97.1	2.9	40.9	16.0	2.0	13.8	27.7
France	76.8	23.2	16.9	13.4	12.8	25.8	28.1
Germany	94.7	5.3	20.9	14.5	5.1	17.4	42.1
Greece	99.1	0.9	18.2	19.2	0.1	11.0	51.1
Hungary	n/a	n/a	n/a	n/a	n/a	n/a	n/a
Iceland	100	0	35.2	n/a	n/a	18.6	33.3
Ireland	100	0	41.4	12.8	0.0	27.6	18.3
Italy	96	4	16.8	16.2	7.6	13.9	45.5
Japan	95.9	4.1	33.8	7.7	6.3	16.0	36.3
Korea	84.7	15.3	53.3	17.3	3.8	25.6	n/a
Mexico	100	0	33.5	12.5	0.0	n/a	53.9
Netherlands	98.1	1.9	25.8	8.9	2.6	10.9	47.2
New Zealand	99.3	0.7	45.1	29.9	n/a	5.8	19.2
Norway	95.8	4.2	23.9	18.9	2.2	10.5	38.8
Poland	n/a	n/a	n/a	n/a	n/a	n/a	n/a
Portugal	98.9	1.1	39.8	17.7	0.6	9.0	33.1
Slovak Republic	93	7	31.6	11.8	n/a	35.1	18.0
Spain	62.7	37.3	36.1	15.4	3.8	3.4	41.1
Sweden	77.8	22.2	11.6	9.7	2.7	20.0	48.9
Switzerland	99.3	0.7	4.7	2.4	n/a	n/a	61.5
Turkey	n/a	n/a	n/a	n/a	n/a	n/a	n/a
UK	69.7	30.3	14.1	32.1	2.9	19.3	31.1
USA	45.6	54.4	12.1	55.2	13.4	11.7	n/a
EU	84.9	15.1	20.6	16.2	6.2	17.4	38.3
OECD Total	70.2	29.8	22.3	27.1	8.5	15.8	24.5

Source: OECD (2003a).

Appendix Table 4 Business enterprise research by sector of performance, 2001 or most recent year, percentages

OECD country	Aerospace (%)	Electronics (%)	Office machinery and computers (%)	Pharmaceuticals (%)	Scientific instruments (%)	Services (%)	Other (%)	Total (%)
Australia	0.1	10.6	2.0	7.3	2.9	42.7	34.4	100
Austria	0.0	28.5	0.2	6.1	2.4	24.0	38.7	100
Belgium	1.2	16.5	0.2	18.6	1.3	19.8	42.3	100
Canada	9.1	39.1	4.7	6.5	2.7	30.7	7.2	100
Czech Republic	3.1	3.2	0.0	3.0	1.6	33.1	56.0	100
Denmark	0.0	4.4	0.9	25.3	6.3	36.2	26.8	100
Finland	0.1	52.3	0.1	5.3	2.8	12.7	26.8	100
France	10.9	14.7	1.6	13.3	7.3	11.4	40.8	100
Germany	7.3	12.0	2.1	6.8	5.5	8.7	57.7	100
Greece	0.4	21.2	0.1	4.3	0.4	35.2	38.3	100
Hungary	0.0	10.9	0.4	45.9	1.8	22.7	18.3	100
Iceland	0.0	0.0	0.0	4.6	3.7	90.4	1.3	100
Ireland	0.3	29.6	4.9	10.2	4.8	23.8	26.4	100
Italy	11.9	21.5	1.3	9.5	4.7	23.4	27.7	100
Japan	0.8	18.4	10.6	6.7	4.4	2.1	56.9	100
Korea	4.3	40.4	8.7	2.5	1.6	14.1	28.6	100
Mexico	0.0	0.9	1.0	3.4	0.3	10.3	84.1	100
Netherlands	0.3	22.3	7.8	10.9	2.1	19.9	36.8	100
New Zealand	0.0	12.1	0.1	1.0	2.7	39.8	44.3	100
Norway	0.3	11.2	0.8	3.6	1.7	39.6	42.8	100
Poland	4.1	6.5	0.2	6.3	2.1	19.9	60.8	100
Portugal	0.0	5.6	0.2	0.0	1.0	45.4	47.8	100
Slovak Republic	0.0	15.0	0.0	7.1	1.1	34.5	42.3	100
Spain	6.1	6.7	1.3	11.4	1.8	43.7	29.0	100
Sweden	2.4	19.3	0.6	13.6	4.7	10.6	48.9	100
Switzerland	0.0	4.8	0.0	0.0	0.0	21.6	73.5	100
Turkey	0.8	14.2	0.0	1.5	0.3	14.8	68.4	100
UK	11.9	9.8	1.0	28.7	4.6	22.4	21.6	100
USA	5.5	13.7	5.5	6.9	10.2	36.3	22.1	100
EU	7.3	13.1	1.7	0.0	4.5	12.5	60.9	100

Source: OECD (2003a).

Appendix Table 5 Sources of funds for research carried out by industry 2001 or nearest year available, percentages

OECD country	Industry (%)	Government (%)	Other national sources (%)	Abroad (%)	Total (%)
Australia	91.5	3.7	0.5	4.3	100
Austria	64.4	5.5	0.1	30.1	100.1
Belgium	88.5	6.2	0	5.3	100
Canada	67.1	2.4	0	30.5	100
Czech Republic	84.3	12.2	1.6	1.9	100
Denmark	89.5	4.1	0.6	5.8	100
Finland	95.6	3.4	0.3	0.7	100
France	81	9.9	0.1	9	100
Germany	90.5	7.1	0.2	2.1	99.9
Greece	75.2	3.5	0	21.3	100
Hungary	75.7	6.1	0.1	16.9	98.8
Iceland	73.1	1.4	0.2	25.3	100
Ireland	92.8	4	0	4.5	101.3
Italy	80.8	12.2	0.2	6.9	100.1
Japan	97.8	0.8	0.8	0.5	99.9
Korea	91.2	8.1	0.2	0.6	100.1
Mexico	80.4	1.1	0	18.5	100
Netherlands	79.3	5.2	0.1	15.4	100
New Zealand	84	9.6	1.2	5.3	100.1
Norway	81.4	10.3	0	8.3	100
Poland	67.6	30.4	0.2	1.8	100
Portugal	94.4	2.1	n/a	3.6	100.1
Slovak Republic	78.3	20.6	0	1.1	100
Spain	82.5	9.5	0.3	7.7	100
Sweden	91.1	5.8	0.1	2.9	99.9
Switzerland	91.4	2.3	0.5	5.8	100
Turkey	92.4	4.3	1.4	1.9	100
UK	64.4	11.9	0	23.7	100
USA	90.2	10.9	0	n/a	101.1
OECD Total of which:	88.8	7.6	0	n/a	96.4
EU	83.5	7.8	0.1	8.4	99.8

Source: OECD (2003a).

Appendix Table 6 Percentage of total R&D paid for by industry, 1975

Country	R&D (%)
USA	39
UK	43
France	38
Germany	58
Japan	50
Italy	n/a

Source: OECD (1993).

REFERENCES

Abbott, F. M. (1998). 'The Enduring Enigma of TRIPS: A Challenge for the World Economic System', *Journal of International Economic Law*, 1(4): 497–521.

Aikenhead, G. (2003). 'Chemistry and Physics Instruction: Integration, Ideologies and Choices', *Chemical Education: Research and Practice* 4(2): 115–30.

Aitken, B. and Harrison, A. (1999). 'Do Domestic Firms Benefit from Direct Foreign Investment? Evidence from Venezuela', *American Economic Review*, 89(3): 605–18.

Akamatsu, K. (1956). 'A Wild Geese Flying Pattern of Japanese Industrial Development: Machine and Tool Industries', *Hitotsubashi Review*, 6(5): 55–87 (in Japanese).

Akrich, M., Callon, M., and Latour, B. (2002). 'The Key to Success in Innovation Part I: The Art of Interessment, and Part II: The Art of Choosing Good Spokespersons', *International Journal of Innovation Management*, 6(2): 187–206, 207–25.

Albert, M. (1991). *Capitalisme Contre Capitalism*. Paris: Seuil.

Albu, A. (1980). 'British Attitudes to Engineering Education: A Historical Perspective', in K. Pavitt (ed.), *Technical Innovation and British Economic Performance*. London: Macmillan.

Alcorta, L. and Peres, W. (1998). 'Innovation Systems and Technological Specialization in Latin America and the Caribbean', *Research Policy*, 26(7–8): 857–81.

Alfranca, O., Rama, R., and von Tunzelmann, N. (2001). 'Cumulative Innovation in Food and Beverage Multinationals', *Global Business & Economics Review, Anthology 2001, Business & Business Society International*: 446–59.

—— —— (2003a). 'Technological Capabilities in Multinational Agribusiness', *International Journal of Agricultural Resources Governance and Ecology*, 2(3–4): 383–98.

—— —— (2003b). 'Competitive Behaviour, Design and Technical Innovation in Food and Beverage Multinationals', *International Journal of Biotechnology*, 5(3–4): 222–48.

Allinson, K. (1993). *The Wild Card of Design: A Perspective on Architecture in a Project Management Environment*. Oxford: Butterworth Architecture.

Amable, B., Barre, R., and Boyer, R. (1997). *Les Systèmes d'innovation á l'ére de la Globalization*. Paris: Economica.

Amsden, A. (1989). *Asia's Next Giant: South Korea and Late Industrialization*. New York: Oxford University Press.

—— and Hikino, T. (1994). 'Project Execution Capability, Organizational Know-How and Conglomerate Corporate Growth in Late Industrialization', *Industrial and Corporate Change*, 3(1): 111–47.

Anderson, B. (2004). 'If "Intellectual Property Rights" Is the Answer, What Is the Question', *Economics of Innovation and New Technology*, 13(5): 417–42.

Aoki, M. (1990). 'Towards an Economic Model of the Japanese Firm', *Journal of Economic Literature*, 28: 1–27.

—— *Information, Corporate Governance and Institutional Diversity*. Oxford: Oxford University Press.

Archibugi, D. and Michie, J. (1995). 'The Globalization of Technology: A New Taxonomy', *Cambridge Journal of Economics*, 19(1): 121–40.

Arditi, D. S., Kale, M., and Tangkar, M. (1997). 'Innovation in Construction Equipment and Its Flow into the Construction Industry', *Journal of Construction Engineering and Management*, 123(4): 371–78.

Arnold, E. and Guy, K. (1986). *Parallel Convergence*. London: Frances Pinter.

Arora, A., Fosfuri, A., and Gambardella, A. (2001). *Markets for Technology*. Cambridge, MA: MIT Press.

Arthur, W. B. (1988). 'Competing Technologies: An Overview', in G. Dosi, C. Freeman, R. Nelson, G. Silverber, and L. Soete (eds.), *Technical Change and Economic Theory*. London: Pinter.

—— (1989). 'Competing Technologies, Increasing Returns and Lock-in by Historical Events', *Economic Journal*, 99(394): 116–31.

AstraZeneca (2000). 'Zeneca Agrochemicals and Cambridge Discovery Chemistry Announce Collaboration', AstraZeneca Website, http://www.astrazeneca.com/news/archive, last accessed 30th April.

Athreye, A. (1998). 'On Markets in Knowledge', *Journal of Management and Governance*, 1(2): 231–53.

—— (2005). 'The Indian Software Industry and its Evolving Service Capability', *Industrial and Corporate Change*, 14(3): 393–418.

—— and Keeble, D. (2000). 'Technological Convergence, Globalization and Ownership in the UK Computer Industry', *Technovation*, 20(5): 227–45.

Atkinson, A. B. and Stiglitz, J. E. (1969). 'A New View of Technological Change', *Economic Journal*, 79(315): 573–8.

Avnimelech, G. and Teubal, M. (2003). 'Evaluating Venture Capital Policies: Methodological Lessons from the Israeli Experience', Advances in the Economic and Social Analysis of Technology (ASEAT) and the Institute of Innovation Research (IoIR) conference, in *Knowledge and Economic and Social Change: New Challenges to Innovation Studies*. Manchester, UK: Oxford Road.

Azpiazu, D. (1997). 'El Nuevo perfil de la elite empresaria', *Realidad Economica*, 145: 7–43.

—— Basualdo, E., and Khavisse, M. (1986). *El Nuevo Poder Economico en la Argentina*. Buenos Aires: Legasa.

Bain, J. (1956). *Barriers to New Competition*. Cambridge, MA: Harvard University Press.

Baran, P. A. and Sweezy, P. M. (1960). *Monopoly Capital*. Harmondsworth, UK: Penguin Books.

Barras, R. (1986a). 'A Comparison of Embodied Technical Change in Services and Manufacturing Industry', *Applied Economics*, 18(9): 941–58.

—— (1986b). 'New Technologies and the New Services', *Futures*, 18(6): 748–72.

—— (1986c). 'Towards a Theory of Innovation in Services', *Research Policy*, 15(4): 161–73.

Bartlett, C. and Ghoshal, S. (1997). 'Managing Innovation in the Transnational Corporation', in M. L. Tushman and P. Anderson (eds.), *Managing Strategic Innovation and Change*. New York: Oxford University Press.

Batt, R. (1995). *Performance and Welfare Effects of Work Restructuring: Evidence from Telecommunications Services*, Ph.D. Dissertation. MIT: Sloan School of Management.

Bauer, M (1988). 'The Politics of State-Directed Privatization: The Case of France', *West European Politics*, 11(4): 49–60.

Baumol, W. J. (1967). 'Macroeconomics of Unbalanced Growth: The Anatomy of Urban Crisis', *American Economic Review*, 57(3): 415–26.

Beer, J. J. (1959). *The Emergence of the German Dye Industry.* Urbana, IL: Illinois University Press.

Belussi, F. (1989). 'Benetton: A Case Study of Corporate Strategy for Innovation in Traditional Sectors', in M. Dodgson (ed.), *Technology Strategy and the Firm: Management and Public Policy.* Harlow: Longman.

—— and Arcangeli, F. (1998). 'A Typology of Networks: Flexible and Evolutionary Firms', *Research Policy*, 27: 415–28.

Best, M. (1990). *The New Competition: Institutions of Industrial Restructuring.* Cambridge, MA: Harvard University Press.

—— (2001). *The New Competitive Advantage: The Renewal of American Industry.* Oxford: Oxford University Press.

—— and Humphries, J. (1986). 'The City and Industrial Decline', in B. Elbaum and W. Lazonick (eds.), *The Decline of the British Economy.* Oxford: Clarendon Press.

Blackaby, F. (ed.) (1979). *De-Industrialization.* London: Heinemann.

Blackwell, B. (1976). 'Culture, Morbidity and the Effects of Drugs', *Clinical Pharmacology and Therapeutics*, 1(5, part 2): 668–74.

Blomstrom, M. and Kokko, A. (1998). 'Multinational Corporations and Spillovers', *Journal of Economic Surveys*, 12(2): 1–31.

Boltho, A. (1996). 'The Assessment: International Competitiveness', *Oxford Review of Economic Policy*, 12(3): 1–15.

Boyer, R. (2005). 'How and Why Capitalisms differ', *Economy and Society*, 34(4): 509–57.

Bozeman, B. and Dietz, J. (2001). 'Research Policy Trends in the United States: Civilian Technology Programs, Defense Technology and the Deployment of the National Laboratories', in P. Larédo and P. Muster (eds.), *Research and Innovation Policies in the New Global Economy.* Cheltenham, UK: Edward Elgar.

Breschi, S., Malerba, F., and Orsenigo, L. (2000). 'Technological Regimes and Schumpeterian Patterns of Innovation', *Economic Journal*, 111(463): 388–410.

Bresnahan, T. Gambardella, A., and Saxenian, A. (2001). '"Old Economy" Inputs for "New Economy" Outcomes: Cluster Formation in the New Silicon Valleys', *Industrial and Corporate Change*, 10(4): 835–60.

Broadman, H. (1994). 'GATTS: The Uruguay Round Accord in International Trade and Investment in Services', *The World Economy*, 17(3): 281–92.

Broetz, E. (2001). 'Can Government Subsidies Compensate for an Unsupportive National System of Innovation to Induce Sustainable Industry Developments? The Case of the German Biotechnology Industry'. M.Sc. Dissertation. Manchester, UK: Manchester School of Management.

Brown, P. (1998). 'Restaurants Press for Ban on Genetic Crops', *The Guardian*, 30 December.

Brusco, S. (1982). 'The Emilian Model: Productive Decentralization and Social Integration', *Cambridge Journal of Economics*, 6(2): 167–84.

Brusco, W. and Pezzini, M. (1990). 'Small-Scale Enterprise in the Ideology of the Italian Left', in F. Pyke, G. Becattini, and W. Sengenberger (eds.), *Industrial Districts and Inter-Firm Co-Operation in Italy.* Geneva: International Labour Organization.

Brusoni, S., Prencipe, A., and Pavitt, K. (2001). 'Knowledge Specialization, Organizational Coupling and the Boundaries of the Firm: Why Firms Know More Than They Make?' *Administrative Science Quarterly*, 46(4): 597–621.

Buckley, P. J. (1989). *The Multinational Enterprise: Theory and Applications*. London: Macmillan.

—— and Casson, M. C. (1976). *The Future of the Multinational Enterprise*. London: Macmillan.

Byé, P. (1999). 'The Food Industry: Still a Craft Industry', in P. Byé and D. Hayton (eds.), *Industrial History and Technological Development in Europe*. Luxembourg: Office for Official Publications of the European Communities, pp. 45–75.

Callon, M. (1986). 'Some Elements of a Sociology of Translation: Domestication of the Scallops and Fisherman of St Brieuc Bay', in J. Law (ed.), *Power, Action and Belief: A New Sociology of Knowledge?* London: Routledge.

—— (1987). 'Society in the Making: The Study of Technology as a Tool for Sociological Analysis', in W. E. Bijker, T. P. Hughes, and T. J. Pinch (eds.), *The Social Construction of Technological Systems*. Cambridge, MA: MIT Press.

—— (1994). 'Is Science a Public Good?', *Science, Technology and Human Values*, 19: 395–424.

—— (2003). 'The Increasing Involvement of Concerned Groups in R&D Policies: What Lessons for Public Powers?', in A. Guena, A. Salter and E. Steinmuller (eds.), *Science and Innovation*. Cheltenam: Edward Elgar.

—— and Law, J. (1995). 'Agency and the Hybrid Collectif', *The South Atlantic Quarterly*, 94: 485.

—— and Rabeharisoa, V. (2003). 'Research "in the Wild" and the Shaping of New Social Identities', *Technology in Society*, 25(2): 193–204.

Calvert, J. (2002). *Making Academic Research Useful: Scientists' Responses to Changing Policy Demands*, Paper presented to the NPRNet Conference, 'Rethinking Science Policy: Analytical Frameworks for Evidence-Based Policy'. Brighton, UK: Science Policy Research Unit, Sussex University.

Cantwell, J. (1989). *Technological Innovation and Multinational Corporations*. Oxford: Basil Blackwell.

—— (ed.) (1992). *Multinational Investment in Modern Europe: Strategic Interaction in the Integrated Community*. Aldershot, UK: Edward Elgar.

—— (1995). 'The Globalization of Technology: What Remains of the Product Cycle Model?' *Cambridge Journal of Economics*, 19(1): 155–74.

—— and Janne, O. (1999). 'Technological Globalization and Innovative Centres: The Role of Corporate Technological Leadership and Locational Hierarchy', *Research Policy*, 28(2–3): 119–44.

—— and Kotecha, U. (1997). 'The Internationalization of Technological Activity: The French Evidence in a Comparative Setting', in J. Howells and J. Michie (eds.), *Technology, Innovation and Competitiveness*. Cheltenham, UK: Edward Elgar, pp. 126–76.

Cardwell, D. S. L. (1957). *The Organization of Science in England* London: Heinemann.

Cassier, M. (2002). 'Private Property, Collective Property and Public Property in the Age of Genomics', *International Social Science Journal*, 54(171): 83–98.

Castells, M. (1992). 'Four Asian Tigers with a Dragon Head: A Comparative Analysis of the State, Economy and Society in the Asian Pacific Rim', in R. P. Appelbaum and J. Henderson (eds.), *States and Development in the Asian Pacific Rim*. London: Sage, pp. 33–70.

Cesaroni, F. (2004). 'Technological Outsourcing and Product Diversification: Do Markets for Technology Affect Firms' Strategies?' *Research Policy*, 33(10): 1547–64.

Chandler, A. D. (1977). *The Visible Hand: The Managerial Revolution in American Business.* Cambridge, MA: Harvard University Press.

Chang, H. J. (2002). *Kicking Away the Ladder: Development Strategy in Historical Perspective.* London: Anthem Press.

Chang, H., Park, H., and Yoo, C. (1998). 'Interpreting the Korean Crisis: Financial Liberalization, Industrial Policy and Corporate Governance', *Cambridge Journal of Economics*, 22(6): 735–46.

Chang, P., Karsteny, G., Mattoo, A., and Richtering, J. (1999). 'GATS, the Modes of Supply and Statistics on Trade in Services', *Journal of World Trade*, 33(3): 93–115.

Chesnais, F. (1988a). 'Multinational Enterprises and the International Diffusion of Technology', in G. Dosi et al. (eds.), *Technical Change and Economic Theory*. London: Pinter.

—— (1988b). 'Technical Co-Operation Agreements between Firms', *STI Review*, 4: 52–119.

—— (1992). 'National Systems of Innovation, Foreign Direct Investment and the Operations of Multinational Enterprises', in B.-A. Lundvall (ed.), *National Systems of Innovation*. London: Pinter.

—— (1996). 'Technological Agreements, Networks and Selected Issues in Economic Theory', in R. Coombs, A. Richards, P. Saviotti, and V. Walsh (eds.), *Technological Collaboration: The Dynamics of Cooperation in Innovation*. Aldershot, UK: Edward Elgar.

—— (1997). *La Mondialisation du Capital*. Paris: Syros.

—— Ietto-Gilles, G., and Simonetti, R. (2000). *European Integration and Global Corporate Strategies*. London: Routledge.

—— and Serfati, C. (1992). *l'Armement en France: Genèse, Ampleur et coût d'une Industrie.* Paris: Nathan.

—— —— (2000). 'Long Term Investment in a Globalised Finance Dominated Accumulation Regime: An Interpretation of the Leveling off of R&D in the 1990s', in F. Chesnais, G. Ietto-Gillies, and R. Simonetti (eds.), *European Integration and Global Corporate Strategies*. London: Routledge.

—— and Simonetti, R. (2000). 'Globalization, Foreign Direct Investment and Innovation', in F. Chesnais, G. Ietto-Gillies, and R. Simonetti (eds.), *European Integration and Global Corporate Strategies*. London: Routledge, pp. 3–24.

—— and Walsh, V. (1994). 'Biotechnology and the Chemical Industry: The Relevance of Some Evolutionary Concepts', EUNETIC conference on Evolutionary Economics of Technological Change: Assessment of Results and New Frontiers, Strasbourg, October.

Choi, B. I. (2001). 'Treatment of Autonomous Liberalization in the WTO New Service Round—To Give Credit Is to Get More', *Journal of World Trade*, 35(2): 363–78.

Cimoli, M., Cingano, F., and Della Giusta, M. (1998). *Historical Modes of Industrial Development, Technological Capabilities and Competitiveness in Mexico*, Mimeo.

Clairmonte, F. F. and Cavanagh, J. H. (1981). *The World in Their Web: Dynamics of Textile Multinationals*. London: Zed Press.

Clarke, L. and Wall. C. (1998). *A Blueprint for Change: Construction Skills Training in Britain.* Bristol, UK: Policy Press.

Clark, J. and Guy, K. (1998). 'Innovation and Competitiveness: A Review', *Technology Analysis and Strategic Management*, 10(3): 363–95.

Coates, D. (2000). *Models of Capitalism: Growth and Stagnation in the Modern Era.* Cambridge, MA: Polity Press.

Cohen, W. M. and Levinthal, D. (1989). 'Innovation and Learning: The Two Faces of R&D', *Economic Journal*, 99(397): 569–96.

Committee of Inquiry into the Engineering Profession (1980). *Engineering Our Future*. London: Her Majesty's Stationery Office.

Coombe, R. (1998). *The Cultural Life of Intellectual Properties: Authorship, Appropriation and the Law*. Durham, NC: Duke University Press.

Coombs, R. (1999). *Innovation in Services: Overcoming the Services-Manufacturing Divide*. Apeldoorn, The Netherlands: Nijmegen Business School, Maklu-Uitgevers.

—— and Richards, A. (1993). 'Strategic Management of Technology in Diversified Companies with De-Centralized R&D', *Technology Analysis and Strategic Management*, 5(4).

—— Saviotti, P., and Walsh, V. (1987). *Economics and Technological Change*. Basingstoke, UK: Macmillan.

—— Harvey, M., and Tether, B. S. (2003). 'Analysing distributed processes of provision and innovation', *Industrial and Corporate Change*, 12(6): 1125–55.

Cornbilt, O. (1967). 'Inmigrantes y empresarios en la politica Argentina', *Desarrollo Economico*, 6(24): 641–91.

Corvers, F. Dankbaar, B., and Hassink, B. (1995). 'Technology Cooperation Across the Border? The Case of a Dutch–Belgium–German Border Region', in L. A. Lefebvre and E. Lefebvre (eds.), *Management of Technology and Regional Planning in a Global Environment*. London: Paul Chapman.

Cowling, K. and Sugden, R. (1987). *Transnational Monopoly Capitalism*. Brighton, UK: Wheatsheaf Books.

David, P. (1985). 'Clio and the Economics of QWERTY', *American Economic Review*, AEA Papers and Proceedings, 75(2): 332–37.

—— (2001). *From Keeping 'Nature's Secrets' to the Institutionalization of 'Open Space'*, University of Siena Lectures on Science as an Institution and the Institutions of Science.

Davies, A. and Brady, T. (2000). 'Organisational Capabilities and Learning in Complex Product Systems: Towards Repeatable Solutions', *Research Policy*, 29(7–8): 931–53.

De Aenelle, C. (1998). 'Mergers Give Industry Boost in Developing New Products', *International Herald Tribune*, November 18: 20.

De Long, J. B. (1991). 'Did J. P. Morgan's Men Add Value? An Economist's Perspective on Financial Capitalism', in P. Temin (ed.), *Inside the Business Enterprise*. Chicago, IL: University of Chicago.

De Solla Price, D. J. (1986). *Little Science, Big Science ... and Beyond*. New York: Columbia University Press (1st edn., 1963).

Delorme (1962). *Anthologie des Brevets sur les Matièrs Plastiques*, 1(3). Paris: Amphora.

Dertouzos, M., Lester, R., and Solow, R. (1989). *Made in America*. Cambridge, MA: MIT Press.

Dicken, P. (1992). *Global Shift: The Internationalization of Economic Activity*. London: Paul Chapman.

Do, T. T., Faulkner, S., and Kolp, M. (2003). Organizational Multi-Agent Architecture for Information Systems. Proceedings of the 5th International Conference on Enterprise Information Systems (ICEIS 2002), Angers, France, April.

Dodgson, M. and Rothwell, R. (1988). 'Small Firm Policy in the UK', *Technovation*, 7(3): 231–47.

—— —— (1994). *The Handbook of Innovation*. Aldershot, UK: Edward Elgar.

Dosi, G. (1982). 'Technological Paradigms and Technological Trajectories: A Suggested Interpretation of the Determinants and Directions of Technical Change', *Research Policy*, 11(3): 147–62.

—— and Soete, L. (1988). 'Technical Change and International Trade', in G. Dosi, K. Pavitt, and L. Soete (eds.), *The Economics of Technical Change and International Trade*. Brighton: Harvester Wheatsheaf.

—— Freeman, C., Nelson, R., Silverberg, G., and Soete, L. (eds.) (1988). *Technical Change and Economic Theory*. London: Pinter.

Dunning, J. H. (1977). 'Trade, Location of Economic Activity and MNE: A Search for an Eclectic Approach', in B. Ohlin, P. O. Hesselborn, and P. M. Wijkman (eds.), *The International Allocation of Economic Activity*. London: Macmillan.

—— (1980). 'Explaining Changing Patterns of International Production: In Defense of the Eclectic Theory', *Oxford Bulletin of Economics and Statistics*, 41(4): 269–95.

—— (1988). *Explaining International Production*. London: Unwin Hyman.

—— (1993). 'Global Strategy and the Theory of International Production', in J. Dunning (ed.), *The Globalization of Business*. London: Routledge, pp. 78–101.

—— (1997). *Alliance Capitalism and Global Business*. London: Routledge.

—— and Wymbs, C. (1999). 'The Geographical Sourcing of Technology-Based Assets by Multinational Enterprises', in D. Archibugi, J. Howells, and J. Michie (eds.), *Innovation Policy in a Global Economy*. Cambridge, UK: Cambridge University Press.

EC (1998). *Communication from the Commission to the Council: The Contribution of Business Services to Industrial Performance—A Common Policy Framework*. Brussels: EC.

—— (2003). *Communication from the Commission to the Council, the European Parliament, the European Economic and Social Committee and the Committee of the Regions: The Competitiveness of Business-Related Services and Their Contribution to the Performance of European Enterprises, COM (3002) 747*. Brussels: EC.

Eccles, R. (1981). 'The Quasi-Firm in the Construction Industry', *Journal of Economic Behaviour and Organisation*, 2(4): 335–57.

Edquist, C. (1997). *Systems of Innovation: Technologies, Institutions and Organizations*. Washington, DC: Pinter.

EFPIA (2001). *G10 Medicines: High Level Group on Innovation and Provision of Medicines, Consultation Paper*. Brussels: European Federation of Pharmaceutical Industry Associations, November.

—— (2003). *The Pharmaceutical Industry in Figures*. Brussels: European Federation of Pharmaceutical Industries and Associations.

Eisenberg, R. (1996). 'Public Research and Private Development: Patents and Technology Transfer in Government Sponsored Research', *Virginia Law Review*, 82(8): 1663–1727.

Elbaum, B. and Lazonick, W. (1986). *The Decline of the British Economy*. Oxford: Clarendon Press.

Epstein, S. (1995). 'The Construction of Lay Expertise: AIDS Activism and the Forging of Credibility in the Reform of Clinical Trials', *Science, Technology and Human Values*, 20(4): 408–437.

—— (1996). *Impure Science: AIDS, Activism and the Politics of Knowledge*. Berkeley, CA: University of California Press.

Epstein, S. (1997). 'Activism, Drug Regulation, and the Politics of Therapeutic Evaluation in the AIDS Era: A Case Study of the ddC and the "Surrogate Markers" Debate', *Social Studies of Science*, 27(5): 691–726.

Ergas, H. (1987). 'Does Technology Policy Matter?' in B. R. Guile and H. Brooks (eds.), *Technology and Global Industry: Companies and Industries in the Global Economy*. Washington, DC: National Academy Press.

Ernst, D. (2002). 'Global Production Networks and the Changing Geography of Innovation Systems: Implications for Developing Countries', *Journal of the Economics of Innovation and New Technologies*, 11(6): 497–523.

—— (2004a). *Searching for a New Role in East Asian Regionalization: Japanese Production Networks in the Electronics Industry*, Hawaii, HI: East-West Center Working Papers Economics Series No. 68.

—— (2004b). *Internationalization of Innovation: Why Is Chip Design Moving to Asia?* Hawaii, HI: East-West Center Working Papers Economics Series No. 64.

—— and Kim, L. (2002). 'Global Production Networks, Knowledge Diffusion and Local Capability Formation', *Research Policy*, 31(8–9): 1417–29.

Etzkowitz, H. and Brisolla, S. (1999). 'Failure and Success: The Fate of Industrial Policy in Latin America and South East Asia', *Research Policy*, 28(4): 337–50.

Fagerberg, J. (1985). *Technology Growth and International Competitiveness*. Oslo: Norwegian Institute of International Affairs (NUPI).

—— (1987). 'A Technology Gap Approach to Why Growth Rates Differ', *Research Policy*, 16(2–4): 87–99.

—— (1988). *Technical Change and Economic Theory*. London: Frances Pinter.

Faulkner, W. and Senker, J. (1995). *Knowledge Frontiers: Public Sector Research and Industrial Innovation in Biotechnology, Engineering Ceramics and Parallel Computing*. Oxford: Clarendon Press.

Finger, J. M. (1991). 'Development Economics and the General Agreement on Tariffs and Trade', in J. de Melo and A. Sapir (eds.), *Trade Theory and Economic Reform: North, South and East*. Cambridge, MA: Basil Blackwell.

Florida, R. and Kenney, M. (1988). 'Venture Capital, Financial Innovation and Technological Change in the USA', *Research Policy*, 17(3): 119–37.

FOE (2004). Friends of the Earth website, http://www.foeeurope.org/GMOs/moratorium.htm, accessed 17th July.

Foray, D. (1995). 'The Economics of Intellectual Property Rights and Systems of Innovation: The Persistence of National Practices versus the New Global Model of Innovation', in J. Hagedoorn (ed.), *Technical Change and the World Economy: Convergence and Divergence in Technology Strategies*. Cheltenham, UK: Edward Elgar.

Fransman, M. (1990). *The Market and Beyond: Cooperation and Competition in Information Technology in the Japanese System*. Cambridge: Cambridge University Press.

—— and King, K. (1984). *Technological Capability in the Third World*. London: Macmillan Press.

Freeman, C. (1979). 'Technical Innovation and British Trade Performance', in F. Blackaby (ed.), *De-industrialisation*. London: Heinemann.

—— (1987). *Technology Policy and Economic Performance: Lessons from Japan*. London: Pinter.

—— (1988). 'Japan: A New National System of Innovation?' in G. Dosi, R. Nelson, G. Silverberg, and L. Soete (eds.), *Technical Change and Economic Theory*. London: Pinter.

—— (1989). 'The Third Kondratieff Wave: Age of Steel, Electrification and Imperialism', in Bohlin et al. (eds.), *Samhällsvetenskap ekonomi och histoia*. Göterborg: Daidalos. Shorter version published in Kihlstrom et al. (eds.), *Fetschrift in Honour of Lars Herlitz*. Gothenburg.

—— (1995). 'The National System of Innovation in Historical Perspective', *Cambridge Journal of Economics*, 19(1): 5–24.

—— and Louçã, F. (2001). *As Time Goes By: From the Industrial Revolutions to the Information Revolution*. Oxford: Oxford University Press.

—— and Perez, C. (1988). 'Structural Crises of Adjustment, Business Cycles and Investment Behaviour', in G. Dosi et al. (eds.), *Technical Change and Economic Theory*. London: Pinter.

—— and Soete, L. (1997). *The Economics of Technological Innovation*. London: Pinter.

Galimberti, I. (1993). 'Large Chemical Firms in Biotechnology: Case Studies in Learning in Radically New Technologies', DPhil. Thesis, University of Sussex.

Gambardella, A., Orsenigo, L., and Pamoli, F. (2000). *Benchmarking the Competitiveness of the European Pharmaceutical Industry*, Background report prepared for DG Enterprise of the European Commission. Brussels: European Commission.

Gann, D. (1994). 'Innovation in the Construction Sector', in M. Dodgson and R. Rothwell (eds.), *The Handbook of Innovation*. Aldershot, UK: Edward Elgar.

—— (1997). 'Should Governments Fund Construction Research?' *Building Research and Information*, 25(5): 257–67.

Gann, D. M. and Salter, A. J. (2000). 'Innovation in Project-Based, Service-Enhanced Firms: The Construction of Complex Products and Systems', *Research Policy*, 29(7–8): 955–72.

Garrido, C. (1994). 'National Private Groups in Mexico, 1987–1993', *CEPAL Review*, 53: 159–76.

Gascoigne, R. M. (1987). *A Chronology of the History of Science, 1450–1900*. New York: Garland.

Gaudillière, J-P. (2005). 'Le cartel des hormones', *Entreprise et Histoire*, 34.

—— (forthcoming). 'Cartel, Patents and Know How: The Appropriation of Biologicals in Interwar Germany', *History of Technology*.

Gereffi, G. (1994). 'The Organization of Buyer-Driven Global Commodity Chains: How US Retailers Shape Overseas Production Networks', in G. Gerreffi and M. Korzeniewicz (eds.), *Commodity Chains and Global Development*. Westport, CT: Praeger.

—— and Korzeniewicz, M. (eds.) (1994). *Commodity Chains and Global Capitalism*. Westport, CT: Praeger.

Gershenkron, A. ([1951] 1966). 'Economic Backwardness in Historical Perspective', in A. Gershenkron (ed.), *A Book of Essays*. Cambridge, MA: Belknap Press of Harvard University Press.

Gerybadze, A. and Reger, G. (1999). 'Globalization of R&D: Recent Changes in the Management of Innovation in Transnational Corporations', *Research Policy*, 28(2–3): 251–74.

Glyn, A. (2004). 'The Assessment: How far has Globalization Gone?' *Oxford Review of Economic Policy*, 20(1): 1–14.

GM Science Review Panel (2004). *GM Science Review First Report* (July 2003) and *Second Report* (January 2004); http://www.gmsciencedebate.org.uk, accessed 17th July.

Goodman, J. (2000). 'Pharmaceutical Industry', in J. Pickstone and R. Cooter (eds.), *Medicine in the Twentieth Century*. London: Harvard Academic Publishers, pp. 143–56.

—— and Walsh, V. (1998). 'Combining the Earth for Cancer Cures', Wellcome Conference on Botany and Medicine. London: Wellcome Foundation, 17 April.

Goodman, J. and Walsh, V. (2001). *The Story of Taxol: Nature and Politics in the Pursuit of an Anticancer Drug*. New York: Cambridge University Press.

Gorg, H. and Strobl, E. (2001). 'Multinational Companies and Productivity Spillovers: A Meta-Analysis', *The Economic Journal*, 111(475): 723–39.

Green, K. and Morphet, C. (1977). *Research and Technology as Economic Activities*. London: Butterworth.

—— Richards, A., and Walsh, V. (eds.) (1998). 'Introduction' (Special edition on styles of innovation), *Technology Analysis and Strategic Management*, 10(4): 403–7.

—— Hull, R., McMeekin, A., and Walsh, V. (1999). 'The Construction of the Techno-Economic: Networks vs. Paradigms', *Research Policy*, 28(7): 777–92.

Greenaway, D. (1997). 'Policy Forum: Competitiveness and Competitiveness Policy', Editorial Note, *Economic Journal*, 107(444): 1484–5.

Greenberg, S. (1998*a*). *Report to the British Working Group, Monsanto*, http://www.greeneace. org.uk/monsanto, accessed November.

—— (1998*b*). *Report to the German Working Group, Monsanto*, http://www.greenpeace.org.uk/ monsanto, accessed November.

Greenpeace (2000). 'Greenpeace Calls European States to Stop Patenting Life', *Press Release 19th November*, http://archive.greenpeace.org/pressreleases/geneng /2000nov19.html

Griliches, A. (1995). 'R&D and Productivity: Econometric Results and Measurement Issues', in P. Stoneman (ed.), *Handbook of the Economics of Innovation and Technological Change*. Oxford: Blackwell.

Grimshaw, D. and Miozzo, M. (2006). 'Institutional Effects on the Market for IT Outsourcing: Analyzing Clients, Suppliers and Staff Transfer in Germany and the UK', *Organization Studies*, forthcoming.

Groak, S. (1994). 'Is Construction an Industry? Notes Towards a Greater Analytic Emphasis on External Linkages', *Construction Management and Economics*, 12(4): 287–93.

Grossman, G. M. and Elhanan, H. (1991). 'Quality Ladders and Product Cycles', *The Quarterly Journal of Economics*, 106(2): 557–86.

Guellec, D. and van Pottelsberghe de la Potterie, B. (2001). 'The Internationalization of Technology Analysed with Patent Data', *Research Policy*, 30(8): 1253–66.

Hagedoorn, J. (2002). 'Inter-Firm R&D Partnerships: An Overview of Major Trends and Patterns Since 1960', *Research Policy*, 31(4): 477–92.

—— and Soete, L. (1991). 'The Internationalization of Science and Technology (Policy): How do 'National Systems Cope?' in H. Inose, M. Kawasaki, and F. Kodama (eds.), *Science and Technology Policy Research, 'What should be done?' What can be done?'* Tokyo: MIT Press, pp. 201–13.

Hannah, L. (1983). 'Entrepreneurs and the Social Sciences', Inaugural Lecture. London: School of Economics and Political Science.

Harvey, M. (2002). 'Markets, Supermarkets and the Macro-Social Shaping of Demand: An Instituted Economic Process Approach', in A. McMeekin, K. Green, M. Tomlinson, and V. Walsh (eds.), *Innovation by Demand: An Interdisciplinary Approach to the Study of Demand and Its Role in Innovation*. Manchester, UK: Manchester University Press, pp. 187–208.

Harvey, P. (1998). 'Exploitable Knowledge Belongs to the Creators of It: A Debate', *Social Anthropology*, 6(1): 109–26.

Hassink, R., Dankbaar, B., and Corvers, F. (1995). 'Technology Networking in Border Regions: Case-Study of the Euregion Maas-Rhine', *European Planning Studies*, 3(1): 63–8.

Hayden, C. (1998). 'A Biodiversity Sampler for the Millennium', in S. Franklin and H. Ragonè (eds.), *Reproducing Reproduction: Kinship, Power and Technological Innovation*. Philadelphia, PA: University of Pennsylvania Press.

Hayes, P. (1987). *Industry and Ideology: I. G. Farben in the Nazi Era*. Cambridge: Cambridge University Press.

Hayter, S. (2005). *The Social Dimension of Global Production Systems: A Review of the Issues*, Working Paper No. 25. Geneva: International Labour Organization.

Hegde, D. and Hicks, D. (2005). *Globalization of US Corporate R&D: More of the Same or Something New*, Working Paper No. 3. Atlanta, GA: Georgia Tech Research Corporation.

Heilbroner, R. (1953). *The Worldly Philosophers*. New York: Simon and Schuster.

Helpman, E. and Krugman, P. (1985). *Market Structure and Foreign Trade*. Cambridge, MA: MIT Press.

Henderson, J. (1998). *Uneven Crisis: Institutional Foundations of East Asian Economic Turmoil*, Working Paper. Manchester, UK: Manchester Business School, University of Manchester.

—— Dicken, P., Hess, M., Coe, N., and Wai-Chung Yeung, H. (2002*a*). *Global Production Networks and the Analysis of Economic Development*, Mimeo. Manchester, UK: Manchester Business School, University of Manchester.

—— —— —— —— —— (2002*b*). 'Global Production Networks and the Analysis of Economic Development', *Review of International Political Economy*, 9(3): 436–64.

Herrigel, G. (1993). 'Large Firms, Small Firms, and the Governance of Flexible Specialization: The Case of Baden-Wurttemburg and Socialized Risk', in B. Kogot (ed.), *Country Competitiveness: Technology and the Organization of Work*. New York: Oxford University Press.

Hicks, D. and Hegde, D. (2005). 'Highly Innovative Small Firms in the Markets for Technology', *Research Policy*, 34(5): 703–16.

Hill, C. (1958). *Puritanism and Revolution: Studies in Interpretation of the English Revolution of the 17th Century*. London: Secker and Warburg.

Hirschman, A. O. (1958). *The Strategy of Economic Development*. New Haven, CT: Yale University Press.

—— (1970). *Exit, Voice, and Loyalty: Responses to Decline in Firms Organizations, and States*. Cambridge, MA: Harvard University Press.

—— (1971). 'The Political Economy of Import-Substituting Industrialization in Latin America', in A. Hirschman (ed.), *A Bias for Hope: Essays on Development in Latin America*. New Haven, CT: Yale University Press, pp. 85–123.

Hirst, P. and Thompson, G. (1999). *Globalization in Question: The International Economy and the Possibilities of Governance*, 2nd edn. Cambridge, MA: Polity Press.

Hobday, M. (1994). 'Export-led Technology Development in the Four Dragons: The Case of Electronics', *Development and Change*, 25: 333–61.

—— (1995). 'The Asian Latecomer Firms: Learning the Technology of Electronics', *World Development*, 23(7): 1171–93.

—— (2000). 'The Project-Based Organization: An Ideal Form for Managing Complex Products and Systems', *Research Policy*, 29(7–8): 895–911.

Hobsbawm, E. (1968). *Industry and Empire: An Economic History of Britain since 1750*. London: Weidenfeld & Nicolson.

Hounshell, D. A. (1984). *From the American System to Mass Production 1800–1932: The Development of Manufacturing Technology in the United States.* Baltimore, MD and London: John Hopkins University Press.

Howells, J. (1995). 'Going Global: The Use of ICT Networks in Research and Development', *Research Policy*, 24(2): 169–84.

—— (1997). 'The Globalization of Research and Technological Innovation: A new Agenda?' in J. Howells and J. Michie (eds.), *Technology, Innovation and Competitiveness.* Cheltenham, UK: Edward Elgar.

—— (2002). 'Mind the Gap: Information and Communication Technologies, Knowledge Activities and Innovation in the Pharmaceutical Industry', *Technology Analysis and Strategic Management*, 14(3): 335–70.

—— and Wood, M. (1993). *The Globalization of Production and Technology.* London: Belhaven Press.

Huang, H. T. and Miozzo, M. (2004). 'Patterns of Technological Specialization in East Asia and Latin American countries: An Analysis of Patents and Trade Flows', *Economics of Innovation and New Technology*, 13(8): 615–53.

Hymer, S. (1976). *The International Operations of National Firms.* Cambridge, MA: MIT Press.

Ietto-Gillies, G. (1992). *International Production: Trends, Theories and Effects.* Cambridge, MA: Polity Press.

Institute for Management Development (2002). *World Competitiveness Yearbook 2002.* Lausaane: Institute for Management Development.

Johnson, C. (1982). *MITI and the Japanese Miracle: The Growth of Industrial Policy, 1925–1975.* Stanford, CA: Stanford University Press.

Kagliwal, M. (2004). *Movement of Small and Medium Sized Indian IT Suppliers up the Value Chain in an Outsourcing Relationship*, M.Sc. Dissertation. Manchester, UK: University of Manchester Institute of Science and Technology.

Kaitin, K. I. (2000). *Impact of the Prescription Drug User Fee Act of 1992 on the Speed of New Drug Development.* Washington, DC: FDP Public Hearing on the Prescription Drug User Fee Act.

Kaldor, M. (1980). 'Technical Change in the Defence Industry', in K. Pavitt (ed.), *Technological Innovation and British Economic Performance.* Basingstoke: Macmillan.

—— (1982). *The Baroque Arsenal.* London and Deutsch, Germany: Abacus.

—— (2001). *Beyond Militarism: Arms Races and Arms Control*, Nobel Peace Prize Centennial Symposium, December 6–8 Social Science Research Council *After September 11.*

Kaldor, N. (1978). 'The Effect of Devaluations on Trade in Manufacturers', in N. Kalsor (ed.), *Further Essays on Applied Economics.* London: Duckworth.

—— (1981). 'The Role of Increasing Returns, Technical Progress and Cumulative Causation in the Theory of International Trade and Economic Growth', *Economie Appliquee*, 43(4): 593–617.

Katz, J. (1984). 'Technological Innovation, Industrial Organization and Comparative Advantages of Latin American Metalworking Industries', in M. Fransman and K. King (eds), *Technological Capability in the Third World.* London: Macmillan Press.

Kay, C. (1989). *Latin American Theories of Development and Underdevelopment.* London: Routledge.

Keefe, J. H. and Batt, R. (1977). 'United States', in H. Katz (ed.), *Telecommunications, Restructuring Work and Employment Relations Worldwide.* Cornell, NY: ILR Press.

Kim, L. (1993). 'National System of Industrial Innovation: Dynamics of Capability Building in Korea', in R. Nelson (ed.), *National Systems of Innovation.* Oxford: Oxford University Press.

Kindleberger, C. P. (1969). *American Business Abroad.* New Haven, CT: Yale University Press.

Kline, S. J. and Rosenberg, N. (1986). 'An Overview of Innovation, in National Academy of Engineering', *The Positive Sum Strategy: Harnessing Technology for Economic Growth.* Washington, DC: National Academy Press.

Kloppenberg, J. (1988). *First the Seed: The Political Economy of Plant Biotechnology.* Cambridge, UK: Cambridge University Press.

Koekkoek, K. A. (1988). 'Trade in Services, the Developing Countries and the Uruguay Round', *The World Economy,* 11(1): 151–5.

Kocka, J. (1994). 'Capitalism and Beaurocracy in German Industrialization before 1914', in P. K. O'Brien (ed.), The Industrial Revolution in Europe. Oxford: Blackwell.

Kondratieff, N. ([1925] 1935). 'The Major Economic Cycles', *Voprosy Konjunktury,* 1(1): 28–79, in (partial translation into English) *Review of Economic Statistics,* 18: 105–15.

Krugman, P. R. (1979). 'A Model of Innovation, Technology Transfer, and the World Distribution of Income', *Journal of Political Economy,* 87(21): 253–66.

—— (1994a). *The Age of Diminished Expectations.* London: MIT Press.

—— (1994b). 'Competitiveness: A Dangerous Obsession', *Foreign Affairs,* 73(2): 28–44.

—— (1995). 'Technical Change in International Trade', in P. Stoneman (ed.), *Handbook of the Economic of Innovation and Technological Change.* Oxford: Blackwell, Chapter 9, pp. 342–65.

—— (1996). 'Making Sense of the Competitiveness Debate', *Oxford Review of Economic Policy,* 12(3): 17–25.

Kuemmerle, W. (1999). 'Foreign Direct Investment in Industrial Research in the Pharmaceutical and Electronics Industries: Results from a Survey of Multinational Firms', *Research Policy,* 28(2–3): 179–93.

Kuhn, T. (1962). *The Structure of Scientific Revolutions.* Chicago, IL: Chicago University Press.

Kutznets, S. (1953). *Economic Change.* New York: Norton.

Laborde, M. and Sanvido, V. (1994). 'Introducing Process Technologies into Construction Companies', *Journal of Construction Engineering and Management,* 120(3): 488–509.

Lall, S. (2000). 'The Technological Structure and Performance of Developing Country Manufactured Exports, 1985–98', *Oxford Development Studies,* 28(3): 338–63.

—— (2001). 'Competitiveness Indices and Developing Countries: An Economic Evaluation of the Global Competitiveness Report', *World Development,* 29(9): 1051–1525.

—— and Teubal, M. (1998). 'Market-Stimulating' Technology Policies in Developing Countries: A Framework with Examples from East Asia', *World Development,* 26(8): 1369–85.

Landes, D. (1969). *The Unbound Prometheus.* Cambridge, UK: Cambridge University Press.

Lang, T. (2003a). 'Battle of the Food Chain', *The Guardian,* 17 May.

—— (2003b). 'Food Industrialization and Food Power', *Development Policy Review,* 21(5): 30–9.

Langlois, R. N. (2002). 'Computers and semiconductors', in B. Steil, D. Victor, and R. Belson (eds.), *Technological Innovation and Economic Performance.* New Jersey: Princeton.

—— (2003). 'The Vanishing Hand: The Changing Dynamics of Industrial Capitalism', *Industrial and Corporate Change,* 12(2): 351–85.

—— and Mowery, D.C. (1986). 'The Federal Government Role in the Development of the American Software Industry: An Assessment', in D.C. Mowery (ed.), *The International Computer Software Industry*. New York: Oxford University Press.

Larédo, P. and Mustar, P. (1996). 'The Techno-Economic Network: A Socio-Economic Approach to State Intervention in Innovation', in R. Coombs, A. Richards, P. Saviotti and V. Walsh (eds.), *Technological Collaboration: The Dynamics of Cooperation in Innovation*. Aldershot: Edward Elgar.

—— and Mustar, P. (2001). *Research and Innovation Policies in the New Global Economy*. Cheltenham, UK: Edward Elgar.

Latour, B. (1993). *We Have Never Been Modern*. Cambridge, MA: Harvard University Press.

Law, J. (1992). 'Notes on the Theory of the Actor-Network: Ordering, Strategy and Heterogeneity', *Systems Practice*, 5: 379–93.

—— and Hassard, J. (1999). *Actor-Network Theory and After*. Oxford: Blackwell.

Lazar, F. (1990). 'Services and the GATT: US Motives and a Blueprint for Negotiations, *Journal of World Trade*, 24(1): 135–45.

Lazerson, M. (1990). 'Suncontracting in the Modena Knitwear Industry', in F. Pyke, G. Becattini, and W. Sengenberger (eds.), *Industrial Districts and Inter-Firm Co-Operation in Italy*. Geneva: International Labour Organization.

Lazonick, W. (1991). *Business Organization and the Myth of the Market Economy*. Cambridge, UK: Cambridge University Press.

—— (1993). 'Industry Clusters Versus Global Webs: Organizational Capabilities in the American Economy', *Industrial and Corporate Change*, 2(1): 1–24.

—— (1999). 'The Japanese and Corporate Reform: What Path to Sustainable Prosperity?' *Industrial and Corporate Change*, 8(4): 607–33.

—— and O'Sullivan, M. (1996). 'Organization, Finance and International Competition', *Industrial and Corporate Chang*, 5(1): 1–49.

Le Monde (1999). La France Mondialisee, 16th March.

Lehrer, M. (2005). 'Science-Driven vs. Market-Pioneering High Tech: Comparative German Technology Sectors in the Late Nineteenth and Twentieth Centuries', *Industrial and Corporate Change*, 14(2): 251–78.

Leontieff, W. (1953). 'Domestic Production and Foreign Trade: The American Position Reexamined', *Proceedings of the American Philosophical Society*, 97.

Levitt, T. (1976). 'The Industrialization of Services', *Harvard Business Review*, 54(4): 63–74.

Lexchin, J. and Mintzes, B. (2004). 'Comments to the Food and Drug Administration on Direct-to-Consumer Advertising of Prescription Drugs' (www.fda.gov/ohrms/dockets/dailys/02/Sep02/091302/02N-0209_emc-000108-01.DOC 2002); accessed 1st June 2004.

Lilley, S. (1949). *Archives Internationales d'Historie des Sciences*, 28: 376–443.

List, F. (1841). *The National System of Political Economy*. London: Longman (English edition 1904).

Lopez, A. and Miozzo, M. (2004). 'Multinationals and Technology Development in East Asia and Latin America', in S. Prasad and P. Ghauri (eds.), *Multinationals in Emerging Nations in the Age of Anxiety*. Connecticut: Praeger.

Lundvall, B.-A. (1985). *Product Innovation and User-Producer Interaction*. Aalborg, Denmark: Aalborg University Press.

—— (1988). 'Innovation as an Interactive Process: From User-Producer Interaction to the National Systems of Innovation', in G. Dosi, C. Freeman, R. Nelson, G. Silverberg, and L. Soete (eds.), *Technical Change and Economic Theory*. London: Pinter.

—— (ed.) (1992). *National Systems of Innovation*. London: Pinter.

Maclean, M. (1999). 'Towards a European Model? A Comparative Evaluation of Recent Corporate Governance Initiatives in France and the UK', *Journal of European Area Studies*, 7(2): 227–45.

Maitland, A. (1996). 'Against the Grain: Controversy around GM Crops May Have Caught Biotech Companies by Surprise', *The Financial Times*, 15 October.

Malecki, E. (1997). *Technology and Economic Development: The Dynamics of Local Regional and National Competitiveness*. Harlow, UK: Longman.

Malerba, F. (2002). 'Sectoral Systems of Innovation and Production', *Research Policy*, 31(2): 247–64.

—— and Orsenigo, L. (1996). 'Schumperian Patterns of Innovation Are Technology Specific', *Research Policy*, 25(3): 451–78.

Marker, R. E., Tsukamoto, T. and Turner, D. (1940). 'Sterols. XCIX. Sterols from Various Sources', *Journal of the American Chemical Society*, 62: 2525–32.

Marks, L. (2001). *Sexual Chemistry*. New Haven: Yale University Press.

Marsh, P. (2003). 'China Ranks Third in R&D Spending', *The Financial Times*, 27 October.

Marx, K. [1867] 1956. *Capital: A Critique of Political Economy*, First published in German. New York: International Publishers.

—— and Engels, F. (1848). *Manifesto of the Communist Party*.

Mason, E. (1957). *Economic Concentration and Monopoly Problem*. Cambridge, MA: Harvard University Press.

Mattoo, A. (2000). 'Developing Countries in the New Round of GATTS Negotiations: Towards a Pro-Active Role', *The World Economy*, 23(4): 471–89.

Mazzoleni, R. and Nelson, R. (1998). 'The Benefits and Costs of Strong Patent Protection: A Contribution to the Current Debate', *Research Policy*, 27(3): 273–84.

McKenna, C. D., Djelic, M.-L., and Ainamo, A. (2002). 'Message and Medium: The Role of Consulting Firms in the Process of Globalization and Its Local Interpretation', in M.-L. Djelic and S. Quack (eds.), *Globalization and Institutions: Redefining the Rules of the Game*. Cheltenham, UK: Edward Elgar.

McMeekin, A. and Harvey, M. (2002). 'The Formation of Bioinformatics Knowledge Markets: An 'Economies of Knowledge' Approach', *Revue D'Economie Industrielle*, 101(4): 47–64.

Méadel, C. and Rabeharisoa, V. (2001). 'Taste as a Form of Adjustment between Food and Consumers', in R. Coombs, K. Green, A. Richards, and V. Walsh (eds.), *Technology and the Market Demand, Users and Innovation*. Cheltenham, UK: Edward Elgar.

Merges, R. and Nelson, R. (1994). 'On Limiting or Encouraging Rivalry in Technical Process: The Effect of Patent Scope Decisions', *Journal of Economic Behaviour and Organization*, 25(1): 1–24

Meyer-Stamer, J. (1997). 'New Patterns of Governance for Industrial Change: Perspectives for Brazil', *The Journal of Development Studies*, 33(3): 364–91.

Miles, I. (1994). 'Innovation in Services', in M. Dodgson and R. Rothwell (eds.), *The Handbook of Innovation*. Aldershot, UK: Edward Elgar.

Miles, I. (1995). *Services Innovation: Statistical and Conceptual Issues*, Report to OECD NESTI Working Group on Innovation Surveys. Manchester, UK: PREST, University of Manchester.

—— (2001). *Knowledge-Intensive Business Services and the New Economy*, presented at the seminar at the (Jena: Evolutionary Economics Unit, Max-Planck Institute for Research into Economic Systems).

—— (2003). *Business Services and Their Contribution to Their Client's Performance: A Review*, ECORYS/CRIC Project, University of Manchester, mimeo.

Mintz, S. W. (1986). *Sweetness and Power: The Place of Sugar in Modern History*. London: Penguin.

—— (1996). *Tasting Food, Tasting Freedom: Excursions into Eating, Culture and the Past*. Boston, MA: Beacon Press.

Miozzo, M. (2000). 'Transnational Corporations, Industrial Policy and the 'War of Incentives': The Case of the Argentine Automobile Industry', *Development and Change*, 31(3): 651–80.

—— (2002). 'Sectoral Specialization in East Asia and Latin America Compared', *Brazilian Journal of Political Economy*, 22(4): 48–68.

—— and Dewick, P. (2002). 'Building Competitive Advantage: Innovation and Corporate Governance in European Construction', *Research Policy*, 31(6): 989–1008.

—— —— (2004). *Innovation in European Construction: A European Analysis*. Cheltenham, UK: Edward Elgar.

—— and Grimshaw, D. (2005). 'Modularity and Innovation in Knowledge-Intensive Business Services: IT Outsourcing in Germany and the UK', *Research Policy*, 34(9): 1419–39.

—— —— (eds.) (2006a). *Knowledge Intensive Business Services: Organizational Forms and National Institutions*. Cheltenham, UK: Edward Elgar.

—— —— (2006b). 'Capabilities of Computer Services Firms', Paper prepared for the 2006 Academy of Management Conference, Atlanta, 11–16 June.

—— and Ivory, C. (2000). 'Restructuring in the British Construction industry: Implications of Recent Changes in Project Management and Technology', *Technology Analysis and Strategic Management*, 12(4): 513–31.

—— and Miles, I. (eds.) (2002). *Internationalization, Technology and Services*. Cheltenham, UK: Edward Elgar.

—— and Ramirez, M. (2003). 'Services Innovation and the Transformation of Work: The Case of UK Telecommunications', *New Technology Work and Employment*, 18(11): 63–80.

—— and Soete, L. (2001). 'Internationalization of Services: A Technological Perspective', *Technological Forecasting and Social Change*, 67(2): 159–85.

Mirowski, P. (1981). 'Is There a Mathematical Neo-Institutional Economics?' *Journal of Economic Issues*, 15(3): 593–613.

Molnár, V. and Lamont, M. (2002). 'Social Categorisation and Group Identification: How African-Americans Shape the Collective Identity through Consumption', in A. McMeekin, K. Green, M. Tomlinson, and V. Walsh (eds.), *Innovation by Demand*. Manchester: Manchester University Press.

Monsanto (2000). 'Scientists Achieve Major Breakthrough in Rice; Data to be Shared with Worldwide Research Community', http://www.monsanto.com/monsanto/layout/media/00/04-04-00.asp; http://monsanto.com/monsanto/layout/careers/timeline/timeline6.asp, last accessed 10th October 2002.

Morris, D. (1984). *Co-Operative Agreements in International Business: Opportunities and Obstacles*. Fontainebleau: Unpublished final report of INSEAD Conference.

Morse, L. (1996). 'From Petri Dish to Supper Plate', *The Financial Times*, 15 October.

Mortimore, M. (1993). 'Flying Geese or Sitting Ducks? Transnationals and Industry in Developing Countries', *CEPAL Review*, 51: 15–34.

Mowery, D. (1983). 'The Relationship between Intrafirm and Contractual Forms of Industrial Research in American Manufacturing 1900–1940', *Explorations in Economic History*, 20(4): 351–74.

—— (1986). 'Industrial Research, 1900–1950', in B. Elbaum and W. Lazonick (eds.), *The Decline of the British Economy*. Oxford: Clarendon Press.

—— (1996). *The International Computer Software Industry*. Oxford: Oxford University Press.

—— (2001). 'The US National Innovation System after the Cold War', in P. Larédo and P. Mustar (eds.), *Research and Innovation Policies in the New Global Economy*. Cheltenam: Edward Elgar.

—— and Nelson, R. (1996). 'The US Corporation and Technical Progress', in C. Kaysen (ed.), *The American Corporation Today*. New York and Oxford: Oxford University Press.

—— and Nelson, R. R. (1999). *Sources of Industrial Leadership: Studies of Seven Industries*. Cambridge, UK: Cambridge University Press.

—— and Rosenberg, N. (1989). *Technology and the pursuit of Economic Growth*. New York: Cambridge University Press.

—— —— (1993). 'The US National Innovation System', in R. Nelson (ed.), *National Innovation Systems*. New York: Oxford University Press.

—— Nelson, R. Sampat, B. and Ziedonis, A. (2001). 'The Effects of the Bayh-Dole Act on US Research and Technology Transfer: An Analysis of Data from Columbia University, the University of California, and Stanford University', *Research Policy*, 30, 99–119.

Mukherjee, N. (1999). 'GATS and the Millennium Round of Multilateral Negotiations—Selected Issues from the Perspective of the Developing Countries', *Journal of World Trade*, 33(4): 87–102.

Mulder, U. (1991). 'Le Fianacement de la R-D au croisement des logiques industrielles, fiancière et politique', in *EC Monitor-FAST Programme, Globalization of the Economy and Technology*. Brussels: European Commission, 5.

Murray, F. (1987). 'Flexible Specialization in the 'Third Italy', *Capital and Class*, 33: 84–95.

Mustar, P. (1991). 'Processes of Integrating Science with the Market: The Creation of Technology-Based Businesses', International Colloquium of Management of Technology, Paris, 27–8 May.

—— (1993). 'La creation d'entreprise par les chercheurs, Thèse pour le doctorat de socio-économie de l'Ecole Nationale des Mines de Paris, June: La politique de l'innovation en France: le colbertisme entamé', in F. Sachwald (ed.), *Les Défis de la Mondialisation: Innovation et Concurrence*. Paris: Masson-IFRI.

Mytelka, L. K. (1995). 'Dancing with Wolves: Global Oligopolies and Strategic Partnerships', in J. Hagedoorn (ed.), *Technical Change and the World Economy: Convergence and Divergence in Technology Strategies*. Cheltenam: Edward Elgar.

—— (1999). *Competition, Innovation and Competitiveness in Developing Countries*. Paris: OECD.

Mytelka, L. K. (2002). 'Mergers, Acquisitions and Inter-Firm Technology Agreements in the Global Learning Economy', in D. Archibugi and B.-A. Lundvall (eds.), *The Globalizing Learning Economy*. Oxford: Oxford University Press.

Nelson, D. (1980). *Frederick W Taylor and the Rise of Scientific Management*. Madison, WI: University of Wisconsin Press.

Nelson, R. (1990). 'US Technological Leadership—Where Did It Come from and Where Did It Go?' *Research Policy*, 19(2): 117–32.

Nelson, R. R. (ed.) (1993). *National Innovation Systems*. New York: Oxford University Press.

—— (1998). 'Institutions Supporting Technical Change in the United States', in G. Dosi, R. Nelson, G. Silverberg, and L. Soete (eds.), *Technological Change and Economic Theory*. London: Pinter.

—— (2003). 'On the Complexities and Limits of Market Organization', in S. Metcalfe and A. Warde (eds.), *Market Relations and the Competitive Process*. Manchester, UK: Manchester University Press.

—— and Winter, S. G. (1977). 'In Search of a Useful Theory of Innovation', *Research Policy*, 6(1): 36–76.

—— —— (1982). *An Evolutionary Theory of Economic Change*. Cambridge, MA: Harvard University Press.

—— and Wright, G. (1992). 'The Rise and Fall of American Technological Leadership: The Postwar Era in Historical Perspective', *Journal of Economic Literature*, 30(4): 1931–64.

New Scientist (2004). 'Full Text: Margaret Beckett's GM speech', 9th March.

Niosi, J. and Zhegu, M. (2005). 'Aerospace Clusters: Local or Global Knowledge Spillovers', *Industry and Innovation*, 12(1): 5–29.

Noble, D. F. (1977). *American by Design*. Oxford: Oxford University Press.

Nottingham, S. (1998). *Eat Your Genes: How Genetically Modified Food Is Entering Our Diet*. London: Zed Books.

Nuffield Council on Bioethics (1999). *Genetically Modified Crops: The Ethical and Social Issues*. London: Nuffield Council on Bioethics.

Odagiri, H. and Goto, A. (1993). 'The Japanese System of Innovation: Past, Present and Future', in R. Nelson (ed.), *National Innovation Systems*. New York: Oxford University Press.

OECD (1992). *Technology and the Economy: The Key Relationships*. Paris: OECD.

—— (1993). *Science, Technology and Industry Indicators Unit*. Paris: OECD.

OECD (2002). *The Measurement of Scientific and Technological Activities: Proposed Standard Practice for Surveys of Research and Experimental Development—Frascati Manual*. Paris: OECD.

—— (2003a). *Main Science and Technology Indicators*. Paris: OECD.

—— (2003b). *Education at a Glance*. Paris: Organisation for Economic Cooperation and Development.

OECD Observer (1998). *Government as Venture Capitalist* (No. 123, August/September).

—— (1999). *Where Risk Capital Ventures* (17 December).

O'Shea, M. and Stevens, C. (1998). 'Governments as Venture Capitalists', *OECD Observer*, 213 (August/September).

O'Sullivan, M. (1998). 'Sustainable Prosperity, Corporate Governance and Innovation in Europe', in J. Michie and J. Grieve-Smith (eds.), *Globalization, Growth and Governance: Creating an Innovative Economy.* Oxford: Oxford University Press.

OTA (1981). *Patent Term Extension and the Pharmaceutical Industry US Government Printing Office Development.* Washington, DC; US Government Printing Office.

Palloix, C. (1973). *Les Firmes Internationalies et le process d'internationalization.* Paris: Francois Maspero.

Pálsson, G. and Harðardòttir, K. E. (2001). *For Whom the Cell Tools: Debates About Biomedicine*, Paper presented at Conference, Innovation, Creation and New Economic Forms: Approaches to Intellectual and Cultural Property. Cambridge: University of Cambridge.

Parker, G. (ed.) (1993). *The Times of Atlas of World History*, 4th edn. Hammond World Atlas Corporation.

Patel, P. (1995). 'Localized Production of Technology for Global Markets', *Cambridge Journal of Economics*, 19(1): 141–53

—— and Pavitt, K. (1991). 'Large Firms in the Production of the World's Technology: An Important Case of Non-Globalization', *Journal of International Business Studies*, 22(1): 1–21.

—— —— (1992). 'Large Firms in the Production of the World's Technology: An Important Case of Non-Globalization', in O. Granstrad, L. Håkanson, and S. Sjölander (eds.), *International R&D and Technology.* Chichester, UK: John Wiley & Sons.

—— —— (1993). *National Systems of Innovation: Why They Are Important and How They Might be Defined, Compared and Assessed* (Document de travail no. 93/05 du seminaire d'analyse économique). France: LATAPSES Unité de Recherche du CNRS, Université de Nice, Sophia Antipolis.

—— and Vega, M. (1997). *Patterns of Internationalization of Corporate Technology: Location Versus Home Country Advantages*, Working Paper (www.sussex.ac.uk/spru). Sussex, UK: University of Sussex, SPRU Electronic.

—— —— (1999). 'Patterns of Internationalization of Corporate Technology: Location versus Home Country Advantages', *Research Policy*, 28(2–3): 145–55.

Pavitt, K. (1980). *Technical Innovation and British Economic Performance.* London: Macmillan.

—— (1984). 'Sectoral Patterns of Technical Change: Towards a Taxonomy and a Theory', *Research Policy*, 13(6): 343–73.

—— (1991). 'Key Characteristics of Large Innovating Firms', *British Journal of Management*, 2(1): 41–50.

—— (1999). *Technology, Management and Systems of Innovation.* Cheltenham, UK: Edward Elgar.

—— (2003*a*). 'Are Systems Designers and Integrators 'Post-Industrial' Firms?' in A. Prencipe, A. Davies, and M. Hobday (eds.), *Systems Integration and Firm Capabilities.* Oxford: Oxford University Press.

—— (2003*b*). 'What Are Advances in Knowledge Doing to the Large Industrial Firm in the 'New Economy?' in J. F. Christensen and P. Maskell (eds.), *The Industrial Dynamics of the New Digital Economy.* Cheltenham, UK: Edward Elgar.

—— and Patel, P. (1997). 'Global Corporations and National Systems of Innovation: Who Dominates Whom?' in D. Archibugi and J. Michie (eds.), *Technology, Globalization and Economic Performance.* Cambridge, UK: Cambridge University Press.

Pavitt, K. and Patel, P. (1999). 'Global Corporations and National Systems of Innovation: Who Dominated Whom?' in D. Archibugi, J. Howells, and J. Michie (eds.), *Innovation Policy in a Global Economy.* Cambridge, UK: Cambridge University Press.

—— and Soete, L. (1980). 'Innovative Activities and Export Shares: Some Comparisons', in K. Pavitt (ed.), *Technical Innovation and British Economic Performance.* London: Macmillan.

Pearce, R. (1999). 'Decentralizing R&D and Strategic Competitiveness: Globalized Approaches to Generation and Use of Technology in Multinational Enterprises', *Research Policy,* 28(2–3): 157–78.

—— and Papanastassiou, M. (1999). 'Overseas R&D and the Strategic Evolution of MNEs: Evidence from Laboratories in the UK', *Research Policy,* 28(1): 23–41.

—— and Singh, S. (1992). *Globalizing Research and Development.* Basingstoke, UK: Macmillan.

Peneder, M., Kaniovaski, S., and Dachs, B. (2003). 'What Follows Tertiarisation? Structural Change and the Role of Knowledge-Based Services', *The Services Industries Journal,* 23(2): 47–66.

Perez, C. (1985). 'Microelectronics, Long Waves and World Structural Change: New Perspectives for Developing Countries', *World Development,* 13(3): 441–63.

—— (1988). 'New Technologies and Development', in C. Freeman and B.-A. Lundvall (eds.), *Small Countries Facing the Technological Revolution.* London: Pinter.

—— (2002). *Technological Revolutions and Financial Capital: The Dynamics of Bubbles and Golden Ages.* Cheltenham, UK: Edward Elgar.

Phillips, A. (1971). *Technology and Market Structure: A Study of the Aircraft Industry.* Lexington, MA: Heath.

Pianta, M. (1988). *New Technologies Across the Atlantic: US Leadership or European Autonomy,* Chapter 4.2 and 4.3. Hemel Hampstead, UK: Harvester Wheatsheaf.

Pilling, D. (2001). 'AstraZeneca Ulcer Drug Wins Six-Month Reprieve', *The Financial Times* (London), 2 May, www.ft.com, accessed 13th March 2004.

Piore, M. and Sabel, C. (1984). *The Second Industrial Divide: Possibilities of Prosperity.* New York: Basic Books.

Pisano, G. (1989). 'Using Equity Participation to Support Exchange: Evidence from the Biotechnology Industry', *Journal of Law, Economics and Organisation,* 5: 109.

—— (1997). *The Development Factory: Unlocking the Potential of Process Innovation.* Boston, MA: Harvard Business School Press.

—— (1990). 'The R&D boundaries of the Firm: an empirical analysis', *Administrative Science Quarterly,* 35: 153–76.

Pitelis, C. (1994). 'Multinational/Transnational Corporations', in Arestis and Sawyer (eds.), *The Elgar Companion to Radical Political Economy.* Aldershot, UK: Edward Elgar.

Polanyi, M. (1967). *The Tacit Dimension.* New York: Doubleday Anchor.

Porter, M. (1985). *Competitive Advantage.* New York: Free Press.

—— (1986). *Competition in Global Industries.* Boston, MA: Harvard Business School Press.

—— (1990a). 'The Competitive Advantage of Nations', *Harvard Business Review,* 90(2): 73–93.

—— (1990b). *The Competitive Advantage of Nations.* Basingstoke, UK: Macmillan.

Posner, M. (1961). *International Trade and Technological Change.* Oxford: Oxford Economic Papers.

Powell, W. W. (2000). 'The Capitalist Firm in the 21st Century', in P. J. DiMaggio (ed.), *The Twenty-First Century Firm.* Princeton, NJ: Princeton University Press.

—— Koput, K. W., Smith-Doerr, L., and Owen-Smith, J. (1999). 'Network Position and Firm Performance: Organizational Returns to Collaboration in the Biotechnology Industry', in S. Andrews and D. Knoke (eds.), *Networks in and Around Organizations*. Greenwich, CT: J. A. J. Press.

Prencipe, A. (2000). 'Breadth and Depth of Technological Capabilities in CoPS: The Case of the Aircraft Engine Control System', *Research Policy*, 29(7–8): 895–911.

Pries, F. and Janszen, F. (1995). 'Innovation in the Construction Industry: The Dominant Role of the Environment', *Construction Management and Economics*, 13(1): 43–51.

Pyke, F., Becattini, G., and Sengenberger, W. (1990). *Industrial Districts and Inter-Firm Co-Operation in Italy*. Geneva: International Labour Organization.

Quigley, J. M. (1982). 'Residential Construction', in R. Nelson (ed.), *Government and Technical Progress: A Cross-Industry Analysis*. New York: Pergamon Press.

Quinn, J. B. (1999). 'Strategic Sourcing: Leveraging Knowledge Capabilities', *Sloan Management Review*, 40(4): 9–21.

Quinn, R. J., de Almedia Leone, P., Guymer, G., and Hooper, J. N. A. (2002). 'Australian Biodiversity via Its Plants and Marine Organisations: A High Throughput Screening Approach to Drug Discovery', *Pure and Applied Chemistry*, 74(4): 519–26.

Rabeharisoa, V. and Callon, M. (2001). 'The Involvement of Patients in Research Activities Supported by the French Muscular Dystrophy Association', in S. Jasanoff (ed.), *States of Knowledge: Science, Power and Political Culture*. Chicago, IL: Chicago University Press.

Rabinow, P. (1992). 'Severing the Ties: Fragmentation and Dignity in Late Modernity', in D. Hess and L. Layne (eds.), *Knowledge and Society: The Anthropology of Science and Technology*. Greenwich, CT: JAI Press, pp. 169–87.

Radford, T. (1997). 'Genetics Bring Speed and Accuracy to an Age-Old Craft', *The Guardian*, 15 December.

Rama, R. (1996). 'Empirical Study on Sources of Innovation in International Food and Beverage Industry', *Agribusiness*, 12(2): 123–34.

—— (1999). 'Productive Inertia and Technological Flows in Food and Drink Processing', in P. Byé and D. Hayton (eds.), *Industrial History and Technological Development in Europe*. Luxembourg: Office for Official Publications of the European Communities, pp. 77–82.

Ramirez, P. (2003). *Globalization, Technology and Organizational Change in the Pharmaceutical Industry*, Ph.D. Thesis. Manchester, UK: University of Manchester Institute of Science and Technology.

—— (2005a). 'The Globalization of Research amongst Leading European and US Pharmaceutical Multinationals: A Case of Uneven Development', *Technological Analysis and Strategic Management*, forthcoming.

—— (2005b). *Personal Communication*. E-Mail dated 12th July.

—— and Tylecote, A. (2004). 'Hybrid Corporate Governance and Its Effects on Innovation: A Case Study of AstraZeneca', *Technology Analysis and Strategic Management*, 16(1): 97–119.

Rausch, L. (1998). *Venture Capital Investment Trends in the United States and Europe*. Washington, DC: National Science Foundation, Directorate for Social, Behavioural and Economic Sciences, NSF 99-303, 16th October.

Reich, R. (1991). *The Work of Nations: Preparing Ourselves for 21st Century Capitalism*. New York: Simon & Schuster.

Reppy, K. (2000). 'Conceptualizing the Role of Defense Industries in the National System of Innovation', in J. Reppy (ed.), *The Place of the Defense Industry in National Systems of Innovation*. Ithaca, NY: Cornell University Peace Studies Program.

Rhodes, M. and van Apeldoorn, B. (1998). 'Capital Unbound? The Transformation of European Corporate Governance', *Journal of European Public Policy*, 5(3): 406–27.

Richards, E. (1988). 'The Politics of Therapeutic Evaluation: The Vitamin C and Cancer Controversy', *Social Studies of Science*, 18(4): 653–701.

—— (1991). *Vitamin C and Cancer: Medicine or Politics*. Basingstoke, UK: Macmillan.

Roberts, T. (2000). 'EPO Patents—Patentability of Plants', *European Intellectual Property Review*, 22(3).

Rose, H. and Rose, S. (1970). *Science and Society*. Harmondsworth, Middlesex, UK: Penguin Books.

Rosenberg, N. (1976). *Perspectives on Technology*. Cambridge, UK: Cambridge University Press.

—— (1982). *Inside the Black Box: Technology and the Economy*. Cambridge, UK: Cambridge University Press.

—— (1986). 'Schumpeter and Marx: How Common a Vision?' in R. MacLead (ed.), *Technology and the Human Prospect*. London: Pinter.

—— (1990). 'Why Do Firms Do Basic Research (With Their Own Money)?' *Research Policy*, 19(2): 165–74.

Rosenfeld, Y. (1994). 'Innovative Construction Methods', *Construction Management and Economics*, 12(6): 521–41.

Rostow, W. W. (1960). *The Stages of Economic Growth, A non-Communist Manifesto*. Cambridge: Cambridge University Row.

Rothwell, R. (1989). 'Small Firms, Innovation and Industrial Change', *Small Business Economics*, 1(1): 51–64.

—— (1992). 'Successful Industrial Innovation: Critical Factors for the 1990s', *R&D Management*. 22(3): 221–39.

Rugman, A. (2001). 'The World Trade Organization and the International Political Economy', in A. Rugman and G. Boyd (eds.), *The World Trade Organization in the New Global Economy: Trade and Investment Issues in the Millennium Round*. Cheltenham, UK and Northampton, MA: Edward Elgar.

—— and Boyd, G. (eds.) (2001). *The World Trade Organization in the New Global Economy: Trade and Investment Issues in the Millennium Round*. Cheltenham, UK and Northampton, MA: Edward Elgar.

Ruiz, R. (1997). 'The Restructuring of the Brazilian Industrial Groups between 1980 and 1993', *CEPAL Review*, 61: 167–86.

Sabel, C., Herrigel, G., Deeg, R., and Kazis, R. (1989). 'Regional Prosperities Compared: Massachusetts and Baden-Wurttemberg in the 1980s', *Economy and Society*, 18(4): 374–404.

SAGB (Senior Advisory Group on Biotechnology) (1990). *Economic Benefits and European Competitiveness*. Brussels: CEFIC (European Chemical Industry Council).

Salter, W. (1962). *Productivity and Technical Change*. Cambridge, UK: Cambridge University Press.

Sato, Y. (2001). 'The Structure and Perspective of Science and Technology Policy in Japan', in P. Laredo and P. Mustar (eds.), *Research and Innovation Policies in the New Global Economy*. Cheltenham, UK: Edward Elgar.

Sauve, P. (2000). 'Developing Countries and the GATTS 2000 Round', *Journal of World Trade*, 34(2): 85–92.

Saxenian, A. (1994). *Regional Advantage: Culture and Competition in Silicon Valley and Route 128*. Cambridge, MA: Harvard University Press.

—— (2002). 'The Silicon Valley Connection: Transnational Networks and Regional Development in Taiwan, China and India', *Industry and Innovation*, 9(2): 183–200.

—— and Hsu, J. (2001). 'The Silicon Valley–Hsinchu Connection: Technical Communities and Industrial Upgrading', *Industrial and Corporate Change*, 10(4): 893–920.

Schumpeter, J. (1934). *The Theory of Economic Development*, First published in German, 1912. Cambridge, MA: Harvard University Press (New York: Oxford University Press, 1961).

—— (1939). *Business Cycles: A Theoretical, Historical and Statistical Analysis*. New York: McGraw-Hill.

—— (1942). *Capitalism, Socialism and Democracy*. New York: Harper and Brothers (Harper Colophon edition, 1976).

Segerstrom, P. S., Anant, T. C. A., and Dinopoulos, E. (1990). 'A Schumpeterian Model of the Product Life Cycle', *American Economic Review*, 80(5): 1077–91.

Senker, J. and Faulkner, W. (1996). 'Networks, Tacit Knowledge and Innovation', in R. Coombs, A. Richards, P. Saviotti, V. Walsh (eds.), *Technological Collaboration: The Dynamics of Cooperation in Industrial Innovation*. Cheltenham: Edward Elgar.

Shapin, S. (1999). *The Moral Equivalence of the Scientist: A Preliminary History Paper*, Paper presented. San Diego, CA: Society of the Social Studies of Science Conference.

Silverberg, G., Dosi, G., and Orsenigo, L. (1998). 'Innovation, Diversity and Diffusion: A Self-Organizing Model', *The Economic Journal*, 98(393): 1032–54.

SIPRI (2001). *Yearbook 2001: Armaments, Disarmament and International Society*. Oxford: Oxford University Press.

Slaughter, E. S. (1998). 'Models of Construction Innovation', *Journal of Construction Engineering and Management*, 124(3): 226–31.

Soete, L. (1981). 'A General Test of Technological Gap Trade Theory', *Weltwirtschaftliches Archiv*, 117(4): 638–66.

—— (1985). 'International Diffusion of Technology, Industrial Development and Technological Leapfrogging', *World Development*, 13(3): 409–22.

—— and Miozzo, M. (1989). 'Trade and Development in Services: A Technological Perspective', MERIT Research Memorandum 89-031. The Netherlands: MERIT.

Solow, R. M. (1957). 'Technical Progress and the Aggregate Production Function', *Review of Economics and Statistics*, 39(3): 312–20.

Stegemann, K. (2000). 'The Integration of Intellectual Property Rights into the WTO System', *The World Economy*, 23(9): 1237–67.

Steward, F. (2001). 'Shaping Technological Trajectories Through Innovation Networks and Risk Networks: Investigating the Food Sector', in O. Jones, S. Conway, and F. Steward (eds.), *Social Interaction and Organisational Change: Aston Perspectives on Innovation Networks*. London: Imperial College Press, pp. 193–210.

Storey, D. and Tether, B. (1998). 'New Technology-Based Firms in the European Union: An Introduction', *Research Policy*, 26(9): 933–46.

Storper, M. (1995). 'Regional Technology Coalitions: An Essential Dimension of National Technology Policy', *Research Policy*, 24(6): 895–911.

Storper, M. (2000). 'Globalization and Knowledge Flows: An Industrial Geographer's Perspective', in J. H. Dunning (ed.), *Regions, Globalization and the Knowledge-Based Economy.* Oxford: Oxford University Press.

Strathern, M. (1996). 'Potential Property: Intellectual Rights and Property in Persons', *Social Anthropology,* 4(1): 17–32.

—— (1997). 'Cutting the Network', *Journal of the Royal Anthropological Institute,* 2: 517–35.

—— (1999). *Property, Substance and Effect.* London: Athlone Press, pp. 179 and 201.

—— da Cunha, M. C., Descola, P., Alberto, C., and Harvey, P. (1998). 'Seconding the Opposition, Exploitable Knowledge Belongs to the Creators of It: A Debate', *Social Anthropology,* 6(1): 109–26.

Sundbo, J. (1998). *The Organization of Innovation in Services.* Aldershot, UK: Edward Elgar.

Sutcliffe, R. and Glyn, A. (2003). 'Measures of Globalization and Their Misinterpretation', in J. Michie (ed.), *The Handbook on Globalization.* Cheltenham, UK: Elgar, pp. 61–80.

Swords-Isherwoods, N. (1980). 'British Management Compared', in K. Pavitt (ed.), *Technical Innovation and British Economic Performance.* London: Macmillan.

Tampubolon, G. (2003). *Globalisation of Innovation in Agricultural Biotechnology,* Unpublished Ph.D. Thesis. Manchester, UK: Manchester School of Management, University of Manchester Institute of Science and Technology.

Tansey, G. and Worsley, T. (1995). *The Food System: A Guide.* London: Earthscan.

Tarabusi, C. and Vickery, G. (1998). 'Globalisation in the Pharmaceutical Industry', *International Journal of Health Services,* 28(2): 281–303.

Tatum, C. B. (1986). 'Potential Mechanisms for Construction Innovation', *Journal of Construction Engineering and Management,* 112(2): 178–87.

—— (1987). 'Process of Innovation in Construction Firm', *Journal of Construction Engineering and Management,* 113(4): 648–63.

Teece, D. J. (1986). 'Profiting from Technological Innovation: Implications for Integration, Collaboration, Licensing and Public Policy', *Research Policy,* 15(6): 285–305.

Teitel, S. (2004). *On Semi-Industrialized Countries and the Acquisition of Technological Capabilities,* International Centre for Economic Research (ICER), Working Paper No. 19.

Tether, B., Miles, I., Blind, K., Hipp, C., de Liso, N., and Cainelli, G. (2001). 'Innovation in Services: An Analysis of CIS-2 Data on Innovation in the Services Sector', *Report for the European Commission (under CIS contract 98/184).*

Teubal, M. (1996). 'R&D and Technology Policy in NICs as Learning Processes', *World Development,* 24(3): 449–60.

Thomas, P. (1999). 'Knowledge Regimes: The WTO, IP and Public Interests in India', *Telematics and Informatics,* 16(4): 219–31.

Tomlinson, M. and McMeekin, A. (2002). 'Social Routines and the Consumption of Food', in A. McMeekin, K. Green, A. Tomlinson, and V. Walsh (eds.), *Innovation by Demand: An Interdisciplinary Approach to the Study of Demand and Its Role in Innovation.* Manchester, UK: Manchester University Press, pp. 75–87.

Toole, T. M. (1998). 'Uncertainty and Home Builders' Adoption of Technological Innovation', *Journal of Construction Engineering and Management,* 124(4): 323–32.

Tsukamoto, T. and Ueno, Y. (1936). *Journal of the Phamaceutical Society of Japan,* 56: 135.

Tylecote, A. and Demirag, I. (1992). 'Short-Termism: Culture and Structures as Factors in Technological Innovation', in R. Coombs, P. Saviotti, and V. Walsh (eds.), *Technological Change and Company Strategies*. London: Academic Press.

—— and Ramirez, P. (2004). 'Hybrid Corporate Governance and Its Effects on Innovation: A Case Study of AstraZeneca', *Technology Analysis and Strategic Management*, 16(1): 97–119.

UN (2001). *World Investment Report 2001: Promoting Linkages*. New York: UN.

UNESCO (2001). *Institute for Statistics: The State of Science and Technology in the World 1996–1997*. Montreal: UNESCO.

UNIDO (2002). *Industrial Development Report 2002/2003: Competing Through Innovation and Learning*. United Nationals Industrial Development Organization.

Utterback, J. M. (1979). 'The Dynamics of Product and Process Innovation in Industry', in C. T. Hill and J. M. Utterback (eds.), *Technological Innovation for a Dynamic Economy*. Oxford: Pergamon.

Vernon, R. (1966). 'International Investment and International Trade in the Product Cycle', *The Quarterly Journal of Economics*, 80(2): 190–207.

Vidal, J. and Milner, M. (1997). 'Food: The £250 Billion Gamble: Big Firms Rush for Profits and Power Despite Warnings', *The Guardian*, 15 December.

Vittas, D. and Kawaura, A. (1995). *Policy-Based Finance, Financial Regulation and Financial Sector Development in Japan*, Policy Research Working Paper WPS 1443. Washington, DC: World Bank Financial Sector Development Department.

von Hippel, E. (1988). *The Source of Innovation*. Oxford: Oxford University Press.

Wade, R. (1990). *Governing the Market: Economic Theory and the Role of Government in East Asian Industrialization*. Princeton, NJ: Princeton University Press.

Walker, W. (1993). 'National Innovation Systems: Britain', in R. Nelson (ed.), *National Innovation Systems*. New York: Oxford University Press.

Walker, W. B. (1980). 'Britain's Industrial Performance 1850–1950: A Failure to Adjust', in K. Pavitt (ed.), *Technical Innovation and British Economic Performance*. London: Macmillan.

Walsh, V. (1980). 'Contraception: The Growth of a Technology', in L. Birke et al. (eds.), *Alice Through the Microscope*. London: Virago.

—— (1984). 'Invention and Innovation in the Chemical Industry: Demand Pull or Discovery Push?' *Research Policy*, 13(4): 211–34.

—— (1988). 'Technology and the Competitiveness of Small Countries: A Review', in C. Freeman and B.-A. Lundvall (eds.), *Small Countries Facing the Technological Revolution*. London: Pinter.

—— (1998). 'Industrial R&D and Its Influence on the Organization and Management of the Production of Knowledge in the Public Sector', in J.-P. Gaudillière and I. Löwry (eds.), *The Invisible Industrialist: Manufactures and the Production of Scientific Knowledge*. London: Macmillan.

—— (2002a). 'Biotechnology and the UK 2000–2005: Globalization and Innovation', *New Genetics and Society*, 21(2): 149–76.

—— (2002b). 'Creating Markets for Biotechnology', *International Journal of Sociology of Agriculture and Food*, 10(2): 33–45.

—— (2004). 'Paradigms in the Evolution of Life Sciences Research, and the Changing Structure of the Innovative Organisation', in K. Grandin (ed.), *Science and Industry in the Twentieth Century*. Canton, MA: Science History Publications.

Walsh, V. and Goodman, J. (1999). 'Cancer Chemotherapy, Biodiversity, Public and Private Property: The Case of the Anti-Cancer Drug Taxol', *Social Science and Medicine*, 49(9): 1215–25.

—— —— (2002). 'From taxol to Taxol®: The Changing Identities and Ownership of an Anticancer Drug', *Medical Anthropology*, 21(3–4): 307–36.

—— and Le Roux, M. (2004). 'Contingency in Innovation and the Role of National Systems: Taxol and Taxotère in the USA and France', *Research Policy*, 33(9): 1307–27.

—— and Lodorfos, G. (2002). 'Technological and Organisational Innovation in Chemicals and Related Products', *Technology Analysis and Strategic Management*, 14(3): 273–98.

—— Townsend, J. Senker, P. and Huggett, C. (1980). 'Technical Change and Skilled Manpower Needs in the Plastics Processing Industry', SPRU Occasional Paper, No. 11, Sept.

—— Niosi, J., and Mustar, P. (1995). 'Small Firm Formation in Biotechnology: A Comparison of France Britain and Canada', *Technovation*, 15(5): 303–27.

—— Ramirez, P., and Tampubolon, G. (2000). 'La mondialisation de l'activité innovatrice dans l'industrie pharmaceutique', in M. Delapierre, P. Moati, and E. M. Mouhoud (eds.), *Connaissance et Mondialisation*. Paris: Economica.

—— Roy, R., Bruce, M., and Potter, S. (1992). *Winning by Design: Technology, Product Design and International Competitiveness*. Oxford: Basil Blackwell.

Warde, A. (1997). *Consumption Food and Taste: Culinary Antinomies and Commodity Culture*. London: Sage.

—— (2000). 'Eating Globally: Cultural Flows and the Spread of Ethnic Restaurants', in D. Kalb, M. van der Land, R. Staring, B. van Steenbergen, and N. Wilterdink (eds.), *The Ends of Globalisation: Bringing Society Back in*. Boulder, CO: Rowman & Littlefield, pp. 299–316.

—— and Martens, L. (2000). *Eating Out: Social Differentiation, Consumption and Pleasure*. Cambridge, UK: Cambridge University Press.

Weber, M. ([1922] 1978) *The Economy and Society* (first published in German). Berkeley: University of California Press.

Weiller, J. (1949). 'Les preferences nationales de structure et le desequilibre structural', *Revue d'Economie Politique*, 414.

Weiner, M. (1981). *English Culture and the Decline of the Industrial Spirit, 1850–1980*. Cambridge, UK: Cambridge University Press.

Whitley, R. (1992). *Business Systems in East Asia: Firms, Societies and Markets*. London: Sage.

Wilkinson, J. (2002). 'Genetically Modified Organism, Organics and the Contested Construction of Demand in the Agrofood System', *International Journal of Sociology of Agriculture and Food*, 10(2): 3–11.

Williamson, O. (1975). *Markets and Hierarchies*. New York: Free Press.

—— (1985). *The Economic Institutions of Capitalism*. New York: Free Press.

Wilson, H. (1992). *The Impact of Venture Capital Funding on the Growth of Small High Technology Manufacturing Firms in the United Kingdom*, Ph.D. Thesis. Edinburgh, UK: Heriot-Watt University.

—— (1995). 'Are the Business Angles of Today the Venture Capitalists of Yesterday?' *The Journal of High Technology Management Research*, 6(1): 145–56.

Winch, G. (1996). 'Contracting Systems in the European Construction Industry—A Sectoral Approach to the Dynamics of Business Systems', in R. Whitley and P. H. Kristensen (eds.), *The Changing European Firm: Limits to Convergence*. London: Routledge.

—— (1998). 'Zephyrs of Creative Destruction: Understanding the Management of Innovation in Construction', *Building Research and Information*, 26(4): 268–79.

—— and Campagnac, E. (1995). 'The Organization of Building Projects: An Anglo-French Comparison', *Construction Management and Economics*, 13(1): 3–14.

Womack, J. P., Jones, D., and Roos, D. (1990). *The Machine That Changed the World*. New York: Macmillan.

World Economic Forum (2003). *The Global Competitiveness Report 2002–2003*. New York and Oxford: Oxford University Press.

World Health Organization (2002–2003). *The Impact of Implementation of ICH Guidelines in non-ICH Countries*. Geneva: Regulatory Support Series No. 9, WHO/EDM/QSM/.

Wrigley, J. (1986). 'Technical Education and Industry in the Nineteenth Century', in B. Elbaum and W. Lazonick (eds.), *The Decline of the British Economy*. Oxford: Clarendon Press.

Wrong, M. (1999a). 'Fodder for the GM Debate', *The Financial Times*, 18 November.

—— (1999b). 'Monsanto Chief Admits Public Relations Disaster', *The Financial Times*, 7 October.

Zysman, J. (1983). *Governments, Markets and Growth: Financial Systems and the Politics of Industrial Change*. Ithaca, NY: Cornell University Press.

INDEX